Programming under Mach

Joseph Boykin

David Kirschen

Alan Langerman

Susan LoVerso

Addison-Wesley Publishing Company
Reading, Massachusetts • Menlo Park, California • New York
Don Mills, Ontario • Wokingham, England • Amsterdam • Bonn
Sydney • Singapore • Tokyo • Madrid • San Juan • Milan • Paris

This book is in the **Addison-Wesley UNIX and Open System Series**
Series Editors: Marshall Kirk McKusick and John S. Quarterman

Deborah R. Lafferty: Sponsoring Editor
Thomas Stone: Senior Editor
Juliet Silveri: Associate Production Supervisor
Robert Donegan: Marketing Manager
Roy E. Logan: Senior Manufacturing Manager
Marshall Henrichs: Cover Designer
Patricia Daly: Copy Editor

Library of Congress Cataloging-in-Publication Data

Programming under Mach / Joseph Boykin ... [et al.].
  p. cm.
Includes bibliographical references and index.
ISBN 0-201-52739-1
1. Mach (Computer Operating System). 2. UNIX. I. Boykin, Joseph.
QA76.8.N49P76   1993
005.4$'$469–dc20
                                            92-18187
                                              CIP

The programs and applications presented in this book have been included for their instructional value. They have been tested with care but are not guaranteed for any particular purpose. The publisher and authors do not offer any warranties or representations, nor do they accept any liabilities with respect to the programs or applications.

Many of the designations used by manufacturers and sellers to distinguish their products are claimed as trademarks. Where those designations appear in this book, and Addison-Wesley was aware of a trademark claim, the designations have been printed in initial caps or all caps.

1 2 3 4 5 6 7 8 9 10-AL-959493

I dedicate this book to the memory of my father, Murray Boykin, who taught me that I can do anything I set my mind to. I miss you dad.

I dedicate this book to the memory of my parents, Rose and Leonard Kirschen, to my wife Marilyn for her support, and to Len and Bob for providing endless hours of pleasant video game musical background for our author meetings.

I dedicate this book to my family and friends with much love and affection. And to Ben & Jerry's and Herrell's for inspiration and padding.

I dedicate this book to my parents, Ray and Alice Wroblewski, who shaped my life, and to my husband, John, whose support was invaluable.

We also dedicate this book to the Book Babies, Michael Boykin and Peter LoVerso. Sometimes we were doing other things when we should have been writing.

UNIX AND OPEN SYSTEM SERIES

Network Management: A Practical Perspective Allan Leinwand
Karen Fang

UNIX, POSIX, and Open Systems: John S. Quarterman
The Open Standards Puzzle Susanne Wilhelm

Practical Internetworking with TCP/IP and UNIX Smoot Carl-Mitchell
John S. Quarterman

Programming under Mach Joseph Boykin
David Kirschen
Alan Langerman
Susan LoVerso

Series Editors

John S. Quarterman
Marshall Kirk McKusick

Series Foreword

Marshall Kirk McKusick
John S. Quarterman

Addison-Wesley is proud to publish the **UNIX and Open Systems Series.** The primary audience for the Series will be system designers, implementors, administrators and their managers. The core of the series will consist of books detailing operating systems, standards, networking, and programming languages. The titles will interest specialists in these fields, as well as appeal more broadly to computer scientists and engineers who must deal with open-systems environments in their work. The Series comprises professional reference books and instructional texts.

Open systems allow users to move their applications between systems easily; thus, purchasing decisions can be made on the basis of cost/performance ratio and vendor support, rather than on which systems will run a user's application suite. Decreasing computer hardware prices have facilitated the widespread adoption of capable multiprocess, multiuser operating systems, UNIX being a prime example. Newer operating systems, such as Mach and Chorus, support additional services, such as lightweight processes. The Series illuminates the design and implementation of all such open systems. It teaches readers how to write application programs to run on these systems, and gives advice on administration and use.

The Series treats as a unified whole the previously distinct field of networking and operating systems. Networks permit open systems to share hardware and software resources, and allow people to communicate efficiently. The exponential growth of networks such as the Internet, and the adoption of protocols such as TCP/IP in industry, government, and academia, have made network and system administration critically important to many organizations. This series will examine many aspects of network protocols, emphasizing the interaction with operating systems. It will focus on the evolution in computer environments, and will assist professions in the development and use of practical networking technologies.

Standards for programming interfaces, protocols, and languages are a key concern as networks of open systems expand within organizations and across the globe. Standards can be useful for system engineering, application programming, marketing, and procurement; but standards that are released too late, cover too little, or are too narrowly defined can be counterproductive. This series will encourage its readers to participate in the standards process by presenting material detailing the use of specific standards to write application programs, and to build modern multiprocess, multiuser computing environments.

Mach, the subject of this book, is a good example of an interesting and popular new operating system. It has found growing acceptance, both in its use in whole or part by various vendors, including Hewlett-Packard, Digital, and IBM, and in its adoption as the basis of the OSF/1 operating system of the Open Software Foundation (OSF).

Mach is based conceptually on UNIX, but discards many redundant features and reimplements the others on top of a small message-passing kernel. Major subsystems such as virtual memory (VM) have been completely redesigned and reimplemented; Mach even supports VM in a user-level server, rather than in the kernel. Yet Mach's VM is faster than many others.

In one sense, Mach is an attempt to redo UNIX in the light of more than twenty years of experience with UNIX. More importantly, Mach provides one foundation for the future. Systems like Mach are permitting distributed computing to move outside the research realm and into the commercial world.

Foreword

Rick Rashid

It has occurred to me from time to time that at least some of the success Mach has achieved may have been derived from my choice of the name for the system. This belief is reinforced by the frequent requests I receive for information on how the name "Mach" was chosen. The story falls into the "strange but true" category.

The Mach project at Carnegie Mellon University was originally called the "Supercomputer Workbench Project." That name came from the title of the original Defense Advanced Research Projects Agency (DARPA) proposal I wrote in 1983 that had as its goal the development of an operating system for experimental multiprocessors being developed by DARPA as next-generation supercomputers. The original four-processor VAX 11/784 that we used for our development was called the "workbench machine" and its four processors were labeled accordingly as "wb1," "wb2," "wb3," and "wb4." There was even some talk of using the name workbench as part of the operating system name, i.e., Workbench Operating System or WOS. Luckily no one really liked that name enough for it to stick.

In fact, no one liked any name well enough for it to stick and the project operated for a considerable time with no real operating system name at all. Finally fed up with receiving reports that contained circumlocutions such as "the operating system that" or "our operating system supports," our program manager at DARPA—Steve Squires—suggested rather forcefully that I come up with a real name for the system. I no longer remember precisely if that "suggestion" contained a threat that he would do it if I did not. Thus "incentivised" the project members generated a rather large number of names that peppered our lunchtime conversation for weeks.

An early name suggested by Robert Baron was "Melange" after the geriatric spice in the Dune books. The rationale for this name was the status of the Supercomputer Workbench Project as a follow-on to Carnegie Mellon's earlier personal computer network project called SPICE. Melange was intended to be the ultimate spice project. Bob was so taken by this name that he began to relabel our machines with names taken from the Dune books such as Arrakis and Atreides. The word Melange started appearing in source code at about that time as well. In retrospect I seriously doubt that we would have been nearly as successful had we used Melange—although we would undoubtedly have appealed to the science fiction market! Luckily one of the key graduate students on the project, Avie Tevanian, so disliked the name that he conducted a guerilla war of machine name reassignment and source code modification that doomed the name to oblivion.

Many other names were suggested. KOMA was suggested as an acronym for Kernel Operating System for Multiprocessor Applications. One obvious problem with that name was the opportunity for other groups to talk about the system going "comatose." Another suggestion that eventually was viewed as the best by many of the graduate students was MOOSE—an acronym for Multiprocessor-Oriented Operating System and Environment. It was never fully clear to me the relationship between this suggestion and the moose head mounted in the office of another of the project's key graduate students, Mike Young. Needless to say, I hated the name—not so much because I disliked large-hoofed animals with antlers, but because I was unhappy with the prospect of getting up in front of 300 of my peers and talking about "my system, MOOSE."

I stumbled onto the name Mach quite by accident. I was in the office of a colleague at CMU discussing with amusement some of the sillier names we had invented. One of the names I mentioned was MUCK, an acronym for Multiprocessor Universal Communication Kernel. This colleague, Darlo Giuse, had been born in Italy and evidently misheard my pronunciation of MUCK because he immediately said "Mach, that is a good name!" Knowing a good thing when I heard it, I replied "Yes, it is!"

The end of this story is perhaps the strangest part of all. Even after I came up with the name Mach there was still a spirited debate within the group between the advocates of Mach (me) and the advocates of MOOSE (nearly everyone else). Using a decision technique I found useful throughout the project, I declared that we would base the choice of operating system name on a flip of a coin. Or, more specifically, we decided to flip three quarters at the same time and base the decision on how all the coins came up, either heads or tails. The coins were flipped, they all came up heads, and the name Mach was chosen. The result has been quite satisfactory.

Of course, the coins were mine and I did the flipping.

Mach has come a long way from those times. It is now a cornerstone of the new operating systems which are being developed in today's industry. This book is a challenge to anyone interested in the development of the Mach operating system. Not only is it written by very authoritative people in the field, but it is a compilation of creative, interactive experiences from authors with years of experience.

FTP Access to Source Code

The example programs presented in this book have been made available on line for your personal, noncommercial use. While we have made every effort to test these programs under Mach Release 2.5 or OSF/1, we cannot warrant that they will run on your system.

The authors encourage readers to send suggested improvements or comments about typographical or other errors found in this book by electronic mail to `Mach-bugs@orca.com`.

The files are available on the Internet on host `world.std.com` (`192.74.137.5`) via anonymous FTP. To access the files from an Internet host, enter the following commands. Output from the system is shown in **bold type**.

```
% ftp world.std.com
Name: anonymous
331 Guest login ok, send email address as password.
Password: <your email address>
230-
230-Hello!
230-
...
ftp> cd AW/Mach
250 CWD command successful.
ftp> get README
```

The `README` file describes the contents of the various subdirectories and files available. You may use additional FTP **get** commands to retrieve files.

Contents

Preface

Why This Book

Not since the development of UNIX at AT&T Bell Laboratories has a new operating system (OS) stirred so much interest in the computer industry. The Mach operating system is the result of research at Carnegie Mellon University (CMU) that began in the mid-1980s and continues today. The goal of that research was to develop a new operating system that would allow computer programmers to exploit modern hardware architectures emerging from vendors, universities, and research laboratories. This operating system was designed to reduce the number of features in the kernel and, in turn, reduce the size of the kernel, thus reversing the growing trend to produce operating systems with many features and excessive complexity. The system would be easy to use, with just five basic programming abstractions.

As interest in the Mach operating system has grown, so has the need for a focused, programmer-oriented book explaining how to use it. This book fills a need for in-depth technical information on using Mach to develop your applications. It introduces you to the fundamental Mach concepts and includes some "nuts and bolts" examples so you can learn how to apply those concepts.

Why a book specifically about Mach? We have been directly involved with Mach since 1986. We have frequently heard the question, "Where can I get information about using Mach?" Unfortunately, there has been no source of introductory material generally available. While there are many good programming introductions for UNIX, Mach is so new that no such resources exist. The largest body of information on Mach is in the form of system-level documentation and papers published in journals and conference proceedings. You can find a reference and reading list of these published documents in Appendix D. This material is of interest to operating system developers and researchers, but it does not provide an organized introduction

1

to using Mach. We felt it was time for a solid, hands-on approach that would take the mystery out of writing programs under Mach.

This book is not a general introduction to programming nor a textbook on operating systems concepts. It is, however, a complete introduction to writing Mach programs. Starting with fundamental examples, the text progresses to more advanced use of Mach services. The approach is based on code fragments as well as entire programs to illustrate practical techniques. This code provides effective ways to illustrate the application of general principles. For instance, Chapter 3 on interprocess communication (IPC) develops a complete client/server application. The design rationale for each segment of code is given so that you can see what kinds of tradeoffs and issues arise in developing programs for Mach.

To get the most out of this book, you should be conversant with programming in the C language and you should have some familiarity with programming on another modern operating system, particularly UNIX. We recommend that you try these examples on a Mach system, although you certainly can learn the basics of Mach from this book without hands-on experience. We encourage you to modify or extend our examples with new features or by using different Mach functions. Note that there are several versions of Mach available. This book was written for Mach version 2.5.

About This Book

We begin our tour of Mach programming with some introductory details on writing Mach programs, such as necessary program declarations and header files, libraries, and programming conventions. The first few chapters of this book describe most of the fundamental concepts of Mach. These chapters lay the foundation for all the remaining chapters. For example,

- While most users will use a library interface to write multithreaded programs, it is important to understand the *tasks* and *threads* model before seeing how the library abstracts the basic concepts. Two such libraries are the C Threads and P Threads packages.

- The basics of IPC must be understood before writing a client and server program using the Mach interface generator program.

- It is important to understand basic virtual memory concepts and the VM/IPC integration before using more advanced virtual memory concepts to manage memory objects.

This book first presents the basic concepts and devotes a chapter to each of the aforementioned advanced topics. Successive chapters build on material presented in the earlier chapters.

The fundamental concepts are interdependent. They are presented in these three chapters: Chapter 2, "Tasks and Threads"; Chapter 3, "Interprocess Communication"; and Chapter 4, "Virtual Memory." We begin a more advanced discussion by exploring how to write a multithreaded program in Chapter 5, "C Threads." This chapter covers topics ranging from the mechanics of creating and managing C Threads to synchronization and its impact.

An often overlooked, but very important, topic is covered in Chapter 6, "Mach Exception Handling." This chapter describes when exceptions may be generated and how they are delivered to your program. It discusses how you use the exception handling facility to make your program more robust by dealing with exceptions as an integral part of the program's design.

The next two chapters continue the discussion of interprocess communication. Additional IPC topics are described in Chapter 7, "Advanced IPC." These topics include passing port rights, sending out-of-line data, and detailed information about port managers. Immediately following, while IPC is still fresh in your mind, is a presentation of the Mach Interface Generator (MIG) in Chapter 8. This facility provides an easy way to write client/server programs that communicate using messages and ports.

One of the most difficult topics, external memory management, is dealt with in Chapter 9. This chapter requires a clear understanding of the virtual memory subsystem from Chapter 4. The seemingly daunting task of writing a user-level program to manage memory objects is explained clearly. A sample memory management program is developed step by step to make the concepts understandable.

The POSIX threads interface, P Threads, is presented in Chapter 10, which discusses OSF/1. The concepts in P Threads are similar to those explained in Chapter 5, but the package represents a standardized interface.

We devote a chapter to practical techniques for programming under Mach in Chapter 11, "Mach Programming." We discuss how to multithread an application from a more philosophical standpoint. This chapter also explains differences between Mach and 4.3BSD. The hazards of mixing UNIX signals and Mach system calls with the task and thread model are discussed.

The interfaces to Mach are presented in their respective chapters. We provide a system call summary in Appendix C.

Acknowledgments

We would like to thank the many people who helped make this book possible, through their input, comments, reviews, and suggestions. We would like to thank the editors at Addison-Wesley for their infinite patience and perseverance. Specifically, we would like to extend our appreciation to Debbie Lafferty, Keith Wollman, and Jim DeWolf (Addison-Wesley), David Black (OSF Research Institute), Richard Draves (Microsoft Corporation), Mary Thompson (Carnegie Mellon University), Isaac Nassi (Apple Computer), Barbara Boykin, John LoVerso, Marilyn Kirschen, and Buster. We would like to extend our appreciation to the following reviewers, whose comments and opinions were very helpful throughout the writing of this book: David Black, Richard Draves, David Finkel, David Mitchell, Barry Shein, David Slattengren, Vance Vaughan, and Stephen Vinoski.

Chapter 1

Introduction

1.1 The Development of Mach

The Mach project at Carnegie Mellon University (CMU) began in 1985 with
funding from DARPA (the Defense Advanced Research Projects Agency).
The first implementation, for a Digital Equipment Corporation (DEC) VAX
minicomputer, was completed in the spring of 1986. A short time later,
an implementation for the IBM PC/RT workstation was started. Then implementations were started for the Sun workstation and the Encore Multimax multiprocessor. Today there are Mach implementations completed or
in progress for almost every major general-purpose computer, from PCs to
supercomputers.

From the beginning, compatibility was a very important concern. For
Mach to become a successful operating system, it had to be easy to use in an
environment with existing systems. The de facto standard operating system
in the DARPA research community was the Berkeley Standard Distribution,
so from the outset it was decided that Mach should be compatible with
Berkeley UNIX (ultimately 4.3BSD). To ensure complete compatibility, the
Mach implementors began with the kernel source code for 4.3BSD, replacing
subsystems with the Mach equivalent and adding new Mach subsystems.
This placed additional constraints on the Mach designers, but the tradeoff
was well worth the extra effort. Programs written for 4.3BSD can generally
be run under Mach with no changes. Of course, vanilla UNIX programs do
not take advantage of the features unique to Mach. This book shows you
how to do that!

Several other operating systems influenced the design of Mach. UNIX
provided a compatibility specification at the system call level. The ACCENT

5

system, also developed at Carnegie Mellon, provided a base for the Mach interprocess communications facility. Some of the virtual memory concepts came from the DEC's Tenex operating system.

While the early Mach implementations were completed at CMU as part of the research there, there are now commercial implementations as well. The first was from Encore Computer Corporation, which optimized Mach for its Multimax multiprocessor. One successful commercial product to date is the release for the NeXT computer system. The most well-known offering is the Mach-based OSF/1 operating system developed by the Open Software Foundation. Other commercial versions are available for the i386, the Macintosh, and many other hardware platforms.

There have been several releases of Mach. The first, Release 1.0, was distributed by CMU to allow other researchers to see how the development of Mach was progressing. This release had the virtual memory and IPC subsystems in place but did not have support for tasks and threads. A more functional release, 2.0, followed. This release contained full support for tasks and threads. This latter release formed the basis for the first commercial products. As Mach became more popular and gained a following, there were requests for additional features, such as an implementation of Sun's Network File System (NFS). The result was Release 2.5. This release also contained support for external memory management.

The research group at CMU found that the effort needed to distribute Mach was becoming too great for a research program. Since January, 1990, the VAX, Sun, and i386 versions have been available from Mt. Xinu, a software firm under contract to Carnegie Mellon. This release, MSD 2.6, is intended to be a complete package, with other software (such as the X Window System) bundled with the operating system.

As sometimes happens, Mach was actually a bit too popular. One of its original goals was a small, compact OS kernel. However, some of the original Berkeley UNIX code was still an integral part of the system. The success Mach enjoyed resulted in the addition of other important features (such as NFS). The result, of course, was that Mach actually became larger than UNIX. Carnegie Mellon has removed the remaining UNIX code from the kernel, providing the standard Berkeley UNIX interface by means of user-level server programs. This slimmed-down kernel is known as Release 3.0, a fully functional *microkernel* version with a 4.3BSD server. This release has caused great excitement in research and development labs.

Mach's popularity has affected the industry at large. Its widespread acceptance is evident in the large number of Mach-related activities. Not only are tutorials about Mach available through several professional organizations, but there have been several symposia dedicated to Mach developments from the Usenix Association and the Open Software Foundation's Research Institute. In addition, Mach was partly responsible for spawning a workshop from the Usenix Association on the general topic of microkernels.

1.2   OSF/1

Several of the major computer manufacturers founded The Open Software Foundation (OSF) in 1988 to develop and deliver software for open systems. The OSF/1 operating system was a key component of that open systems strategy. The OSF received clear requirements for the OSF/1 operating system from its member organizations. The members' requirements for OSF/1 included

- Good multiprocessor support

- Excellent portability to differing architectures

- Compatibility with the POSIX standard

- UNIX System V compatibility

- Support for security certification

- Internationalized commands and libraries

- A strategy for long-term OS development.

With these requirements in mind, the OSF chose Mach as the base kernel technology for OSF/1. Major subsystems (STREAMS, the kernel virtual filesystem architecture, security features, internationalized commands and libraries) were obtained from a variety of suppliers (including IBM, UC Berkeley, SecureWare, and Mentat). The OSF worked with Encore Computer Corporation to optimize the UNIX portions of the Mach kernel for high performance on multiprocessor machines. The authors were principals of that multiprocessor effort. The result was Release 1.0 of the OSF/1 operating system, released to licensees in December, 1990. The information presented in the other chapters of this book is applicable to OSF/1 as well as to Mach. OSF/1 was developed by starting with Mach 2.5 and replacing or adding subsystems, but the Mach portion of the kernel *is* Mach 2.5. All

of the examples in this book have been tested on a Mach 2.5 or an OSF/1
Release 1.1 system.

This book concentrates on Release 2.5, since that release is currently
more prevalent due to its use in commercial offerings such as those from
Mt. Xinu, NeXT, and OSF. The concepts presented in this book remain
the same across all versions of Mach. While the Mach interfaces will evolve
with newer versions, this book explains the most commonly available version
of Mach. The fundamental abstractions and rationale behind the services
provided remain unchanged.

1.3   Fundamental Mach Concepts

Mach offers five programming abstractions, which are the basic building
blocks of the system. These abstractions were chosen as the minimum necessary to produce a useful system on top of which the typical complex operations could be built. You will become very familiar with these primitives
as you learn how Mach programs are designed:

Task: The traditional UNIX process is divided into two separate components in Mach, as shown in Fig. 1.1. The first is the *task*, which
contains all of the resources for a group of cooperating entities. Examples of resources in a task are virtual memory and communications
ports. A task is a passive collection of resources; it does not run on a
processor.

Thread: The second component of the UNIX process is the active execution environment. Each task may support one or more concurrently
executing computations, called *threads*. For example, a multithreaded
program may use one thread to compute scientific calculations while
another thread monitors the user interface. A Mach task may have
many threads of execution, all running simultaneously. Much of the
power of the Mach programming model comes from the fact that all
threads in a task share the task's resources. For instance, they all have
the same virtual memory (VM) address space. However, each thread
in a task has its own private execution state. This state consists of
a set of registers, such as general-purpose registers, a stack pointer, a
program counter, and a frame pointer.

Port: The communications channel through which threads communicate
with each other is a *port*. A port is a resource and is owned by a

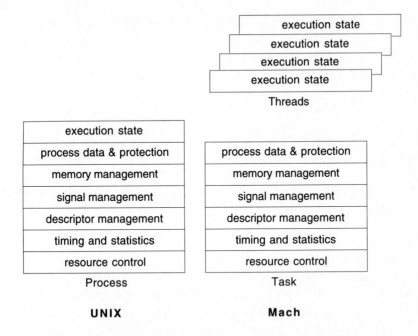

Figure 1.1: UNIX Process and Mach Task and Threads

task. A thread gains access to a port by virtue of belonging to a task. Cooperating programs may allow threads from one task to gain access to ports in another task. An important feature of ports is that they are location transparent. This capability facilitates the distribution of services over a network without program modification.

Message: Threads in different tasks communicate with each other by exchanging *messages*. A message contains typed collections of data. This data can range from program-specific data such as numbers or strings to Mach-related data such as transferring capabilities of a port from one task to another.

Memory Object: The ability to perform traditional OS functions in user-level programs is a key feature of Mach. For example, Mach supports virtual memory paging policy in a user-level program. *Memory objects* are an abstraction to support this capability.

All of these concepts are a fundamental part of Mach programming and are used by the Mach kernel itself. Each of these concepts is explained in this book in detail, and complete examples support these explanations. We believe it is important to understand these basic components fully before continuing on to more advanced features.

1.4   Getting Started with Mach

This section describes some of the basics of writing and compiling Mach programs. Nearly every Mach program requires the headers and libraries presented here. This section also discusses how to compile your program and what libraries you need to use. Fortunately, the mechanics of building a Mach program are simple.

1.4.1   Header Files

There is one very important header file that all Mach programs must include. This header is `mach.h`, and it encompasses all the typedefs and interfaces necessary to program under Mach.

Certain special packages require their own additional header files. For instance, the C Threads library requires the `cthreads.h` header file. The MIG facility uses `mach/mig_errors.h` for error codes. The OSF/1 P Threads library requires the `pthread.h` include file. This file must be the *first* header file specified in a P Threads program.

One important note regarding header files is that their location differs among the various versions of Mach released by different vendors. Header files for Mach programs exist in a variety of places, but they can generally be found in

- `/usr/include`

- `/usr/include/mach`

- `/usr/include/sys`

- `/usr/include/servers`

If a program example does not compile due to header file errors, it will most likely be due to this variance.

1.4.2   Compilation and Libraries

To build your Mach program, you need to use the appropriate libraries to provide the functions described in this book. There is a library archive,

`libmach.a`, which contains many of the functions discussed. So the typical
Mach program would be compiled as follows:

```
cc -o prog prog.c -lmach
```

Again, the threads packages have their own libraries that also must be
specified to use those packages. Those archives are `libthreads.a` for the
C Threads library and `libpthreads.a` for the P Threads library. When
using those packages, it is important to specify the threads library before
the Mach library. The P Threads library uses a re-entrant (i.e., thread-safe)
version of the C library. The order shown here is very important to compile
a C Threads or P Threads program:

```
cc -o cthreads_prog cthreads_prog.c -lthreads -lmach
cc -o pthreads_prog pthreads_prog.c -pic-none -lpthreads -lmach -lc_r
```

Chapter 2

Tasks and Threads

One of the central elements of Mach is its program execution environment. This advanced environment easily allows applications to optimize performance by using concurrently running computations called *threads*. To exploit this capability, it must be possible to share data and other resources among threads conveniently and efficiently. Mach implements this sharing by grouping resources together in a *task*. Every thread belongs to a single task and may access all of that task's resources. Any number of threads may be associated with the same task. Tasks and threads permit the design of applications that automatically take advantage of multiple processors while running on single CPU machines without change.

In contrast, UNIX combines a running computation and its resources into a *process*. Mach separates these two aspects of a program, permitting the application designer control over each one independently. Mach models a traditional UNIX process as a task with a single thread.

The Mach task and thread model provides advantages over the corresponding UNIX model of program execution. *Parallel processing* (multiple computations running at once applied to the same problem) is more natural with tasks and threads. Information sharing is more straightforward and requires less setup. Creating threads is less costly in CPU time than creating UNIX processes.

This chapter presents the Mach kernel's task and thread capabilities. A thorough knowledge of tasks and threads is important because tasks and threads play a key role in the operation of many aspects of Mach applications. For instance, the ports used for Mach interprocess communication (IPC) are resources associated with a task. Similarly, Mach's virtual memory

13

mechanisms operate on tasks. The exception handling facility is specifically designed to work with tasks and threads. You will find many more examples as you learn more about Mach. Understanding how to control tasks and threads is as important for the Mach programmer as understanding processes is for the UNIX programmer.

The remainder of this chapter shows how to use Mach kernel calls directly to create and use tasks and threads in your applications, and contains:

- A discussion of the use of Mach tasks

- An exploration of programming with Mach threads

- A description of the Mach thread system calls

- An example multithreaded application.

The material in this chapter provides a solid foundation for further exploration of Mach programming.

2.1   Using Mach Tasks

What is a Mach task, and how does it differ from a UNIX process? In Mach, a task is a container for a collection of resources (see Fig. 2.1). Mach tasks are *passive*. They do not execute program code. This separation between an executing calculation and its resources is a key difference between Mach and UNIX. A Mach task is different from a UNIX process, which includes both resources, such as file descriptors and memory, and an executing computation.

Just as most UNIX applications use one process, most Mach applications use one task. But Mach allows designing applications with multiple tasks, as well. Let's look at some of the reasons for using more than one task in your application.

2.1.1   Designing Applications with Multiple Tasks

You design an application with more than one task when you need the following:

- Protection for a set of resources

- A different set of resources

- Additional resources.

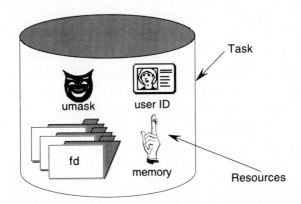

Figure 2.1: Mach Tasks Are Resource Containers

All three of these considerations spring from the fact that a Mach task is a repository for resources. Let's look at each of them in more detail.

A task encapsulates a program to provide a protection boundary. Thus when a program requires protection from other software, you use a separate task. For example, it is not possible for one task to refer directly to the memory of another without mediation by the Mach kernel. This separation of tasks means that, for instance, damage to the memory of one task (e.g., from an errant program) cannot affect the memory of another task.

Application designers would use multiple tasks, then, whenever a protection boundary is required between two or more parts of an application. Client/server applications often fall into this category. The clients and servers are typically implemented as separate tasks so that, for example, malfunctions in the client cannot adversely affect the server. A database server with front-end client programs might be structured in this way. A debugger is another example of an application needing a protection boundary, in this case between the debugger and the target program. Damage to resources in the program being debugged (e.g., clobbered memory) cannot be allowed to affect the debugger itself. The common solution involves using one task for the debugger and a separate task for the target program.

Another reason for multiple tasks is to obtain additional or different resources. For instance, the UNIX concept of a *current working directory* is implemented as a per-task resource in Mach.[1] Thus you might employ more

---

[1]This implementation of the current working directory is specific to Mach 2.5. Mach 3.0 and later versions do not associate a task with a current working directory.

than one task in your application if you need more than one current working
directory.

Additional address space might also be the impetus for using more than
one task in your application. A sparse memory layout or an unusual thirst
for memory might require multiple address spaces. Such a design would
entail using a separate Mach task for each address space.

Most traditional programs do not need to use more than one task. Mach
provides you with the flexibility to do so, however, if your application requires
such a design. Note that multiple processes are sometimes employed in UNIX
to obtain performance improvement by running more than one computation
at a time. This scheme is not necessary in Mach because a single task can
support concurrently executing calculations by using multiple threads.

2.1.2   Talking about Tasks

Unlike UNIX processes, Mach tasks are not related to their creating task.
Nonetheless, for convenience we often refer to a newly created task as a *child
task*. Similarly, we refer to the creating task as the *parent task*.

Also unlike UNIX, there are no a priori control relationships between
Mach tasks, even between parent and child tasks. Strictly speaking, only a
valid *task identifier* is required to perform operations on another task. Task
identifiers are actually Mach IPC ports. Usually a parent knows the identity
of its children, but not vice versa. However, a task may explicitly supply its
identifier to another task (even to a child task), thereby allowing itself to be
the target of task operations.

Note that we sometimes colloquially refer to a task as though it is an
executing program (e.g., "The parent task creates a child task"). We really
mean, "An executing thread in the parent task creates a child task," but
this verbose construction quickly becomes cumbersome. Remember, tasks
are just repositories for resources in Mach.

2.1.3   Spawning a New Task

In Mach 2.5 you create a new task as a byproduct of creating a new UNIX
process with the **fork()** call. Because **fork** produces a UNIX process, it
actually does much more than just create a new task. Specifically, **fork** will

- Create a new task, the child

- Copy the parent (creating) task's memory into the child

- Create one new thread belonging to the child

- Initialize the child's UNIX-related information, such as user IDs and process ID

- Start the execution of the newly created thread.

Mach 3.0 and later versions permit applications to create tasks directly, without invoking the **fork** system call. Mach 3.0 applications must be prepared to initialize the child's memory and other resources, create an initial thread, and so on.

2.1.4   Identifying Mach Tasks

Many Mach system calls accept a task identifier as an input parameter. For example, you must specify a task when creating a new thread, examining a task's address space, or obtaining information about a task. The most common case entails the *current task* (i.e., the task that contains the thread issuing the system call). In both Mach 2.5 and Mach 3.0, you specify this task using the **task_self()** function.

How do you obtain a task identifier for a child task? In Mach 3.0 the **task_create()** call used to spawn a task returns the new task's identifier. Because Mach 2.5 employs the **fork** system call for creating new tasks, there is no mechanism for returning the identifier of new tasks at creation time. Instead, Mach provides the **task_by_unix_pid()** call for this purpose:

```
kern_return_t status;
task_t        target_task;
pid_t         child_pid;
task_t        child_task;

status = task_by_unix_pid(target_task, child_pid, &child_task);
```

The **task_by_unix_pid** call accepts a UNIX process ID, *child_pid*, specifying the process whose task identifier is desired. You also supply a task identifier as input (*target_task*). This task identifier was originally intended to specify the network host on which Mach looks for the specified process; you should supply **task_self** for this argument. Mach returns the task identifier for the process named by *child_pid* in *child_task*.

If the **task_by_unix_pid** call completes successfully, Mach returns the code KERN_SUCCESS in *status*. If *child_pid* specifies an invalid process, the kernel returns KERN_INVALID_ARGUMENT.

Mach restricts your query to processes with the same UNIX user identification (UID) as the process issuing the call. Note that the restriction does not limit *child_pid* to descendents of the calling process, as long as the UIDs match. The *root* UID is an exception and may request the task identifier for any process. Mach returns KERN_PROTECTION_FAILURE if you specify a process in *child_pid* with a different UID than the calling process.

The following short program demonstrates the use of the **task_by_unix_pid** call. The program (let's call it tbup, for **task_by_unix_pid**) creates a child task using **fork**, determines the corresponding task identifier with **task_by_unix_pid**, and then prints the process ID and the task ID.

```
#include <mach.h>

main()
{
        /*
         * Note: child_pid is a "pid_t" in OSF/1
         *   and a "short" in Mach 2.5
         */
        pid_t         child_pid;
        task_t        child_task;
        kern_return_t status;

        child_pid = fork();
        if (child_pid == 0) {    /* child */
                sleep(5);
                exit(0);
        } else {                  /* parent */
                status = task_by_unix_pid(task_self(),
                                        child_pid, &child_task);
                printf("pid: 0x%x  task: 0x%x\n",
                        child_pid, child_task);
                exit(0);
        }
}
```

Here is the output from program tbup:

```
pid: 0xb6b  task: 0xb
```

2.2   Using Mach Threads

Previously we noted that multiple Mach tasks are not required to execute
more than one computation at a time. Instead, Mach offers the ability to
employ one or more *threads*. Mach threads are essentially *virtual processors*,
with their own set of registers and their own state information. Figure 2.2
shows a conceptual model of a thread, a hypothetical *Sparkler CPU*, fetching
instructions from its task's memory and executing them. The thread in Fig.
2.2, for instance, is about to fetch the instruction at location 18.

Mach threads are *active*. They execute program code stored in the address space of a Mach task. Each thread belongs to one task, and several
threads may be, and often are, associated with the same task. The threads
in a task run concurrently.[2] Figure 2.3 extends our conceptual illustration
to show three threads executing code in the same task. Two of these threads
happen to be executing the same instruction—the threads run independently.
Nothing prevents more than one thread from running in a given function or,
as in this case, executing the same instruction.

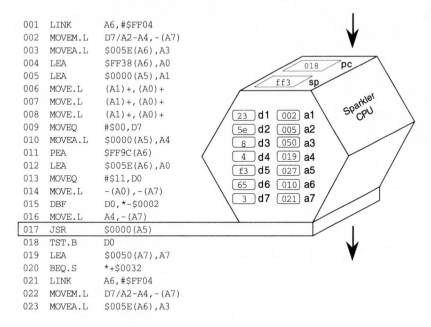

001	LINK	A6,#$FF04
002	MOVEM.L	D7/A2-A4,-(A7)
003	MOVEA.L	$005E(A6),A3
004	LEA	$FF38(A6),A0
005	LEA	$0000(A5),A1
006	MOVE.L	(A1)+,(A0)+
007	MOVE.L	(A1)+,(A0)+
008	MOVE.L	(A1)+,(A0)+
009	MOVEQ	#$00,D7
010	MOVEA.L	$0000(A5),A4
011	PEA	$FF9C(A6)
012	LEA	$005E(A6),A0
013	MOVEQ	#$11,D0
014	MOVE.L	-(A0),-(A7)
015	DBF	D0,*-$0002
016	MOVE.L	A4,-(A7)
017	JSR	$0000(A5)
018	TST.B	D0
019	LEA	$0050(A7),A7
020	BEQ.S	*+$0032
021	LINK	A6,#$FF04
022	MOVEM.L	D7/A2-A4,-(A7)
023	MOVEA.L	$005E(A6),A3

Figure 2.2: A Thread Is a *Virtual Processor*

---

[2]On a single CPU machine, the Mach scheduler apportions the available processor
time among the runnable threads. On a multiple processor system, threads can truly run
concurrently.

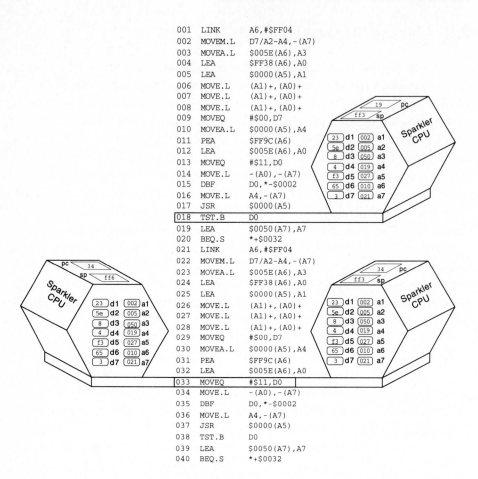

```
001   LINK      A6,#$FF04
002   MOVEM.L   D7/A2-A4,-(A7)
003   MOVEA.L   $005E(A6),A3
004   LEA       $FF38(A6),A0
005   LEA       $0000(A5),A1
006   MOVE.L    (A1)+,(A0)+
007   MOVE.L    (A1)+,(A0)+
008   MOVE.L    (A1)+,(A0)+
009   MOVEQ     #$00,D7
010   MOVEA.L   $0000(A5),A4
011   PEA       $FF9C(A6)
012   LEA       $005E(A6),A0
013   MOVEQ     #$11,D0
014   MOVE.L    -(A0),-(A7)
015   DBF       D0,*-$0002
016   MOVE.L    A4,-(A7)
017   JSR       $0000(A5)
018   TST.B     D0
019   LEA       $0050(A7),A7
020   BEQ.S     *+$0032
021   LINK      A6,#$FF04
022   MOVEM.L   D7/A2-A4,-(A7)
023   MOVEA.L   $005E(A6),A3
024   LEA       $FF38(A6),A0
025   LEA       $0000(A5),A1
026   MOVE.L    (A1)+,(A0)+
027   MOVE.L    (A1)+,(A0)+
028   MOVE.L    (A1)+,(A0)+
029   MOVEQ     #$00,D7
030   MOVEA.L   $0000(A5),A4
031   PEA       $FF9C(A6)
032   LEA       $005E(A6),A0
033   MOVEQ     #$11,D0
034   MOVE.L    -(A0),-(A7)
035   DBF       D0,*-$0002
036   MOVE.L    A4,-(A7)
037   JSR       $0000(A5)
038   TST.B     D0
039   LEA       $0050(A7),A7
040   BEQ.S     *+$0032
```

Figure 2.3: Several Threads Can Run Concurrently

2.2.1   Designing Applications with Multiple Threads

Recall that the task provides the set of resources used by its threads: Memory, IPC ports, and UNIX resources such as file descriptors, umask, user IDs, and other UNIX items are all part of the Mach task. All threads in a task share that task's resources.

The most noticeable effect of this resource sharing is that all threads in a task use the same memory. This memory sharing makes it easy for threads to cooperate in solving problems that need several calculations with the same data. For example, a multiuser appointment manager might be implemented as a multithreaded server under Mach, as illustrated in Fig. 2.4. Such an application could retain the appointment database in memory

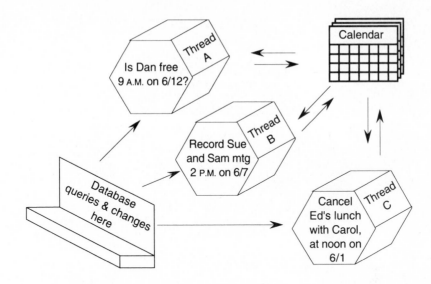

Figure 2.4: A Multithreaded Appointment Manager

and might be designed so a separate thread handles each service request. As queries and changes to the appointment database arrive, the next available thread services each request as other threads complete their work on previous requests. All of these threads would operate on the same set of shared data, such as the client calendars in our example. All threads in a Mach task share the same memory, and this facilitates the close cooperation.

Of course, sharing data carries a responsibility to synchronize changes to that data. Failure to consider this responsibility results in program failures that are difficult to reproduce and debug. Because synchronizing access to shared data is so important when writing multithreaded programs, user-level thread libraries often include synchronization facilities for just this purpose. Section 5.1 describes the synchronization mechanisms provided by the C Threads library often provided with Mach.

While all of the memory in a task is shared among the task's threads, in practice each thread does not use the entire address space. By convention, each thread has an area of the address space designated as its own private stack. All thread stacks are physically accessible to all threads in a task, but typically each thread references only its own assigned stack area. Mach does not enforce this behavior, so it is possible to access (or even overwrite) another thread's stack. Figure 2.5 illustrates a typical memory layout for a multithreaded task. The figure depicts the address space as it would appear after a program creates two additional threads.

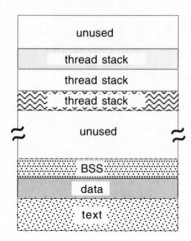

Figure 2.5: Typical Memory Layout for a Multithreaded Task

You might consider the following points when designing your next application. Should you design your application to utilize more than one thread? If so, how many threads should be used? How should the work of an application program be partitioned among multiple threads? There are no universal answers to these questions, but we explore some of the issues in the following sections.

2.2.2   Modular Program Design

Threads can simplify program design when each thread is given a small, focused role. Consider again the hypothetical appointment manager application. A traditional program (i.e., a UNIX process) contains one thread for receiving and dispatching incoming service requests as well as processing the requests. The processing entails querying or changing the database and returning a response message to service requestors. If a separate thread handles this work, the processing code can easily be developed and tested independently of the code to receive and dispatch service requests. While the same separation is theoretically possible with a more monolithic design, threads make it simpler and easier to achieve such a clean, modular application architecture.

2.2.3   Increased Performance

Using threads in your application can provide better performance in three situations:

1. When computing can be overlapped with I/O

2. When computing jobs are frequently created and destroyed

3. When the hardware provides more than one processor.

Let's look at each possibility in more detail.

When Computing Can Be Overlapped with I/O

When a UNIX process performs I/O, it stops until the I/O completes. This delay may be significant, for example, if it is necessary to wait until output data reaches a device, or for input operations from a network. If the machine has no other work, the processor is idle during this waiting period.

By using more than one thread, your application can perform I/O and continue execution at the same time. As long as the computations do not require data from the I/O operations, the two activities can overlap. Figures 2.6 and 2.7 show two time sequences comparing the time needed for a fixed amount of work. In Fig. 2.6, the CPU running Thread X pauses after each I/O call. In Fig. 2.7, Thread A executes during the I/O operations performed concurrently by Thread B, reducing the total time needed for the program to finish.

When Computing Jobs Are Frequently Created and Destroyed

The client/server paradigm can be applied to UNIX processes as well as to Mach threads. But when the frequency of requests becomes too high,

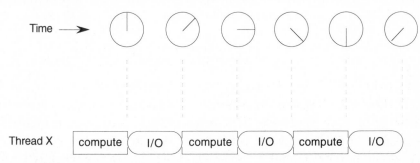

Figure 2.6: One Thread Alternating Calculation and I/O Operations

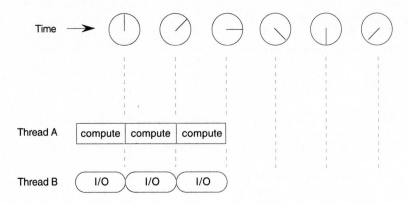

Figure 2.7: Two Threads Concurrently Calculating and Performing I/O

the overhead of creating and destroying UNIX processes becomes a limiting factor in the application's performance. For instance, one might design the appointment manager application using processes. Whenever a new request to query or modify the appointment database arrives, a new UNIX process would be created to service the request. For infrequent requests, this design is adequate, but it does not scale well as service requests arrive at a higher rate.

It takes significantly less CPU time to create and destroy Mach threads than UNIX processes. The difference arises because threads include much less information than UNIX processes. All of the resource data normally part of a UNIX process are associated with a task in Mach. Creating a new thread, unlike executing a **fork** call to create a new process, does not require duplicating an address space. In addition, threads do not include any of the UNIX-specific information, such as user IDs and mask settings. Threads can therefore be created with less cost in terms of CPU time than processes. In situations like the appointment manager, threads may be a better choice than processes when processes must be created and destroyed often.

When the Hardware Provides More Than One Processor

A key advantage of threads is that Mach runs more than one thread at a time if there are available processors. It is not necessary to change your application to take advantage of this feature. Multithreaded applications run unchanged on both single processor and multiprocessor systems. The execution of more than one computation at a time can significantly improve your application's performance.

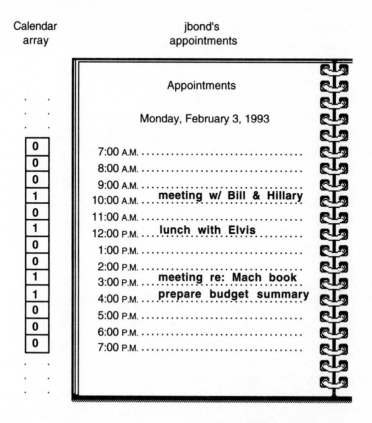

Figure 2.8: Array of One-Hour Time Slots

Finally, not all problems can be solved more efficiently using multiple threads. Small calculations are sometimes accomplished faster without the added complexity of creating and managing threads. The "breakeven" point varies with the application and differs if you employ a threads library such as C Threads or P Threads.

2.2.4   Sharing Data among Threads

Until now, we have glossed over a key concept in programming with threads. Using multiple threads requires *synchronizing* access to shared data. Let's look at why this is true and then discuss the implications for writing Mach programs.

To facilitate our exploration of shared data usage, consider the multi-user appointment manager we discussed earlier in this chapter. Assume this program uses an in-memory array representing each hour in a client's week to track empty time slots. A zero (0) in an entry represents an available hour, while the value one (1) indicates a used time slot. Figure 2.8 shows this *calendar* array for user jbond. Each thread in our program that handles an incoming request for jbond's time checks the *calendar* array to see if the desired time slot is open, and if so marks the slot as in-use. To illustrate the importance of synchronizing access to shared data, suppose that two requests for a 9:00 A.M. Monday meeting with jbond have arrived. Two threads (let's call them Thread X and Thread Y) both execute the following code at the same time:

```
#define AVAIL 0
#define TAKEN 1

struct client *jbond;

/*
 * mark_hour_if_free:  check calendar slot for indicated
 *      day and hour;  if available, mark it as taken.
 *      Sunday is day 0, hours are numbered 0-23.
 */

mark_hour_if_free(day, hour_of_day)
int day, hour_of_day;
{
        int calendar_index;

        calendar_index = (day * 24) + hour_of_day;

        if (jbond->calendar[calendar_index] == AVAIL)
                jbond->calendar[calendar_index] = TAKEN;
}
```

Refer to Fig. 2.9 and watch what happens as the two threads move through this function. For 9:00 A.M. Monday, day is 1 and hour_of_day is 9. Thread X first stores 33 ($1 * 24 + 9 = 33$) into *calendar_index*, an automatic variable local to Thread X. Thread Y also calculates a value of 33 for its instance of *calendar_index*. Thread X now performs the first part of the if statement and finds that the 9:00 A.M. Monday time slot is free. Thread Y then executes the first part of the if statement and also determines that the entry for 9:00 A.M. Monday is available. Thread X, having found the slot free, now sets the entry to 1 (TAKEN). Thread Y, having found the entry free, also sets it to TAKEN. Poor jbond now has two meetings at the same time!

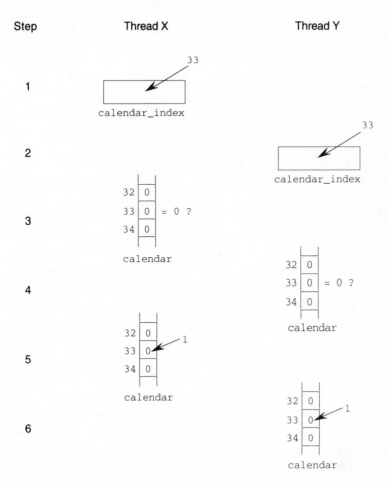

Figure 2.9: Two Threads Running Concurrently

This problem is called a *race*. The difficulty lies in the unrestricted access to the shared *calendar* array. This sharing of data is quite common in multithreaded programs and is one of the reasons for using multiple threads: Sharing of data is easy. However, we must also ensure that only one thread at a time actually manipulates shared data. The solution is quite simple.

All that is necessary is a way of *locking* the shared data. Locking is a mechanism that causes a thread to pause in its execution if another thread has already locked the shared data. An important characteristic of such a locking facility is that it is *atomic*. That is, the checking for other threads that have locked the data and the subsequent locking must be a single, indivisible operation. Only one thread at a time may safely modify shared data and some sort of lock operation is needed to achieve this serialization.

2.2.5   Multithreading Existing Programs

How do we take an existing single-threaded program and modify it to use more than one thread? There are two key design activities to consider:

- Partitioning the problem

- Protecting shared data.

Once these issues have been addressed, the mechanics of using multiple threads become straightforward. To illustrate this point, in Section 2.4 we walk through the process of adding multiple threads to an existing program. In this section we take a closer look at these two application design questions.

Let's begin with partitioning the problem. To divide your application into pieces suitable for multiple threads, recall the goals of increased performance and simplicity. Higher performance is achieved by executing previously serial operations concurrently. Divide your program into its natural portions, and see if those sections can run simultaneously. Does each part you have identified operate without needing the result from another part? Do the parts have clear, infrequent interactions? If so, each of these pieces is a good candidate for execution in a separate thread.

An important caveat: Partitioning can easily be carried too far. If each thread in your application performs a small enough piece of the total job, the threads will need to exchange information frequently. The greater the interaction between the threads, the more CPU time is devoted to interthread communication, and the less CPU time is applied to solving your problem.

Now we consider the question of shared data. Checking the usage of global data is the key technique here. For single-threaded programs, global data is not normally considered "shared" in the sense that we have used the term in this chapter. But changing your program to execute some pieces concurrently invalidates this otherwise safe assumption. You must synchronize access to this shared data.

2.2.6   Thread-Safe Libraries

Complete Mach programs require not just your own code, but also supporting functions in libraries. UNIX programmers are familiar with the standard

C library (*libc*). You may also have local libraries available on your system. When they can be called simultaneously by multiple threads, library routines linked with your Mach program are subject to the requirements discussed in Section 2.2.5 for correct operation.

2.3   Mach Thread Calls

This section presents several of the Mach system calls you need in working with Mach threads. After discussing these calls, we use them in a multi-threaded application example so you can see how all the pieces fit together.

Let's begin with a look at requesting and starting a new thread. Newly created threads do not execute immediately. They are created in a dormant state and must be explicitly initialized and then started. The next three sections present the Mach system calls used to create, initialize, and start a thread.

2.3.1   Spawning a New Thread

Mach provides the **thread_create()** call for requesting a new thread:

```
kern_return_t status;
task_t        parent_task;
thread_t      new_thread;

status = thread_create(parent_task, &new_thread);
```

If the **thread_create** call completes without error, a new thread is created in *parent_task*, an identifier for the new thread is placed in *new_thread*, and the kernel returns KERN_SUCCESS in *status*. The call can fail if either *parent_task* is not a valid task (KERN_INVALID_ARGUMENT) or if there are insufficient resources in the kernel (KERN_RESOURCE_SHORTAGE).

Mach kernel calls are designed to be as general as possible. For example, you can create a new thread belonging either to the task executing the **thread_create** call or to another accessible task. To create a thread in another task, simply specify the desired task as the first parameter to **thread_create**. The **task_self()** call is often used as the first argument to **thread_create**:

```
status = thread_create(task_self(), &new_thread);
```

This construction indicates that the new thread will belong to the same task as the thread executing the **thread_create** call.

2.3.2   Preparing the New Thread to Run

A newly created thread cannot yet execute. First, the thread must be prepared by setting various pieces of information. These data include such items as the stack pointer, the address of the first instruction to execute, the state of various flags (such as a carry bit or an arithmetic overflow indicator), and so on. Unfortunately, the specific list of elements to be considered depends on the machine. Typically, the state is composed of the hardware machine registers. Each system architecture requires the setup of a unique set of such *state information* to run a thread.

Use the **thread_set_state()** call to specify the state information for a thread. This state data is contained in a *thread_state_t* structure defined in the header file <thread_status.h>. By convention the name of the structure usually includes the architecture name. Examples include mips_thread_state for systems based on a MIPS architecture, ns32000_thread_state for machines using the National 32000-series architecture, and i386_thread_state for systems based on the Intel 386 architecture.

An architecture's state information is sometimes partitioned into sets, or *flavors*, of related register data. Two examples are state information related to floating point operations, and state information specific to a particular processor type within an architecture family. Table 2.1 shows the data structure names for several of these state information varieties.

You specify the state information for a thread using the Mach **thread_set_state** system call:

```
kern_return_t       status;
thread_t            th;
int                 flavor;

thread_state_t      new_state;
unsigned int        count;

status = thread_set_state(th, flavor, new_state, count);
```

This call stores the state information *new_state* for the specified thread *th* in the Mach kernel. The *flavor* argument indicates which set of state information to store (e.g., i386_THREAD_STATE versus i386_FLOAT_STATE). For machines with more than one flavor of state information, a **thread_set_state**

Standard Registers	Floating Registers	Other CPU Registers
i386_THREAD_STATE	i386_FLOAT_STATE	
NS32000_THREAD_STATE		NS32532_THREAD_STATE
MIPS_THREAD_STATE	MIPS_FLOAT_STATE	

Table 2.1: Thread State Flavors

call may be required for each flavor to specify the thread state. Mach does not interpret or use the state information at the time of the **thread_set_state** call. The data are simply stored away for use when the indicated thread is run later.

A *thread_state_t* type is defined as an array of integers. In practice, the state information is not usually declared as a *thread_state_t*. Instead, the *new_state* parameter is typically one of the machine-specific thread state structures, such as mips_thread_state, cast to type *thread_state_t* in the call to **thread_set_state**.

For convenience, most Mach implementations include a symbol defining the size of the state information array in `<thread_status.h>`. By convention this size is named by taking the flavor name and appending _COUNT. Examples include i386_THREAD_STATE_COUNT and i386_FLOAT_STATE_COUNT.

The *count* argument to **thread_set_state** reflects the size of *new_state* in units of integers. Storing only a portion of a thread's state information is disallowed. In this case the kernel returns KERN_INVALID_ARGUMENT. The kernel also returns KERN_INVALID_ARGUMENT if *th* specifies the calling thread or does not specify a valid thread.

Note that a Mach application that employs the **thread_set_state** call is not portable among multiple hardware architectures. Source code portability is an important impetus for using a threads library such as C Threads or P Threads, which hides this machine-specific aspect of Mach kernel threads.

Some programs, debuggers for instance, need the ability to modify some of the state information for a thread. In this case, the current state must be obtained, individual items changed, and the new state stored in the kernel. Use the **thread_get_state()** system call to retrieve the current state information:

```
kern_return_t      status;
thread_t           th;
int                flavor;
```

```
thread_state_t      cur_state;
unsigned int        count;

status = thread_get_state(th, flavor, cur_state, &count);
```

This call returns the current state information for thread *th* as specified by *flavor*. The *count* argument must be set to the maximum size of the area to hold the new state *cur_state*, in units of integers. The kernel updates this count to indicate how much data (in units of integers) were actually stored. If *cur_state* is too small to hold the state information, MIG_ARRAY_TOO_LARGE is returned. The kernel returns KERN_INVALID_ARGUMENT if *th* does not specify a valid thread.

2.3.3   Running a New Thread

When a thread is first created, Mach sets its initial state to *suspended*. In this condition, the thread does not execute. To start the thread running, execute the **thread_resume()** system call:

```
kern_return_t status;
thread_t      th;

status = thread_resume(th);
```

The **thread_resume** call decrements a *thread suspend count*, maintained in the kernel, for the specified thread *th*. Mach sets this suspend count to 1 when creating the thread. When the count reaches zero, the thread is allowed to run.[3] You can obtain a snapshot of a thread's suspend count via the **thread_info()** system call discussed in Section 2.6.3.

You can stop a running thread by using the **thread_suspend()** system call:

```
kern_return_t status;
thread_t      th;

status = thread_suspend(th);
```

---

[3]Mach makes no guarantee that the thread *will* run immediately. The Mach kernel determines which threads run at any given time based on relative thread priorities and the available processor resources.

This operation increments the specified thread's suspend count, preventing Mach from running the thread. Note that a thread does not necessarily run after a **thread_resume()** call. Any previous **thread_suspend** calls must be balanced by the same number of **thread_resume** calls before a thread can execute.

Threads do not cease execution immediately when suspended. If the thread being suspended is running in the kernel—for example, to perform an I/O system call such as **read()** or **write()**—the thread is suspended when the system call completes. If the thread being suspended is running in user mode, it continues to run until it *traps* to the kernel. Traps occur for a variety of reasons, including clock interrupts at the end of a scheduler time slice, system calls, I/O interrupts, and page faults. Thus there might be a short delay before a thread stops running. The **thread_suspend** call is synchronous; when it returns, the specified thread has been stopped.

2.3.4   The Demise of a Thread

When a thread has completed its work, it may be disposed of using the **thread_terminate()** call:

```
kern_return_t status;
thread_t       unneeded_thread;

status = thread_terminate(unneeded_thread);
```

Specifying **thread_self()** as the first argument to the **thread_terminate** call causes the running thread to commit suicide. In Mach 2.5, the last thread in a task must call **exit()** instead of **thread_terminate**. The **exit** system call performs cleanup operations that are required to terminate cleanly; omitting the call to **exit** causes your program to hang. Note that **exit** terminates all threads in the task, not just the calling thread.

2.4   A Multithreaded Example

We now know enough about Mach threads to implement a program that uses them. To illustrate the calls described in Section 2.3, we develop a multithreaded version of a matrix multiplication program. Since our goal is to illustrate the techniques involved in using Mach threads, we emphasize multithreading concepts and issues while keeping the matrix multiplication

$$\begin{pmatrix} \text{result}_{00} & \text{result}_{01} \\ \text{result}_{10} & \text{result}_{11} \end{pmatrix} = \begin{pmatrix} \text{mat\_1}_{00} & \text{mat\_1}_{01} & \text{mat\_1}_{02} \\ \text{mat\_1}_{10} & \text{mat\_1}_{11} & \text{mat\_1}_{12} \end{pmatrix} * \begin{pmatrix} \text{mat\_2}_{00} & \text{mat\_2}_{01} \\ \text{mat\_2}_{10} & \text{mat\_2}_{11} \\ \text{mat\_2}_{21} & \text{mat\_2}_{21} \end{pmatrix}$$

$$\text{result}_{jk} = \sum_{i=1}^{P} \text{mat\_1}_{ji} * \text{mat\_2}_{ik}$$

Figure 2.10: An Example Matrix Multiplication

aspects of our program as simple as possible. Our motivation for using multiple threads is higher performance. Note that on a multiprocessor machine, Mach automatically executes more than one thread at a time. You need not perform any special operations to take advantage of this important Mach feature.

2.4.1   Single-Threaded Design

Let's start by looking at a version of the matrix multiplication program that does not use multiple threads. This will provide a base for later comparison with the multithreaded version of the same application. The single-threaded smat program computes a result matrix *result* by multiplying two input matrices, *mat_1* and *mat_2*. Matrix *mat_1* consists of N rows by P columns and matrix *mat_2* contains P rows by M columns. These sizes yield a result matrix *result* of N rows by M columns. For instance, Fig. 2.10 shows the problem where matrix *mat_1* has N = 2 rows and P = 3 columns, and matrix *mat_2* contains P = 3 rows and M = 2 columns.

The three matrices are implemented as statically allocated, fixed size arrays. We statically initialize the two input matrices with small integers just to simplify the example. When executed, program smat prints the two input matrices and the *result* matrix:

```
mat_1:
    1    2    3    4
    5    6    7    8
    9    0    1    2
mat_2:
    3    4    5    6    7
    8    9    0    1    2
    3    4    5    6    7
    8    9    0    1    2
```

```
result:
   60    70    20    30    40
  148   174    60    86   112
   46    58    50    62    74
```

The file "`mat.h`" defines the sizes of the matrices:

```
/*
 * mat.h - Common definitions for programs smat, mmat
 */

#define N 3
#define P 4
#define M 5
```

Here is the single-threaded matrix multiplication program, smat:

```
/*
 * Program smat - Singlethreaded Matrix Multiply
 *                (implemented and tested on OSF/1)
 */

#include <stddef.h>
#include <stdlib.h>
#include "mat.h"

int mat_1[N][P] = {{1, 2, 3, 4},
                   {5, 6, 7, 8},
                   {9, 0, 1, 2}};

int mat_2[P][M] = {{3, 4, 5, 6, 7},
                   {8, 9, 0, 1, 2},
                   {3, 4, 5, 6, 7},
                   {8, 9, 0, 1, 2}};

int result[N][M];

main()
{
        matrix_multiply();      /* Multiply the matrices */
        matrix_print();         /* Print the result      */
        exit(0);
}

/*
 * Multiply matrices mat_1 * mat_2
```

```
 */
matrix_multiply()
{
        int i, j, l;
        for (i=0; i < N; i++) {
                for (j=0; j < M; j++) {
                        result[i][j] = 0;
                        for (l=0; l < P; l++) {
                                result[i][j] +=
                                        mat_1[i][l] * mat_2[l][j];
                        }
                }
        }
}
```

The code to print the matrices will be used again for the multithreaded
version of the program, so we keep it in a separate file:

```
/*
 * matprt.c - Print matrices for smat, mmat programs
 */

#include "mat.h"

extern int mat_1[N][P], mat_2[P][M], result[N][M];

void
matrix_print()
{
        int i, j;

        printf("mat_1:\n");
        for (i=0; i < N; i++) {
                for (j=0; j < P; j++)
                        printf("%4d  ", mat_1[i][j]);
                putchar('\n');
        }

        printf("mat_2:\n");
        for (i=0; i < P; i++) {
                for (j=0; j < M; j++)
                        printf("%4d  ", mat_2[i][j]);
                putchar('\n');
        }
```

```
printf("result:\n");
for (i=0; i < N; i++) {
        for (j=0; j < M; j++)
                printf("%4d  ", result[i][j]);
        putchar('\n');
}
}
```

2.4.2   Multithreading Design

Before launching into the details of applying multiple threads to our matrix multiplication problem, we consider the applicability of multithreading.
Matrix multiplication lends itself to a multithreaded solution because the
calculation of each element in the result matrix is independent of the calculation for the other elements. This independence means that no interaction
is required among our computing threads; each thread can proceed without
waiting for any of the others. This situation represents the best case—no
thread need pause until another thread completes some or all of its work, so
performance is optimized.

A multithreaded approach to matrix multiplication also requires shared
data. The elements of the input matrices must be accessible to every thread
contributing to the formation of the result matrix. Such accessibility is precisely why threads are suited to this type of problem: All threads in a Mach
task share the same memory, so the input matrices are automatically available to each thread. Of course, UNIX processes could be used to achieve
similar sharing, but with much more effort. Sharing would need to be explicitly established (e.g., using System V shared memory segments). The
requirement to share data makes Mach threads a perfect vehicle for solving
this kind of problem.

The single-threaded version of the program was quite straightforward.
Let's consider what we need to change in order to use multiple threads.
The first activity is to partition the problem so each thread can work on its
own assignment in parallel with other threads. For matrix multiplication,
the smallest sensible unit of work is the computation of one element in the
result matrix. It is possible to divide the work into even smaller chunks,
but any finer division would not be useful. For example, calculating each
result matrix element requires P additions. These additions could be divided
among more than one thread, but there are two disadvantages:

- The overhead of determining which part of the calculation each thread performs becomes too costly.

- The result of each thread's calculation would have to be combined with the results of the other threads working on the same matrix element.

The second point implies not just additional work, but also an important design constraint: Since the partial results from all threads computing a given element must be combined, the threads must now synchronize their activities. This synchronization would lengthen the time needed to solve the overall problem. By assigning each thread the job of calculating a unique element in the result matrix, the synchronization requirement is avoided.

Note that shared data must be protected. Referring to program smat, the global data are the two input matrices and the result matrix. Program smat does not modify the input matrices, so there is no need to synchronize access to them. It *is* necessary to synchronize access to the result matrix, since more than one thread modifies it concurrently. However, we have designed the multithreaded version of the program, mmat, so only one thread at a time changes a given matrix element. This scheme eliminates the need to synchronize access to the result matrix.

In the multithreaded version of the program, mmat, we keep the basic structure of the smat program intact. But now the routine to multiply the two matrices, **matrix_multiply**, does not do the actual work itself. Instead, it calls a function **thread_fork** to create each thread, prepare the thread for execution, and start it running. The individual threads each then perform a portion of the matrix multiplication. Here is the new version of function **matrix_multiply**:

```
/*
 * Create & start NTHREADS threads
 * to multiply matrices mat_1 * mat_2
 */
matrix_multiply()
{
        int thread_num;

        for (thread_num = 0; thread_num < NTHREADS; thread_num++) {
                threads[thread_num] = THREAD_NOT_DONE;
                thread_fork(thread_num);
        }
        wait_for_threads();
}
```

Before creating and starting a thread, **matrix_multiply** notes that the
thread has not completed its work. This notation is maintained in a *threads*
table, with one entry for each thread. The mmat program will use this information later to determine when the calculation of the result matrix has
finished.

2.4.3   Creating the Threads

Let's take a look at the details of initiating the threads in **thread_fork**.
Three steps are needed:

- Request a new thread from the kernel.

- Set up the thread's state information.

- Start running the thread.

We have already seen the **thread_create** call used to obtain a new thread
from the kernel. The state setup happens in a new routine, **setup_thread()**,
which we examine later. Function **thread_fork** then starts the new thread
executing with a **thread_resume** system call.   Here is the complete
thread_fork function:

```
/*
 * Create, setup, and start a thread
 */
thread_fork(thread_num)
int thread_num;
{
        kern_return_t status;
        thread_t      th;

        status = thread_create(task_self(), &th);
        if (status != KERN_SUCCESS) {
                mach_error("thread_create:", status);
                exit(1);
        }
        setup_thread(th, thread_num);
        status = thread_resume(th);
        if (status != KERN_SUCCESS) {
                mach_error("thread_resume:", status);
                exit(2);
        }

}
```

2.4.4   Preparing the New Thread for Execution

The **setup_thread** function prepares a new thread for execution. Before a newly created thread can run, its state information must be initialized. This entails at a minimum allocating an area for the thread's stack, setting the thread's stack pointer and program counter registers, and performing any other machine-specific setup. The matrix multiplication example presented here runs on an Intel i386-based system. You will need to change this machine-specific code to perform whatever unique setup is appropriate to your hardware. The hardware-dependent code is clearly marked (/***/) in the example.

In addition to the machine-specific preparation, generic setup work is needed for all implementations. Each thread requires a key, *thread_num*, that determines which portion of the overall computation each thread will do. We pass this key to each thread as an input argument (*arg*). The code to prepare the thread for execution thus comprises these steps:

1. Allocate space for the thread's stack.

2. Initialize pointers to the start and end of the stack.

3. Clear the structure holding the thread's new state.

4. Set the thread's register values in the state structure and set up the stack.

5. Store the new state in the Mach kernel (**thread_set_state**).

Step 4 includes setting the value of the program counter register to the beginning of the function **thread_multiply**. All new threads will begin running in this routine. Then we initialize the stack so it appears as though **thread_multiply** was called with one argument, *arg* (representing a sequence number for the thread). The next section discusses this startup processing in more detail.

Here is the code to implement these five steps in program mmat:

```
#define STACKSIZE 8192
#define NTHREADS 8

char stacks[NTHREADS][STACKSIZE];

/*
 * Prepare a thread for execution
```

```
 */
setup_thread(th, arg)
thread_t th;         /* ID of thread to setup            */
int      arg;        /* Argument to thread's start routine */
{
        char                    *stack;
        register int            *top;
/***/   struct i386_thread_state state, *ts;
        kern_return_t           status;

        /*
         * 1.  Allocate space for the stack
         */

        /*
         * (In this program, the stack is statically allocated,
         * so no further action is required)
         */

        /*
         * 2.  Initialize pointers to start, end of stack
         */
        stack = (char *) &stacks[arg];
        top = (int *) (stack + STACKSIZE - sizeof(void));

        /*
         * 3.  Clear the area to hold the new state
         */
        bzero((char *) &state, sizeof(state));

        /*
         * 4. Set up i386 call frame and registers.
         *    One argument (arg) will be on the stack.
         */
/***/   ts = (struct i386_thread_state *) &state;
        /*
         * Store the address of the start
         *  routine (thread_multiply)
         */
/***/   ts->eip = (int)(int(*)())thread_multiply;
/***/   *--top = (int) arg;      /* argument to function th_mul  */
/***/   *--top = 0;              /* fake pc                      */
/***/   ts->uesp = (int) top;
```

```
        /*
         * 5.   Advise the kernel of the new thread state
         */
/***/    status = thread_set_state(th, i386_THREAD_STATE,
                                   (thread_state_t) &state,
                                   i386_THREAD_STATE_COUNT);
         if (status != KERN_SUCCESS)
                 mach_error("setup_thread", status);
}
```

Note that we avoid using library routines like **malloc()**, since not all library
routines are safe in a multithreaded program.[4] Instead, we allocate space
for the thread's stack using static declarations.

The lines preceded by /***/ indicate hardware-specific operations that
you will need to replace with code for your computer. This aspect of Mach
threads is a hindrance to portability. The code must be adapted for each
new machine on which you use it. For this reason, it is unusual to employ
Mach's thread facilities directly. Instead, you should use one of the threads
libraries described in later chapters. But do not skip ahead just yet—our
discussion of Mach kernel threads is important for understanding the threads
libraries.

2.4.5   Performing the Computation

The last action of the routine **thread_fork** is to start each newly created
thread running by executing the **thread_resume** system call. Each thread
will begin executing code in its *start routine*. All threads in our matrix
multiplication application use the same start routine, **thread_multiply**.
This function determines which elements of the result matrix each thread will
compute. The calculation has been broken down for clarity and now resides
in a new function **compute_element()**. Here is routine **thread_multiply**:

```
/*
 * Do one thread's multiplications
 */
thread_multiply(thread_num)
int thread_num;
{
        kern_return_t status;
        int i, j;
```

---

[4]However, in this case only one thread executes the function **setup_thread** at a time,
so **malloc** could be used with no ill effect.

```
    for (i=0; i < N; i++) {
            for (j=thread_num; j < M; j += NTHREADS)
                    result[i][j] = compute_element(i, j);
    }

    threads[thread_num] = THREAD_DONE;
    status = thread_terminate(thread_self());
    if (status != KERN_SUCCESS)
            mach_error("thread_terminate:", status);
}
```

As program mmat creates each thread, it numbers them, from 0 to
NTHREADS-1. The parameter *thread_num* supplied to **thread_multiply** is
this sequence number.   Thus the first thread created calls **thread_
multiply(0)**, the second thread calls **thread_multiply(1)**, and so on. The
function **thread_multiply** uses the thread sequence number to determine
which elements of the result matrix to compute. For instance if we use two
threads (i.e., NTHREADS = 2), then in the first thread, routine **thread_
multiply** calls **compute_element** to calculate the result matrix elements
$result_{00}$, $result_{02}$, $result_{04}$, ... In the second thread, **thread_multiply** will
call **compute_element** for matrix elements $result_{01}$, $result_{03}$, $result_{05}$, ...
The two threads thus divide the work involved in computing the result matrix. The same approach handles any number of threads simply by modifying
NTHREADS, with no change needed in the coding of **thread_multiply**.
    Where is the invocation of the routine **thread_multiply**? There is no ex-
plicit call to this routine. Instead, mmat designates **thread_multiply** as the
start routine for each thread. For each newly created thread, **setup_thread**
sets the memory address of **thread_multiply** as the thread's program
counter value. When **thread_fork** calls **thread_resume** for the thread,
it begins running in routine **thread_multiply**. Similarly, **setup_thread**
stores the sequence number for the thread (*arg*, the argument to the thread's
start routine) on the thread's stack. When Mach begins executing the thread
in **thread_multiply**, the parameter *thread_num* contains the sequence number.
    Although the calculation has not changed in our multithreaded version
of the program, for completeness we present **compute_element**:

```
/*
 * Compute one result matrix element
```

```
 */
compute_element(i, j)
int i, j;
{
        int l, element;

        element = 0;
        for (l=0; l < P; l++)
                element += mat_1[i][l] * mat_2[l][j];
        return(element);
}
```

2.4.6   When Are We Done?

When using multithreaded programs you must determine when all the application's work has been completed. When our application used only one thread to compute the result matrix, it was clear when the calculations were finished. At that point the program could terminate because it had performed all of its work. With our multithreaded program, there are several computing threads as well as the thread executing the main program. The routine **matrix_multiply** now only *initiates* other threads to perform the computation and then returns to the main program. If we simply call **exit** at this point, the program is likely to be in the middle of its calculations. Later we will see how to employ synchronization mechanisms for multithreaded programs. For now, we use a simpler scheme to ensure that all the computation threads have finished their assigned matrix elements before the program exits.

Recall that each thread stored a THREAD_NOT_DONE flag in the *threads* table when it was first created in **matrix_multiply**. As each thread completes its portion of the overall job, it changes this entry in the table to THREAD_DONE before terminating. The main program now defers its **exit** call until all of the table entries contain THREAD_DONE. This synchronization is handled by the new routine **wait_for_threads**:

```
/*
 * Poll until all threads are done
 */
wait_for_threads()
{
        int thread_num;
```

```
        for (thread_num = 0; thread_num < NTHREADS; thread_num++) {
                while(threads[thread_num] == THREAD_NOT_DONE)
                        sleep(1);
        }
}
```

We have now covered all of the central ideas in our multithreaded matrix multiplication program. In the next section, we put all of the pieces together.

2.4.7   The Complete Multithreaded Program

```
/*
 * Program mmat - Multithreaded Matrix Multiply
 */

#include <stddef.h>
#include <stdlib.h>
#include <stdio.h>
#include <mach.h>
#include "mat.h"

int mat_1[N][P] = {{1, 2, 3, 4},
                   {5, 6, 7, 8},
                   {9, 0, 1, 2}};

int mat_2[P][M] = {{3, 4, 5, 6, 7},
                   {8, 9, 0, 1, 2},
                   {3, 4, 5, 6, 7},
                   {8, 9, 0, 1, 2}};

int result[N][M];

#define THREAD_NOT_DONE 0
#define THREAD_DONE     1

#define STACKSIZE 8192
#define NTHREADS 8

int threads[NTHREADS];
char stacks[NTHREADS][STACKSIZE];

main()
{
        matrix_multiply();      /* Multiply the matrices   */
```

```
        matrix_print();              /* Print the result matrix */
        exit(0);
}

/*
 * Create & start NTHREADS threads
 * to multiply matrices mat_1 * mat_2
 */
matrix_multiply()
{
        int thread_num;

        for (thread_num = 0; thread_num < NTHREADS; thread_num++) {
                threads[thread_num] = THREAD_NOT_DONE;
                thread_fork(thread_num);
        }
        wait_for_threads();
}

/*
 * Create, setup, and start a thread
 */
thread_fork(thread_num)
int thread_num;
{
        kern_return_t status;
        thread_t      th;

        status = thread_create(task_self(), &th);
        if (status != KERN_SUCCESS) {
                mach_error("thread_create:", status);
                exit(1);
        }
        setup_thread(th, thread_num);
        status = thread_resume(th);
        if (status != KERN_SUCCESS) {
                mach_error("thread_resume:", status);
                exit(2);
        }
}

/*
 * Compute one result matrix element
 */
```

```
compute_element(i, j)
int i, j;
{
        int l, element;

        element = 0;
        for (l=0; l < P; l++)
                element += mat_1[i][l] * mat_2[l][j];
        return(element);
}


/*
 * Do one thread's multiplications
 */
thread_multiply(thread_num)
int thread_num;
{
        kern_return_t status;
        int i, j;

        for (i=0; i < N; i++) {
                for (j=thread_num; j < M; j += NTHREADS)
                        result[i][j] = compute_element(i, j);
        }

        threads[thread_num] = THREAD_DONE;
        status = thread_terminate(thread_self());
        if (status != KERN_SUCCESS)
                mach_error("thread_terminate:", status);
}


/*
 * Prepare a thread for execution
 */
setup_thread(th, arg)
thread_t th;        /* ID of thread to setup          */
int      arg;       /* Argument to thread's start routine */
{
        char                    *stack;
        register int            *top;
/***/   struct i386_thread_state state, *ts;
        kern_return_t           status;

        /*
```

```
                 * 1.  Allocate space for the stack
                 */


             /*
              * (In this program, the stack is statically allocated,
              * so no further action is required)
              */


             /*
              * 2.  Initialize pointers to start, end of stack
              */
             stack = (char *) &stacks[arg];
             top = (int *) (stack + STACKSIZE - sizeof(void));


             /*
              * 3.  Clear the area to hold the new state
              */
             bzero((char *) &state, sizeof(state));


             /*
              * 4. Set up i386 call frame and registers.
              *    One argument (arg) will be on the stack.
              */
/***/        ts = (struct i386_thread_state *) &state;
/***/        ts->eip = (int)(int(*)())thread_multiply; /* Start Routine*/
/***/        *--top = (int) arg;     /* argument to function th_mul    */
/***/        *--top = 0;             /* fake pc                        */
/***/        ts->uesp = (int) top;


             /*
              * 5.  Advise the kernel of the new thread state
              */
/***/        status = thread_set_state(th, i386_THREAD_STATE,
                                     (thread_state_t) &state,
                                     i386_THREAD_STATE_COUNT);
             if (status != KERN_SUCCESS)
                     mach_error("setup_thread", status);
}

/*
 * Poll until all threads are done
 */
wait_for_threads()
{
```

```
    int thread_num;

    for (thread_num = 0; thread_num < NTHREADS; thread_num++) {
        while(threads[thread_num] == THREAD_NOT_DONE)
                sleep(1);
    }
}
```

2.5 Mach Task Calls

This section covers the task-related system calls available to your application. All of these calls involve threads as well as tasks. Therefore the material is presented here, after the discussion of threads, rather than in the earlier discussion of tasks in Section 2.1.1. These calls accept a task identifier (of type task_t) as an argument.

2.5.1 Suspending and Resuming All Threads in a Task

For convenience, Mach permits you to suspend all threads in a task with a single system call. This capability is useful, for example, when dealing with exceptions. The **task_suspend()** call increments a *task suspend count* and stops all threads in the specified task. Mach initializes this count to zero when creating new tasks. When the task suspend count is positive, newly created threads will not run. The **task_suspend** call is synchronous (i.e., it does not return until all threads in the task have been suspended). To suspend all threads in the task with the task identifier **a_task**, you invoke the **task_suspend** call as follows:

```
kern_return_t status;
task_t        a_task;

status = task_suspend(a_task);
```

Note that the task suspend count is independent of the suspend counts for each thread in a task. A thread can be runnable only if both its own thread suspend count and its task's suspend count are zero. You can obtain a snapshot of a task's suspend count using the **task_info()** system call described later in this section.

Suspended tasks may be resumed using the **task_resume()** call:

```
kern_return_t status;
task_t        a_task;

status = task_resume(a_task);
```

This call decrements the specified task's suspend count. If the count becomes zero, any threads in the task with zero thread resume counts are allowed to execute.

The **task_resume** call returns KERN_FAILURE if the task suspend count is already zero (it may not be decremented past zero). Both the **task_suspend** and **task_resume** calls return KERN_INVALID_ARGUMENT if the specified task is not a valid task identifier.

2.5.2   Finding All Threads in a Task

Mach provides the **task_threads()** system call for obtaining a list of all threads in a task:

```
kern_return_t  status;
task_t         a_task;
thread_array_t thread_list;
int            thread_count;

status = task_threads(a_task, &thread_list, &thread_count);
```

When you issue the **task_threads** call, the kernel allocates an area of memory in the calling task, fills the area with a list of identifiers for the threads in *a_task*, stores the address of the list in *thread_list*, and places the number of identifiers stored in *thread_count*. You can use the identifiers returned in other calls that accept a *thread_t*.[5] The list of thread identifiers is not in any particular order. Note that although the kernel allocates the memory for the list, your application must explicitly free the allocated storage using the Mach **vm_deallocate()** call. The **task_threads** call returns KERN_INVALID_ARGUMENT if *a_task* is not a valid task.

2.5.3   Requesting Task Information

You can obtain various information about a task using the **task_info()** system call. Most Mach applications rarely need this call. Its primary purpose

---

[5]In addition to storing the identifier for each thread in the list, the kernel grants the caller *send rights* to the thread's kernel port. Chapter 3 describes send rights in detail.

is for the UNIX ps program, which displays various items of information
about processes. In Mach, some of this data is actually task information,
and the ps program uses **task_info** to retrieve information about tasks, for
instance when memory usage information is requested. In this section we
show the use of the **thread_info** call to retrieve and print a task's virtual
and resident memory sizes and its task suspend count.

Mach's designers realized that the future is likely to bring new requirements. For this reason, the **task_info** call is designed to facilitate future
expansion. You specify a designator to indicate the particular set of task
information desired. Mach 2.5 defines only one set, the basic task data designated by the constant TASK_BASIC_INFO.[6] You also supply the address of
a memory area and a maximum size for that area. The kernel writes the
task information into that area. Thus you issue the **task_info** call like this:

```
kern_return_t status;
task_t        a_task;
int           which_info;
task_info_t   info_array;
unsigned int  *info_array_size;

status = task_info(a_task, which_info,
                   info_array, info_array_size);
```

Mach returns the requested information (specified by *which_info*) for task
a_task in the area that *info_array* points to. The length of the area is given
in *info_array_size*, in units of integers. Mach replaces this value with the
size of the data returned, in units of integers (even though some of the data
returned are not integer-size items). The following items comprise the basic
task data returned by **task_info**:[7]

```
struct task_basic_info {
        int        suspend_count;  /* suspend count for task  */
        int        base_priority;  /* base scheduling priority */
        vm_size_t  virtual_size;   /* virtual mem size in bytes*/
        vm_size_t  resident_size;  /*
                                    * resident memory size
                                    *  in bytes
```

---

[6]The expansion capability has already been used. For example, the OSF/1 operating
system provides two additional sets of task data.

[7]The Mach 2.5 *Kernel Interface Manual* incorrectly documents the virtual and resident
size fields as being in units of pages. The values returned for these fields are in bytes.

```
                                          */
        time_value_t user_time;          /*
                                          * total user run time for
                                          *  terminated threads
                                          */
        time_value_t system_time;        /* total system run time for
                                          *  terminated threads
                                          */
};
```

The header file `<task_info.h>` provides you with several type definitions for use with the **task_info** call:

```
typedef int         *task_info_t;              /* varying array of int */
typedef struct task_basic_info  task_basic_info_data_t;
typedef struct task_basic_info  *task_basic_info_t;
#define TASK_BASIC_INFO_COUNT   \
                (sizeof(task_basic_info_data_t) / sizeof(int))
```

The kernel returns the code KERN_INVALID_ARGUMENT if *a_task* is not a valid task or *which_info* is not a legitimate designator—only TASK_BASIC_INFO is valid in Mach 2.5. If the memory area specified by *info_array* is not large enough to hold all of the data, Mach returns the code MIG_ARRAY_TOO_LARGE and fills the area as much as possible. In this case *info_array_count* is set to the number of integer-size items that would be returned if there were enough room.

Let's look at an example of the use of the **task_info** system call. The program task_info performs the following steps:

1. Allocate a memory area to receive task information.

2. Request the basic task information from the kernel for the running task.

3. Print the current task's virtual and resident memory sizes and the task's suspend count.

Here is the code for program task_info:

```
/*
 * task_info - Program to demonstrate the task_info call
 */
```

```
#include <mach.h>
#include <stdio.h>

main()
{
        kern_return_t       status;
        task_basic_info_t   the_info;
        unsigned int        info_count;

        /*
         * 1. Allocate an area of memory to receive
         *            the task information
         */
        the_info = (task_basic_info_t)
                            malloc(TASK_BASIC_INFO_COUNT);
        if (the_info == NULL) {
                perror("task_info");
                exit(1);
        }
        /*
         * 2. Request the basic thread information from the kernel
         */
        bzero(the_info, TASK_BASIC_INFO_COUNT*sizeof(int));
        info_count = TASK_BASIC_INFO_COUNT;
        status = task_info(task_self(), TASK_BASIC_INFO,
                            (task_info_t) the_info, &info_count);
        if (status != KERN_SUCCESS) {
                mach_error("task_info:", status);
                exit(2);
        }
        /*
         * 3. Print the current task's virtual memory size
         *            and suspend count
         */
        printf("For task_self():\n");
        printf("\tresident size: %3d bytes\n",
                the_info->resident_size);
        printf("\t virtual size: %3d bytes\n",
                the_info->virtual_size);
        printf("\tsuspend count: %3d\n",
                the_info->suspend_count);

        exit(0);
}
```

When we run task_info we expect nonzero displays for the resident and virtual memory sizes. Since the task has a running thread (the only thread, the one executing the **task_info** call), we know that the current task is not suspended. The task suspend count should therefore be zero. These are the results of running the program task_info:

```
For task_self():
        resident size: 319488 bytes
         virtual size: 9338880 bytes
        suspend count:   0
```

2.5.4   Specialized Task IPC Ports

Mach creates new tasks with two Mach IPC ports already set up.[8] The first is the *task notify port*. The kernel directs messages to the notify port to advise a task that a port to which it holds send rights has been destroyed. The kernel allocates a notify port for a task when the task is first created. The second preallocated task IPC port is the *task exception port*. Mach directs messages to the task exception port when an exception has occurred and the thread that caused the exception has no registered thread exception port. The task exception port is inherited from the parent task at task creation time.

You register a port as a task notify port or task exception port using the Mach **task_set_special_port()** system call:

```
kern_return_t status;
task_t        a_task;
int           which_port;
port_t        special_port;

status = task_set_special_port(a_task, which_port, special_port);
```

This call registers the supplied IPC port *special_port* as the notify or exception port for task *a_task*. The designator *which_port* is one of the constants TASK_NOTIFY_PORT or TASK_EXCEPTION_PORT. If *a_task* does not specify a valid thread or *which_port* is not one of these two constants, the kernel returns the code KERN_INVALID_ARGUMENT.

For convenience in coding, Mach supplies two macros to invoke the **task_set_special_port** call:

---

[8] A third port, the *bootstrap port*, is defined but not used in Mach 2.5.

- task_set_notify_port(task, port)

- task_set_exception_port(task, port)

These macros are defined in the header file `<task_special_ports.h>`.

You ask the kernel for the currently registered exception port or notify port using the **task_get_special_port()** call:

```
kern_return_t status;
task_t        a_task;
int           which_port;
port_t        returned_port;

status = task_get_special_port(a_task, which_port, &returned_port);
```

The kernel stores the special port for task *a_task* designated by the constant *which_port*, TASK_NOTIFY_PORT or TASK_EXCEPTION_PORT, at the location specified by *returned_port*.[9]

For convenience in coding, Mach supplies two macros to invoke the **task_get_special_port** call:

- task_get_notify_port(task, port)

- task_get_exception_port(task, port)

These macros are defined in the header file `<task_special_ports.h>`.

2.6   Miscellaneous Thread Calls

Thus far we have presented the most commonly used Mach thread calls. In this section, we look at several additional thread-related capabilities. Some of these calls also relate to Mach's interprocess communication mechanism.

2.6.1   Aborting Threads Cleanly

Mach programs often employ the Mach interprocess communications (IPC) facility to send and receive information. We now explore the correct method for stopping a thread that might be performing an IPC operation.

Consider the job of simulating delivery of a UNIX signal using Mach system calls. The desired effect is to stop a specified thread, cause it to

---

[9]In addition to storing the requested port, Mach grants *send rights* to the port. Chapter 3, "Interprocess Communication," explains send rights in detail.

begin executing in its signal handler function, and then return to the point of interruption.

Recall from Section 2.3.3 that the effect of the **thread_suspend** system call is not immediate. In particular, if the specified thread is executing a system call, the call is allowed to complete before the thread is stopped. This design poses a problem in the case of system calls that run for long or indefinite periods. For instance, the Mach **msg_receive()** system call may wait indefinitely for an incoming message. How can a thread performing a **msg_receive** be suspended?

To address this problem you employ the **thread_abort()** call. This system call cleanly aborts the **msg_send**, **msg_receive**, or **msg_rpc** operations. The aborted call returns a code, either SEND_INTERRUPTED or RCV_INTERRUPTED, indicating that it was interrupted.

In our example, these are the steps involved in simulating a UNIX signal delivery:

1. Stop the target thread using **thread_suspend**.

2. Interrupt any in-progress system calls using **thread_abort**.

3. Modify the target thread's program counter using **thread_set_state**, so when it continues running it will begin executing in the signal handler function.

4. Cause the target thread to start running again using **thread_resume**.

This sequence of operations ensures that the target thread can be cleanly stopped before executing the signal handler code.

2.6.2   Specialized Thread IPC Ports

In this section we consider Mach system calls pertinent to both threads and the Mach IPC facility. Every Mach thread has a set of Mach IPC ports. These ports are not intended for general communication among threads; rather they serve specialized functions. Mach 2.5 defines two such ports:

reply port Mach system calls are generally implemented as Mach IPC message exchanges between a thread and the kernel. When your application includes a Mach system call such as **port_allocate()**, code in the libmach library sends an IPC message to the Mach kernel, receives the response message, and returns the appropriate status to your application. But there is a "chicken and egg" problem here—how can the kernel issue the reply message before your application has allocated an IPC port? The answer is that every thread is created with a *reply port* for this purpose.

exception port When your thread encounters an exception such as arithmetic overflow, Mach reacts by sending an IPC message. The message is directed to a port reserved for this purpose, called the *thread exception port.*

You assign a (previously allocated) port as a thread's reply or exception port with the **thread_set_special_port()** call:

```
kern_return_t status;
thread_t      th;
int           which_port;
port_t        special_port;

status = thread_set_special_port(th, which_port, special_port);
```

This call stores the supplied IPC port *special_port* with the data maintained by the kernel for thread *th*. The designator *which_port* is one of the constants THREAD_REPLY_PORT or THREAD_EXCEPTION_PORT. If *th* does not specify a valid thread or *which_port* is not one of these two constants, the kernel returns the code KERN_INVALID_ARGUMENT.

For convenience in coding, Mach supplies two macros to invoke the **thread_set_special_port** call:

- thread_set_reply_port(thread, port)

- thread_set_exception_port(thread, port)

These macros are defined in the header file <thread_special_ports.h>.

You ask the kernel for the current exception port or reply port using the **thread_get_special_port()** call:

```
kern_return_t status;
thread_t      th;
int           which_port;
port_t        returned_port;

status = thread_get_special_port(th, which_port, &returned_port);
```

The kernel stores the special port for thread *th* designated by the constant *which_port*, THREAD_REPLY_PORT or THREAD_EXCEPTION_PORT, at the location specified by *returned_port*.[10]

For convenience in coding, Mach supplies two macros to invoke the **thread_get_special_port** call:

- thread_get_reply_port(thread, port)

- thread_get_exception_port(thread, port)

These macros are defined in the header file <thread_special_ports.h>.

2.6.3   Requesting Thread Information

You can obtain various information about a thread using the **thread_info()** system call. Most Mach applications rarely need this call. Its primary purpose is for the UNIX ps program, which uses **thread_info** to retrieve information about threads when the -m option is given. In this section we use the **thread_info** call to demonstrate that new threads are indeed created in a suspended state.

Mach's designers realized that the future is likely to bring new requirements. For this reason, the **thread_info** call is designed to ease future expansion. You specify a designator to indicate the particular set of thread information desired. Mach 2.5 defines only one set, the basic thread data designated by the constant THREAD_BASIC_INFO.[11] You also supply the address of a memory area and a maximum size for that area. The kernel writes the task information into that area. Thus you issue the **thread_info** call like this:

```
kern_return_t status;
thread_t      th;
int           which_info;
thread_info_t info_array;
unsigned int  info_array_size;

status = thread_info(th, which_info, info_array, &info_array_size);
```

---

[10]In addition to storing the requested port, Mach grants *send rights* to the port. For the reply port, *receive rights* and *ownership* rights are also granted. Chapter 3 explains these concepts in detail.

[11]The expansion capability has already been used. For example, the OSF/1 operating system provides two additional sets of thread data.

Mach returns the requested information specified by *which_info* for thread *th* in the area that *info_array* points to. The length of the area is given in *info_array_size*, in units of integers. Mach replaces this value with the size of the data returned, in units of integers (even though some of the data returned are not integer-size items). The following items comprise the basic thread data returned by **thread_info**:

```
struct thread_basic_info {
        time_value_t user_time;      /* user run time           */
        time_value_t system_time;    /* system run time         */
        int          cpu_usage;      /* scaled usage percentage */
        int          base_priority;  /* base scheduling priority */
        int          cur_priority;   /* current sched priority  */
        int          run_state;      /* run state               */
        int          flags;          /* various flags           */
        int          suspend_count;  /* suspend count for thread */
        long         sleep_time;     /* number of seconds that
                                      * thread has been sleeping
                                      */
};
```

The header file `<thread_info.h>` provides you with several type definitions for use with the **thread_info** call:

```
typedef int        *thread_info_t;              /* varying array of int */
typedef struct thread_basic_info thread_basic_info_data_t;
typedef struct thread_basic_info *thread_basic_info_t;
#define THREAD_BASIC_INFO_COUNT \
                (sizeof(thread_basic_info_data_t) / sizeof(int))
```

The kernel returns the code KERN_INVALID_ARGUMENT if *th* is not a valid thread or *which_info* is not a legitimate designator—only THREAD_BASIC_INFO is valid in Mach 2.5. If the memory area specified by *info_array* is not large enough to hold all of the data, Mach returns the code MIG_ARRAY_TOO_LARGE and fills the area as much as possible. In this case *info_array_count* is set to the number of integer-size items that would be returned if there were enough room.

Let's return now to our discussion of thread suspend counts for a new thread. The program th_info performs the following steps:

1. Allocate a memory area to receive thread information.

2. Request the basic thread information from the kernel for the running thread.

3. Print the current thread's user CPU time and suspend count.

4. Create a new thread.

5. Request the basic thread information from the kernel for the new thread.

6. Print the new thread's user CPU time and suspend count.

Here is the code for the program th_info:

```
/*
 * th_info - Program to demonstrate the thread_info call
 */

#include <mach.h>
#include <stdio.h>

main()
{
        kern_return_t        status;
        thread_basic_info_t  the_info;
        unsigned int         info_count;
        thread_t th;

        /*
         * 1. Allocate an area of memory to receive
         *            the thread information
         */
        the_info =
             (thread_basic_info_t) malloc(THREAD_BASIC_INFO_COUNT);
        if (the_info == NULL) {
                perror("th_info");
                exit(1);
        }
        /*
         * 2. Request the basic thread information from the kernel
         */
        info_count = THREAD_BASIC_INFO_COUNT;
```

```
status = thread_info(thread_self(), THREAD_BASIC_INFO,
                (thread_info_t)the_info, &info_count);
if (status != KERN_SUCCESS) {
        mach_error("thread_info:", status);
        exit(2);
}
/*
 * 3. Print the current thread's user cpu time
 *            and suspend count
 */
printf("For thread_self():\n");
printf("\t    user time: %3d seconds %3d microseconds\n",
        the_info->user_time.seconds,
        the_info->user_time.microseconds);
printf("\tsuspend count: %3d\n", the_info->suspend_count);
/*
 * 4. Create a new thread
 */
status = thread_create(task_self(), &th);
if (status != KERN_SUCCESS) {
        mach_error("thread_create:", status);
        exit(3);
}
/*
 * 5. Request the basic thread information from the
 *            kernel for the new thread
 */
status = thread_info(th, THREAD_BASIC_INFO,
                (thread_info_t)the_info, &info_count);
if (status != KERN_SUCCESS) {
        mach_error("thread_info:", status);
        exit(4);
}
/*
 * 6. Print the new thread's user cpu time and suspend count
 */
printf("For a new thread:\n");
printf("\t    user time: %3d seconds %3d microseconds\n",
        the_info->user_time.seconds,
        the_info->user_time.microseconds);
printf("\tsuspend count: %3d\n", the_info->suspend_count);

exit(0);
}
```

What should th_info display? Because the first values are for the running thread, we expect a nonzero CPU time and a zero thread suspend count. For the new thread, we expect just the opposite: zero CPU time (the thread has not yet begun executing) and a suspend count of one. Here is the output from the program th_info:

```
For thread_self():
            user time:    0 seconds 43430 microseconds
        suspend count:    0
For a new thread:
            user time:    0 seconds    0 microseconds
        suspend count:    1
```

Chapter 3

Interprocess Communication (IPC)

Since the invention of multiprogrammed systems, in which more than one program can run at the same time, programmers have wanted application programs to send data to one another. Communication allows you to solve complex problems through separate application programs working together. The communication between two programs, sometimes called processes, is called *interprocess communication*, or IPC.

Early attempts at IPC used disk files as the communications medium. One program would write to a file, and another would read from the file. Unfortunately, this approach did not perform very well. There were two problems: the speed of disk I/O, which can be slow, and synchronization between the two programs. How would the reader know when the writer had made data available in the file? Most often, the reader would repeatedly test for the existence of the file or for a change in its length. This test reduces the amount of time the application can spend working on a problem, consumes operating system resources, and is limited by the speed of the disk drive.

A better solution was needed. Early IPC implementors experimented with separate programs sharing memory. Although this was an excellent mechanism for sharing data and was significantly faster than disk I/O, there were several problems. Simply storing data in memory was not sufficient. The application programs needed to implement a framework for passing organized messages. With such a framework in place, synchronization mechanisms between sender and receiver needed to be found. A shared memory location that indicated "data available" provided a common synchronization

63

mechanism. Unfortunately, this mechanism required the receiver to waste CPU cycles by regularly polling memory.

Rather than requiring an application program to create its own message system, for example, on top of shared memory, the obvious approach was to provide IPC mechanisms as an integral part of the operating system. Many operating systems provide such capabilities. Examples include:

- UNIX pipes

- Berkeley UNIX (4.2 and later) *sockets*

- AT&T System V **msgop()**

- DEC's VAX/VMS "mailbox" facility

- IBM VM/370 IUCV (Inter User Communication Vehicle) and VMCF (Virtual Machine Communication Facilities).

The idea of interprocess communication mechanisms within the operating system was not new when Mach was designed. However, the Mach designers made several observations that affected the way they implemented IPC.

First, networking, and in particular local area networks (LANs), had become commonplace by the mid-1980s. Mach fully integrates the IPC mechanism with the network. IPC messages may be passed between tasks running on different computer systems. Messages between programs running on different machines are sent in the same manner as messages between programs running on the same machine. Further, unlike when using UNIX sockets, neither the sending nor receiving task needs to be aware when a message is transmitted across the network.

Second, high performance must also be a primary goal of any IPC implementation. The Mach design integrates the IPC and virtual memory (VM) subsystems to increase performance significantly over other existing implementations. Using special VM techniques, large messages may be mapped into the receiver's address space rather than being copied. Large IPC messages sent across the network have also been optimized by transmitting only when the receiving task accesses the data.

Let's compare Mach IPC with other UNIX implementations. The System V **msgop()** family of system calls resembles Mach IPC, with three significant differences:

1. Mach allows network transparent transmission of messages, while System V does not.

2. System V does not integrate the IPC and VM subsystems as Mach does. Thus Mach transfers large messages much more efficiently than does System V.

3. Mach IPC messages are typed collections of data. System V transmits a byte stream that the user must interpret.

While Berkeley sockets do provide an IPC mechanism, many limitations exist. For example, to achieve optimum performance, the programmer must know a priori whether the communicating program is on the local or remote host. Similar to System V, sockets provide a simple byte stream with no data typing, forcing the programmer to convert data types when sending messages between different computers. Using sockets also requires frequent copying of data, which limits performance. In brief, sockets provide a solid foundation for IPC but do not provide the functionality and flexibility that some application programmers desire.

Since the early 1970s, UNIX systems have implemented the *pipe*. Pipes provide an I/O stream between two processes and may be considered a primitive form of IPC, but their many limitations make them a poor choice as an IPC mechanism:

- Processes must be related; in other words, one process must be the parent or ancestor of the other. Unrelated processes may not use pipes. Recent versions of UNIX provide *named pipes*, which may be used by unrelated processes. Standard and named pipes may not be used interchangeably, however.

- Processes on different computer systems may not communicate with each other.

- Data appear as a simple byte stream, without data typing.

- Traditionally, pipes are unidirectional and provide for only a single sender and receiver.

The common use of redirecting output from one program into another make pipes useful. However, this does not make them adequate as an IPC mechanism.

Interprocess communication may be used by many types of applications. Consider a database application consisting of two main pieces: a user interface and a file storage system. The user interface accepts input from a

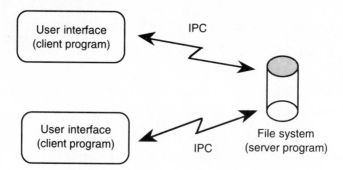

Figure 3.1: A Database Using IPC

terminal, provides a graphical interface, and formats queries for the under-
lying file storage system but does not read or modify the actual database.
This program would be the *client*, making requests of the database's file
system server. There may be many instances of the client (potentially each
on a separate computer system) making requests of one or more servers.

The file storage system accepts queries, processes them, and returns the
result. Requests to this system might include reading or writing a record
within the database. The program that performs the functions of the file
storage system acts as a *server* to programs that request file services.

These two complex functions can easily be made into separate programs.
IPC messages may be used for communication between the two programs,
as shown in Fig. 3.1.

Dividing the database into separate programs allows for easier software
development and support. In addition, this separation removes limitations
placed on a single program regarding size, number of open files, amount of
memory, and so on. Finally, since Mach has the ability to send IPC messages
to another computer via the network, the two programs can run on different
machines, providing increased flexibility and performance.

In the remainder of this chapter we will discuss basic concepts behind
Mach IPC. By the end of this chapter you will know how to create an IPC
communication channel and send and receive messages, and you will understand the format and use of the various data structures required for Mach
IPC. Although IPC has many details, its use is straightforward. Mach also
provides an interface generator (MIG) that can conveniently hide many of
these details.

To demonstrate Mach IPC capabilities, we will write two small programs
that use many of the Mach IPC features. The first program, a server, provides the time of day, in either numeric or string form, on request from a

client program. The second program, the client, requests the time from the server. These two programs illustrate the use of Mach IPC system calls and associated data structures.

3.1 General IPC Concepts

Mach defines the communication channel used to pass data as a *port*. Ports are implemented as a queue of *messages* that the kernel manages. Messages contain a typed collection of data objects. The programmer defines what data are passed in a message and the type of data, such as characters, 32-bit integers, and so on.

3.1.1 Access Rights

A set of *access rights* defines the IPC operations a task may perform. A task may have any combination of *send, receive,* or *ownership*[1] rights to a port. Only tasks with a send right to a port may successfully send an IPC message to that port. A receive right allows a task to receive a message from a port. Many tasks may have send rights to a port; however, only one task may receive messages enqueued to that port. Because ports are a resource that the task holds, any thread within a task may send or receive messages to a port belonging to the task.

Ownership rights provide a backup mechanism when the receiving task terminates. As with receive rights, only one task may hold the ownership right to a port. Ownership rights are only used when a task with the receive right has given up that right. This may happen voluntarily or when the task terminates. When a task with the receive right to a port relinquishes that right, the receive right automatically transfers to the task with the ownership right. When a task with the ownership right to a port relinquishes that right, the ownership right automatically transfers to the task with the receive right. If no task exists with receive or ownership rights, the kernel deallocates the port and sends a notification message to all tasks with send rights.

If a task acquires receive or ownership rights, it will automatically acquire the send right to that port. A task receives all three access rights when it

---

[1]Ownership rights are *deprecated* in the current release of Mach. It is expected that the concept of ownership rights will be deleted in a future version. Although for completeness we describe ownership rights in the remainder of this book, programmers should limit their use of this feature.

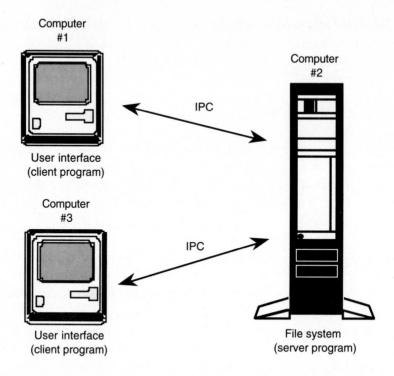

Figure 3.2: Distributed Database Access Using Mach IPC

creates a port. Access rights may be passed to another task at any time by sending an IPC message to the target task.

The database example we described earlier could benefit if the two programs run on separate computers (see Fig. 3.2). These computers would be equipped as appropriate to do the required job optimally. For example, the computers running the user interface program might be small workstations with high-speed, bit-mapped color graphics but a minimum of disk and memory. The file storage system runs on Computer #2. This machine has a high throughput I/O system to satisfy file storage system requests quickly.

3.1.2   Seamless Distributed Computing

Distributed computing models often hide the existence of the network. A program sending a message does not know or care whether the recipient is on the same machine or a different one. Communicating tasks can execute as easily on separate machines as on the same one. This seamless, network-wide IPC transmission provides a simple model for distributed computing. Our database example would benefit from a seamless IPC model: Neither the database server nor its clients would require special programming to handle the case in which both programs run on the same machine or the case in which they run on separate machines. Unlike the traditional IPC mechanisms we have already described, Mach provides a seamless IPC mechanism that invisibly accommodates messages exchanged between programs on the same machine or different machines.

To initiate a connection between communicating tasks, a Mach server "advertises" a port on which it accepts service requests. A client program "looks up" the server, obtains a send right to the port, and uses the port for communication. A special Mach server handles both the advertising and look-up activities and isolates regular servers and clients from all knowledge of the network. By using this intermediary, a client may obtain a send right to a server port without having to know how to talk directly to the server. The use of Berkeley sockets, on the other hand, requires knowledge of network addresses and other issues that make the network all too visible when initiating a connection.

Should an IPC message cross the network, Mach assures that the remote computer will be able to read the data, even if the computers have different data representations. This conversion is made possible by requiring the programmer to include the data type of each block of data. This information is both necessary and sufficient to allow Mach to translate data from one machine representation to another. In contrast, Berkeley sockets use untyped data streams, forcing the programmer to convert data types between different machines.

Mach imposes no restriction on the amount of data that can be sent in a message. You need not worry about whether a message will be too large for the local machine or for the network. Limitations on message size severely limit the usefulness of other traditional IPC mechanisms.

3.1.3   Port Names

Each port is known by a unique *name*, which is implemented as an integer value. Different tasks may have their own, potentially different, name for the same port. For example, if two tasks, A and B, are sending messages to a server, task A may be using a port named twelve while task B knows that port as port seven. The server receiving the messages may know that port as port forty-two. Figure 3.3 illustrates this example.

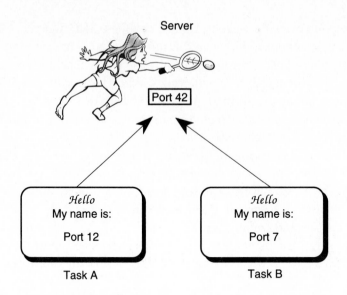

Figure 3.3: Sending Messages with Ports of Different Names

3.2   The Time Server

We use a simple time server program to illustrate IPC concepts. These concepts are also applicable to more complex programs, such as the database server we described in the previous section.

Let's begin by analyzing what the server must do. The first step is initialization. Once initialized, the server waits for an incoming message containing a request for the current time. When the message arrives, the server processes the request and returns the result in another IPC message. When it is finished with the request, the server loops back to wait for the next message. The next three sections describe these steps in more detail.

3.2.1   Initialization

The first operation allocates a new port for receiving service requests. The **port_allocate()** and **port_deallocate()** system calls allocate and deallocate ports respectively. These calls are issued as follows:

```
#include <mach.h>

kern_return_t   ret;
port_name_t     server_port;
```

```
/*
 * Sample Port Allocation
 */
ret = port_allocate(task_self(), &server_port)
if (ret != KERN_SUCCESS) {
        mach_error("port_allocate:", ret);
        exit(1);
}

/*
 * Sample Port Deallocation
 */
ret = port_deallocate(task_self(), server_port);
if (ret != KERN_SUCCESS) {
        mach_error("port_deallocate:", ret);
        exit(1);
}
```

The first argument to both system calls names the task in which the port will be allocated or deallocated. Remember, under Mach most system calls permit you to allocate or deallocate resources in tasks other than the current one, as long as the calling task has the appropriate permission. The argument **task_self()** names the current task as the task to contain the port, the most common case.

The second parameter names the port to be allocated or deallocated. **Port_allocate** accepts a pointer to local storage in which the kernel returns the name of the allocated port. This name is used when deallocating a port. Note that deallocating a port does not necessarily destroy the port. Other tasks may use the port as long as the task with the receive right to the port does not terminate. Only the task that **port_deallocate** operates on loses its ability to use the port.

Ports are defined with the *port_name_t* type. Other compatible declarations are also available, including *port_t, port_rcv_t, port_own_t* and *port_all_t*.[2] These names specify a port with send, receive, ownership, and both receive and ownership rights, respectively. However, the Mach kernel has no way to distinguish between any of these declarations; these different names ultimately declare the same object, a port. Mach therefore cannot guarantee that a port has only the rights indicated by the port type name you use. You may use these names to provide mnemonic assistance, but do not expect additional error checking.

---

[2]Earlier versions of Mach provided only the *port_t* type name.

The kernel returns the constant KERN_SUCCESS when the system call succeeds. **Port_allocate** can fail with KERN_RESOURCE_SHORTAGE if the kernel has depleted memory allotted for ports. **Port_deallocate** may also fail with KERN_INVALID_ARGUMENT if the task does not have rights to the port or the port does not exist.

Allocating a port without taking any other action does not permit another task to send messages to that port. The task that allocated the port must somehow give a cooperating task a send right to the port. Consider an analogy from UNIX file manipulations. A process may create a file, but for another process to use it the first process must somehow inform the second of the file's name. Further, the creating process must set appropriate read and write permissions on the file. Similarly, the responsibility of passing a send right to another task initially falls on the task that allocated the port.

Port rights are passed by sending them in an IPC message to another task. Data typing within the IPC message identifies rights being passed. The Mach kernel uses these data types to identify and transfer port rights from one task to another. Sending this IPC message requires having a send right to a port belonging to the target task. There are two ways in which the sending task can obtain this right. If the sending task created the receiving task, the sending task automatically gains access to the task control port of the newly created, receiving task. The sending task can then insert a port it created into the receiving task's port space. Besides being cumbersome, this method does not work for unrelated tasks. Alternately, the sending task can use a send right for the receiving task that the sender acquires from a third task. Once a send right has been acquired, it may be passed on to any other task. However, this alternative still begs the question, How do the sending and third-party tasks acquire send rights to each other in the first place?

Providing every task with a send right to a common, trusted third-party server solves this problem. The server provided with Mach-based systems is called the *network message server* (netmsgserver).[3] Mach automatically endows a new task with a send right to the netmsgserver, solving the problem of acquiring the first send right.

A program wishing to pass send rights registers an ASCII name and the port with the network message server. This name has no relation to the port name referred to in Section 3.1.3. Another program may obtain the send right to that port by querying the name server using the same ASCII name.

---

[3]Another server, the *environment manager* (envmgr), is also provided with Mach systems. Section 7.10.2 describes this name server and its interface.

The two programs, most often a server and its clients, must therefore have agreed on a name in advance. The name may be any sequence of characters up to eighty characters long, including a terminating ASCII NULL (0). The declaration of this string is done with the *netname_name_t* type definition.

Using the netmsgserver, our time server registers the newly allocated port with the **netname_check_in()** call.

```
#include <servers/netname.h>

kern_return_t    ret;
netname_name_t   name;

strcpy(name, "Time-Server-Port");

ret = netname_check_in(name_server_port, name,
                       task_self(), server_port);
if (ret != NETNAME_SUCCESS) {
        mach_error("netname check in:", ret);
        exit(1);
}
```

The check-in request is sent to the port provided as the first argument to the function call. In our example we use the *name_server_port*, a global variable initialized during program creation and initialization.

The second argument, of type *netname_name_t*, is the ASCII name of the port we want to register. In our example we use the name Time-Server-Port. Remember that the server and client must both use the same name.

The third argument, known as the *signature*, prevents unauthorized tasks from deleting our port's name from the netmsgserver's name space. Signature must be a port to which the calling task has send rights. The netmsgserver records the signature port for the checked-in name. A future request to delete the name must also include the same port, or the netmsgserver will reject the request. Using PORT_NULL for the signature disables protection of the name. In our example we use **task_self()** as the port. This port is unique to the server task and is convenient. Of course, in general you should not hand out the **task_self** port because it can be used to control the task. However, the netmsgserver can be trusted.

The last argument is *server_port*, and it is the port we are going to check in. We showed the allocation of this port using the **port_allocate** system call earlier in this section.

If the **netname_check_in** operation succeeds, the constant NETNAME_
SUCCESS is returned. Error codes, as well as a complete description of other
interfaces and capabilities of the netmsgserver, are described in Section 7.10.1.

3.2.2   Receiving a Message

Our server is almost ready to receive a message. Before the server can
receive any messages, it must give Mach a little information. For all receive
operations, a program must supply two pieces of information: the port on
which to receive the data and the maximum size of a message it will accept.
These are provided in a message header.

In the following example, the server uses a structure that contains a
message header, a type descriptor we will describe later, and an integer that
will specify the format to use when returning the time. We will call this
structure *request_msg* and declare it in a header file called <time_server.h>.
This header file will also contain other declarations that will be used in our
time server and in the client program. The content of this file is as follows:

```
/*
 * Time_server.h
 *
 * Structure definitions and manifest constants for
 *  use by the time server and its clients.
 */

/*
 * Structure used to make a request of the server.
 */
struct request_msg {
        msg_header_t    hdr;
        msg_type_t      type;
        int             request;
};

/*
 * Format of the structure the server sends in response.
 */
struct reply_msg {
        msg_header_t    hdr;
        msg_type_t      type;
        union {
```

```
                  /*
                   * Numeric version of time is returned
                   *   as 'time_t'.
                   * String version of the time is provided as
                   *   a character string as returned by ctime(2),
                   *   which has a maximum length of 26 characters.
                   */
                  time_t  ntime;
                  char    ctime[26];
          } time;
};

/*
 * Define request codes used for format specifier.
 */
#define TS_NUMERIC_FORM      (0)
#define TS_STRING_FORM       (1)
```

The header and type structure are data structures defined by the kernel and used for all IPC messages. Organizing these two data structures and an integer into a single data structure is specific to this program; the Mach kernel does not require it. The declaration and initialization of the fields required to receive a message are handled as follows:

```
#include <mach/message.h>
#include "time_server.h"

struct request_msg request_msg;

request_msg.hdr.msg_local_port = server_port;
request_msg.hdr.msg_size = sizeof(struct request_msg);
```

The *msg_local_port* field specifies the port on which the server will receive the message. In this example, we use the port *server_port*, which was allocated earlier. The *msg_size* field specifies the maximum size message the server will accept. The remaining fields within the message header and type structure will be described when we discuss sending messages.

To receive a message, the server issues the **msg_receive()** system call. This system call takes three parameters: the address of the message header, a set of option specifications, and a timeout value, as shown here:

```
#include <mach/message.h>
#include <mach/port.h>
#include "time_server.h"

msg_return_t     ret;

ret = msg_receive(&request_msg.hdr, MSG_OPTION_NONE, 0);
if (ret != RCV_SUCCESS) {
        mach_error("msg_receive:", ret);
        exit(1);
}
```

The option specification consists of one or more of the constants shown in Table 3.1 logically OR'd together.

Option Name	Meaning
MSG_OPTION_NONE	A place holder to specify that no options are desired.
RCV_TIMEOUT	When specified, the third argument to **msg_receive** is a timeout. The timeout argument specifies the number of milliseconds to wait before aborting the receive operation. If this option is not specified, the thread will wait indefinitely for a message to arrive. If no receive timeout is desired, a zero is used as a "place holder" for the system call. The kernel does not use or examine the value.
RCV_INTERRUPT	Specifies that the call should return when a software interrupt has occurred in this thread. If not specified, interrupts that the **thread_abort()** system call generates will be ignored.
RCV_NO_SENDERS	The system call will return immediately if no tasks with send rights to the port, other than the task(s) with receive or ownership rights, exist. This option has not been implemented as of the CMU Release 2.5 of Mach.

Table 3.1: Message Receive Options

The thread executing the **msg_receive** system call will be suspended until a message is received or an error occurs. On return from the system call, the constant RCV_SUCCESS indicates that the call succeeded. If an error occurs, one of the error codes shown in Table 3.2 is returned.

Error Code	Meaning
RCV_INVALID_MEMORY	The address of the message header, or a portion of the receiving task's virtual address space necessary to store the message, was not a valid memory location.
RCV_INVALID_PORT	The task does not have the receive right to the port, or the port was deallocated while waiting for the incoming message.
RCV_TOO_LARGE	The incoming message was larger than the value specified by the *msg_size* field. On return, the *msg_size* field contains the minimum size necessary to receive the message.
RCV_NOT_ENOUGH_MEMORY	The incoming message contains more out-of-line data than can be allocated.
RCV_TIMED_OUT	The RCV_TIMEOUT option was specified, and no message arrived within *timeout* milliseconds.
RCV_ONLY_SENDER	No tasks, other than the task(s) with receive and ownership rights, have send access to the port. This feature is unimplemented in the CMU Release 2.5 of Mach.
RCV_INTERRUPTED	The RCV_INTERRUPT option was specified and the call was interrupted.
RCV_PORT_CHANGE	The port was moved into a port set by the task with the receive right while the **msg_receive** call was waiting for an incoming message.

Table 3.2: Message Receive Error Codes

3.2.3   Process and Reply

Now that we have received the message containing the client request, we must process the request and send a reply. The processing code is simple because the time server is only asked to provide data in either numeric or string form. Numeric format is the standard UNIX time format: a 32-bit integer containing the number of seconds since January 1, 1970. String format is an ASCII string, as returned by the **ctime()** library function. To determine which of these formats the server should use, the client supplies an integer as a format specifier. Values of zero and one specify returning numeric and string format, respectively.

A type structure precedes and describes each user data structure within an IPC message. The *msg_type_t* declaration defines a type structure. Thus our client's message must contain both a type structure and the immediately following format specifier.

Because one or more *msg_type_t* structures are part of every IPC message, the Mach designers felt it was important to make this structure as small as possible. The overhead of transmitting a large structure with each message could have slowed IPC message transmission significantly. For this reason, the *msg_type_t* structure is defined as bit fields within a single integer. This structure contains six fields:

msg_type_name (8 bits): This field specifies the type of data comprising the object. Common formats are integers of various lengths, characters, character strings, and floating point numbers. In addition, Mach permits ports and port set names (see Section 7.3) to be transmitted. When sending ports, it is possible to send any combination of send, receive, and ownership rights.

Mach uses these type definitions in two ways. The first is when port rights are passed between tasks. The kernel transfers port rights as specified. The second is when data is transferred between machines with different architectures. Integers and floating point numbers may need to be converted to the machine-dependent format required on the target machine. The kernel does not use any of the other data types.

The application programmer uses these definitions to determine the type of data being sent. In combination with other fields within the type structure, the user knows the size and number of data elements.

The data type definitions are:

- MSG_TYPE_UNSTRUCTURED
- MSG_TYPE_BOOLEAN
- MSG_TYPE_INTEGER_32
- MSG_TYPE_PORT_RECEIVE
- MSG_TYPE_PORT
- MSG_TYPE_BYTE
- MSG_TYPE_REAL
- MSG_TYPE_STRING_C
- MSG_TYPE_BIT
- MSG_TYPE_INTEGER_16
- MSG_TYPE_PORT_OWNERSHIP
- MSG_TYPE_PORT_ALL
- MSG_TYPE_CHAR
- MSG_TYPE_INTEGER_8
- MSG_TYPE_STRING

As this book went to press, no Mach release had implemented conversion of floating point numeric formats (MSG_TYPE_REAL) within IPC messages sent between computer systems. In addition, when transferring integers, Mach does not check the **msg_type_size** field to see if the bit size matches the sixteen or thirty-two bits implied by the MSG_TYPE_INTEGER_16 and MSG_TYPE_INTEGER_32 names.

Port send rights are the most common rights to pass. These are passed with the name MSG_TYPE_PORT. Receive and ownership rights are passed with the MSG_TYPE_PORT_RECEIVE and MSG_TYPE_PORT_OWNERSHIP names, respectively. All three rights may be passed using the name MSG_TYPE_PORT_ALL.

msg_type_size (8 bits):   This field specifies the number of bits in the object named in the **msg_type_name** field. Several of the aforementioned data formats have implied bit lengths. For example, MSG_TYPE_INTEGER_32 implies a 32-bit integer. Other data formats are machine specific and have no implied length.

How many bits does it take to store a floating point number? Some systems use thirty-two, and others use sixty-four. The ability to specify these values allows more flexible communication between application programs running between computer systems with different architectures.

The eight-bit size of this field limits the size of any single piece of data to 255 bits. The longform version of this structure removes this limitation.

msg_type_number (12 bits):   This field describes the number of data items being sent. The twelve-bit size of this field limits the number of items that can be sent to 4095. The longform version of this structure removes this limitation.

msg_type_inline (1 bit):   The data or a pointer to the data is included in the message. The **msg_type_inline** field specifies which. When this field is set to TRUE, the data described by the type structure will immediately follow the type structure. This case is called *in-line* data. When this field is set to FALSE, a pointer to the data immediately follows the type structure. Sending the data separate from the type structure is termed *out-of-line* data and is described in Section 7.1.

msg_type_longform (1 bit):   When the value to be stored in the **msg_type_name**, **msg_type_size**, or **msg_type_number** fields is larger than fits in the field, an alternate structure is used to describe the data. This is known as the *longform* version of the structure. When this field is set to TRUE, the longform version is used and supersedes the standard fields in the type structure. When this field is set to FALSE, the standard structure is used.

msg_type_deallocate (1 bit):   This boolean field is used to control whether memory or port rights are removed from the sending task when the message has been successfully queued. If this field is set to TRUE and data is being sent, the portion of the address space containing transmitted data is deallocated from the sending task. If port rights are being sent, the sending task will no longer have rights to the port. If this field is set to FALSE, the memory or port rights remain as they were prior to the call.

Figure 3.4 illustrates the general format of an IPC message. A single header structure describes the overall message contents. Multiple type structures describe the data being sent.

In our example, the client will send a single format specifier (an integer); hence the standard version of the structure will be used. Our processing code will retrieve the value, check for validity, and then return the requested information.

```
#include <mach.h>
#include <sys/time.h>
#include "time_server.h"

struct  timeval  timeofday;

/*
 * We're expecting an integer as a format specifier.
```

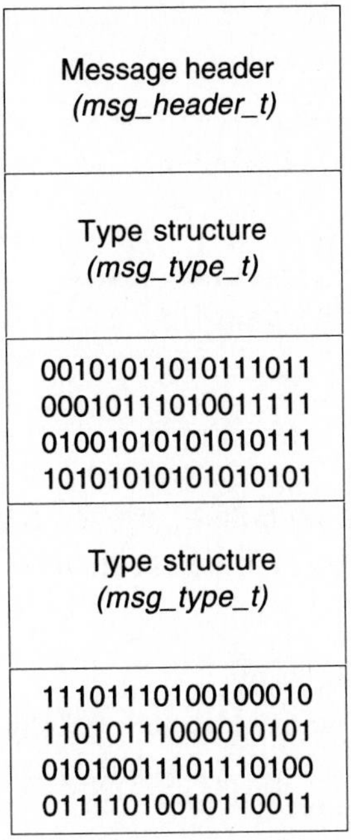

```
┌─────────────────────────┐
│                         │
│     Message header      │
│     (msg_header_t)       │
│                         │
├─────────────────────────┤
│                         │
│     Type structure      │
│      (msg_type_t)       │
│                         │
├─────────────────────────┤
│  00101011010111011      │
│  000101110100011111     │
│  01001010101010111      │
│  10101010101010101      │
├─────────────────────────┤
│                         │
│     Type structure      │
│      (msg_type_t)       │
│                         │
├─────────────────────────┤
│  11101110100100010      │
│  11010111000010101      │
│  01010011101110100      │
│  01111010010110011      │
└─────────────────────────┘
```

Figure 3.4: IPC Message with Multiple Type Structures

```
 *   Print an error if that isn't what we receive.
 */
if (request_msg.type.msg_type_name != MSG_TYPE_INTEGER_32) {
        fprintf(stderr, "Unexpected message type\n");
        return;
}

/*
 * Get time of day from the system.
 */
gettimeofday(&timeofday, (struct timezone *)0);

/*
 * Return the data in the format requested.
 */
switch (request_msg.request) {

    case TS_NUMERIC_FORM:
            reply_msg.time.ntime = timeofday.tv_sec;
            break;
```

```
case TS_STRING_FORM:
        strcpy(reply_msg.time.ctime,
                ctime(&timeofday.tv_sec));
        break;

default: strcpy(reply_msg.time.ctime,
            "Invalid Request");
        break;
}
```

When the processing is complete, we send the information back to the client task. We must fill in a message header structure when sending a message as follows:

```
reply_msg.hdr.msg_simple = TRUE;
reply_msg.hdr.msg_size = sizeof(struct reply_msg);
reply_msg.hdr.msg_type = MSG_TYPE_NORMAL;
reply_msg.hdr.msg_local_port = PORT_NULL;
reply_msg.hdr.msg_remote_port = request_msg.hdr.msg_remote_port;
reply_msg.hdr.msg_id = request_msg.hdr.msg_id;
```

Msg_simple is a boolean assigned a value of FALSE if we will be sending ports or out-of-line data and a value of TRUE otherwise. The *msg_size* field specifies the number of bytes contained in the message, including the header, all type structures, and in-line data. Our example always sends twenty-six bytes of data, even though when we return the time in numeric format we only need to send four bytes (the size of the numeric time field). We will presume that the client will correctly interpret the results regardless of how much data we send.

The *msg_type* field is used to describe some general characteristics of the message. The constants defined next are found in the include files <mach/message.h> and <mach/msg_type.h> and are logically OR'd together for the assignment. Only MSG_TYPE_NORMAL, used to define normal priority messages, and MSG_TYPE_EMERGENCY,[4] used to define high-priority messages, are interpreted by the Mach kernel. The remainder are available for use by the application program.

---

[4]MSG_TYPE_EMERGENCY is a *deprecated* feature in the current release of Mach. It is expected that the use of this type will be deleted in a future version. Although for completeness we describe this feature in the remainder of this book, programmers should limit their use of this feature.

MSG_TYPE_NORMAL: This is the most common type of message. Unless one of the following type descriptors applies to your application, use this type code.

MSG_TYPE_EMERGENCY: Emergency messages have several characteristics. These are delivered before other messages, and they are transmitted even when the port backlog has been reached. Similar types of facilities are often termed *out-of-band* or *urgent* data in other contexts. Emergency messages should rarely be used, as their indiscriminate use may cause kernel resource shortages.

Emergency messages also cause the signal SIGEMSG to be delivered to the task, although this signal must be explicitly enabled with the usual UNIX signal system calls to be processed. It is anticipated that this feature will be removed in future releases of Mach.

MSG_TYPE_CAMELOT: This type is reserved for use by the Camelot Transaction server.

MSG_TYPE_ENCRYPTED: This type specifies that the message has been encrypted. The encryption is not performed by the kernel but by the sending application. It is therefore the responsibility of the receiver to decrypt the message when this option is specified.

MSG_TYPE_RPC: This type is used to indicate that a reply to this message is expected. Most often, the message was sent using the **msg_rpc()** system call.

Our example initializes the *msg_local_port* field to PORT_NULL. If we were expecting a reply, we would have instead specified the port we wanted the reply sent to. Mach will give a send right for that port to the task receiving the message.

The *msg_remote_port* field specifies the destination port. We must have send rights to this port, or an error will be returned. In our example, notice that we are using the *msg_remote_port* field from the received message. When the message was sent, the *msg_local_port* field was assigned the port name of where the reply is to be returned. Mach swapped the local and remote port fields when the message was sent. The reply must therefore be sent to the port now contained in the *msg_remote_port* field. It is a common programming error to use the wrong field when sending a reply.

Finally, we fill in the *msg_id* field with the value we received. While there is no requirement that we do so, the receiver may use the value to identify our reply. For example, automated remote procedure call interface generators such as MIG use this field to distinguish between messages in a group of interfaces.

While each message contains a single header, a message may contain more than one type structure, each of which has data associated with it. The type structure is immediately followed by the data it describes. To send more than one type of data, another type structure and data would follow the data from the previous entry. Our example sends only one type of data, but the type is dependent on the request.

```
if (request_msg.request == TS_NUMERIC_FORM) {
        /*
        * Return a single, 32-bit integer.
        */
        reply_msg.type.msg_type_name = MSG_TYPE_INTEGER_32;
        reply_msg.type.msg_type_size = sizeof(int)*8;
        reply_msg.type.msg_type_number = 1;
} else {
        /*
        * Return a NULL-terminated character string.
        */
        reply_msg.type.msg_type_name = MSG_TYPE_CHAR;
        reply_msg.type.msg_type_size = sizeof(char)*8;
        reply_msg.type.msg_type_number =
                        strlen(reply_msg.time.ctime) + 1;
}
/*
* These fields are initialized identically,
*   regardless of format.
*/
reply_msg.type.msg_type_inline = TRUE;
reply_msg.type.msg_type_longform = FALSE;
reply_msg.type.msg_type_deallocate = FALSE;
```

We are now ready to send the data to the client. To send a message, the server issues the **msg_send()** system call. This system call takes a form similar to that of the **msg_receive** call we have already used. The **msg_send** system call takes three parameters: the address of the message header, a set of option specifications, and a timeout value. The option specification consists of one or more of the constants shown in Table 3.3 logically OR'd together.

Option Name	Meaning
MSG_OPTION_NONE	This definition is a place holder to specify that no options are desired.
SEND_TIMEOUT	The system call will be terminated after the number of milliseconds specified by the system call's third option has expired.
SEND_NOTIFY	If the destination port is full, the sender is typically suspended until the receiver has received a message and made space in the queue. This option permits a task to send one message to the destination port when the queue is full without being suspended. The kernel will send a message to the sending task's notification port when the target task receives the message. If both the SEND_TIMEOUT and SEND_NOTIFY options are specified, the kernel will wait until the timeout has elapsed before invoking the SEND_NOTIFY option.
SEND_INTERRUPT	Specifies that the call should return when a software interrupt has occurred in this thread. If not specified, interrupts that **thread_abort()** generates will be ignored.

Table 3.3: Message Send Options

The server will not need any of these options; hence the message is returned to the client using the following code:

```
msg_return_t  ret;

ret = msg_send(&msg_send.hdr, MSG_OPTION_NONE, 0);
if (ret != SEND_SUCCESS) {
        mach_error("msg_send:", ret);
        exit(1);
}
```

The thread executing the system call will be suspended only until the message is enqueued by the kernel, *not* until the receiver has received the message. On return from the system call, the constant SEND_SUCCESS indicates that the call succeeded. If an error occurs, one of the error codes shown in Table 3.4 is returned.

3.2.4   The Complete Time Server

In previous sections we have put together all the major pieces needed to build our time server. This section integrates all of these pieces in a complete program.

Error Code	Meaning
SEND_INVALID_MEMORY	Some portion of the message was within a portion of the calling task's address space which was not readable.
SEND_INVALID_PORT	This error code indicates one of several possible errors regarding ports. The caller may not have send rights to the destination port, or the destination port may have already been deallocated (with **port_deallocate**).
SEND_TIMED_OUT	The SEND_TIMEOUT option was specified and the timeout has expired. The message was not sent to the remote port.
SEND_WILL_NOTIFY	When the SEND_NOTIFY option is set, this return code is used if the destination port is full. When the message can be posted to the receiving port, the calling task will receive a message from the kernel on its notification port.
	If the notification message is NOTIFY_MSG_ACCEPTED, the kernel was able to enqueue the message to the receiver. A notification message of NOTIFY_PORT_DELETED indicates that the destination port was deleted during the time the kernel was waiting for space to enqueue the message.

Table 3.4: Message Send Error Codes

Error Code	Meaning
SEND_NOTIFY_IN_PROGRESS	The SEND_NOTIFY option was specified, but there already exists an outstanding notification request from this task to the target port.
SEND_KERNEL_REFUSED	The kernel refused to send the message. This code is returned when a message is being sent across the network and the remote host is not accessible.
SEND_INTERRUPTED	The thread was interrupted while waiting for the message to be enqueued.
SEND_MSG_TOO_LARGE	The message is larger than 8192 bytes. Mach will not send messages (including header, type structures, and in-line data) which are larger than 8 KB. Out-of-line data is not limited in this manner.
SEND_MSG_TOO_SMALL	This error code is returned when the message size is smaller than the kernel expects. This may occur if the message header specified a size which was smaller than the size of a message header structure. It can also occur when a type description specified more data than was specified by the message size in the header.

Table 3.4   *Continued*

```
/*
 * Mach Time Server.
 *
 * Process requests for current time of day in two formats.
 */

#include <mach.h>
#include <servers/netname.h>
#include <mach/message.h>
#include <mach/port.h>
```

```
#include <sys/time.h>
#include "time_server.h"

#define ZERO_TIMEOUT    (0)

port_name_t      server_port;

/*
 * Main routine simply calls 'init' for program
 *  initialization, then 'process' which does all the
 *  real work.
 */
main(argc, argv)
int     argc;
char    *argv[];
{
        init();

        process();
}

/*
 * Program Initialization.
 *
 * Allocate a new port and check the name in.
 */
init()
{
        kern_return_t   ret;
        netname_name_t  name;

        /*
         * Allocate a new port.
         */
        ret = port_allocate(task_self(), &server_port);
        if (ret != KERN_SUCCESS) {
                mach_error("port_allocate:", ret);
                exit(1);
        }

        /*
         * Check the name in.  The ASCII name will be
         *  "Time-Server-Port"; any client wishing to
         *  communicate with the time server must
```

```
              *   know to use this name.
              */
             strcpy(name, "Time-Server-Port");
             ret = netname_check_in(name_server_port, name,
                                task_self(), server_port);
             if (ret != NETNAME_SUCCESS) {
                     mach_error("netname check in:", ret);
                     exit(1);
             }
}

process()
{
             struct request_msg request_msg;
             struct reply_msg   reply_msg;
             struct timeval     timeofday;
             msg_return_t       ret;

             /*
              * This is an infinite loop which waits for messages to
              *  arrive and then processes them.
              */
             for (;;) {
                     /*
                      * Wait for an incoming request.
                      */
                     request_msg.hdr.msg_local_port = server_port;
                     request_msg.hdr.msg_size =
                                     sizeof(struct request_msg);

                     ret = msg_receive(&request_msg.hdr,
                                     MSG_OPTION_NONE, ZERO_TIMEOUT);
                     if (ret != RCV_SUCCESS) {
                             mach_error("msg_receive:", ret);
                             continue;
                     }

                     /*
                      * We're expecting an integer as a format specifier.
                      *  Print an error if that isn't what we receive.
                      */
                     if (request_msg.type.msg_type_name
                                     != MSG_TYPE_INTEGER_32)
                             continue;
```

```
/*
 * Get time of day from the system.
 */
gettimeofday(&timeofday, 0);

/*
 * Return the data in the format requested.
 */
switch (request_msg.request) {

    case TS_NUMERIC_FORM:
            reply_msg.time.ntime = timeofday.tv_sec;
            break;

    case TS_STRING_FORM:
            strcpy(reply_msg.time.ctime,
                    ctime(&timeofday.tv_sec));
            break;


    default: strcpy(reply_msg.time.ctime,
                    "Invalid Request");
            break;
}

/*
 * Setup the reply message.
 */
reply_msg.hdr.msg_simple = TRUE;
reply_msg.hdr.msg_size = sizeof(struct reply_msg);
reply_msg.hdr.msg_type = MSG_TYPE_NORMAL;
reply_msg.hdr.msg_local_port = PORT_NULL;
reply_msg.hdr.msg_remote_port =
                request_msg.hdr.msg_remote_port;
reply_msg.hdr.msg_id = request_msg.hdr.msg_id;
if (request_msg.request == TS_NUMERIC_FORM) {
        reply_msg.type.msg_type_name =
                MSG_TYPE_INTEGER_32;
        reply_msg.type.msg_type_size =
                sizeof(int) * 8;
        reply_msg.type.msg_type_number = 1;
} else {
        reply_msg.type.msg_type_name =
```

```
                              MSG_TYPE_CHAR;
                reply_msg.type.msg_type_size =
                        sizeof(char) * 8;
                reply_msg.type.msg_type_number =
                        strlen(reply_msg.time.ctime) + 1;
        }
        reply_msg.type.msg_type_inline = TRUE;
        reply_msg.type.msg_type_longform = FALSE;
        reply_msg.type.msg_type_deallocate = FALSE;

        /*
         * All done, send it back!
         */
        ret = msg_send(&reply_msg.hdr, MSG_OPTION_NONE,
                        ZERO_TIMEOUT);
        if (ret != SEND_SUCCESS) {
                mach_error("msg_send:", ret);
                continue;
        }
    }
}
```

3.2.5   Server Compilation and Execution

The time server is easy to compile. It requires only a single source file and the standard Mach library. If the time server resides in the file time_server.c, the following command will build the server:

```
cc -o time_server time_server.c -lmach
```

The time server takes no command line arguments and produces no output. However, it should be run as a background task. Hence we execute the server as follows:

```
% ./time_server &
[1] 3192

%
```

3.3   The Client

The time server is complete, and we now turn to writing the client program. The IPC code within the client is almost identical to that in the server.

When the client sends a message, it can use the same **msg_send** system call, as does the server. To receive the reply from the server, it can use the **msg_receive** system call. Our example starts by using these calls. We then change the example to use a slightly more efficient mechanism.

As we did for the server, let us begin by analyzing what the client must do. The first step will be initialization. Once the client is ready to run, it will send a message to the server requesting the time. Finally, the client will display the returned data and exit. The next two sections describe these steps in more detail.

3.3.1   Client Initialization

The first step in initializing the program is to identify the port on which the server is listening. In Section 3.2.1 we showed how the server allocates a port and registers that port with the netmsgserver. To find that port and obtain the rights necessary to send to that port, the client must do a look-up as follows:

```
kern_return_t    ret;
netname_name_t   name;
port_name_t      server_port;

strcpy(name, "Time-Server-Port");

ret = netname_look_up(name_server_port, "*", name, &server_port);
if (ret != NETNAME_SUCCESS) {
        mach_error("netname look up:", ret);
        exit(1);
}
```

The first parameter to this function is the port on which the netmsgserver will be listening. The second parameter is the name of the host on which to look. If a host name is specified, only that host will be interrogated. A null string specifies the local host. An asterisk, as in the example, specifies all hosts on the local area network (LAN). Should the same name be checked in on multiple hosts, the netmsgserver picks the response to supply to the user. This scenario provides the most flexibility—there is no need to know on which host a server is running, and the server can be moved from one host to another if the load gets too high. However, using a server from another machine on the network will always be somewhat less efficient than using a server running on the local host.

The third parameter is the ASCII name identifying the port. The client must use the exact same name as the server used when it issued the **netname_check_in** call.

The last parameter is a pointer to a variable that will contain the port if the look-up operation was successful.

If the look-up operation succeeded, the constant NETNAME_SUCCESS is returned and the variable that the fourth parameter pointed to contains a port identifier for the time server.

Error codes, as well as a complete description of other interfaces and capabilities of the netmsgserver, are described in Section 7.10.1.

3.3.2   Sending the Message

The message sent to the server includes an integer whose value determines the format of the data to be returned. Sending the message to the server is nearly identical to the server sending a message to the client. The complete code for the client program is shown in Section 3.3.3.

If you examine this program, you will see that the header and type structures are filled in identically as for the server. The request field is initialized to TS_STRING_FORM to request the time in string format. There are two significant differences between this code and that of the server. The first is the initialization of the *msg_local_port* field with the variable *client_reply_port*. By initializing the *msg_local_port* field with this port identifier, we specify that the server should reply to *client_reply_port*. The Mach kernel automatically grants the recipient of the message send rights to the port specified in the *msg_local_port* field. The server sets this field to PORT_NULL, as it does not expect a reply.

The second difference is the initialization of the *msg_id* field with the value 123. The Mach kernel does not interpret this field; it is passed through to the receiver unchanged. The sender and receiver may use this field for any purpose they choose. Most often, it is used when the same IPC port is used to transfer different types of messages. We will use the *msg_id* field to ensure that the reply to our request comes from the time server.

Receipt of the message from the time server is done in a manner similar to the time server receiving messages from clients. This is shown in the next section with the source code for the complete client program.

3.3.3   The Complete Client Program

```
/*
 * Mach Client Program
 *
 * Send request for time of day to the Time Server.
 */

#include <mach.h>
#include <servers/netname.h>
#include <mach/message.h>
#include <mach/port.h>
#include <sys/time.h>
#include "time_server.h"

#define ZERO_TIMEOUT        (0)

port_name_t        server_port;
port_name_t        client_reply_port;

/*
 * Main routine simply calls 'init' for program
 *   initialization, then 'process' which does all the
 *   real work.
 */
main(argc, argv)
int     argc;
char    *argv[];
{
        init();

        process();
}


/*
 * Program initialization:
 *    Look up the server port
 *    Allocate a port for the server to send a reply message.
 */
init()
{
        kern_return_t    ret;
        netname_name_t   name;
```

```
          /*
           * Look up the server port using the name
           * "Time-Server-Port".  If the lookup fails, the server
           * is not running anywhere on the local area network and
           * we will exit as there is nothing to do.
           */
          strcpy(name, "Time-Server-Port");
          ret = netname_look_up(name_server_port, "*",
                              name, &server_port);
          if (ret != NETNAME_SUCCESS) {
                  mach_error("netname look up:", ret);
                  exit(1);
          }

          /*
           * Allocate a port for the server to send back the reply.
           *  If we cannot allocate the new port, we exit as there is
           *  no way to get a reply back from the server.
           */
          ret = port_allocate(task_self(), &client_reply_port);
          if (ret != KERN_SUCCESS) {
                  mach_error("port_allocate:", ret);
                  exit(1);
          }
}

/*
 * Do all the real work.
 *  Send a message requesting the time to the time server.
 *  Receive the reply and print it.
 */
process()
{
          struct request_msg request_msg;
          struct reply_msg   reply_msg;
          msg_return_t        ret;

          /*
           * Fill in the message header.
           */
          request_msg.hdr.msg_simple = TRUE;
          request_msg.hdr.msg_size = sizeof(struct request_msg);
          request_msg.hdr.msg_type = MSG_TYPE_NORMAL;
```

```
request_msg.hdr.msg_local_port = client_reply_port;
request_msg.hdr.msg_remote_port = server_port;
request_msg.hdr.msg_id = 123;

/*
 * Fill in the type structure.  The request code is
 * sent as an integer.
 */
request_msg.type.msg_type_name = MSG_TYPE_INTEGER_32;
request_msg.type.msg_type_size = sizeof(int) * 8;
request_msg.type.msg_type_number = 1;
request_msg.type.msg_type_inline = TRUE;
request_msg.type.msg_type_longform = FALSE;
request_msg.type.msg_type_deallocate = FALSE;

/*
 * Specify that we want the time in string form.
 */
request_msg.request = TS_STRING_FORM;

/*
 * Send the request to the time server.
 */
ret = msg_send(&request_msg.hdr, MSG_OPTION_NONE,
               ZERO_TIMEOUT);
if (ret != SEND_SUCCESS) {
      mach_error("msg_send:", ret);
      exit(1);
}

/*
 * Wait for the reply.
 */
reply_msg.hdr.msg_local_port = client_reply_port;
reply_msg.hdr.msg_size = sizeof(struct reply_msg);

/*
 * Loop waiting for the response from the
 * time server -- this is denoted with a msg_id
 * of 123.  While unnecessary for this program, it
 * would be used if the same port (client_reply_port)
 * were used for communication with multiple servers.
 */
do {
```

```
                  ret = msg_receive(&reply_msg.hdr,
                                   MSG_OPTION_NONE, ZERO_TIMEOUT);
                  if (ret != RCV_SUCCESS) {
                          mach_error("msg_receive:", ret);
                          exit(1);
                  }
          } while (reply_msg.hdr.msg_id != 123);

          printf("Time is: %s\n", reply_msg.time.ctime);
}
```

3.3.4   Client Compilation and Execution

Compilation of the client is similar to the time server. It requires only a single source file and the standard Mach library. If the client resides in the file time_client.c, the following command will build the server:

```
cc -o time_client time_client.c -lmach
```

The client takes no command line arguments and outputs the time string obtained from the server. Output from the client should appear as follows:

```
% ./time_client
Time is: Thu Jun 18 10:33:11 1992
```

Chapter 4

Virtual Memory

4.1   Introduction

Mach provides control over a program's memory as one of its basic facilities. Mach introduces the notion of treating memory as a resource that programmers can handle directly. As Mach gives the programmer complete control over tasks, threads, IPC messages, and ports, so too does Mach allow complete control of a program's memory layout through the virtual memory system calls. Using these interfaces, a program can allocate, deallocate, protect, and share arbitrary ranges of memory in any task. These memory ranges need not be contiguous and, in fact, may be scattered throughout a program's entire address space.

In contrast, UNIX was designed before the advent of modern virtual memory systems. A UNIX program can only alter the amount of memory consumed by the *heap*, a region extending from the end of the uninitialized data (*bss*) segment. The **sbrk()** system call adjusts the "break," the demarcation between allocated and unallocated memory (see Fig. 4.1). Some versions of UNIX also implement an interface whereby programs can share memory, but UNIX does not provide the generality found in the Mach virtual memory system.

The Mach virtual memory subsystem combines broad functionality with ease of use and high performance. Memory from a single page to a complete address space may be manipulated quickly; invisibly to the user, Mach uses deferred evaluation techniques to speed operations. In fact, Mach virtual memory implementations permit the user to allocate or copy very large

99

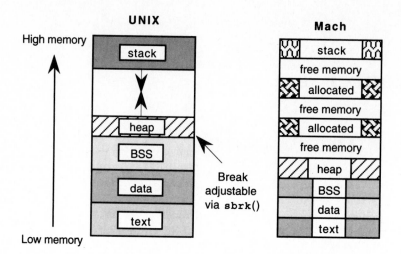

Figure 4.1: UNIX **sbrk** versus Mach Memory Allocation

amounts of memory with only a tiny penalty until a program actually accesses that memory.

The virtual memory primitives can operate on the calling task itself, another task on the same machine, or even a program on a different machine, with no change to their interfaces. The Mach virtual memory interface remains the same on all machines supporting Mach, from workstations to mainframes, from uniprocessors to large-scale multiprocessors.

We will begin this chapter by discussing the need for virtual memory as opposed to ordinary, physical memory. Then we will describe the fundamental abstractions and data types of the Mach memory interfaces. The remaining sections of the chapter detail the various memory management primitives, illustrating their use with small programs. Advanced virtual memory features will be analyzed in Chapter 9.

4.2   The Problems and the Remedy

On some computing systems, such as small personal computers, a program has unmediated access to the computer's hardware address space. The memory addresses that the executing program generates are used directly by the hardware to look up data in main memory. Unfortunately, this scheme places burdens on the programmer. When a program becomes too large to fit into main memory, the implementor must divide it into pieces and arrange to bring each piece into memory when needed. Alternately, when a program

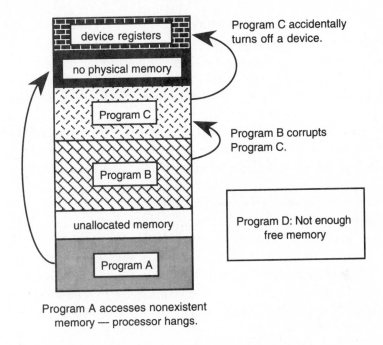

Figure 4.2: Problems with Unmediated Access to Memory

fits into memory, those portions not being used waste precious memory. Programs loaded simultaneously have no alternative but mutual trust; through malice or mistake, one program can corrupt another's data. A program can even attempt to access memory that does not exist, or inadvertently tinker with physical devices such as disk drive controllers, with potentially disastrous results. Figure 4.2 illustrates these problems.

To overcome these drawbacks, many computers provide a hardware memory management unit (MMU) that permits an operating system, such as Mach, to control a program's address space. Mach assigns each application program its own *virtual address space*. In other words, the kernel configures the computer's memory management unit to translate memory addresses that a program generates into hardware addresses. Each program has its own map of virtual to physical translations that the kernel sets up. The MMU will reject a program's attempt to access memory that the kernel has not already mapped. Thus one program has no way to manipulate memory belonging to another program without the operating system's prior arrangement. Furthermore, the kernel programs the MMU to forbid access by user programs to nonexistent memory, or sensitive regions such as memory-mapped device registers. With the aid of the MMU, the kernel can prevent applications from corrupting or crashing the machine.

In particular, Mach only supports *paged* memory management units (PMMUs). Such hardware divides an address space into *page*-sized pieces. While on any given machine the page size remains constant, across platforms page sizes vary from 512 to 8192 bytes or more. The PMMU's translation and protection mechanisms, mentioned earlier, apply on a per-page basis. Therefore the PMMU translates all addresses on one virtual page to a single hardware page; but two pages adjacent in virtual memory can be located on discontiguous hardware pages (see Fig. 4.3).[1]

Use of the PMMU enables Mach to manage memory automatically for programs. The kernel invisibly splits programs into page-sized pieces, not all of which need be simultaneously resident in physical memory. Typically, the data file containing the program's pages resides on a secondary storage device. Whenever a program generates a reference to an address on a page not in memory, the PMMU alerts Mach. In turn, Mach fetches the missing page from secondary storage, changes the PMMU translation table appropriately, and resumes the program where it left off. As a result, a program larger than main memory can be made to work without requiring extra effort by the program's author.

Furthermore, the PMMU permits Mach to manage main memory frugally. Only those program pages actively in use need reside in main memory. Unneeded pages can be retained on secondary storage. Thus more memory can be made available to run programs simultaneously or to run larger programs. Refer to Fig. 4.3 for an illustration of two programs sharing a computer's memory on a page basis.

Mach employs additional strategies to minimize memory use, which also depend on the use of the PMMU. For example, Mach makes heavy use of a feature called *copy-on-write* (COW), which optimizes the frequent operation of copying the contents of one page onto another. In the traditional case, making a copy of a page requires reserving a second (virtual) page and allocating a physical page to match it. Then the kernel executes a loop, copying each and every byte from the first page onto the second page.

---

[1]In practice, a larger virtual page size is often built from the native hardware page size. For example, an 8192-byte virtual page can be constructed from two contiguous 4096-byte hardware pages. Addresses on one virtual page always map to the same, contiguous physical pages; but adjacent virtual pages may still map to discontiguous *sets* of physical pages.

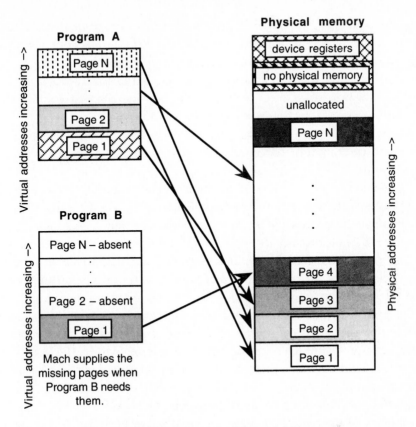

Figure 4.3: Programs in Virtual Memory

Like the traditional method, the copy-on-write strategy reserves a second virtual page for the copied data. However, the COW strategy defers both the allocation of a new physical page and the physical data copy. Both virtual pages can share the same physical page as long as no attempt is made to modify data on either virtual page. After all, until modified, the contents of both pages will be identical. Mach sets up the PMMU to detect an attempted modification of either virtual page; if that happens, the kernel allocates a new physical page and performs the data copy as outlined earlier. Then the program attempting to modify the data can be permitted to continue. The key concept to remember is that the data are effectively duplicated at the time the copy is requested. The fact that Mach may postpone or avoid the actual copy operation until a later time is a detail.

In practice, data are frequently copied without subsequently being changed, so the COW optimization saves physical memory space by avoiding

allocating new physical pages. Copy-on-write also saves time by avoiding unneeded data copies. For instance, the UNIX **fork()** and **exec()** system calls
benefit substantially from the application of COW techniques. The **fork** call
causes the address space of a process to be copied as part of creating a new
process. However, **exec** often follows **fork**, causing the just-copied address
space to be overlaid with a new program (see Fig. 4.4).

With the COW optimization, **fork** becomes much less expensive and the
fork/exec combination becomes much less wasteful of memory and time
(see Fig. 4.5).

Additionally, Mach virtual memory has been closely integrated with
Mach's interprocess communication facilities (IPC). As a result, Mach messages can include portions of a task's address space, which will be transferred
efficiently to another task using the copy-on-write technique. Because the
data copy can be deferred, sending large IPC messages can be performed
very quickly. Further description of Mach IPC's use of virtual memory can
be found in Section 7.1.

The copy-on-write optimization is one instance of a broader class of optimizations called *deferred evaluation* (or, more informally, *lazy evaluation*).
Rather than performing a requested operation immediately, the kernel defers
most of the work involved because it may never be needed. The kernel does
only the minimal amount of work necessary to detect cases later when the
requested operation must actually be carried out. With COW techniques,
for instance, Mach records enough information to perform the copy should
a program ever attempt to modify the "copied" data. In other cases, Mach
may defer changing memory protections until the change becomes unavoid-
able, or defer allocating physical memory until actually needed, and so on.
Applying deferred evaluation techniques to virtual memory requires the use
of a PMMU so that the kernel can intercept accesses to lazily evaluated
memory regions.

Finally, Mach can configure a PMMU to support full, read/write sharing
of memory between tasks. One or more tasks may use the same physical
memory, although it might be located at different virtual addresses in each
task. Any task's modifications to such memory are visible to all tasks having
the memory mapped for full sharing. Full sharing can be combined with
copy-on-write. In other words, Mach understands how to copy fully shared
memory using copy-on-write techniques. Consider Fig. 4.6. Tasks A and
B fully share a page of memory. Both tasks see changes to the contents of
that page. After task B **fork**s a new task, due to the copy-on-write and
lazy evaluation optimizations that Mach applies, all three tasks continue to

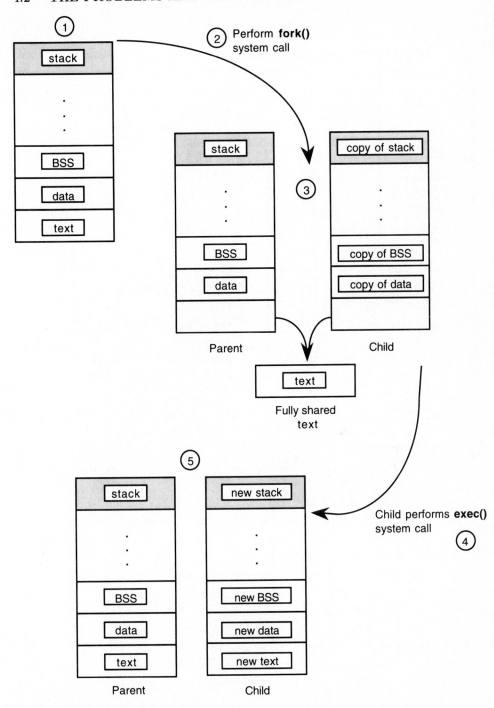

Figure 4.4: **fork()/exec()** without Copy-on-Write

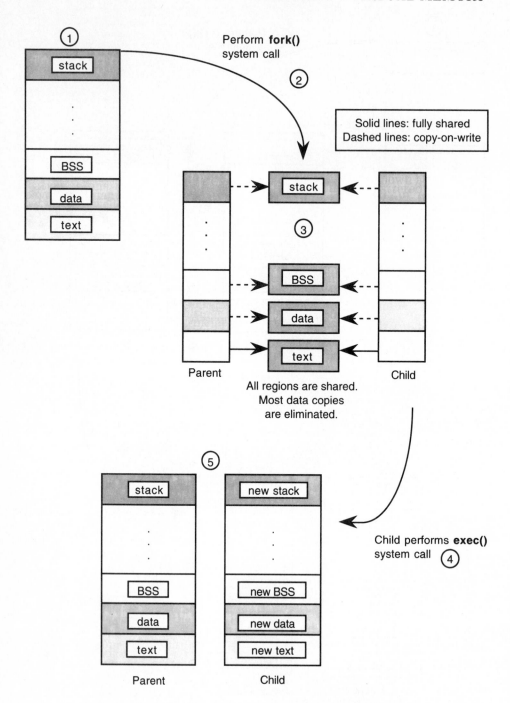

Figure 4.5: Copy-on-Write Applied to **fork()**/**exec()**

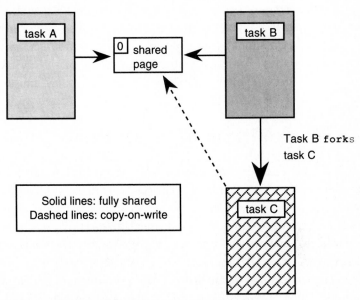

(a) Memory shared between tasks A and B, immediately
after task B `fork`s task C.

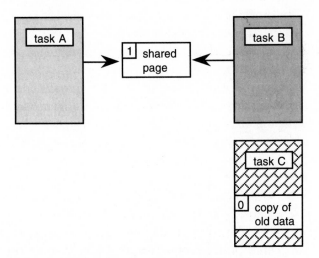

(b) Task B changed the contents of the shared page. This
results in task C obtaining a copy of the original data.

Figure 4.6: Memory Sharing Combined with Copy-on-Write

share the same physical page. A subsequent change to the contents of the
page by any of these tasks causes Mach to copy the page; tasks A and B
share one copy of the page while task C receives a second copy of the page.
Therefore, after the **fork**, tasks A and B's modifications of the page continue
to be visible to each other but are not apparent to task C. Any changes to
the page by task C are not visible to either of the original tasks.

4.3   Mach Virtual Memory Basics

Each Mach task has its own virtual address space that all threads within the
task share fully. The memory locations within an address space are numbered sequentially from a lower bound to an upper bound that the operating
system or hardware imposes. Each location contains a single byte (8 bits).
For instance, most of the current popular microprocessors offer a "32-bit"
address space (i.e., 2^{32} addressable bytes), so virtual memory can theoretically occupy addresses zero through four gigabytes. A Mach implementation
may have other uses for some of that memory, so the virtual address space
available to a program may be smaller. In all but the rarest cases, a Mach
programmer need not worry about the exact limit on the address space.

The UNIX model of an address space is oriented toward contiguous memory. Consider the program in Fig. 4.7 running under UNIX. UNIX puts the
text, data, and bss segments together and defines a *break* between the bss
segment and unallocated memory. Dynamic memory is allocated by moving
the break. There is also a stack that grows downward from high memory.
The result is that the address space only has a few contiguous areas that
UNIX must manage. Some UNIX versions are more sophisticated—they can
handle several regions but are still oriented toward mostly contiguous memory. On machines with large address spaces, UNIX essentially still confines
the programmer to memory that grows up from the bss segment or grows
down from the stack.

Unlike UNIX, Mach has been designed to handle large memory spaces
efficiently. These address spaces typically are *sparse*, which means that
there may be memory allocated at many locations separated by large gaps.
For example, the same UNIX program from Fig. 4.7 when run under Mach
might have an address space similar to that of Fig. 4.8. While the text,
data, and bss segments are still there (after all, it *is* a UNIX program),
further memory allocation can happen anywhere in the program's address
space. The programmer can easily allocate chunks of memory ranging from

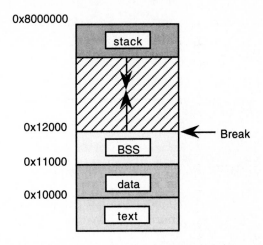

Figure 4.7: Memory Model of a UNIX Program

very small to very large, without any requirement that these chunks be
contiguous. Always remember that, under Mach, a piece of memory literally
can be anywhere in the entire address space, unlike the more restrictive
UNIX memory model.

    While threads share all of a task's address space, different tasks can also
share portions of their address spaces. You should keep in mind that Mach
encourages sharing to the greatest extent possible. In this chapter, we will

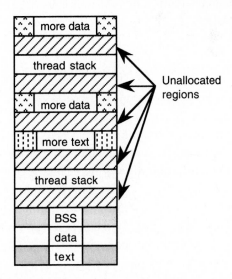

Figure 4.8: Memory Model of a Mach Program

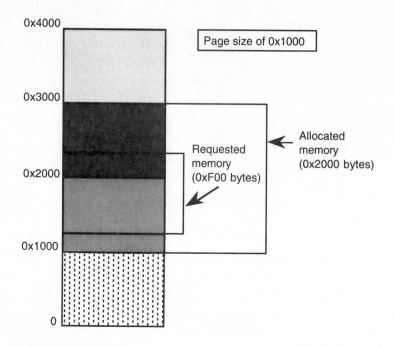

Figure 4.9: Mach Converts Memory Ranges to Page Ranges

discuss the case in which a parent task shares parts of its address space with one or more child tasks. Chapter 9, "External Memory Management," analyzes the sharing of memory between entirely unrelated tasks.

4.3.1   Page Sizes and Ranges

The Mach virtual memory primitives take as arguments a range within the address space specified by a beginning address and a total length in bytes. Thus you always view memory as a linear array of bytes, within which operations can be performed on any byte sequence. However, you must remain aware that Mach kernel always manipulates memory in page units. An operation on an arbitrary memory range will be converted to an operation on a page range. Consider a request starting at *address* and extending for *size* bytes (see Fig. 4.9). Mach will make *address page-aligned* by *truncating* it to the nearest page boundary. Mach then computes the end of the page range by summing *address* and *size* and then *rounding up* that result to the nearest page boundary. Mach operates on page ranges because memory management hardware cannot operate on any unit smaller than a page.

To avoid hard-coding page size constants into programs, Mach provides a global variable, *vm_page_size*, to each running program. When a program starts, Mach initializes the *vm_page_size* variable to the system's virtual memory page size. You should use *vm_page_size* to avoid writing code that depends on a specific page size.

4.3.2   Data Types

The Mach virtual memory functions repeatedly use a few data types, so we will discuss them before analyzing the functions themselves.

All Mach VM primitives take as their first argument a *vm_task_t*, which identifies the task on which to operate. In practice, a *vm_task_t* names a task control port, or *task_t*. The Mach manual pages specify their arguments using *vm_task_t*, but in fact you may use this data type interchangeably with *task_t*.[2]

If you specify something other than a *vm_task_t* or a *task_t* to one of the Mach virtual memory functions, your program will behave strangely. If the argument is not a valid port, you will get an IPC error. If the argument is a valid port but not a task control port, then Mach will send a message to that port; this message will request a virtual memory operation. The receiver of the port probably will not understand what to do with this message, so your program may just appear to hang in the original virtual memory function call.

Mach represents address ranges as starting addresses and lengths. The *vm_address_t* type holds a specific virtual memory address. Mach always uses the *vm_size_t* to store the length of an address range.

Mach provides a few other data types for less common cases. For example, the *vm_inherit_t* represents memory inheritance values (see Section 4.7). The *vm_prot_t* abstracts the page protection features that a PMMU provides in a machine-independent form. We will discuss these types in greater detail later in this chapter.

---

[2]For the insatiably curious among you: Most Mach system calls are implemented with MIG. The kernel must translate the task argument differently for the virtual memory calls than for the task manipulation calls. Thus while as a user you see exactly the same data types and values for task arguments, the kernel defines a different data type to force MIG to do different translations. Do not worry about all this—it works.

4.4   Memory Allocation

Before doing anything with virtual memory, you must first be able to create it. While every program starts up with virtual memory containing its initial code, data, and stack, most programs at some time require new virtual memory allotted "on the fly." This run-time allocated memory is also known as dynamic memory. The Mach virtual memory subsystem offers the **vm_allocate()** system call to create new memory for a task.

Mach processes allocation requests quickly because Mach uses lazy evaluation to postpone much of the required work. Physical memory will only be assigned to a newly allocated virtual page when a program attempts to use the page, as discussed in Section 4.2. Mach also defers the assignment of backing storage until Mach needs to flush pages from main memory, further speeding allocation requests.

When assigning a physical page to a virtual page, Mach clears the contents of the physical page to erase any data remaining from previous uses of the page. Thus all memory obtained through **vm_allocate** initially contains zeroes. We mention these details to point out that you can request large chunks of memory from **vm_allocate** without penalty; you only force the system to assign resources for virtual memory when you actually use it.

Vm_allocate only creates memory in units of a Mach page and further constrains the newly allocated memory to be aligned on a page boundary. The caller usually permits **vm_allocate** to allocate whatever portion of the program's address space may be most convenient for the operating system. However, **vm_allocate** can also be given an explicit address at which the new memory should be created. The **vm_allocate** interface requires four arguments:

```
kern_return_t   status;              /* function result */
vm_task_t       target_task;
vm_address_t    new_memory;          /* in/out */
vm_size_t       size;
boolean_t       find_space;
```

```
status = vm_allocate(target_task, &new_memory, size, find_space);
if (status != KERN_SUCCESS)
        mach_error("vm_allocate", status);
```

The first argument, *target_task*, specifies which task receives the newly allocated memory. Because of the generality of Mach, one task can in fact allocate memory in another task's address space. Of course, this allocation will only succeed if the calling task has access to the target task's control port. Commonly, you specify **task_self()** as the first argument, indicating that the new memory should be allocated in the calling task's address space.

The second argument, *new_memory*, serves both as an input parameter and an output result. That is why you pass a pointer to the variable rather than just its contents. Mach always returns the page-aligned address of the newly allocated memory in *new_memory*. We will expand on the use of this argument in a moment.

The third argument, *size*, indicates the number of bytes requested for this allocation. *Size* should be a multiple of the number of bytes in a Mach page. If you request a memory allocation not aligned on page boundaries, Mach will align your request as described in Section 4.3.1.

The *new_memory* argument can be used to tell Mach where the new memory should be allocated in the task's address space. When you set the last argument, *find_space*, to FALSE, the contents of *new_memory* specify the exact address at which you want the new memory to reside. Mach returns the error KERN_INVALID_ADDRESS if you attempt to allocate new memory over existing memory. Beware: If the address you supply does not start on a page boundary, the kernel silently truncates the address to a page boundary. When set to TRUE, *find_space* instructs Mach to ignore the initial value of *new_memory* and search the task's address space for an otherwise-unallocated, contiguous area large enough to hold the requested memory. Upon finding such an area, the operating system reserves sufficient memory from it to satisfy the **vm_allocate** request, leaving the remainder marked as unallocated.

Besides rejecting a request to allocate memory within an already-allocated region, the **vm_allocate** function can fail in only one other case. If a task's virtual address space does not have enough contiguous memory left to satisfy an allocation request, Mach returns KERN_NO_SPACE. Otherwise, when **vm_allocate** succeeds, Mach returns KERN_SUCCESS. Figure 4.10 illustrates the application of **vm_allocate** to a program's address space.

Along with a way to allocate memory dynamically, there must be some way to dispose of it when it has no further use. While a task's virtual address space may seem huge, in fact the virtual address space can be exhausted by programs that use large amounts of address space or that frequently allocate memory and fail to free it when no longer needed. You should be careful to clean up dynamically allocated memory and especially memory received in out-of-line messages. Otherwise, memory will leak, slowly degrading the efficiency of the entire system and eventually causing your program to fail.

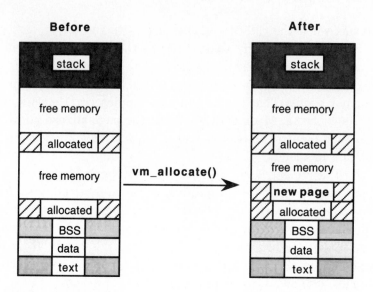

Figure 4.10: Address Space before and after **vm_allocate**

Deallocating unused memory permits Mach to manage the computer's physical memory and paging space more efficiently.

A **vm_deallocate()** call requires three arguments:

```
kern_return_t    status;                    /* function result */
vm_task_t        target_task;
vm_address_t     address;
vm_size_t        size;

status = vm_deallocate(target_task, address, size);
if (status != KERN_SUCCESS)
        mach_error("vm_deallocate", status);
```

Like **vm_allocate**, the user must indicate which task's address space Mach should alter. Most often, you specify **task_self()** for *target_task*. Of course, you can operate on the address space of another task if you hold a send right to that task's control port. Otherwise, Mach will return KERN_INVALID_TASK should you specify an illegal value for *target_task*.

The second and third arguments, *address* and *size*, collectively specify the range of memory Mach should deallocate. As with **vm_allocate**, Mach converts the memory range to a page range. Mach always internally converts deallocation requests from a byte range to an integral number of pages.

Mach does *not* require that the user deallocate precisely the same memory originally allocated. Deallocation requests need not precisely match

previous allocations. For example, Mach permits you to allocate eight pages
at one time and then deallocate four pages in the middle later. Furthermore, Mach will not return an error if the memory region you specify does
not wholly contain allocated memory, or even any allocated memory at all.
Vm_deallocate simply guarantees that the specified portion of the address
space has been removed by the time the call completes.

A **vm_deallocate** request on a task's memory does not affect any other
task that may be sharing the same memory. In Fig. 4.11, tasks A, B, and
C fully share a memory region while task D has a copy-on-write copy of the
same region. If task B removes the region by calling **vm_deallocate**, tasks
A and C continue to share the same memory fully while task D still has its
copy of that memory. **Vm_deallocate** removes memory from a single task,
but not from any tasks sharing or copying that memory.

Both the **vm_allocate** and **vm_deallocate** interfaces permit you to
operate on whatever byte range you prefer. However, recall that the kernel always operates on entire pages, so your request may be truncated and
rounded as needed to span an integral page range. For this reason, you cannot treat these system calls in the same way you would the UNIX **malloc()**
and **free()** library calls. **Malloc** and **free** accept arbitrary sizes and addresses, which need not correspond with the operating system page size.

To demonstrate the use of the memory allocation and deallocation functions, consider the following small program. The dynamic_memory.c program requests a few pages of memory and then, to prove the memory exists,
scribbles a byte on each page. The program then reads the bytes back
and prints them out. Finally, dynamic_memory.c frees the newly allocated
memory and attempts to reuse it, deliberately causing the program to die
suddenly.

```
/*
 * dynamic_memory.c:  demonstrate creating and freeing
 * memory at run-time.
 */

#include <mach.h>
#include <stdio.h>

/*
 * Define the size of the virtual region with which to experiment.
 * We will use a few pages, and isolate the program from page-size
 * dependencies by using the vm_page_size variable automatically
```

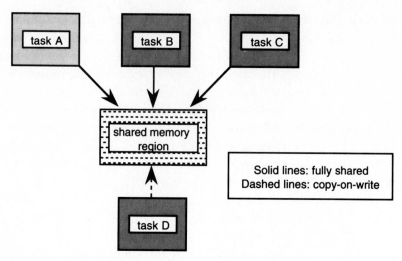

(a) Memory fully shared between tasks A, B, and C;
shared copy-on-write with task D.

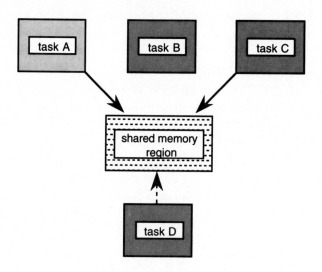

(b) After task B `vm_deallocate`'s shared region.

Figure 4.11: Memory before and after **vm_deallocate**

```
 * set up by Mach.
 */
#define NUM_PAGES        3
#define REGION_SIZE      (NUM_PAGES * vm_page_size)
```

```
main()
{
        vm_address_t      new_memory;
        kern_return_t     kr;
        char              *nm;
        int               i;

        /*
         * 1.  Allocate a few pages of memory wherever Mach finds
         * it most convenient.
         */
        if ((kr = vm_allocate(task_self(), &new_memory,
                        REGION_SIZE, TRUE)) != KERN_SUCCESS) {
                mach_error("vm_allocate", kr);
                exit(1);
        }

        nm = (char *) new_memory;        /* treat as array of chars */

        /*
         * 2.  Prove the memory exists by scribbling a byte on each
         * page; arbitrarily, we choose to alter the 18th byte.
         * Note that the virtual memory we just allocated won't have
         * physical pages assigned to it until we try to write to it
         * in this step.  The pages will be filled with zeroes,
         * except for the eighteenth byte.
         */
        for (i = 0; i < REGION_SIZE; i += vm_page_size)
                *(nm + i + 17) = 'a';

        /*
         * 3.  Now read the bytes back and print them.
         */
        for (i = 0; i < REGION_SIZE; i += vm_page_size)
                printf("%c\n", *(nm + i + 17));

        /*
         * 4.  Attempt to free up the new memory.
         */
        if ((kr = vm_deallocate(task_self(), new_memory,
                        REGION_SIZE)) != KERN_SUCCESS) {
                mach_error("vm_deallocate error (impossible)," kr);
```

```
        }

        /*
         * 5.  Now try to access the freed memory.
         */
        printf("The program will die now.\n");
        (void) fflush(stdout);
        printf("One of the characters is... %c\n", *(nm + 17));

        /*
         * 6.  It should be impossible to get to this step.
         */
        (void) fflush(stdout);
        printf("The memory was not deallocated!\n");
        exit(0);
}
```

When run, dynamic_memory.c produces output like this:

```
%        ./dynamic_memory
a
a
a
The program will die now.
Segmentation fault (core dumped)
```

The three *a* characters come from the loop, proving that we allocated
and initialized the new memory region. The program dies, as anticipated, attempting to access memory that **vm_deallocate** removed from the address
space.

4.5   Memory Movement Operations

From time to time, it may be necessary to copy large chunks of data within
an address space or even move data between the address spaces of two distinct tasks. Mach provides three virtual memory operations—**vm_read()**,
vm_write, and **vm_copy**—that have been optimized for these chores. In
particular, whenever it can, Mach employs copy-on-write techniques to map
the data from one address space to another rather than copying the data
byte by byte.

IPC messages can be used to send data from one task to another. In
fact, a message can handle very large amounts of data. When moving data

between programs, either the VM or the IPC interface can be used for much the same purpose. There are three important distinctions to consider when choosing between VM operations and IPC messages.

First, to employ Mach's memory movement system calls, the calling task must have send rights to the task control port of the affected task. Thus the affected task must trust the calling task. To avoid the issue of trust, we have limited the examples in this chapter to altering the currently running program's address space.

The second difference between using VM and messages to send data lies in the responsibilities of the program receiving the data. To receive data in a message, the target task must be *active*; it must be prepared to receive a message on the necessary port. With VM, on the other hand, the target task can be completely passive. All operations take place at the behest of the calling task and without the target task's intervention.

A third distinction to consider is the control that the VM interfaces permit over the layout of the target task's address space. The VM system calls allow you to specify regions in the target task's virtual memory. On the other hand, out-of-line data sent in a message appears in the target's address space wherever Mach decides to put it.

4.5.1   Reading and Writing Memory

The **vm_read** and **vm_write** operations transfer data between the address space of the current task and that of a target task. **Vm_read** retrieves data from a target task and places it in the current task.

```
kern_return_t    status;                    /* function result */
vm_task_t        target_task;
vm_address_t     address;
vm_size_t        size;
pointer_t        data;
unsigned int     data_count;

status = vm_read(target_task, address, size, &data, &data_count);
if (status != KERN_SUCCESS)
        mach_error("vm_read", status);
```

There are a few considerations to remember when using **vm_read**. The first argument, of course, indicates the task whose memory will be read. The implicit destination of the read is the address space of the task executing the **vm_read** call. The second and third arguments, *address* and *size*, specify the boundaries of the memory on which Mach will operate. Mach expects that *address* and *size* collectively define an integral number of pages. *Size*, of course, must be supplied in units of bytes. For **vm_read**, Mach does *not* convert your request to a page range. If you supply arguments that do not already meet these restrictions, **vm_read** will fail.[3]

The data read from *target_task* appears in the calling task's address space as newly allocated pages. Mach fills in the *data* argument with a pointer to the new memory pages. Mach also sets the *data_count* argument to the number of bytes transferred. Because *size* must be a multiple of the page size, *data_count* will always be the same value as *size* and thus has no apparent use. In fact, *data_count* exists because Mach system call interfaces are generated by the Mach Interface Generator (MIG), which treats the newly read region as a variable-sized array. MIG generates a starting address and a length for all variable-sized arrays that a function call returns, so the **vm_read** system call must have the otherwise-useless *data_count* argument.

Vm_read returns KERN_SUCCESS when the data can be read from *target_task* into the current task without error. However, the system call may fail in any one of several ways. One common mistake is specifying an originating region that is not an aligned, integral number of pages. Attempting to read a partially allocated region, or one that simply does not exist, causes **vm_read** to fail. The **vm_read** call also fails if *target_task*'s memory does not have read permission set (see Section 4.6). Table 4.1 lists error codes that can arise from **vm_read**.

The complementary system call **vm_write** moves data from the caller's address space into the target task's address space. The interface to **vm_write** resembles that of **vm_read**:

```
kern_return_t   status;                  /* function result */
vm_task_t       target_task;
vm_address_t    address;
pointer_t       data;
int             data_count;

status = vm_write(target_task, address, data, data_count);
if (status != KERN_SUCCESS)
        mach_error("vm_write", status);
```

---

[3]Eventually, Mach 3.0 will rationalize this interface so that it behaves like other virtual memory interfaces, converting your request from an address range to a page range as you would expect. As of this writing, most—possibly all—implementations of Mach 2.5 as well as Mach 3.0 have this restriction on **vm_read**.

Error Code	Meaning
KERN_INVALID_ARGUMENT	The *address* or *size* parameter is incorrect. *Address* must be aligned on a page boundary and *size* must be an integral multiple of the page size.
KERN_NO_SPACE	The caller of **vm_read** does not have room left in the address space for the data.
KERN_PROTECTION_FAILURE	The permissions on the target task's region do not allow the memory to be read.
KERN_INVALID_ADDRESS	*Address* contains an illegal value, or specifies an unallocated region of the target task, or in conjunction with *size* designates an only partially allocated region of the target task's memory.

Table 4.1: Error Codes that **vm_read** Returns

Similar to **vm_read**, you must obey a few restrictions when using **vm_write**. The *address* parameter indicates the starting point in *target_task* where the new data will be written, and it must be page aligned. The *data* and *data_count* arguments collectively designate the area of memory to write from the caller's address space into that of *target_task*. This region need *not* be page aligned, although data_count must still specify an integral number of pages. Additionally, Mach requires that the entire target region in the destination task is already allocated. One easy way to allocate the target region is with **vm_allocate** (see Section 4.4). The target region must also be writable (see Section 4.6). Table 4.2 lists error codes that may result from a **vm_write** call.

4.5.2 Copying Memory

Copying data within the virtual memory of the current task can be done using **vm_read** or **vm_write** and specifying **task_self()** as the *target_task* argument. If you care only about making a copy of existing data but not about where the copy resides, you can use **vm_read**. Mach will decide where to place the copied data. On the other hand, by using **vm_write**, you can control the destination of the data as well as its source.

Error Code	Meaning
KERN_INVALID_ARGUMENT	*Address* or *data_count* is erroneous. *Address* must be page aligned and *data_count* must specify an integral number of pages.
KERN_PROTECTION_FAILURE	The permissions on *target_task*'s region do not allow memory to be written.
KERN_INVALID_ADDRESS	An illegal value was specified for *address*, or there was no memory in *target_task* at that location, or *address* and *data_count* specified a memory region not entirely allocated in *target_task*.

Table 4.2: Error Codes that **vm_write** Returns

However, using **vm_read** or **vm_write** to copy data within a second task becomes tricky. Neither of these system calls can perform the copy in one step because both system calls expect to use the calling task's address space as either source or destination for the copy. In fact, to copy the data you would have to write a sequence of calls like this:

```
#include <mach.h>

/*
 * Copy memory range <source,size> to <dest,size>
 * in an arbitrary task.  Assume source and dest
 * are already page-aligned and size is a multiple
 * of the Mach page size.  Return TRUE on success,
 * FALSE on failure.
 */
boolean_t
copy_memory_in_task(target_task, source, size, destination)
vm_task_t               target_task;
vm_address_t            source;
vm_size_t               size;
vm_address_t            destination;
{
        kern_return_t           status;
        pointer_t               data;
        int                     data_count;
        boolean_t               success;
```

```
/*
 * 1.  Assume target_task != task_self.
 * Therefore, must read data from target_task
 * into a temporary copy in our address space.
 */
if ((status = vm_read(target_task, source, size, &data,
                      &data_count)) != KERN_SUCCESS) {
        mach_error("vm_read", status);
        return FALSE;
}

/*
 * 2.  Data and data_count specify the location of the bytes
 * read from target_task into our address space.  Now write
 * them back to the desired destination in target_task.  We
 * assume that the destination region already exists and is
 * writable.
 */
success = TRUE;
if ((status = vm_write(target_task, destination,
                       data, data_count)) != KERN_SUCCESS) {
        mach_error("vm_write", status);
        success = FALSE;
}

/*
 * 3.  Clean up to avoid cluttering our address space with
 * temporary data copies from other tasks.  Ignore errors,
 * there shouldn't be any.
 */
(void) vm_deallocate(task_self(), (vm_address_t) data,
                     (vm_size_t) data_count);

        return success;
}
```

Copying data in this fashion, using **vm_read** and **vm_write**, has two penalties in addition to the extra effort required of the programmer. First, two data copies must be done rather than just one. Mach optimizes both data copies using copy-on-write techniques, but additional overhead remains. Second, the calling task's address space becomes cluttered. It may be necessary to include yet another system call, **vm_deallocate**, to remove the temporary copy from the calling task's memory.

Therefore when the same task is both source of and destination for a memory movement operation, Mach offers the **vm_copy** system call. The **vm_copy** call can execute in one step the copy of one region to another within the same task. Naturally, by calling **vm_copy** on **task_self()**, a program can copy portions of its own memory. Using **vm_copy** eliminates concerns about performance and address space clutter.

```
kern_return_t   status;                    /* function result */
vm_task_t       target_task;
vm_address_t    source_address;
vm_size_t       count;
vm_address_t    dest_address;

status = vm_copy(target_task, source_address,
                 count, dest_address);
if (status != KERN_SUCCESS)
        mach_error("vm_copy", status);
```

The *source_address* and *count* parameters must together specify a page-aligned, page-multiple region of *target_task*'s address space. This source region must already exist and be readable. The destination region must also exist and be writable, and *dest_address* must be page aligned. These restrictions are identical to those you would encounter emulating **vm_copy** by using **vm_read** and **vm_write**. See Table 4.3 for details on the return values from **vm_copy**.

4.5.3   Demonstrating Memory Movement Operations

The following program, vm_copyops.c, illustrates the system calls we have just discussed. Vm_copyops.c allocates a few pages of memory, initializes them, and then reads, writes, and copies data from place to place.

```
/*
 * vm_copyops.c:  demonstrate reading, writing and
 * copying memory.
 */

#include <mach.h>
#define NUM_PAGES       3
#define REGION_SIZE     (NUM_PAGES * vm_page_size)
```

Error Code	Meaning
KERN_SUCCESS	The copy completed without error.
KERN_INVALID_ARGUMENT	*Source_address* or *count* is erroneous. *Source_address* must be page aligned and *count* must specify an integral number of pages.
KERN_PROTECTION_FAILURE	The source region is not readable or the destination region is not writable. See Section 4.6 for details on memory protections.
KERN_INVALID_ADDRESS	All or part of either the source region or the destination region does not exist.

Table 4.3: Error Codes that **vm_copy** Returns

```
void                    initialize_memory();
void                    verify_memory();

main()
{
        vm_address_t    region1;
        vm_address_t    region2;
        vm_address_t    region3;
        vm_size_t       region2_size;
        kern_return_t   kr;

        /*
         * 1.  Allocate two new pieces of memory, called
         * region1 and region3.  Their sizes will both be
         * REGION_SIZE.
         */
        kr = vm_allocate(task_self(), &region1,
                        REGION_SIZE, TRUE);
        if (kr != KERN_SUCCESS) {
                mach_error("vm_allocate region1", kr);
                exit(1);
        }
        kr = vm_allocate(task_self(), &region3,
                        REGION_SIZE, TRUE);
        if (kr != KERN_SUCCESS) {
                mach_error("vm_allocate region3", kr);
                exit(1);
```

```
}

/*
 * 2.   Initialize the contents of region1 to an
 * interesting value.
 */
initialize_memory(region1, REGION_SIZE, 'x');

/*
 * 3.   Read from our own address space.  New pages
 * will be allocated automatically; the address of
 * the start of the newly read region will be
 * returned in region2.
 */
kr = vm_read(task_self(), region1, REGION_SIZE,
             (pointer_t *) &region2,
             (unsigned int *) &region2_size);
if (kr != KERN_SUCCESS) {
        mach_error("vm_read", kr);
        exit(1);
}

/*
 * 4.   N.B. Expect region2_size, returned by Mach,
 * to equal the requested REGION_SIZE; further, the
 * returned size should be an integral multiple of
 * the system page size (as was the original request).
 * This check would not be done in a production
 * environment, as Mach will read everything requested
 * or return an error.
 */
if (region2_size != REGION_SIZE ||
    region2_size % vm_page_size != 0) {
        printf("Size of region2 seems wrong (%#X).\n",
               region2_size);
        exit(1);
}

/*
 * 5.   Verify that the newly read memory region has
 * the contents we expect.
 */
verify_memory(region2, REGION_SIZE, 'x', "5");
```

```
/*
 * 6.  Change the contents of region2 to a new value.
 * The contents of region1 should remain unchanged.
 */
initialize_memory(region2, REGION_SIZE, 'r');
verify_memory(region1, REGION_SIZE, 'x', "6");


/*
 * 7.  Now, write the data from region2 to region3.
 * The source region and destination region are already
 * conveniently aligned.
 */
if ((kr = vm_write(task_self(), region3,
                   (pointer_t) region2,
                   REGION_SIZE)) != KERN_SUCCESS) {
        mach_error("vm_write", kr);
        exit(1);
}


/*
 * 8.  Verify the contents of region3.  Give region3
 * new values, then verify region2 remains unchanged.
 */
verify_memory(region3, REGION_SIZE, 'r', "8a");
initialize_memory(region3, REGION_SIZE, 'q');
verify_memory(region2, REGION_SIZE, 'r', "8b");


/*
 * 9.  Copy the data from region3 back to region1.
 */
kr = vm_copy(task_self(), region3, REGION_SIZE, region1);
if (kr != KERN_SUCCESS) {
        mach_error("vm_copy", kr);
        exit(1);
}


/*
 * 10.  Verify the contents of region1.  Give region3
 * new values, then verify region1 remains unchanged.
 */
verify_memory(region1, REGION_SIZE, 'q', "10a");
initialize_memory(region3, REGION_SIZE, 'h');
verify_memory(region1, REGION_SIZE, 'q', "10b");
```

```
        /*
         * 11.  Clean up.
         */
        (void) vm_deallocate(task_self(), region1, REGION_SIZE);
        (void) vm_deallocate(task_self(), region2, REGION_SIZE);
        (void) vm_deallocate(task_self(), region3, REGION_SIZE);
        printf("Read, wrote and copied data successfully.\n");
        exit(0);
}


void
initialize_memory(address, size, value)
vm_address_t    address;
vm_size_t       size;
char            value;
{
        register char   *cp;

        for (cp = (char *) address;
             cp < (char *) address + size; ++cp)
                *cp = value;
}


void
verify_memory(address, size, value, step)
vm_address_t    address;
vm_size_t       size;
char            value;
char            *step;
{
        register char   *cp;

        for (cp = (char *) address;
             cp < (char *) address + size; ++cp)
                if (*cp != value) {
                        printf("Step %s fails verification.\n",
                                step);
                        exit(1);
                }
}
```

4.6   Memory Protections

Mach provides the ability to alter protections (also known as "permissions") on a range of memory. Normally, once memory has been allocated, we assume that we can read it, write it, or execute program instructions from it as we wish. In fact, that assumption need not be the case. Mach offers a way to change memory permissions on individual pages and page ranges.

With the **vm_protect()** system call, you can control memory protection on any piece of allocated memory. For instance, dynamically created tables can be marked as read-only to catch erroneous attempts to modify them. More esoterically, permission to read or write memory can be explicitly revoked (for instance, to catch attempts to reference beyond the end of an array). Figure 4.12 illustrates the placement of guard pages around a stack. You can use guard pages to surround the stack of a new thread. Without read or write permission, a stack overflow or underflow results in an exception that can be detected and handled (see Chapter 6, "Mach Exception Handling").

Protections are any combination of

VM_PROT_READ: permission to examine the contents of a page

VM_PROT_WRITE: permission to modify the contents of a page

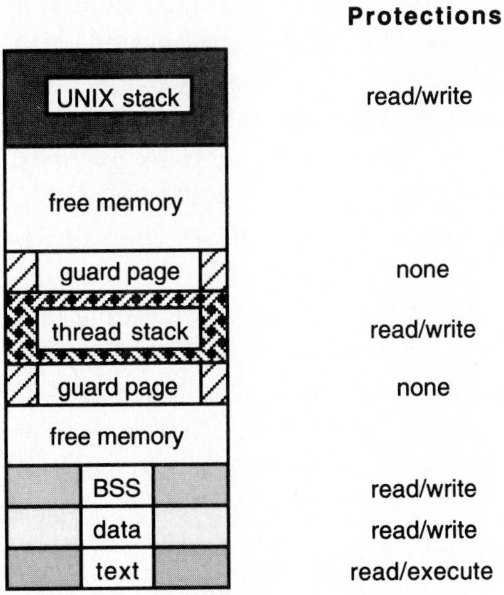

Figure 4.12: Guard Pages around a Thread Stack

VM_PROT_EXECUTE: permission to use the contents of a page as program instructions

VM_PROT_ALL: read, write, and execute permission[4]

VM_PROT_NONE: the page cannot be read, written, or executed but may still exist and contain valid data.[5]

Form combined protection values by logically ORing the individual values together: for example, (VM_PROT_READ|VM_PROT_WRITE).

Memory obtained by calling **vm_allocate()** or by receiving out-of-line data (see Section 7.1) will have both read and write permissions enabled. Older implementations of Mach 2.5, and especially Mach 2.0, may also have execute permission enabled. However, you should assume that newly allocated memory has only read and write access. Always set execute permission explicitly.

The VM_PROT_EXECUTE permission has a special purpose: Specifying this value informs Mach that the indicated memory region may include program instructions. On some machines, instruction execution happens the same way as normal reads and writes from memory, so Mach may ignore VM_PROT_EXECUTE. However, on machines that rely on hardware memory caches or other performance-enhancing techniques, instruction execution may be handled specially. For instance, in a system with one or more caches between main memory and the processor, it might be necessary to flush the caches before executing program instructions. Otherwise the system might fetch stale data from a cache and treat it as an instruction, causing unpredictable program errors. You may set VM_PROT_EXECUTE on a memory range whenever you wish so long as you set the value before attempting to execute instructions from that memory.

As we have just shown, Mach may use machine-independent protection values in machine-dependent ways. Unfortunately, most computers do not implement the full range of protections that Mach allows. Setting protections on such machines may provide less access than you expect. In general, Mach will allow no more access to memory than that specified in a **vm_protect** call.

---

[4]As you would expect, combining any other protection with VM_PROT_ALL still results in VM_PROT_ALL.

[5]Because VM_PROT_NONE is the absence of all the other memory protections, VM_PROT_NONE will be ignored if combined with any of the other protections.

For example, setting VM_PROT_EXECUTE alone on a memory region theoretically should provide "execute-only" memory. An attempt to read or write the memory as normal data should fail, but an attempt to execute a program from that memory should succeed. In fact, most machines support read and write protections but do not provide hardware support for execute-only memory. Mach has no efficient way to emulate the execute-only property, so enabling VM_PROT_EXECUTE on a memory region with no other permissions results in absolutely no access to the region! The same surprise may result from attempting to create "write-only" memory by specifying only VM_PROT_WRITE on a region.[6]

For portability, when setting protections on memory you should write code that obeys the following two assumptions. First, all implementations of Mach guarantee the following protection modes:

All permissions: VM_PROT_READ|VM_PROT_WRITE|VM_PROT_EXECUTE, or simply VM_PROT_ALL

Read/write memory: VM_PROT_READ|VM_PROT_WRITE

Write prohibited: VM_PROT_READ|VM_PROT_EXECUTE, or simply VM_PROT_READ

No access: VM_PROT_NONE.

Second, avoid specifying unusual combinations of memory protections. Avoid the two special and largely useless cases of write-only and execute-only memory.

Mach provides another important restriction on the protection that can be set on a given memory region. Each region has a *maximum* protection associated with it as well as a current protection. Under no circumstances will Mach allow the current protection to exceed the maximum protection. In other words, a protection cannot be set that permits greater access to memory than that specified by the maximum. For instance, if the maximum protection on a region is VM_PROT_READ and VM_PROT_EXECUTE, an attempt to set the protection to VM_PROT_WRITE will fail.

Moreover, the maximum protection can itself be set—but only to a value equal to or lower than its current value. When resetting the maximum

---

[6]Unfortunately, older versions of Mach—including earlier versions of Mach 2.5—work in the opposite fashion. These versions of Mach will grant *at least* as much access to memory as requested. For example, setting VM_PROT_EXECUTE might also result in being able to read the contents of memory.

protection, Mach will also reset the current protection to the minimum of the current protection and the new maximum protection. Thus one task can give memory to or share memory with another task but restrict the latter task's access to that region.

In particular, resetting the maximum protection on a memory region allows a program control over the sharing of memory between tasks related through **fork()**.[7] A parent task can pass any region in its address space to a child task, as we will explain in Section 4.7. By using **vm_protect** before calling **fork**, the parent can forbid the child from arbitrary memory operations. For instance, the parent can **vm_allocate** new memory, then use **vm_protect** to make the memory read-only. By changing the maximum protection, the parent guarantees that the child cannot restore write permission to the memory region.

4.6.1 Mechanics of vm_protect

This is the **vm_protect** interface:

```
kern_return_t   status;                /* function result */
vm_task_t       target_task;
vm_address_t    address;
vm_size_t       size;
boolean_t       set_maximum;
vm_prot_t       new_protection;

status = vm_protect(target_task, address, size, set_maximum,
                    new_protection);
if (status != KERN_SUCCESS)
        mach_error("vm_protect", status);
```

The *address* and *size* arguments collectively indicate the region of memory for the operation. **Vm_protect** converts your request from an address range to a page range, as described in Section 4.3.1. *New_protection* contains one or more of the protection values listed at the beginning of this section. Passing TRUE for *set_maximum* causes **vm_protect** to change the value of the maximum protection on the region to that specified by *new_protection*. Remember, however, that Mach does not allow the maximum protection to increase. Applying *new_protection* to the region's current protection can be done by passing in FALSE for *set_maximum*. Refer to Table 4.4 for details of the errors **vm_protect** can generate.

---

[7]Or **task_create()** in Mach 3.0.

Error Code	Meaning
KERN_SUCCESS	The requested protection change completed without error.
KERN_PROTECTION_FAILURE	The protection that *new_protection* designates would increase the current or maximum protection beyond the old maximum protection.
KERN_INVALID_ADDRESS	Collectively, *address* and *size* specify a region wholly or in part unallocated.

Table 4.4: Error Codes that **vm_protect** Returns

4.6.2   A vm_protect Example

The following small program illustrates the use of **vm_protect** in an unusual way. The program consists only of a small **main()** function that invokes a trivial subroutine, **dummy_func()**. Before calling **dummy_func**, **main** revokes all access permissions on the memory containing **dummy_func**. Rather than successfully calling **dummy_func** and exiting normally, the program terminates abruptly as soon as it tries to fetch instructions from the now-inaccessible region of memory.[8]

```
/*
 * protect_demo.c:  demonstrate memory protection.
 */

#include <mach.h>

main()
{
        void            dummy_func();
        kern_return_t   status;

        printf("Program should terminate prematurely.\n");

        /*
         * 1.  Disable all possible access to the memory
```

---

[8]The program may terminate before the call to **dummy_func**. The program loader might place **main** and possibly even the **vm_protect** C library code on the same memory page containing **dummy_func**. The program would fail fetching the first instruction after the call to **vm_protect**, or sooner still in the C stub implementing **vm_protect**.

```
        * page containing dummy_func.
        */
       status = vm_protect(task_self(), (vm_address_t) dummy_func,
                     vm_page_size, FALSE, VM_PROT_NONE);
       if (status != KERN_SUCCESS)
              printf("Program can't reprotect text segment.\n");


       /*
        * 2.  This program should die attempting to fetch
        * instructions on the way into dummy_func because
        * dummy_func and the memory surrounding it does not
        * have read or execute permission.
        */
       dummy_func();

       printf("Program exits unexpectedly gracefully.\n");
       exit(0);
}


void
dummy_func()
{
       printf("Dummy_func is working after all.\n");
}
```

Protect_demo suffers an untimely death, as shown in the following output.
After printing its initial message, disabling all access to the memory containing **dummy_func** causes the program to terminate.

```
%  ./protect_demo
Program should terminate prematurely.
Segmentation fault (core dumped)
```

4.7   Memory Inheritance between Related Tasks

As we observed in Chapter 2, Section 2.1.2, unlike UNIX processes that
have parent and child relationships, once created Mach tasks have no further
relationship with each other. Nevertheless, for convenience we will refer to
the task causing the creation as the parent and the task being created as the
child. In Mach, we use **fork()** to create a new task.[9]

---

[9]Or **task_create()** in Mach 3.0.

When creating a task, Mach copies the contents of the parent's address space into the child's address space. Of course, Mach uses copy-on-write and lazy evaluation techniques rather than physically copying each byte of memory. The receipt of memory by the child from the parent is called *inheriting memory.*

Memory inheritance defaults to copy-on-write. Memory obtained from **vm_allocate** or received as out-of-line data in a message (see Section 7.1) will be copied into the child task's address space rather than fully shared between parent and child. However, sometimes it is useful to be able to share read/write memory between related tasks or even to prevent memory from being inserted into a new task's address space.

Mach provides an interface, **vm_inherit()**, that allows you to adjust the inheritance attribute for a memory region. A memory range marked as noninheritable in the parent task will be absent in the child. Alternately, memory marked as fully shareable can be read and written by both parent and child, with each task's changes visible to the other. The third option for passing memory from parent to child is copy-on-write. Because memory inheritance defaults to copy-on-write, **fork** under Mach behaves as it does under UNIX unless you set new inheritance attributes. **Vm_inherit** looks like this:

```
kern_return_t    status;                    /* function result */
vm_task_t        target_task;
vm_address_t     address;
vm_size_t        size;
vm_inherit_t     new_inheritance;

status = vm_inherit(target_task, address, size,
                    new_inheritance);
if (status != KERN_SUCCESS)
        mach_error("vm_inherit", status);
```

The *target_task* argument, of course, indicates the task whose memory space should be modified. The *address* and *size* arguments collectively specify the region of memory to be inherited. If needed, the kernel automatically converts the requested address range to a page range. Finally, the *new_inheritance* parameter specifies the inheritance attribute to apply to the memory region. This attribute may be one of the following:

VM_INHERIT_NONE: The memory region will not exist in a new task.

VM_INHERIT_SHARE: The memory region will be shared with subsequently created tasks.

VM_INHERIT_COPY: The memory region will be inserted copy-on-write into a newly created task.

Vm_inherit may return one of two results: KERN_INVALID_ADDRESS if the user specifies a memory region that does not wholly exist, or KERN_SUCCESS if the operation succeeds.

You may wonder why the basic virtual memory functionality permits full sharing of read/write memory between two tasks only through inheritance. Since IPC hides the location of tasks, fully supporting shared read/write memory between independent tasks implies being able to support shared memory between tasks on separate machines. Sharing memory between tasks separated by a network is much more complex than sharing memory between tasks on the same machine. Because the child of a task can only be created on the same machine as the parent, restricting shared memory to related tasks eliminates the problem of sharing memory across the network. Unfortunately, this restriction implies that there is no way to share memory between unrelated tasks using only the functions described in this chapter. Chapter 9, "External Memory Management," presents another mechanism whereby memory can, in fact, be fully shared between unrelated tasks executing on the same or different machines.

4.7.1 Vm_inherit in Action

We demonstrate the use of **vm_inherit** with the following program. The parent task allocates three regions to illustrate the three inheritance options. The parent marks one region to be shared with its child (*shared_region*) and marks another to remain private to itself (*private_region*). The parent leaves the rest of its address space alone, so the third region defaults to copy-on-write inheritance (*cow_region*). Figure 4.13 shows the memory layout of parent and child after calling **fork**.

We test **vm_inherit** by changing values in the parent's memory after creating the child. The parent changes one value in *shared_region* and changes another in *cow_region*. The child detects the first change but not the second.

Upon activation, the child task first sleeps briefly to give the parent task a chance to alter the aforementioned values. In reality, both parent and child

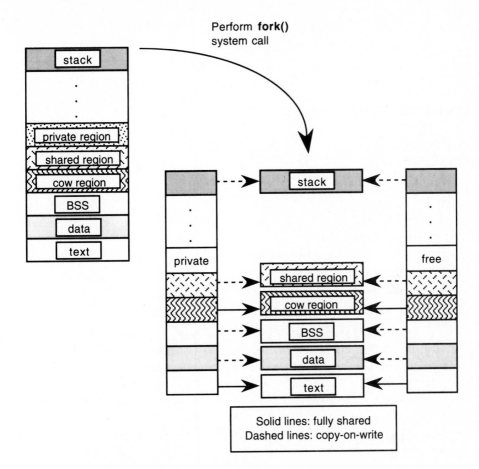

Figure 4.13: Memory Layout Resulting from **vm_inherit**

should use some guaranteed synchronization method to ensure that the parent alters the values before the child examines them. Chapter 5 discusses such synchronization. However, for the purposes of this discussion, suspending the child task for a brief time gives the parent task the opportunity to accomplish its job.

The child prints out the values in *shared_region* and *cow_region*, demonstrating the difference in the regions caused by **vm_inherit**. The child then attempts to access *private_region*, causing the child to terminate prematurely because it did not inherit that region.

```
/*
 * inherit_demo.c:  demonstrate vm_inherit.
 */
```

```
#include <mach.h>
#include <stdio.h>
#include <sys/wait.h>

#define REGION_SIZE      vm_page_size

vm_address_t             shared_region;
vm_address_t             cow_region;
vm_address_t             private_region;

main()
{
        kern_return_t    kr;
        int              pid;
        union wait       status;
        vm_task_t        myself = task_self();

        /*
         * 1.  Allocate three memory regions, one to be fully
         * shared with the child, one to be shared copy-on-write,
         * and one to be visible only to the parent.
         */
        if ((kr = vm_allocate(myself, &shared_region, REGION_SIZE,
                           TRUE)) != KERN_SUCCESS) {
                mach_error("vm_allocate shared_region", kr);
                exit(1);
        }

        if ((kr = vm_allocate(myself, &cow_region, REGION_SIZE,
                           TRUE)) != KERN_SUCCESS) {
                mach_error("vm_allocate cow_region", kr);
                exit(1);
        }

        if ((kr = vm_allocate(myself, &private_region, REGION_SIZE,
                           TRUE)) != KERN_SUCCESS) {
                mach_error("vm_allocate private_region", kr);
                exit(1);
        }

        printf("Parent:  shared region at %#X\n", shared_region);
        printf("Parent:  COW region at %#X\n", cow_region);
        printf("Parent:  private region at %#X\n", private_region);
```

```
(void) fflush(stdout);

/*
 * 2.  Make one region fully shared with any descendants.
 */
if ((kr = vm_inherit(myself, shared_region, REGION_SIZE,
                VM_INHERIT_SHARE)) != KERN_SUCCESS) {
    mach_error("vm_inherit shared_region", kr);
    exit(1);
}


/*
 * 3.  cow_region will be inherited copy-on-write by
 * default across a fork; nothing else to do here.
 */


/*
 * 4. Make one region private to the parent task; it will
 * not be seen by any child tasks.
 */
if ((kr = vm_inherit(myself, private_region, REGION_SIZE,
                VM_INHERIT_NONE)) != KERN_SUCCESS) {
    mach_error("vm_inherit private_region", kr);
    exit(1);
}


/*
 * 5.  Write some identifiable values into the shared,
 * COW and private regions.
 */
*((int *) shared_region) = 123;
*((int *) cow_region) = 456;
*((int *) private_region) = 789;
printf("Parent, before fork:  shared value = %d\n",
        *((int *) shared_region));
printf("Parent, before fork:  COW value = %d\n",
        *((int *) cow_region));
printf("Parent, before fork:  private value = %d\n",
        *((int *) private_region));


/*
 * 6.  Create a child task.  When this call returns, the
 * child's memory contains those regions of the parent
 * task marked as inheritable (VM_INHERIT_SHARE or
```

```
 * VM_INHERIT_COPY).  Other properties of those regions
 * may vary.  For instance, the code of this program will
 * probably be marked VM_PROT_READ|VM_PROT_EXECUTE but
 * will be fully shared via VM_INHERIT_SHARE.  The pages
 * containing statically allocated data, such as the
 * program's global variables, will be marked read/write
 * but will be copy-on-write (COW) because they were
 * originally marked VM_INHERIT_COPY.  The vm_allocated'd
 * region, pointed to by shared_region, will also be
 * read/write but fully shared because of the vm_inherit
 * call above.  (Older implementations of Mach, including
 * earlier versions of Mach 2.5, might also have execute
 * permission set on the statically allocated data and
 * the vm_allocate'd region.)
 */
pid = fork();
switch (pid) {
    case -1:                        /* error trying to fork */
        perror("fork");
        exit(1);
        break;

    default:                        /* parent process */
        /*
         * 7.  The parent immediately changes the shared
         * and COW values to demonstrate that one region is
         * in fact fully shared with the child while the
         * other is copy-on-write.
         */
        *((int *) shared_region) = 222;
        *((int *) cow_region) = 333;
        printf("Parent, after fork:  shared value = %d\n",
                *((int *) shared_region));
        printf("Parent, after fork:  COW value = %d\n",
                *((int *) cow_region));

        pid = wait(&status);

        printf("Parent: child pid %d exited, status %d\n",
                pid, status.w_status);
        printf("Parent: normal exit\n");
        break;

    case 0:                         /* child process */
```

```
                        /*
                         * 8.   Give parent time to act.
                         */
                        sleep(2);

                        /*
                         * 9.   Did child see parent's change to shared
                         * value?  How about parent's change to COW value?
                         */
                        printf("Child: shared value = %d, COW value = %d\n",
                                *((int *) shared_region),
                                *((int *) cow_region));
                        (void) fflush(stdout);

                        /*
                         * 10.   Bravely, but foolishly, the child attempt
                         * to investigate the region the parent marked
                         * VM_INHERIT_NONE.  The child dies now.
                         */
                        printf("Child: peering at 'private' region %#X\n",
                                private_region);
                        (void) fflush(stdout);
                        printf("Child: private value = %d\n",
                                *((int *) private_region));
                        printf("Child: normal exit\n");
                        break;
                }

        exit(0);
}
```

When run, inherit_demo produces output like this:

```
%  ./inherit_demo
Parent:  shared region at 0x1B000
Parent:  COW region at 0x1C000
Parent:  private region at 0x1D000
Parent, before fork:  shared value = 123
Parent, before fork:  COW value = 456
Parent, before fork:  private value = 789
Parent, after fork:  shared value = 222
Parent, after fork:  COW value = 333
Child: shared value = 222, COW value = 456
Child: peering at 'private' region 0X1D000
```

```
Parent: child pid 2033 exited, status 139
Parent: normal exit
```

In the memory region inherited with VM_INHERIT_SHARE, the child finds the value 222 written by the parent. In the copy-on-write memory region, the child finds the value 456 written by the parent *before* the parent **fork**ed the child. The parent's subsequent change of that value to 333 therefore goes unnoticed by the child. Last, the child attempts to probe the memory region marked with VM_INHERIT_NONE by the parent. The child exits with a nonzero status because the region does not exist in its address space.

4.8   Reporting on Memory Regions

When in doubt about what areas of memory have been allocated in an address space, the Mach kernel can provide a description of the task's memory layout through the **vm_region()** system call. Of course, if you examine the regions in an active task, the information that **vm_region** returns may be stale. You might want to suspend the task before inspecting its memory (see Section 2.5.1). Invoke **vm_region** as follows:

```
kern_return_t    status;                 /* function result */
vm_task_t        target_task;
vm_address_t     region_address;         /* in/out */
vm_size_t        size;
vm_prot_t        cur_protection;
vm_prot_t        max_protection;
vm_inherit_t     inheritance;
boolean_t        shared;
port_t           object_name;
vm_offset_t      offset;

status = vm_region(target_task, &region_address, &size,
                &cur_protection, &max_protection,
                &inheritance, &shared,
                &object_name, &offset);
if (status != KERN_SUCCESS)
        mach_error("vm_region", status);
```

Vm_region searches the specified task's address space for an allocated memory region. The search begins at *region_address*, which the caller supplies: If the address falls within a memory region, **vm_region** will report on it.

Otherwise **vm_region** searches forward through the address space to find
the next allocated region. If **vm_region** finds no allocated region at an
address greater than or equal to *region_address*, it returns the error code
KERN_NO_SPACE.

When the call succeeds (KERN_SUCCESS), **vm_region** returns a region's
starting address in *region_address* and that region's associated attributes
in the obvious parameters listed in the interface. These attributes include
the region's size in bytes, its current and maximum protections, and its
inheritance setting. When TRUE, the *share* parameter indicates that some
other task fully shares the region's pages. For a shared copy-on-write region
as well as a private region, Mach sets *share* to FALSE.

In addition, **vm_region** returns a port right, *object_name*, associated
with the memory object that backs the region and the offset into that object
where the region resides. If the memory region has no memory object,
Mach returns PORT_NULL. (Refer to Chapter 9 for a discussion of memory
objects and offsets.) Regardless of any other use of this port right, if it is
not PORT_NULL, you should deallocate it when done to avoid cluttering the
task's port name space.

A small loop that lists the contents of an address space may be written
using repeated calls to **vm_region**. Here is an example:

```
/*
 * vm_region.c:  demonstrate listing areas of allocated memory
 *               via vm_region.
 */

#include <mach.h>
#include <stdio.h>
#include <string.h>

char Banner1[] =        "    Address      Size Prot Max_Prot";
char Banner2[] =        " Inherit Shared Object   Offset";
char Format1[] =        "%#10X %#8X %4s      %4s";
char Format2[] =        "   %5s     %3s     %#3X %#8X";

#define FORMATSIZE      100

char                    *prot_to_str();
char                    *inh_to_str();

show_vm_regions(target_task, prompt)
vm_task_t       target_task;
```

```
char            *prompt;
{
        kern_return_t   kr;
        vm_address_t    region_address;
        vm_size_t       size;
        vm_prot_t       cur_protection;
        vm_prot_t       max_protection;
        vm_inherit_t    inheritance;
        boolean_t       shared;
        port_t          object_name;
        vm_offset_t     offset;
        char            format[FORMATSIZE];
        char            buf1[10], buf2[10], buf3[10];

        /*
         * 1.  Miscellaneous initialization.
         */
        if (prompt != NULL)
                printf(prompt);
        printf("  %s%s\n", Banner1, Banner2);
        (void) sprintf(format, "  %s%s\n", Format1, Format2);

        /*
         * 2.  Begin searching the address space
         * from the lowest possible address.
         */
        region_address = (vm_address_t) 0;

        /*
         * 3.  As long as a region can be found, print
         * out its information.  Mach never wraps the
         * search past the end of the address space, so
         * this loop will always terminate.
         */
        while ((kr = vm_region(target_task, &region_address,
                        &size, &cur_protection,
                        &max_protection, &inheritance,
                        &shared, &object_name,
                        &offset)) == KERN_SUCCESS) {

                printf(format, region_address, size,
                        prot_to_str(cur_protection, buf1),
                        prot_to_str(max_protection, buf2),
                        inh_to_str(inheritance, buf3),
```

```
                        shared ? "yes" : " no",
                        object_name, offset);

                /*
                 * 4.   Remember when done to deallocate the
                 * port right, if any, returned by vm_region.
                 */
                if (object_name != PORT_NULL) {
                        kr = port_deallocate(task_self(),
                                                object_name);
                        if (kr != KERN_SUCCESS) {
                                mach_error("port_deallocate", kr);
                                exit(1);
                        }
                }

                /*
                 * 5.   Important:  must skip over the exact
                 * size of the current region or the search
                 * might report a region multiple times, or
                 * miss a region, or enter an infinite loop.
                 */
                region_address += size;
        }
        (void) fflush(stdout);
}

char *
prot_to_str(protection, buf)
vm_prot_t       protection;
char            *buf;
{
        if (protection == VM_PROT_NONE) {
                (void) strcpy(buf, "none");
                return buf;
        }

        (void) strcpy(buf, "    ");
        if (protection & VM_PROT_READ)
                buf[0] = 'r';
        if (protection & VM_PROT_WRITE)
                buf[1] = 'w';
        if (protection & VM_PROT_EXECUTE)
                buf[2] = 'x';
```

```
            return buf;
}

char *
inh_to_str(inheritance, buf)
vm_inherit_t    inheritance;
char            *buf;
{
        if (inheritance == VM_INHERIT_NONE)
                (void) strcpy(buf, "none");
        else if (inheritance == VM_INHERIT_COPY)
                (void) strcpy(buf, "copy");
        else if (inheritance == VM_INHERIT_SHARE)
                (void) strcpy(buf, "share");
        return buf;
}
```

To demonstrate **show_vm_regions()**, add two calls to it from the inherit_
demo program of Section 4.7.1. (Recall that inherit_demo creates a child
process to demonstrate inheriting memory regions from the parent.) Place
one invocation prior to the sixth step of inherit_demo, in **main()**, after new
regions have been created but before **fork**ing the child:

```
        show_vm_regions(task_self(), "Regions Before Fork\n");
```

Place the other immediately prior to the ninth step of the same function,
before the child attempts to access the nonexistent region.

```
        show_vm_regions(task_self(), "\nRegions In Child\n");
```

Recompile inherit_demo, linking it with vm_regions.o. When you run the
program again, you should see output like this:

```
%  ./inherit_demo
Parent:   shared region at 0x1B000
Parent:   COW region at 0x1C000
Parent:   private region at 0x1D000
Parent, before fork:   shared value = 123
Parent, before fork:   COW value = 456
Parent, before fork:   private value = 789
Regions Before Fork
```

Address	Size	Prot	Max_Prot	Inherit	Shared	Object	Offset
0	0X10000	none	none	share	no	0	0
0X10000	0X9000	r x	rwx	copy	no	0xB	0
0X19000	0X1000	rwx	rwx	copy	no	0xC	0
0X1A000	0X1000	rwx	rwx	copy	no	0	0
0X1B000	0X1000	rwx	rwx	share	no	0	0x1000
0X1C000	0X1000	rwx	rwx	copy	no	0	0x2000
0X1D000	0X1000	rwx	rwx	none	no	0	0x3000
0X1E000	0X3000	rwx	rwx	copy	no	0	0x4000
0XBFF80000	0X80000	rwx	rwx	copy	no	0	0

Parent, after fork: shared value = 222
Parent, after fork: COW value = 333

Regions In Child

Address	Size	Prot	Max_Prot	Inherit	Shared	Object	Offset
0	0X10000	none	none	share	yes	0	0
0X10000	0X9000	r x	rwx	copy	no	0xb	0
0X19000	0X1000	rwx	rwx	copy	no	0xc	0
0X1A000	0X1000	rwx	rwx	copy	no	0	0
0X1B000	0X1000	rwx	rwx	share	yes	0	0x1000
0X1C000	0X1000	rwx	rwx	copy	no	0	0x2000
0X1E000	0X3000	rwx	rwx	copy	no	0	0
0XBFF80000	0X80000	rwx	rwx	copy	no	0	0

Child: shared value = 222, COW value = 456
Child: peering at 'private' region 0x1d000
Parent: child pid 2003 exited, status 139
Parent: normal exit

The output reveals that the program created two new regions visible to the child, one fully shared at address 0x1B000 and the other copy-on-write at address 0x1C000.[10] The child inherited both of these regions. The region at 0x1B000 has *Shared* = *yes* in the child's report but not in the parent's report because at the time the child prints its report, both parent and child actually share the region. The parent created a third region, at 0x1D000, but marked it with **VM_INHERIT_NONE**, preventing the child from inheriting it.

You may be curious why such a small program has so many regions. On this computer, an Intel 486, with this implementation of Mach, the page size is 4096 (0x1000) bytes. The first region, extending from address 0 for 0x10000 bytes, has been created by Mach with **VM_PROT_NONE** to

---

[10]Note that this particular implementation of Mach, based on earlier Mach 2.5 code, sets **VM_PROT_ALL** rather than **VM_PROT_READ|VM_PROT_WRITE** on newly allocated memory.

catch attempts to dereference null pointers. The region starting at address 0x10000 contains the program's code, so it is marked with read and execute permissions. The regions at 0x19000 and 0x1A000 contain the program's data and bss segments, respectively. As we have already discussed, the regions at 0x1B000, 0x1C000, and 0x1D000 were created by inherit_demo itself. Finally, the half-megabyte region starting at 0xBFF80000 contains the program's UNIX stack.

4.9   System Call Summary

The virtual memory system calls sometimes differ in their requirements for specifying address ranges. Many calls automatically convert the supplied address range into a page range.[11] A few calls actually force you to specify page-aligned addresses and page-multiple sizes. Failing to obey these restrictions on such a system call causes Mach to reject the operation completely. Of course, we encourage you always to specify complete page ranges for all virtual memory calls rather than rely on Mach to do the conversion. However, for convenience we have included Table 4.5, which summarizes the virtual memory system calls and their restrictions.

System Call	Alignment Restriction?
vm_allocate	No
vm_deallocate	No
vm_read	Yes—source region must be a page range
vm_write	Yes—source region must be a page range, destination must be page aligned
vm_copy	Yes—source region must be a page range, destination must be page aligned
vm_protect	No
vm_inherit	No
vm_region	No—Mach automatically finds the nearest region, if any

Table 4.5: Virtual Memory System Call Alignment Restrictions

---

[11]As we've mentioned, eventually Mach 3.0 will fix these interfaces to be consistent.

Chapter 5

C Threads

Mach provides a C language interface library to lessen the hardship of creating multithreaded programs. This interface allows the programmer to create and use multiple threads of control without using low-level threads primitives. The user accesses the interface through routines contained in a library called the *C threads* library.

There are many reasons for using the C threads library over the threads system calls presented in Chapter 2. Let us contrast the use of the system calls to that of the library. One major reason to use the C threads library is portability. While using the threads primitives allows complete control of a thread, it also requires handling machine dependencies. You must manually set up the machine state of the thread, including all of its registers. The C threads library allows you to program with threads using machine-independent function calls. Multithreaded applications may then be easily ported to many different hardware platforms.

While the user must write synchronization mechanisms to coordinate threads created through the threads system calls, the library provides synchronization primitives to control C threads. This package handles the maintenance details of synchronization. We discuss various types of synchronization in Section 5.1.

This chapter will familiarize you with many additional issues involved in multithreaded programs. We begin by describing methods of synchronization, why they are necessary, where they are necessary, and how to use them. We also introduce the C threads primitives and how they compare with the thread primitives. A practical example, along with a detailed analysis, shows how you might use the library. We conclude with a discussion of some less common, but certainly useful, functions.

149

5.1   Synchronization

Recall from Chapter 2 that all threads within a single task share the same address space. Therefore when multiple threads are running in a task, they share data. In a multithreaded application, threads accessing shared data must *synchronize* with each other. Failure to do so typically results in lost or corrupted data. In this section we describe several synchronization concepts and the routines in the C threads library that implement them.

5.1.1   Mutual Exclusion

Since you cannot use threads without using shared data, the potential for data corruption exists. Consider the simple example of a task with two threads, A and B, that manipulate a shared counter, running on a multi-processor machine. Both threads happen to update the counter at the same time. Each thread executes along the same code path. The intent of the following code fragment is that the counter will be incremented once each time the fragment is executed. We provide the C language statement and generic assembly language showing what some typical instructions might be like. Let us see what can happen:

```
C                              Assembler
counter++;                     mov    counter, r0
                               add    $1, r0
                               mov    r0, counter
```

In this example, assume both threads run in lock step, fetching the value of the counter, incrementing it, and writing it back at the same time. Thus both threads store the same value back into the counter, losing one of the increments, as shown in Fig. 5.1. Both threads store the value one into the counter. This situation is known as a *race condition*. The threads "race" with each other to update the value of the counter. The resulting counter value is incorrect since we really wanted it incremented twice. A method to serialize access to the counter must be used.

Mutual exclusion locks, or *mutex locks*, provide the ability to serialize access to shared data. The library guarantees that only one thread can acquire the mutex lock. The lock itself has no inherent meaning; it is only the mechanism providing serial access. The presence of locking functions in the code preceding and following the manipulations of vulnerable data provides serialization. Proper coding is a requirement to guarantee the correctness of

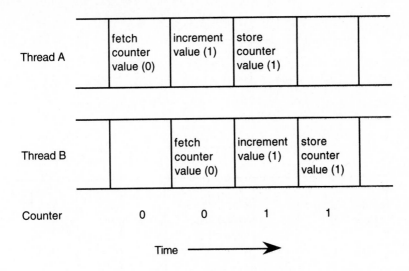

Figure 5.1: Two Threads Corrupting a Counter

data. For example, in an application where threads may be manipulating a shared queue, a lock must be placed around all portions of the code manipulating that queue. Placing a lock around only the enqueueing operations will not prevent queue corruption.

Let us illustrate the use of mutex locks with the example shown in Fig. 5.2. In this example, thread A will get the lock, while thread B will go to sleep waiting to acquire the lock. Thread A can now manipulate the counter, knowing no other thread will access it. When thread A is done manipulating the counter, it releases the lock. This action wakes up thread B and any other threads that were waiting for the lock. Thread B can now acquire the lock and perform its update of the counter. Thus the threads cooperate without corrupting the data and the counter is correctly incremented twice.

If multiple threads are waiting on the mutual exclusion lock, the C threads package guarantees that at most one of those waiting threads will acquire the lock. For efficiency, you should only hold a lock for manipulations relating to the data it guards.

5.1.2   Condition Variables

Occasionally, threads synchronize the occurrence of events with other threads in their task. The *condition variable* construct in the C threads package implements this kind of synchronization.

Thread A

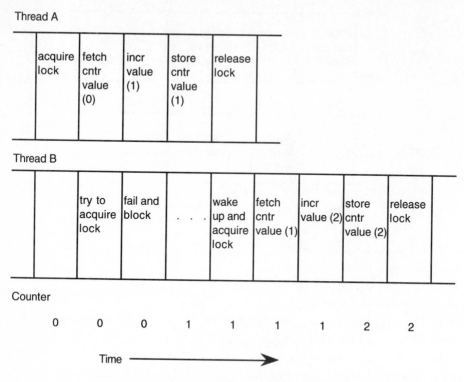

Figure 5.2: Using a Mutual Exclusion Lock

Consider a task with two threads, a producer and a consumer. Suppose this task has a shared queue. The producer places items on this queue, and the consumer removes items from this queue and processes them. Of course, all queueing operations are done under a mutex lock protecting the queue. The consumer must recognize when the producer has added an item to the queue. There are several ways that the notification could be accomplished:

- The consumer could continually check, or *spin*, waiting for new items to appear on the queue.

- The consumer could check the queue at fixed intervals or *poll* for new items.

- The consumer could wait, or *block*, on the queue until the producer signals that some items are there.

The first solution, spinning, clearly wastes processing resources. The second approach, polling, while better than spinning, also wastes resources. The

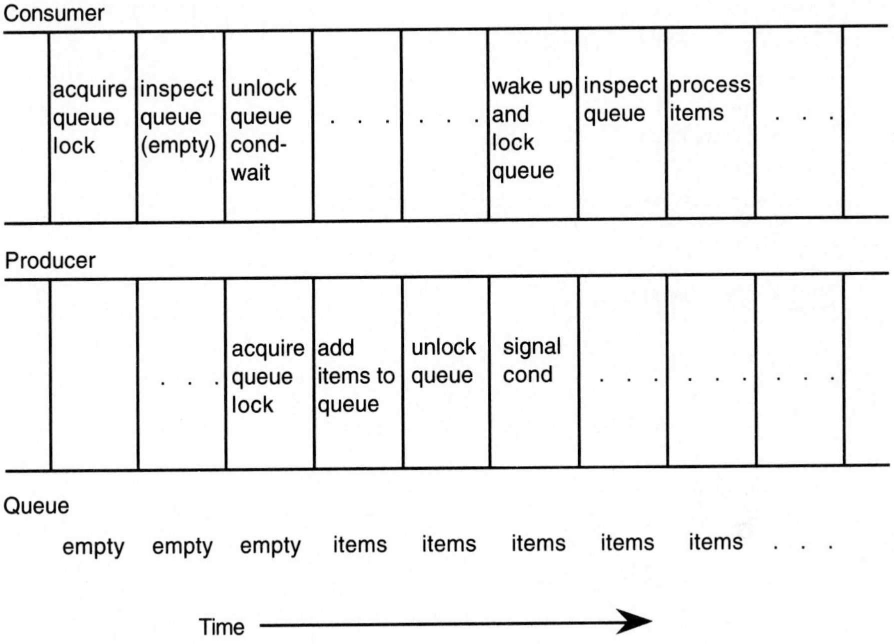

Consumer

	acquire queue lock	inspect queue (empty)	unlock queue cond-wait		. . . . . .		wake up and lock queue	inspect queue	process items	. . .	

Producer

		. . .	acquire queue lock	add items to queue	unlock queue	signal cond	. . .	. . .	. . .	

Queue

empty	empty	empty	items	items	items	items	items	. . .

Time ————————————————————➤

Figure 5.3: Using Condition Variables

third approach provides the best solution. The consumer checks the queue for items. If none are found, the thread is suspended pending notification. The producer, when it adds items to the queue, signals that the event has occurred. Condition variables implement such a notification scheme.

As shown in Fig. 5.3, the consumer acquires the lock protecting the queue and inspects the queue to see if there is any work to do. If not, the consumer waits on a condition, with the **condition_wait()** call. The **condition_wait** function implicitly unlocks the global queue lock the consumer thread holds, and the consumer thread blocks. The following code fragment shows how the consumer program uses conditions in this type of example:

```
/*
 * Mutex lock and condition declarations
 */
mutex_t      queue_lock;
condition_t  queue_condition;

/*
 * Check status of the queue while holding the mutex lock.
 */
```

```
mutex_lock(queue_lock);
while (queue_is_empty(queue)) {
        /*
         * While the queue is empty, wait for the
         * condition to be signaled.
         */
        condition_wait(queue_condition, queue_lock);
}
/*
 * Dequeue the element.
 */

/*
 * Unlock the mutex once we have the element.
 */
mutex_unlock(queue_lock);

/*
 * Do something with the element.
 */
```

Since the **condition_wait** unlocks the global queue lock, the producer
can now acquire the lock protecting the queue and add items. Once the item
is present, it unlocks the queue and signals the consumer thread, with the
condition_signal() call. The consumer is awakened and implicitly reac-
quires the queue lock. It should now reinspect the queue and process any
items found. The C threads library (not the programmer) performs the
implicit unlocking and locking within the **condition_wait** function.

The consumer should check the queue before waiting and must make
sure it synchronizes properly with the producer. Conditions signaled with
no waiting threads are lost, and threads waiting on conditions never signaled
will wait forever.

The **condition_signal** mechanism only allows one thread waiting on
the condition to be awakened. Sometimes many threads may be waiting
on a condition, and they should all be awakened. This "broadcasting" of a
condition is done with the (surprise!) **condition_broadcast()** call. Using
condition_wait and **condition_broadcast**, a *barrier* method of synchronization can be achieved. A barrier is a synchronization primitive to ensure
that a set of threads all reach the same point in their processing before
proceeding further.

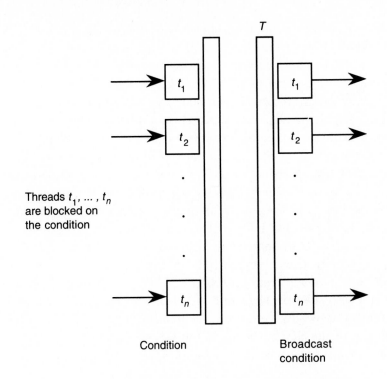

Figure 5.4: Barrier Synchronization

As illustrated in Fig. 5.4, threads $t_1, \ldots, t_n$ wait on the condition. When the condition is broadcast, by thread T, all waiting threads awaken and continue their processing. In this instance, however, the barrier remains. Threads that have not yet come to it will block when they do until the barrier is cleared again.

All of the synchronization and lock primitives described here can only be used with C threads. Non-C threads, such as those created using the primitives described in Chapter 2, cannot use these functions. Also, these locking and condition primitives can be used to create higher-level synchronization mechanisms, such as semaphores and monitors.

5.2   Multithreaded Search

We will now demonstrate how to use the C threads library by writing a multi-threaded application. We have chosen a simple, yet useful, text matching program, which we call "Text Search." The program searches for a string in a list of files and prints out matching lines. Text Search also lends itself naturally to multithreading. How does it do that? Normally, a program like Text Search would be written to search each file sequentially and print out any matching lines it finds. In this example, the searching of one file does not depend on or affect the result of searching any other file. Therefore it is possible to have many threads, each working on a different file simultaneously. This design will result in completing the search of all the files faster. On a multiprocessor, running multiple threads on different processors can result in a significant overall reduction in the time it takes to complete the search. Even on a uniprocessor it is likely that a multithreaded application will yield better performance than its sequential counterpart. For example, when one thread blocks pending I/O, another thread can run in its place.

Let us analyze what Text Search must do and how to do it. We will allow the user to specify how many threads to run, through a PARALLEL environment variable. We will create (PARALLEL−1) child threads, since the parent thread will also share in the work. The code fragments throughout this section intend to show how to use the C threads library. (The complete example at the end of the chapter contains full error checking.)

The program requires the following global data structures:

- List of files to be searched

- File list lock

- Count of threads doing work

- Thread count lock

- Output lock

- Thread termination condition.

Let us look at each in detail and describe the issues that surround their existence.

There is a global list of all files to be searched. Each thread must access this list to determine the next file to search. When a thread finishes searching its current file, it retrieves the next file from the global list. Therefore each thread repeatedly chooses a file to search until all files are searched. Since all threads must share the pointer into this list, access to it must be protected by a mutex lock. Without a lock some files might be searched more than once, similar to the example with the counter earlier in this chapter.

Similarly, we maintain a count of the number of running threads. Each thread, upon termination, will decrement this count. Since this count is a shared variable and multiple threads can be exiting at the same time, we must protect that count with a mutex lock.

Another issue that must be considered is output. The C language standard I/O (stdio) functions use global buffers. Therefore if multiple threads are writing characters using **printf()**, you will see intermixed text. So, again, we must protect stdio calls with a mutex lock.

Some vendors supply a thread-safe version of the C library. If such a library is used, you do not have to lock around output explicitly. Our example does not assume such a library.

Another issue is terminating the program. The parent thread must be the last thread terminated in the task. The current implementation of C threads terminates the entire program when **main()** returns, through an explicit or implicit call to **exit()**. Since the parent will also be sharing the work load, a mechanism is needed so it will know when all the work has been completed. Therefore when the parent is ready to exit, there are two situations that may arise:

1. The parent completes while at least one child thread is still working.

2. The parent completes after the child threads finish.

To handle this problem we use the global count of working threads, protected by the mutex lock, of course. When the file list is exhausted, the child threads terminate, but the parent still has additional work to do. When the parent exits the search function, it will return and check this global thread count. If this count is not zero, at least one child thread still exists. The parent does a condition wait on that count. Every child thread completing its work signals that condition. Remember, the condition signal will just be ignored if no threads wait on that condition. So each child thread can signal the condition even if the parent is not waiting for it. Note that we chose to handle termination this way to illustrate the use of conditions. Termination could also be implemented in a variety of other ways.

The following program example is broken into several sections. We describe the declarations and the global variables used, detailing those mentioned earlier. We then describe initialization, thread creation, and program termination. Finally we discuss the work that each thread does.

5.2.1   Declarations and Global Variables

This section discusses in detail the declarations and global variables that are relevant to our example.

```
#include <stdio.h>
#include <cthreads.h>

#define CHILD   0        /* identify child threads */
#define PARENT  1        /* identify parent thread */
#define MAXNTH  20       /* maximum number of threads to create */
```

All programs that use C threads primitives must include the header file `<cthreads.h>`. We identify the parent thread so it can be distinguished from the child threads in the search function. We also define the maximum number of threads we will allow the user to create.

Now we declare the global data structures described earlier:

```
mutex_t file_lock;        /* lock for file list */
mutex_t stdio_lock;       /* lock for output */
mutex_t count_lock;       /* lock for thread count */

condition_t th_cond;      /* condition for exiting threads */

void search();            /* declare the search function */
char *str;                /* string to search for */
char **files;             /* files to be searched */
int  th_count;            /* count of threads doing work */
```

We need three mutual exclusion locks for this program. The *file_lock* protects against simultaneous accesses to the *files* variable, pointing to the list of files. As discussed earlier, each thread will examine the file list, under lock, to obtain new work. This lock guarantees that every file listed is searched once and only once. The *stdio_lock* serializes access to the standard I/O functions and guarantees ungarbled output. Finally the *count_lock* protects access to the global count of threads doing work, *th_count*.

We also have a condition variable, *th_cond*. This is the condition on which the parent waits for the child threads to complete.

Str contains the string to be matched. The string is considered read-only, meaning that once it is set up at the beginning of the program, its value will never change. As such, access to it need not be protected.

5.2.2   Set Up

This section describes the initialization that Text Search requires.

```
char *parallel;

str = argv[1];
argc -= 2;              /* account for program name and string */
files = &argv[2];       /* argv[2] - argv[argc-1] */

if ((parallel = getenv("PARALLEL")) == NULL)
        th_count = 1;
else
        th_count = atoi(parallel);
/*
 * First set th_count to the parallel environment value
 * or the maximum allowed.
 * Then set th_count to argc if there are fewer files
 * to search than the number of allowed threads.
 */
th_count = (th_count > MAXNTH) ? MAXNTH : th_count;
th_count = (argc < th_count) ? argc : th_count;
```

Str is set to the first argument, which is the string to be matched. Then *files* points to the remaining arguments, the list of files to be searched. We have to determine how many child threads to create. We start by obtaining the value of the PARALLEL environment variable. If it is not set, we set the number of threads to one. We then check the number of threads against the number of files. If the user specifies fewer files than possible threads, we will only create the necessary number of threads. It is wasteful to create superfluous threads that will not have any work to do.

The following code fragment of Text Search does the initialization.

```
cthread_init();

file_lock = mutex_alloc();
stdio_lock = mutex_alloc();
count_lock = mutex_alloc();
th_cond = condition_alloc();
```

Before any C threads routines can be used, the library must be initialized with the **cthread_init()** call. We allocate the three mutual exclusion locks using the **mutex_alloc()** function. This function dynamically allocates a *mutex object* of type *struct mutex*, initializes the mutex, and returns a pointer to it. This object can then be used in the mutex synchronization calls.

Similarly, we dynamically allocate the condition variable by calling **condition_alloc()**. This function returns an object of type *condition_t*, which we will use to signal the termination condition. This is a pointer to a *struct condition*.

5.2.3   Thread Creation

In this section we create all of the child threads we need.

```
cthread_t thread;

for (i = 1; i < th_count; i++) {

        thread = cthread_fork(search, CHILD);
        cthread_detach(thread);
}

/*
 * Parent thread does work too.
 */
search((any_t)PARENT);
```

We call **cthread_fork()** once for each thread we wish to create. This function call is the means of creating new threads using the C threads library. Intermixing C threads calls and thread system calls is not recommended. In our example, we have a function called **search()** that performs the search for the string. When the thread is created, it will call the function that the first parameter specifies. The second parameter to **cthread_fork** is a pointer. The C threads library does not interpret this parameter but passes it directly to the given function. This function becomes the entry function of the newly created thread. If the function requires more than one parameter, the user must create a method of passing a single address into the function and getting all the information needed. This would typically be done by passing the address of a structure containing all pertinent information. In our example all child threads pass in *CHILD* to indicate that they are a child thread. The **cthread_fork** function returns an object of type *cthread_t*, a pointer to a C thread structure.

The C threads library requires that every child thread be detached or joined exactly once. When a child thread is joined, via the **cthread_join()**

function, the caller suspends until the given thread exits via the **cthread_exit()** call. The value that **cthread_exit** receives is passed back to the caller, and the caller resumes. The **cthread_join** function takes the cthread_t of the child thread as an argument. For example, thread P creates a new thread, C, via **cthread_fork** call and then wants to join with thread C. Thread P suspends until thread C terminates. When thread C exits, thread P is resumed, receiving the value that thread C exited with.

In contrast, if a parent thread is not interested in joining with a child thread, then the child thread should be detached. The **cthread_detach()** function, which also takes a *cthread_t* as an argument, indicates that the thread will never be joined. Since detached threads can never be joined again, any value a detached thread passes to **cthread_exit()** will be ignored. Typically when a thread is forked, it is known whether it will ever be joined. In our example, we always want to detach the child threads and therefore call **cthread_detach** immediately after we fork the threads.

We only have to lock access to the *th_count* variable after we have created the child threads. Until this point, only the parent thread has existed; therefore it could manipulate the variable without any locking considerations. Now that the child threads have been forked, access to th_count must be serialized with a mutex lock.

5.2.4   Termination

Recall that earlier we stated that the parent thread must be the last thread to exit the program. Let us now examine how the termination of the program is handled.

```
mutex_lock(count_lock);
while (th_count != 0)
        condition_wait(th_cond, count_lock);
mutex_unlock(count_lock);
```

We make a special case of the parent thread. After it cannot find any more files to search, it will return to **main()**. Here it will wait until all the threads have completed their searches. The parent will check the thread count, *th_count*, until it sees that all child threads have exited. It will take the mutex lock protecting the thread count, *count_lock*, before checking whether all threads are done.

If this is not the last thread, the parent calls **condition_wait()**. Recall that in Section 5.1.2 we discussed conditions. In this example we use them to coordinate the termination of the child threads and the parent thread. Condition_wait takes a condition as its first argument and a mutex lock as the second argument. In our case, this is *th_cond* and *count_lock*, respectively. The lock will be released before the calling thread is suspended. When the thread resumes, the library ensures that the lock will be taken before condition_wait returns. There is no guarantee that the condition will be true when the thread is awakened. Another thread could have acquired the lock and changed the data. In this example, the loop required because each child thread signals the condition and the parent may be required to execute the condition_wait again.

```
mutex_free(file_lock);
mutex_free(stdio_lock);
mutex_free(count_lock);
condition_free(th_cond);
cthread_exit(0);
```

Before exiting, the parent thread deallocates all of the mutex locks and condition variables that were allocated at the beginning of the program. The space would have been deallocated automatically when the task is destroyed, but we will explicitly show it here. Mutex locks are deallocated by calling **mutex_free()**. That function takes a *mutex_t* as an argument. We had three mutex locks in our program, and we deallocate each of them with a **mutex_free** call. Similarly, condition variables are deallocated with the **condition_free()** call. Not surprisingly, this call takes a *condition_t* as an argument. We have only one condition variable, *th_cond*, to deallocate. Finally the parent exits with the **cthread_exit()** call.

5.2.5   The String Search

This section describes the top-level control loop that each thread executes as it searches the files for the pattern string. The textual search is not yet ready to be performed. First, each thread obtains a file to search.

```
void
search(parent_flag)
int parent_flag;
{
        char *cur_file;

        mutex_lock(file_lock);
```

```
        while (*files != NULL) {
                cur_file = *files++;
                mutex_unlock(file_lock);
                search_file(cur_file);
                mutex_lock(file_lock);
        }
        mutex_unlock(file_lock);

        mutex_lock(count_lock);
        th_count--;
        mutex_unlock(count_lock);
        if (parent_flag != PARENT) {  /* We are a child thread */
                condition_signal(th_cond);
                cthread_exit(0);
        }
}
```

Every thread will enter **search()** with *parent_flag* set to CHILD if it is
a child thread, and PARENT if it is the parent. The local variable *cur_file*
points to the current file this thread should search. If there are still files to
search, *cur_file* is assigned the next file. The **search_file()** function is called
to search that particular file. Since local variables are not shared among
threads, each thread has its own private *cur_file* variable.

The *file_lock* mutex lock protects access to the global list of files. This
guarantees that only one thread can fetch a new file at a time. Each file will
be searched exactly once, by using the lock. We hold the *file_lock* when we
are checking for the end of the list at the top of the while loop, in addition
to holding it when we assign the next file. The C threads package guarantees
that only one thread gets the lock at a time. If more than one thread tries
to acquire the lock at the same time, all but one will block.

Once all files have been assigned, each thread leaving the function will
decrement the global count of working threads. Of course, access to this
count is serialized with a mutex lock, *count_lock*. If a child thread is exiting,
indicated when *parent_flag* is CHILD, it will signal the condition, *th_cond*. As
mentioned earlier, the **condition_signal()** call signals the condition variable
given as its argument. Again, if no thread waits on the condition, the signal
is ignored. If more than one thread is waiting on the condition, then only one
thread will be awakened. It is not guaranteed which thread will be awakened
when more than one are waiting. If all threads should be awakened, the
condition_broadcast() function should be used.

This next code fragment describes the pieces of actually searching for the string. It describes the interesting activity related to the individual threads.

```
search_file(file)
char *file;
{

        FILE *fp;
        char line[BUFSIZ];
        int  match_found;

        mutex_lock(stdio_lock);
        if ((fp = fopen(file, "r")) == NULL) {
                mutex_unlock(stdio_lock);
                perror(file);
                return(1);
        }
        mutex_unlock(stdio_lock);

        while (fgets(line, BUFSIZ, fp) != NULL) {
                /*
                 * [ Code to actually match the string goes here. ]
                 *    . . .
                 * Look for match of the string & set match_found
                 * accordingly.
                 */
                if (match_found) {
                        mutex_lock(stdio_lock);
                        printf("%s: %s",file, line);
                        mutex_unlock(stdio_lock);
                }
        }
        fclose(fp);
        return(0);

}
```

The mechanism of searching for the string is shown in the full program at the end of this chapter. We open the file that the **search** function passed in. The **fopen()** function is part of the stdio routines that manipulates a global file structure array. We protect access to it by acquiring the *stdio_lock* before opening the file. Then for each line in the file, we look for a match of the pattern string. If one is found, we want to output that line, along with the filename. As discussed earlier, the output buffer is a global resource, so the *stdio_lock* is taken to ensure that only one thread is writing to the buffer at the same time.

5.3 Additional C Thread Functions

There are other functions worthy of mention that were not applicable to the example program. Most of these have to do with mutex locks and conditions, but there are also a few dealing directly with threads.

5.3.1 C Threads

The **cthread_self()** function returns the thread identifier of the caller. It does not take any arguments. It returns an object of type *cthread_t*. This is the same value that was returned to the parent thread by the **cthread_fork** function. This value uniquely identifies the thread.

The **cthread_set_data()** and **cthread_data()** functions allow the user to associate arbitrary data with a thread. The **cthread_set_data** call takes two arguments. The first argument is a C thread identifier (for instance, the value that **cthread_self** returns). The second argument is a pointer to the data. The **cthread_data** call takes a thread identifier as an argument and returns a pointer to the data associated with the thread. The user can then implement a sophisticated set of functions using these primitives. An example would be a per-thread hash table implementation or per-thread property lists. Since **cthread_set_data** takes a thread identifier, one thread may modify the data of another thread. If the application requires this type of data manipulation, mutex locks must be used to serialize access to the data. The following code fragment shows how these functions would be used in Text Search. The name of the file each thread is working on is stored as data:

```
void
search(parent_flag)
int parent_flag;
{
        char *cur_file;

        mutex_lock(file_lock);
        while (*files != NULL) {
                cur_file = *files++;
```

```
            mutex_unlock(file_lock);
            cthread_set_data(cthread_self(), (any_t)cur_file);
            search_file();
            mutex_lock(file_lock);
        }
        mutex_unlock(file_lock);

        /*
         * Remainder of function is the same.
         */
}

search_file()
{

        char *file;
        FILE *fp;
        char line[BUFSIZ];
        int  match_found;

        file = cthread_data(cthread_self());
        /*
         * Remainder of function is the same.
         */
}
```

Each thread stores the current file it is searching with the **cthread_set_data** function. Then, in the **search_file** function, the name of the file is retrieved with the **cthread_data** routine.

5.3.2   Mutex Locking

There is another locking function that is very useful for mutex locks. This is the **mutex_try_lock()** function. Like other locking routines, it takes an object of type *mutex_t* as an argument. There are many uses for the **mutex_try_lock** function. The **mutex_try_lock** will attempt to acquire the given lock. It returns TRUE if the lock attempt succeeds and FALSE if the lock attempt fails.

One use of **mutex_try_lock** involves deadlock avoidance. For instance, if your program requires taking one mutex lock while holding another mutex lock, take care to avoid deadlock states. Deadlock can occur when multiple locks must be held at the same time and those locks are acquired in different orders. For instance, a deadlock can result if thread 1 acquires lock A and then tries to take lock B. At the same time, thread 2 acquires lock B and then attempts to take lock A. Thread 1 waits forever for lock B because thread 2 has it, and thread 2 waits forever for lock A because thread 1 has it.

We can avoid the deadlock state described by using the **mutex_try_lock** function. First a prescribed order must be established for acquiring the locks (for example, lock A must be taken before lock B). If a thread needs to acquire the locks in a different order, then it uses **mutex_try_lock**. If the function returns TRUE, then we successfully acquired the lock and can proceed. However, if the function returns FALSE, then the lock is held and the potential for deadlock exists. The thread may treat the inability to acquire the lock as an error. It may also decide to avoid the deadlock but continue to try and acquire the lock. The following fragment shows how code that takes the locks in the reverse order might avoid deadlock situations:

```
tryagain:
        mutex_lock(&lockB);
/*
        * This thread now needs to acquire lock A.
        * This is the wrong order for the locks, so
        * use the mutex_try_lock function.
        */
        if (mutex_try_lock(&lockA) == FALSE) {
                /*
                 * Lock A is already held.  Avoid the deadlock and
                 * try again.
                 */
                mutex_unlock(&lockB);
                goto tryagain;
        }
```

Eventually the thread that holds the locks will release them, and this thread can acquire both. The advantage of this scheme is that it avoids deadlock. The disadvantage is that it is inefficient in the case where we must try again. Hopefully the program is written so that retries happen rarely. Remember, **mutex_try_lock** was used to avoid the potential for deadlock. If you are concerned about this overhead, an examination of your code may reveal a circumstance that will alleviate some of the spinning.

5.3.3   Condition Signaling

As described in Section 5.1.2, the **condition_signal()** function only wakes up one thread that is waiting on the given condition. Recall that the C threads library provides a function called **condition_broadcast**, which works as **condition_signal** does, except it wakes up all threads waiting on the given condition. This is useful for implementing a *barrier* mechanism for synchronization. The following line of code demonstrates the use of the broadcast function to clear a barrier:

```
#define barrier_clear(cond)        condition_broadcast(cond)
```

To clear the barrier, we simply call condition_broadcast, and all threads waiting on that condition will be awakened.

5.3.4   Mutex and Condition Management

There are several routines that allow additional manipulations of mutex locks and condition variables. The **mutex_alloc()** and **condition_alloc()** calls will allocate and initialize a mutex structure or a condition, respectively, and return a *pointer* to that structure. Sometimes it may be necessary to initialize an already existing structure. The C threads library provides such a mechanism.

The **mutex_init()** and **condition_init()** calls initialize an object of type *struct mutex* or *struct condition*, respectively. Each routine takes a pointer to its respective structure and initializes it.

The most common use of these routines is when you want to have a structure resident within another structure (rather than a pointer to it). A motive for having the lock within a larger structure would be efficiency of storage and access. Each lock would then be initialized with the **mutex_init** call.

In fact, the **mutex_alloc** and **condition_alloc** routines could themselves be written in terms of the initialization routines.

```
condition_t
condition_alloc()
{
        condition_t c;

        c = (condition_t) malloc(sizeof(struct condition));
        if (c != NULL)
```

```
                condition_init(c);
        return(c);
}
```

The **mutex_alloc** routine would be very similar to the preceding implementation of the **condition_alloc** function.

    The C threads library also provides a finalization function for mutex locks and condition variables. They are called **mutex_clear()** and **condition_clear()**, respectively. Again, each takes a pointer to a mutex structure or a condition structure. It should be plain to see how the **mutex_free** and **condition_free** routines could be implemented in terms of finalization functions:

```
condition_free(c)
condition_t c;
{
        condition_clear(c);
        free((char *)c);
}
```

5.3.5   Naming

The C threads library allows the user to associate an ASCII name with a thread, mutex, or condition. The name can then be used for application-specific debugging information. The following example shows how to use these functions for mutual exclusion locks:

```
mutex_t
my_mutex_alloc(name)
char *name;
{
        mutex_t m;

        m = mutex_alloc();
        if (debug)
                mutex_set_name(m, name);
}

my_mutex_lock(m)
mutex_t m;
{
        mutex_lock(m);
        if (debug)
```

```
            printf("Acquired %s mutex\n",mutex_name(m));
}
```

The **mutex_set_name()** function takes a *mutex_t* and a character string as its arguments. The given name becomes associated with the mutex lock. Similarly the **cthread_set_name()** and the **condition_set_name()** functions take a *cthread_t* or a *condition_t* as the first argument, respectively. The **mutex_name()** function returns a pointer to the string associated with the given *mutex_t*. As before, the **cthread_name()** and **condition_name()** functions return the name associated with the respective *cthread_t* or *condition_t* given as the argument.

If **cthread_name**, **mutex_name**, or **condition_name** is called without first setting the name, a "?" is returned. The sole exception is if the original thread calls **cthread_name**. In this case the name "main" is returned.

5.4   Complete Program Example

```
#include <stdio.h>
#include <cthreads.h>

#define CHILD    0          /* identify child threads */
#define PARENT   1          /* identify parent thread */
#define MAXNTH       20

char *str;              /* string to search for */
char **files;           /* files to be searched */
int  th_count;          /* number of files */

mutex_t        file_lock;           /* lock for index */
mutex_t        stdio_lock;          /* lock for output */
mutex_t        count_lock;          /* lock for thread count */

condition_t    th_cond;         /* condition for exiting threads */

void search();
extern char *getenv();
extern char *index();

main(argc, argv)
int argc;
char **argv;
{
```

```
int i;
char *parallel;
cthread_t thread;

/*
 * For this example, we require at least one file.
 */
if (argc < 3) {
        usage(argv[0]);
        exit(1);
}
str = argv[1];
argc -= 2;
files = &argv[2];
if ((parallel = getenv("PARALLEL")) == NULL)
        th_count = 1;
else
        th_count = atoi(parallel);
th_count = (th_count > MAXNTH) ? MAXNTH : th_count;
/*
 * If there are fewer files than potential threads,
 * only create as many threads as needed.
 */
if (argc < th_count)
        th_count = argc;

cthread_init();
/*
 * Allocate mutex locks and condition variables.
 */
file_lock = mutex_alloc();
stdio_lock = mutex_alloc();
count_lock = mutex_alloc();
th_cond = condition_alloc();

/*
 * Fork off all the child threads.
 */
for (i = 1; i < th_count; i++) {
        thread = cthread_fork(search, CHILD);
        cthread_detach(thread);
}

/*
```

```
      * Parent thread does work too.
      */
      search((char *) PARENT);

      /*
       * Wait for all child threads to finish.
       */
      mutex_lock(count_lock);
      while (th_count != 0)
              condition_wait(th_cond, count_lock);
      mutex_unlock(count_lock);

      /*
       * Free up all the stuff we allocated.
       */
      mutex_free(file_lock);
      mutex_free(stdio_lock);
      mutex_free(count_lock);
      condition_free(th_cond);
      cthread_exit(0);
}

/*
 * Search all the files for the string.  If we
 * are a child thread (parent_flag == NULL),
 * then signal the condition.
 */
void
search(parent_flag)
char *parent_flag;
{
      char *cur_file;

      mutex_lock(file_lock);
      while (*files != NULL) {
              cur_file = *files++;
              mutex_unlock(file_lock);
              search_file(cur_file);
              mutex_lock(file_lock);
      }
      mutex_unlock(file_lock);

      mutex_lock(count_lock);
      th_count--;
```

```
                mutex_unlock(count_lock);
                if (parent_flag != (char *)PARENT) {
                        /*
                         * We are a child thread.
                         */
                        condition_signal(th_cond);
                        cthread_exit(0);
                }
}


/*
 * Search the given file for the string.  For each line that
 * matches, print it out.
 */
search_file(file)
char *file;
{
        FILE *fp;
        int match_found;
        char *line[BUFSIZ];
        char *p, *p1;
        char *s, *s1;

        mutex_lock(stdio_lock);
        if ((fp = fopen(file, "r")) == NULL) {
                mutex_unlock(stdio_lock);
                perror(file);
                return(1);
        }
        mutex_unlock(stdio_lock);

        while (fgets(line, BUFSIZ, fp) != NULL) {
                s = str;
                match_found = 0;
                p = line;
                while ((p = index(p, *s)) && !match_found) {
                        if (strncmp(p, str, strlen(str)) == 0)
                                match_found = 1;
                        p++;
                }
                if (match_found) {
                        mutex_lock(stdio_lock);
                        printf("%s: %s",file, line);
                        mutex_unlock(stdio_lock);
```

```
            }
        }
        fclose(fp);
        return(0);
}

usage(prog)
char *prog;
{
        printf("usage: %s str file1 file2 ...\n",prog);
}
```

Chapter 6

Mach Exception Handling

Frequently, programs are interrupted in the normal course of their execution. In this chapter we look at *exceptions*, one category of such interruptions. Exceptions are interruptions of a program's normal instruction processing that the program itself causes. They occur for a variety of reasons, ranging from explicit design, to program bugs, to human intervention. Examples include exceeding arithmetic limits (for instance, overflow), trying to use virtual memory that does not exist, or hitting a debugger breakpoint. We explicitly exclude from this discussion interruptions due to external events (called *interrupts*), such as the expiration of timers or user requests for program termination.

You should understand exception handling if you want to program effectively. All but the most trivial programs must handle exceptions correctly. While simple programs do not always require the precise control over exception handling described in this chapter, you should design practical applications to respond appropriately to exceptions. This "defensive programming" style is good programming practice.

Exception handling takes on greater importance for applications that process exceptions as an integral part of their operation. Examples include language run-time systems, compatibility packages, and debuggers. The run-time system implementor specifies precise responses to events such as division by zero or other unusual arithmetic conditions. Compatibility packages often emulate hardware instructions in software. Debuggers use breakpoints, synchronous interruptions that permit examination of a program's state. All of these application classes depend on exceptions for their correct functioning. Exceeding arithmetic limits, emulating instructions, and implementing breakpoints are three causes of exceptions. We present the complete list of exception types in Section 6.2.3.

For many straightforward programs, exceptions can be handled with the UNIX signal mechanism. UNIX signals are used for both exceptions and for interrupts, such as notification of process termination requests or changes in process state. In the Mach environment, however, the traditional UNIX signal model does not provide a good match for Mach's support of more than one thread per task. The Mach exception handling facility is designed expressly for this environment. Section 6.5 describes the differences between exception processing in Mach and UNIX.

Exception handling is, of necessity, partially machine dependent, because exceptions are so closely tied to hardware operation. The design of the Mach exception handling facility abstracts many of the common elements involved in processing exceptions. This scheme yields the greatest portability for applications designed to run on multiple hardware architectures. Still, when an exception occurs some of the relevent data is unique to the particular hardware platform, such as the platform-specific exception codes described in Section 6.3.1.

In this chapter we will describe the Mach calls and data structures needed to respond to exceptions. You will learn the general concepts involved in handling exceptions under Mach. We will then illustrate these concepts with three sample programs that demonstrate how to deal with exceptions in practical application programs.

6.1   Overview of Mach Exception Handling

6.1.1   Exception Handling Philosophy

Mach separates the response to an exception from the execution environment where the exception occurred. The kernel suspends a *victim thread* encountering an exception and notifies a *handler thread* of the condition. This design solves several problems inherent in dealing with exceptions directly in the victim thread:

- The interrupted program may be in an inconsistent state. For example, touching an inaccessible page indicates a possible coding problem, such as a reference through a null pointer.

- It can be difficult to handle multiple interruptions at the same time. Normally only a single exception occurs at any point in time, and performance is not usually an issue when responding to an exception. However, a multithreaded program may generate concurrent exceptions (for instance, when emulating floating point instructions in software).

- The code handling an exception may need some of the same resources used in the victim thread. Stack space, for instance, could be a problem if the interruption was due to exhausting the available stack.

Let us look at how the Mach exception mechanism addresses each of these points. First, the code reacting to the exception runs in a separate handler thread and so is not itself vulnerable to inconsistencies in the victim's state. Second, Mach notifies the handler thread of the exception in the victim by sending a message via the Mach IPC facility. This design allows one handler thread to serialize its processing of multiple exceptions or allows for multiple handler threads that process several exceptions simultaneously. Finally, using a separate handler thread helps reduce the dependence on the resources used in the victim thread. The handler thread, for example, runs on its own stack.

Note that applications using the Mach exception handling facility always contain at least two threads: the victim thread (in which the exception occurred) and the handler thread (which receives the IPC message advising of the exception in the victim). Typically the victim and handler threads execute in the same task. Of course, with the generality of the Mach IPC mechanism, the notification message could go to a thread in another task or even to a thread on a different machine!

6.1.2   The Steps in Exception Processing

When an exception occurs in the victim thread, the operating system sends an IPC message to the handler thread. How does Mach know which thread is the handler? Recall from Chapter 3 that a Mach IPC message is sent not to a particular thread but rather to a specified port. Any thread in the task with receive rights to the port may retrieve the message. With this in mind, we can now be more precise about what happens when an exception occurs: The kernel suspends the victim thread and sends an IPC message to a special port, the *thread exception port*. This is the first of four steps involved in Mach exception processing. Figure 6.1 illustrates the sequence.

The next three steps happen in the handler thread. Step two occurs when the handler thread receives an exception notification message from the

1.   Victim thread encounters an exception:

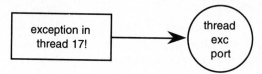

2.   Kernel sends an IPC message to thread exception port:

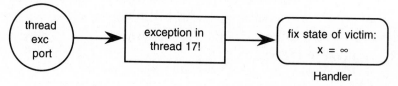

3.   Handler thread receives message, processes exception:

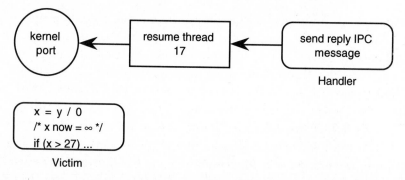

4.   Handler sends reply message, kernel resumes victim:

Figure 6.1: Steps in Exception Processing

thread exception port. Step three entails taking the appropriate action in response to the exception. The handler performs step four by replying to the notification IPC message, causing the Mach kernel either to continue or terminate the victim thread. Usually the handler thread repeats this sequence indefinitely, receiving, acting on, and replying to exception notification messages sent to the exception port.

The handler thread's actions, when notified of an exception, differ with each application. For instance, some programs simply print a message and terminate on encountering a divide-by-zero condition. Other programs log the error, substitute a zero result, and continue. The correct response depends on the details of the application. After processing the exception as appropriate, the handler thread sends an IPC message to the Mach kernel. This response message indicates to the kernel whether or not the exception has been processed successfully.

6.2 Exception Ports

6.2.1 Registering the Thread Exception Port

A thread designates a port as its thread exception port with the Mach call **thread_set_special_port()**, introduced briefly in Section 2.6.2:

```
kern_return_t ret;

thread_t th;        /* Register the port for this thread */
int code;           /* Indicates which special port      */
port_t port;        /* The port to register              */

ret = thread_set_special_port(th, code, port);
if (ret != KERN_SUCCESS) {
        mach_error("exc1: set_special_port failed", ret);
        exit(1);
}
```

The first argument (*th*) names the thread whose exception port is being designated. Often the running thread sets its own thread exception port by supplying **thread_self** for this argument, although any thread may be given. The *code* parameter indicates which of the "special" ports are being designated: The constant THREAD_EXCEPTION_PORT instructs the kernel to direct subsequent notifications of exceptions in this thread to the port supplied in the third argument (*port*).

6.2.2   Using the Thread Exception Port

Let us look at how the **thread_set_special_port** call is used in practice. Consider the simplest situation, a program with two threads. Thread A performs the application's computations, and thread B handles any exceptions. Thread A typically allocates a port and stores its name in a global variable, say, *exc_port*. Thread A then executes the **thread_set_special_port** call to register the port stored in *exc_port* as its own thread exception port. Thread B enters its infinite loop (receive, process, reply), using the global variable *exc_port* to determine which port to specify in its **msg_receive** operation (see Fig. 6.2). Whenever thread A subsequently generates an exception, the kernel finds that thread A has registered an exception port (port 17 in our example). The kernel then sends an IPC message to port 17, which thread B will receive and process.

The same general model applies to multithreaded programs. For example, let us consider a multithreaded graphics application in which arithmetic exceptions are a normal part of its operation. With a multithreaded program design, we might designate one thread in this application as the handler for exceptions in all of the other threads. This handler thread allocates an IPC port for receiving exception notifications and "publishes" the identity of the port so the other threads can find it. Publishing may be as simple as storing the port identifier in a global variable if all the application's threads are in one task. For an application distributed across a network, publishing might entail registering the port under a well-known name. In either case, the other threads in the application obtain the exception port's name and use the **thread_set_special_port** call to set their exception port to that name.

Alternatively, some applications might contain more than one exception handler. Using multiple exception handlers enables an application's individual threads to respond differently to a particular exception. One type of application requiring such flexibility would be an emulator that loads and interprets target programs originally intended for execution on another computer. These emulated programs contain instructions with operation codes legal on the target machine but illegal on the computer running the emulator.

The emulator would be designed to run the target program in another thread, so that both the emulator itself and the emulated program can use individual exception handlers. Since the emulated instructions are not permissable operations on the system running the emulator, the emulator thread should not execute these instructions. Executing them in the emulator produces an exception, which the emulator thread's exception handler treats as

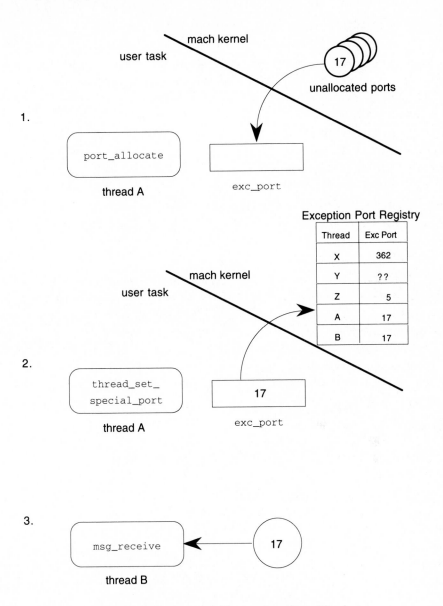

Figure 6.2: Typical Exception Port Usage

an error. The exception handler for the emulated program, however, simulates the target machine's instruction. We implement this arrangement with separate IPC ports for each of the exception handlers, corresponding to the different actions to be taken in each case. Figure 6.3 shows this design.

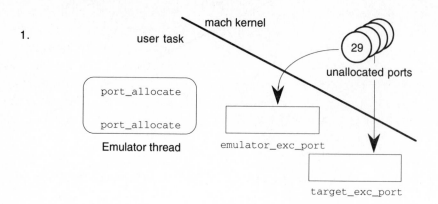

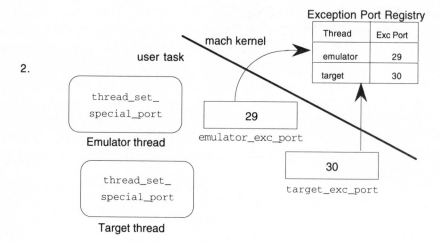

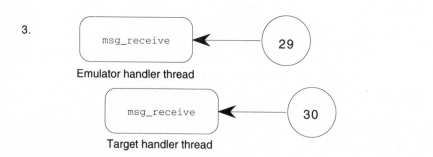

Figure 6.3: Multiple Exception Handlers

Performance also motivates designs using multiple exception handlers. For example, suppose a multithreaded application emulates a complex arithmetic instruction in software. With a single exception handler, only one such instruction can be emulated at once, even if several threads execute emulated instructions simultaneously. With multiple exception handlers, each operates concurrently with the others, performing as many emulations at one time as there are handler threads. With this organization, we use a single thread exception port, since all of the handlers perform the same actions. Figure 6.4 illustrates this arrangement.

6.2.3   The Task Exception Port

Occasionally an exception affects all threads in the application rather than one specific thread. For example, when one thread executes a debugger breakpoint, *all* threads in the task should stop until the user explicitly continues the program. Another example is an unexpected reference to nonexistent virtual memory, indicating a programming error in the application. The handler thread will terminate the application cleanly, and during the cleanup all threads in the program should be suspended. Notice that suspending all threads in the task during the cleanup requires that the handler run in a separate task.

To address this type of exception, an application may specify a *task exception port.* This is the port to which an exception notification will be sent if either

- The victim thread has not set its thread exception port, or

- The handler determines that the IPC message received from the thread exception port is not of interest and instructs the kernel to forward the notification to the task exception port.

Mach always sends notification IPC messages to the thread exception port first. If the reply IPC message from the handler indicates that the exception was not processed, Mach then sends the notification message to the task exception port. Section 6.3 describes these messages in more detail.

Let us amplify what happens when a debugger is interposed to work with another program. Assume the program was originally written to handle and recover from arithmetic overflow. We want to arrange the exception handling such that the program can use its own thread exception handler to process the overflow exceptions while allowing a debugger to handle breakpoints.

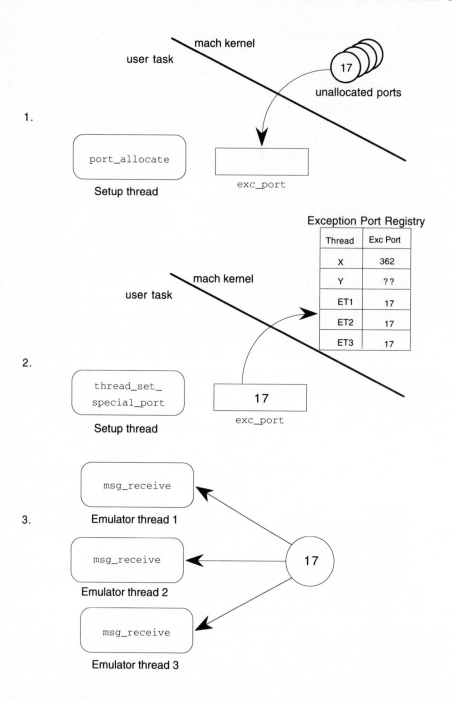

Figure 6.4: Multiple Copies of an Exception Handler

A debugger could simply receive notifications from the program's thread exception port to capture the breakpoint notifications. But the program itself already receives messages from the thread exception port to obtain the overflow notifications. If the debugger also used this same port, there would be no way for the program to handle its overflow conditions.

Instead the debugger receives notifications from the *task* exception port. The program's exception handler thread still deals with overflow events directly, and the debugger never receives notification of these events. Notices of breakpoint exceptions are also initially sent to the program's thread exception port. The program's own exception handler does not process these messages but instead instructs the kernel to forward them to the task exception port. The debugger can now receive the IPC message advising of the breakpoint from the task exception port. This hierarchical design allows the program to function unchanged, while the debugger can process exceptions not handled in the program itself.

When a thread is created, its thread exception port is initially set to the null port (that is, no port is registered). In this case the Mach kernel directs exception notification messages to the task exception port (unless it is also null). Newly created tasks inherit their task exception port from the parent task. So, for instance, a debugger can register a task exception port, and the child programs being debugged will inherit that port.

6.3   Exception IPC Messages

6.3.1   The Notification Message

The IPC message sent to the exception port provides the information that the handler thread needs to process the exception. This processing requires identifying the vicitim thread and determining what exception occurred.

Code	Meaning
EXC_BAD_ACCESS	Could not access memory
EXC_BAD_INSTRUCTION	Instruction failed
EXC_ARITHMETIC	Arithmetic exception
EXC_EMULATION	Emulation instruction
EXC_SOFTWARE	Software-generated exception
EXC_BREAKPOINT	Trace, breakpoint, etc.

Table 6.1: Machine-Independent Exception Codes

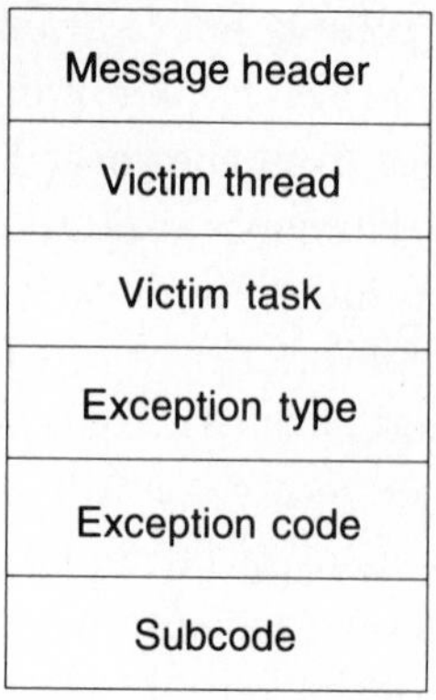

Figure 6.5: The Notification IPC Message

Several items are provided for this purpose in the notification message:
The *thread* and *task* identify the victim. The *type* indicates the general
nature of the exception. Table 6.1 lists these machine-independent exception
types (defined in the header file `<exception.h>`). The *code* further qualifies
the condition, and the *subcode* supplies additional useful data. Figure 6.5
shows the layout of the IPC notification message.

Correctly handling an exception usually requires more information than
just the generic exception type. For instance, if an illegal memory reference
occurs, the specific address referenced is important diagnostic information
and should be recorded. The notification message includes the *code* and
subcode fields to convey such additional data. For example, integer overflow

Code	Meaning
EXC_MIPS_INT	Interrupt
EXC_MIPS_DBE	Data bus error
EXC_MIPS_SYSCALL	System call
EXC_VAX_PRIVINST	Privileged instruction
EXC_VAX_RESOPND	Reserved operand
EXC_VAX_RESADDR	Reserved address
EXC_VAX_COMPAT	Instruction emulation
EXC_I386_BOUND	Array index out of range
EXC_I386_DIV	Division by zero
⋮	⋮

Table 6.2: Machine-Dependent Exception Codes

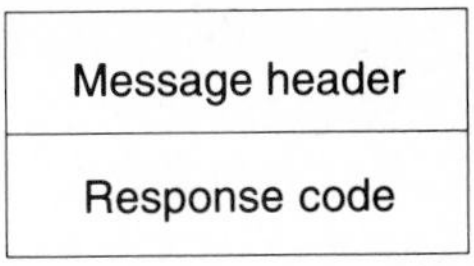

```
┌─────────────────────┐
│   Message header    │
├─────────────────────┤
│   Response code     │
└─────────────────────┘
```

Figure 6.6: The Reply IPC Message

on the Encore Multimax results in an exception type of EXC_ARITHMETIC, a code of EXC_NS32K_FPU, and a subcode of EXC_NS32K_FPU_INTOVF. Note that the meaning of the *code* and *subcode* fields varies with the type of exception and the particular Mach implementation. Some representative examples are shown in Table 6.2. The Encore Multimax, for instance, reports divide-by-zero events as type EXC_ARITHMETIC, with a code of EXC_NS32K_DVZ. Intel i386-based Mach systems report division by zero as type EXC_ARITHMETIC, with a code of EXC_I386_DIV.

6.3.2   The Reply Message

The exception handler returns a response code to the Mach kernel indicating whether or not the exception has been processed. The response code is placed in an IPC message sent back to the kernel. The format of this reply message is shown in Fig. 6.6. A nonzero response code means that the exception was not processed.

6.4   Three Sample Exception Handlers

We now present three simple but complete program examples showing how to handle exceptions under Mach. Our three programs are intended to demonstrate the concepts presented in this chapter, starting with basics and then illustrating progressively more complex ideas. In each case, we will test our code with a short main program that generates a divide-by-zero condition. The victim thread will always be continued. To keep our discussion simple, the exception handler thread will always run in the same task as the victim thread.

Actual examples must be written for a specific hardware platform. You probably will have to modify the programs presented in this section for your own system, for example by using the appropriate symbol for the structure holding the thread's saved registers.

Each of the next three sections will first present several code fragments to illustrate the ideas discussed in this chapter. Some details (like the specific

code to create a new thread) have been covered in earlier chapters. The
complete program is included after the key portions of the code have been
presented.

6.4.1   Developing a Simple Exception Handler

Our first example will just print an appropriate message when an exception
occurs. Then we resume the suspended thread at the following instruction.
Let us begin with the main program. First we allocate a port to which
notification messages can later be sent:

```
port_t exc_port;
kern_return_t ret;

ret = port_allocate(task_self(),&exc_port);
if (ret != KERN_SUCCESS) {
        mach_error("exc1: port_allocate failed", ret);
        exit(1);
}
```

Now we advise the kernel that future notification messages should be
directed to this port:

```
ret = thread_set_special_port(thread_self(),
                                THREAD_EXCEPTION_PORT,
                                exc_port);
if (ret != KERN_SUCCESS) {
        mach_error("exc1: set_special_port failed", ret);
        exit(1);
}
```

This completes the setup for the main program. Any exceptions occurring in this thread will now result in a notification message being sent to the
exception port.

Next we write the code to receive the notification, process it, and send
back a response message. When we put all of these individual operations
together, this exception handling code will run in a separate thread. This
thread's first action, receiving the notification message, is nearly identical to
code in the time server example of Chapter 3:

```
struct msg_rcv {
        msg_header_t      rcv_hdr;
```

```
        msg_type_t       thread_type;
        thread_t         victim_thread;
        msg_type_t       task_type;
        task_t           victim_task;
        msg_type_t       exception_type;
        int              exception;
        msg_type_t       code_type;
        int              code;
        msg_type_t       sub_code_type;
        int              sub_code;
} exc_msg;

exc_msg.rcv_hdr.msg_local_port = exc_port;
exc_msg.rcv_hdr.msg_size = sizeof(exc_msg);
mret = msg_receive(&exc_msg.rcv_hdr, MSG_OPTION_NONE, 0);
if (mret != KERN_SUCCESS) {
        mach_error("exc1: msg_receive failed", ret);
        exit(1);
}
```

One of the advantages of Mach's task and thread model is that it is easy to dedicate threads to specific purposes. In our example program the handler thread can be completely dedicated to its single job and just waits for notification messages. This focus on a single responsibility means that no timeout need be specified for the **msg_receive** call, since the handler thread has no duties other than receiving and processing exception messages.

The MIG file `exc.defs` defines the format of the notification IPC message. The structure definition *exc_msg* in our program expresses the same definition. In the second example program, we will look at how to handle exceptions without knowledge of the specific notification message layout.

After receiving a notification message, the next step entails processing the exception as appropriate for the specific application. Our illustrative program is only intended to demonstrate the idea, so we simply print an informative message on `stderr`. We will use a handy library routine to accomplish this:

```
mach_exception("exc1: Exception - ", exc_msg.exception);
```

The **mach_exception** routine is similar to the UNIX **perror()** function. It prints the string given as the first argument, then substitutes and prints a descriptive text string for the exception type code supplied as the second argument.

Next we advise Mach that the exception has been processed successfully. This is done by replying to the notification IPC message, sending back a response code. The reply message contains the usual IPC header and the response code (*retcode*):

```
struct {
        msg_header_t  head;
        msg_type_t    retcodetype;
        kern_return_t retcode;    /* Response Code */
} rep_msg;
```

Here is the code that constructs the reply message:

```
#define RESPONSE_CODE 0

rep_msg.head.msg_simple = TRUE;
rep_msg.head.msg_size = sizeof(rep_msg);
rep_msg.head.msg_type = exc_msg.rcv_hdr.msg_type;
rep_msg.head.msg_local_port = PORT_NULL;
rep_msg.head.msg_remote_port =
            exc_msg.rcv_hdr.msg_remote_port;
rep_msg.head.msg_id = exc_msg.rcv_hdr.msg_id + 100;

rep_msg.retcodetype.msg_type_name = MSG_TYPE_INTEGER_32;
rep_msg.retcodetype.msg_type_size = sizeof(int) * 8;
rep_msg.retcodetype.msg_type_number = 1;
rep_msg.retcodetype.msg_type_inline = TRUE;
rep_msg.retcodetype.msg_type_longform = FALSE;
rep_msg.retcodetype.msg_type_deallocate = FALSE;

rep_msg.retcode = RESPONSE_CODE;
```

The Mach kernel expects *msg_id* in the reply message to be 100 greater than the *msg_id* field in the notification message. This requirement stems from the use of MIG to define the IPC interface for exception messages, as explained in Chapter 8. Only the setting of the *retcode* field is specific to our sample program. Most of the preceding code comprises the usual setup for sending an IPC message.

The handler thread's final action is to return the response message to the kernel. In practice, the exception handler would then wait for another notification message, repeating the same sequence of steps for each subsequent exception message received. In our example program the exception handler simply exits.

```
mret = msg_send(&rep_msg.head, MSG_OPTION_NONE, 0);
if (mret != KERN_SUCCESS) {
        mach_error("exc1: msg_send failed", mret);
        exit(1);
}
```

The complete example program follows. Several **printf** statements have been
added to show the sequence in which the various functions are executed.

6.4.2   Sample Program 1

```
/*
 *  exc1.c  -  Sample exception handling program
 *
 *  This program is intended to demonstrate basic concepts of
 *  Mach-style exception handling.  The steps are:
 *
 *         1.   Allocate a thread exception port (th_exc_port)
 *         2.   Create and detach an exception handler thread
 *         3.   In the exception handler thread:
 *         3a.   Wait for an exception notification message
 *         3b.   On receiving an exception msg, return TRUE
 *         4.   Execute a divide-by-zero, causing an exception
 *         5.   When continued after the exception, exit
 *
 *  To follow the sequence of steps, printf statements are
 *  used throughout the code.
 */

#include <mach.h>
#include <sys/message.h>
#include <sys/port.h>
#include <cthreads.h>
#include <mach_exception.h>
#include <sys/mig_errors.h>
#include <machine/thread_status.h>

int     th_exc_handler();
port_t th_exc_port;

#define RESPONSE_CODE 0

main()
{
```

```
        kern_return_t ret;
        cthread_t exc_thread;
        int i, j;

        cthread_init();
        ret = port_allocate(task_self(), &th_exc_port);
        if (ret != KERN_SUCCESS) {
                mach_error("exc1: port_allocate failed", ret);
                exit(1);
        }

        ret = thread_set_special_port(thread_self(),
                                THREAD_EXCEPTION_PORT,
                                th_exc_port);
        if (ret != KERN_SUCCESS) {
                mach_error("exc1: set_special_port failed", ret);
                exit(1);
        }

        exc_thread = cthread_fork(th_exc_handler, 0);
        cthread_detach(exc_thread);

        i = 6;
        j = 0;
        i = 7 / j;     /* Generate divide-by-zero exception */

        printf("exc1: After divide-by-zero, result = %d\n", i);
}

th_exc_handler(dummy)
char *dummy;            /* not used */
{
        msg_return_t mret;

        struct msg_rcv {
                msg_header_t   rcv_hdr;
                msg_type_t     thread_type;
                thread_t       victim_thread;
                msg_type_t     task_type;
                task_t         victim_task;
                msg_type_t     exception_type;
                int            exception;
                msg_type_t     code_type;
                int            code;
```

```
        msg_type_t     sub_code_type;
        int            sub_code;
} exc_msg;

struct {
        msg_header_t   head;
        msg_type_t     retcodetype;
        kern_return_t  retcode;
} rep_msg;

exc_msg.rcv_hdr.msg_local_port = th_exc_port;
exc_msg.rcv_hdr.msg_size = sizeof(exc_msg);

mret = msg_receive(&exc_msg.rcv_hdr, MSG_OPTION_NONE, 0);
if (mret != KERN_SUCCESS) {
        mach_error("exc1: msg_receive failed", mret);
        exit(1);
}

printf("exc1: Exception Msg Received");
printf(" (Thread Exception Port)\n");

mach_exception("exc1: Thread Exception Encountered",
                    exc_msg.exception);

rep_msg.head.msg_simple = TRUE;
rep_msg.head.msg_size = sizeof(rep_msg);
rep_msg.head.msg_type = exc_msg.rcv_hdr.msg_type;
rep_msg.head.msg_local_port = PORT_NULL;
rep_msg.head.msg_remote_port =
                        exc_msg.rcv_hdr.msg_remote_port;
rep_msg.head.msg_id = exc_msg.rcv_hdr.msg_id + 100;

rep_msg.retcodetype.msg_type_name = MSG_TYPE_INTEGER_32;
rep_msg.retcodetype.msg_type_size = sizeof(int) * 8;
rep_msg.retcodetype.msg_type_number = 1;
rep_msg.retcodetype.msg_type_inline = TRUE;
rep_msg.retcodetype.msg_type_longform = FALSE;
rep_msg.retcodetype.msg_type_deallocate = FALSE;

rep_msg.retcode = RESPONSE_CODE;

mret = msg_send(&rep_msg.head, MSG_OPTION_NONE, 0);
if (mret != KERN_SUCCESS) {
```

```
            mach_error("exc1: msg_send failed", mret);
            exit(1);
    }

        cthread_exit(0);
}
```

Our sample program `exc1` produces the following output:

```
exc1: Exception Msg Received (Thread Exception Port)
exc1: Thread Exception Encountered: Arithmetic(3)
exc1: After divide-by-zero, result = 7
```

6.4.3   Illustrating the Exception Port Hierarchy

Let us look at an example that demonstrates the interaction between the thread and task exception ports described in Section 6.2.3. We receive the notification message from the thread exception port as in program `exc1`. But unlike our first program, `exc2` returns a code specifying that further handling is required instead of indicating that the handler has successfully processed the exception. The kernel then sends the notification IPC message to the *task* exception port. Program `exc2` includes a second exception handler thread that listens for notification messages sent to the task exception port. This task exception handler "processes" the exception and continues the victim thread.

One additional change simplifies processing the exception notification message. In `exc2`, we use the Mach library routine **exc_server()** to minimize the work involved in dissecting the notification IPC message and in constructing the response message. This routine makes it easy to reply to the exception RPC.

Routine **exc_server()** is a MIG-generated function. It calls a user-supplied routine, **catch_exception_raise()**, to act on the exception. The **exc_server()** function understands the format of the notification message. It extracts the relevant information (victim thread, exception type, etc.) from the message and supplies it to **catch_exception_raise**. This means that your code does *not* need to be concerned with the format of the notification message.

The real work in handling the exception occurs in function **catch_exception_raise**. Here is where, for instance, an informative message is issued, or the state of the victim thread is changed. Routine **exc_server** places

the return status from **catch_exception_raise** into the response message returned to the kernel. A return status of FALSE advises the kernel that the
exception was processed successfully. If **exc_server** had been used for our
first sample program (exc1), **catch_exception_raise** would return FALSE,
indicating to **exc_server** that the exception had been processed without
error:

```
catch_exception_raise(port, thread, task, exception, code, subcode)
port_t   port;
thread_t thread;
task_t   task;
int      exception, code, subcode;
{
        return(FALSE);   /* Exception was processed */
}
```

For program exc2, we "share" the **catch_exception_raise** routine between the thread and task exception handlers. Our example program always
returns TRUE in the thread exception handler, indicating that the exception
was not processed. This is the action your application's exception handler
would take when presented with exceptions it was not designed to handle,
such as a breakpoint exception.

Our example program will always return FALSE in the task exception
handler, indicating that the exception was processed successfully. This is
what a debugger would do after completing the processing for a breakpoint
exception, for example.

Note that a practical application would check the exception type information to determine whether it can actually handle the condition. Our
demonstration program's thread exception handler is written to pass all
notification messages to the task exception port. Our task exception handler "processes" all exceptions. All of this activity occurs in the shared
catch_exception_raise routine, which determines which exception handler
(thread or task) invoked it and then returns the appropriate status:

```
catch_exception_raise(port, thread, task, exception, code, subcode)
port_t   port;
thread_t thread;
task_t   task;
int      exception, code, subcode;
{
        if (port == th_exc_port) {
                /*
                 * A realistic application would test exception,
```

```
             *  code, and subcode here, to see if it can
             *  process the exception.  We just print a
             *  message, and ask the kernel to send the IPC
             *  msg to the task exception port.
             */
            mach_exception("exc2: Thread Exception Encountered",
                           exception);
            return(TRUE); /* Thread: exception not yet handled */
      } else {
             /*
             * Here is where the application processes
             *  1notification messages sent to the task
             *  exception port.  A debugger would handle
             *  breakpoints here, or print an informative
             *  message for arithmetic exceptions.  We just
             *  print a message, and indicate that the
             * exception has been processed.
             */
            mach_exception("exc2: Task Exception Encountered",
                           exception);
            return(FALSE); /* Task: Note exception handled */
      }
}
```

6.4.4   Sample Program 2

```
/*
 *  exc2.c  -  Sample exception handling program
 *
 *  This program is intended to demonstrate basic concepts of
 *  Mach-style exception handling.  The steps are:
 *
 *     1.    Allocate a thread exception port (th_exc_port)
 *     2.    Create and detach two exception handler threads
 *     3.    In each exception handler thread:
 *       3a.    Wait for an exception notification message
 *       3b.    On receiving an exception msg,
 *                - Return FALSE in thread exception handler
 *                - Return TRUE in task exception handler
 *     4.    Execute a divide-by-zero, causing an exception
 *     5.    When continued after the exception, exit
 *
 *  To follow the sequence of steps, printf statements are
 *  used throughout the code.
```

```
 */

#include <mach.h>
#include <sys/message.h>
#include <sys/port.h>
#include <cthreads.h>
#include <mach_exception.h>
#include <sys/mig_errors.h>
#include <machine/thread_status.h>

port_t th_exc_port, task_exc_port;
int th_exc_handler(), task_exc_handler();

/*
 * Exception Notification Message
 */
struct msg_rcv {
        msg_header_t  rcv_hdr;
        int           msg_data[5*2]; /* 5 type, item pairs */
};

/*
 * Handler's Response Message
 */
struct msgrep {
        msg_header_t  head;
        int           msg_data[1*2]; /* 1 type, item pair */
} rep_msg;

main()
{
        kern_return_t ret;
        cthread_t thread_exc_thread, task_exc_thread;
        int i, j;

        cthread_init();

        ret = port_allocate(task_self(), &th_exc_port);
        if (ret != KERN_SUCCESS) {
                mach_error("exc2: port_allocate failed", ret);
                exit(1);
        }

        ret = port_allocate(task_self(), &task_exc_port);
```

```
        if (ret != KERN_SUCCESS) {
                mach_error("exc2: port_allocate failed", ret);
                exit(1);
        }


        ret = thread_set_special_port(thread_self(),
                                THREAD_EXCEPTION_PORT,
                                th_exc_port);
        if (ret != KERN_SUCCESS) {
                mach_error("exc2: set_special_port failed", ret);
                exit(1);
        }
        ret = task_set_special_port(task_self(),
                                TASK_EXCEPTION_PORT,
                                task_exc_port);
        if (ret != KERN_SUCCESS) {
                mach_error("exc2: set_special_port failed", ret);
                exit(1);
        }


        thread_exc_thread = cthread_fork(th_exc_handler, 0);
        task_exc_thread = cthread_fork(task_exc_handler, 0);

        cthread_detach(thread_exc_thread);
        cthread_detach(task_exc_thread);

        i = 6;
        j = 0;
        i = 7 / j;     /* Generate divide-by-zero exception */

        printf("exc2: Result after divide-by-zero is %d\n", i);
}

int
catch_exception_raise(port, thread, task, exception, code, subcode)
port_t   port;
thread_t thread;
task_t   task;
int      exception, code, subcode;
{
        if (port == th_exc_port) {
                mach_exception("exc2: Thread Exception Encountered",
                         exception);
                return(TRUE); /* Thread: exception not yet handled */
```

```
        } else {
              mach_exception("exc2: Task Exception Encountered",
                               exception);
              return(FALSE); /* Task: Indicate exception handled */
        }
}

th_exc_handler(dummy)
char *dummy;
{
        msg_return_t mret;

        struct msg_rcv exc_msg;
        struct msgrep  rep_msg;

        exc_msg.rcv_hdr.msg_local_port = th_exc_port;
        exc_msg.rcv_hdr.msg_size = sizeof(exc_msg);

        mret = msg_receive(&exc_msg.rcv_hdr, MSG_OPTION_NONE, 0);
        if (mret != KERN_SUCCESS) {
                mach_error("exc2: msg_receive failed", mret);
                exit(1);
        }

        printf("exc2: Thread Exception Handler invoked\n");

        exc_server(&exc_msg, &rep_msg);

        mret = msg_send(&rep_msg.head, MSG_OPTION_NONE, 0);
        if (mret != KERN_SUCCESS) {
                mach_error("exc2: msg_send failed", mret);
                exit(1);
        }

        cthread_exit(0);
}

task_exc_handler(dummy)
char *dummy;
{
        msg_return_t mret;

        struct msg_rcv exc_msg;
        struct msgrep  rep_msg;
```

```
            exc_msg.rcv_hdr.msg_local_port = task_exc_port;
            exc_msg.rcv_hdr.msg_size = sizeof(exc_msg);

            mret = msg_receive(&exc_msg.rcv_hdr, MSG_OPTION_NONE, 0);
            if (mret != KERN_SUCCESS) {
                    mach_error("exc2: msg_receive failed", mret);
                    exit(1);
            }

            printf("exc2: Task Exception Handler invoked\n");

            exc_server(&exc_msg, &rep_msg);

            mret = msg_send(&rep_msg.head, MSG_OPTION_NONE, 0);
            if (mret != KERN_SUCCESS) {
                    mach_error("exc2: msg_send failed", mret);
                    exit(1);
            }

            cthread_exit(0);
}
```

The value of variable *i* after the exception has been processed is machine specific. When run on a NeXT workstation, program exc2 produces the following sequence of messages:

```
exc2: Thread Exception Handler invoked
exc2: Thread Exception Encountered: Arithmetic(3)
exc2: Task Exception Handler invoked
exc2: Task Exception Encountered: Arithmetic(3)
exc2: Result after divide-by-zero is 7
```

6.4.5   Modifying the Victim Thread

Our third example demonstrates how an exception handler goes about manipulating the state of the victim thread. Our simple program will modify the result of the divide-by-zero operation, substituting the value −1. Notice that such operations are inherently machine dependent. We must know precisely which register to modify to achieve the desired result. A real-world application might instead set the value of the victim thread's program counter to resume the victim at a known cleanup routine. The details will vary depending on the application.

We also use program exc3 to show another small coding simplification. We use a macro, **thread_set_exception_port()**, to register the port to which exception messages should be directed. A corresponding macro exists for the task exception port.

To modify the result of the interrupted arithmetic operation in the victim thread, routine **catch_exception_raise** will invoke the user-supplied function **fixup()**. This routine uses the **thread_get_state()** call to obtain the values of the victim thread's registers at the time of the divide by zero. The register holding the result is then changed, and the new register values are written using the **thread_set_state** call. The complete program follows (coded for a NeXT workstation).

6.4.6   Sample Program 3

```
/*
 *  exc3.c  -  Sample exception handling program
 *
 *  This program is intended to demonstrate how an exception
 *  handler can modify the state of the victim thread.   The
 *  steps are:
 *        1.    Allocate a thread exception port
 *        2.    Create and detach an exception handler thread
 *        3.    In the exception handler thread:
 *        3a.     Wait for an exception notification message
 *        3b.     On receiving an exception msg:
 *                  - Set the computed value in the victim to -1
 *                  - return TRUE
 *        4.    Execute a divide-by-zero, causing an exception
 *        5.    When continued after the exception, exit
 *
 *  To follow the sequence of steps, printf statements are
 *  used throughout the code.
 */

#include <mach.h>
#include <sys/message.h>
#include <sys/port.h>
#include <cthreads.h>
#include <mach_exception.h>
#include <sys/mig_errors.h>
#include <machine/thread_status.h>
```

```
port_t th_exc_port;
int    th_exc_handler();

main()
{
        kern_return_t ret;
        cthread_t exc_thread;
        int i, j;

        cthread_init();

        ret = port_allocate(task_self(), &th_exc_port);
        if (ret != KERN_SUCCESS) {
                mach_error("exc3: port_allocate failed", ret);
                exit(1);
        }

        ret = thread_set_exception_port(thread_self(),
                                        th_exc_port);
        if (ret != KERN_SUCCESS) {
                mach_error("exc3: set_special_port failed", ret);
                exit(1);
        }

        exc_thread = cthread_fork(th_exc_handler, 0);
        cthread_detach(exc_thread);

        i = 6;
        j = 0;
        i = 7 / j;     /* Generate divide-by-zero exception */

        printf("exc3: After divide-by-zero, result = %d\n", i);
}

int
catch_exception_raise(port, thread, task, exception, code, subcode)
port_t   port;
thread_t thread;
task_t   task;
int      exception, code, subcode;
{
        printf("exc3: catch_exception_raise\n");
        mach_exception("exc3: Thread Exception Encountered",
                        exception);
```

```
        fixup(thread);    /* Fix result in victim        */
        return(FALSE);    /* Exception handled successfully */
}


th_exc_handler(dummy)
char *dummy;     /* Not used */
{
        kern_return_t ret;
        msg_return_t mret;

        /*
         * Exception Notification Message
         */
        struct msg_rcv {
                msg_header_t rcv_hdr;
                int          msg_data[5*2]; /* 5 type, item pairs */
        } exc_msg;

        /*
         * Handler's Response Message
         */
        struct msgrep {
                msg_header_t  head;
                int           msg_data[1*2]; /* 1 type, item pair */
        } rep_msg;

        exc_msg.rcv_hdr.msg_local_port = th_exc_port;
        exc_msg.rcv_hdr.msg_size = sizeof(exc_msg);

        mret = msg_receive(&exc_msg.rcv_hdr, MSG_OPTION_NONE, 0);
        if (mret != KERN_SUCCESS) {
                mach_error("exc3: msg_receive failed", mret);
                exit(1);
        }

        printf("exc3: Thread exception Handler invoked\n");

        exc_server(&exc_msg, &rep_msg);

        mret = msg_send(&rep_msg.head, MSG_OPTION_NONE, 0);
        if (mret != KERN_SUCCESS) {
                mach_error("exc3: msg_send failed", mret);
                exit(1);
        }
```

```
        cthread_exit(0);
}

fixup(thread)
thread_t thread;
{
        union {
                thread_state_data_t mi_state;
                struct NeXT_thread_state_regs md_state;
        } state;

        unsigned int count = THREAD_STATE_MAX;

        kern_return_t      ret;

        printf("exc3: fixing thread state\n");
        ret = thread_get_state(thread, NeXT_THREAD_STATE_REGS,
                                state.mi_state, &count);
        if (ret != KERN_SUCCESS) {
                mach_error("thread_get_state", ret);
                exit(1);
        }

        state.md_state.dreg[0] = -1;   /* Fix result */
        count = sizeof(struct NeXT_thread_state_regs);
        ret = thread_set_state(thread, NeXT_THREAD_STATE_REGS,
                                state.mi_state, count);
        if (ret != KERN_SUCCESS) {
                mach_error("thread_set_state", ret);
                exit(1);
        }
}
```

Here is the output produced when program exc3 is run on a NeXT work-station:

```
exc3: Thread exception Handler invoked
exc3: catch_exception_raise
exc3: Thread Exception Encountered: Arithmetic(3)
exc3: fixing thread state
exc3: After divide-by-zero, result = -1
```

6.5   Mach Exceptions versus UNIX Signals

In UNIX, exceptions are one of several events that result in a *signal* being sent to a process. Other such events are timer expiration, receipt of
a terminal quit signal, or certain changes in the UNIX process hierarchy.
UNIX signals were not designed to operate in the Mach programming environment. The UNIX signal mechanism has several shortcomings when used
in this environment:

- The victim's resources may be needed to process the signal.

- Processing must occur on the victim's machine in the victim's context.

- Signal behavior is undefined with multiple threads.

- The victim's entire state is not available.

- Signal handlers cannot block or acquire locks.

Let us look at how the Mach exception facility improves each of these areas.
   UNIX signal handlers execute in the victim process. So the handler
must share the resources of the victim. The most notorious shared resource
is the victim's stack, and UNIX has evolved a way to avoid this sharing. By
running on a special *signal stack*, a process can avoid the problem. But the
signal stack is typically small, and it is difficult for the handler to access the
stack frames in the victim that caused the original interruption.
   Mach exception handlers execute in a separate thread, even in a separate
task if desired. The handler thread has its own resources, including its own
stack. So there is no need to depend on the resources of the victim in
handling the exception.
   The UNIX operating system invokes signal handlers simply by starting
the victim process in the handler function. Mach exception handlers are
invoked by sending an IPC message. They can reside on either the victim
thread's machine or on a remote system. The processing is identical in either
case.
   Because UNIX has no concept of threads, signals are not designed for a
multithreaded environment. But all programs in Mach Version 2.5 are run
as UNIX processes, even if they contain multiple threads. What happens
if a signal is generated in this case? Mach's UNIX emulation code in the
kernel arbitrarily chooses a thread to receive the signal. Other implementations would have been possible (for instance, create a new thread to handle

the signal, designate one thread as the signal-handler thread, round-robin delivery among all threads, etc.). But no matter what algorithm is used, the end result will appear arbitrary, because UNIX has no concept of threads.

The state of the victim is communicated to the signal handler through a generic *sigcontext* structure. Unfortunately, processing exceptions is inherently a machine-specific operation. Although there is provision in the *sigcontext* structure for machine-specific data, library code in some implementations uses registers of interest to an exception handler.

The Mach exception handler is provided with a machine-dependent context structure. This provides the handler access to all of the victim's registers and other state information.

Finally, care must be taken to ensure that a UNIX signal handler does not operate in a dangerous fashion. For instance, either the handler cannot take locks, or signals must be prevented explicitly when the victim process holds a lock. Failure to follow these rules could result in deadlock, since a lock that the signal handler takes could already be held by the victim thread. Similarly a signal handler is not permitted to sleep.

Mach exception handlers address this problem by running in a normal thread context. They may acquire locks, they may sleep, and they may generally operate independently of the victim thread.

6.6   Summary

Exceptions are interruptions of a program's execution that the program itself causes. Exception processing under Mach occurs in a separate thread, and Mach IPC is used to communicate relevant data between the kernel and the exception handler. This design fits nicely with Mach's task and thread facility and generalizes well in a distributed environment.

Chapter 7

Advanced IPC

This chapter continues our discussion of Mach IPC by exploring more advanced concepts and functionality. Application programs can be built using only the send and receive primitives described in Chapter 3. However, large application programs, such as a database server, usually require more than the ability to send and receive messages. Analogously, UNIX applications require capabilities beyond those to open, close, read, and write a file. Features such as **ioctl()** and **fcntl()** give UNIX applications control over the environment and ease the programming burden.

Similarly, Mach provides more than the ability to create an IPC queue and transfer messages. Some of these additional facilities include

- Transmitting out-of-line data

- Logically grouping ports together

- Querying the status of an IPC queue

- Controlling the maximum number of queued messages

- Naming ports

- Registering ports.

In this chapter we will describe many of these advanced capabilities and demonstrate how they may be used as part of a large system.

7.1   Out-of-Line Data

One of the most common, time-consuming operations that programs perform
is copying data. For instance, when a user reads from disk the operating
system typically caches the data and then copies the data to the user's
address space. When sending data across the network, the operating system
copies the message from the program's virtual address space into a buffer
within the kernel. That data may be copied several more times before it has
been transmitted across the network. The same circumstance exists when
sending data with IPC messages. Messages are copied from the sender into
the operating system and then to the receiver.

The Mach designers recognized an opportunity to optimize large data
transfers. IPC messages can be sent more quickly by using a feature that
causes data to be shared between sending and receiving tasks rather than
copying data to the target task. This optimization requires the close integration of the IPC and virtual memory systems and is known as *out-of-line
data*.

When using in-line data transfers, data is copied from the sender to the
kernel and again from the kernel to the receiver. Out-of-line data requires
no such copy operations. The receiver sees the data as a newly allocated
portion of its address space.

When a message containing out-of-line data is received, the kernel allocates a region in the receiver's virtual address space for the message. This
region uses the same physical pages in the sending task's address space that
contain the message. Mach's manipulation of internal data structures that
describe the two tasks' virtual address spaces is a very fast operation.

Although these pages are initially shared, the tasks are *not* using a shared
memory model for communication. The pages of data are marked *copy-on-
write* so that modifications by either sender or receiver are not seen by the
other. If either task attempts to modify the data, the operating system
first makes a copy of the original data for each task before permitting the
data to be changed. Only the page containing the newly modified data is
copied; all other pages remain shared. Sharing the same physical pages, and
using copy-on-write to ensure that data remains consistent, is transparent
to the programmer. However, because of additional copy operations, programs wishing to achieve maximum efficiency should avoid modifying data
transferred using out-of-line IPC messages.

The receiving task should deallocate the data by using the **vm_
deallocate()** system call when the data is no longer needed. The reader

is referred to Chapter 4 for more details on the virtual memory system and copy-on-write semantics.

We have already mentioned that Mach IPC is network transparent. That is, messages may be transferred across the network without the application programmer needing to take any specific action. Out-of-line data messages are also sent transparently over the network when appropriate. It is important to note, however, that Mach transfers the entire message, not only those pages that the receiving task accesses.

One important security aspect must be considered when using out-of-line data. Mach sends complete pages even when the amount of data specified in the type structure is not a multiple of the page size. Therefore the first and last page may contain additional data that the sending task did not explicitly send. Mach does *not* zero or otherwise hide the data that was implicitly sent. The programmer must ensure that the first and last page do not contain data the receiving program should not see. This security consideration is another important reason to use **vm_allocate** for the contents of all messages, as **vm_allocate** allocates zero-filled page-aligned memory.

Compared to sending in-line data, there are three changes required to send out-of-line data:

1. The *msg_simple* field of the header structure must be set to FALSE.

2. The *msg_type_inline* field within the type structure must be set to FALSE.

3. A pointer to the data follows the type structure.

Figure 7.1 illustrates a message with both in-line and out-of-line data segments. When receiving out-of-line data the receiver examines the *msg_type_inline* field and, when FALSE, uses the pointer following the type structure to locate the data.

The following code fragments demonstrate the use of out-of-line data. The first provides structure definition and manifest constants used in our example. We will place these definitions in the file <ooldefs.h>.

```
#define MAXINLINE       (128)
#define MAXSIZE         (2048)

struct message {
        msg_header_t    hdr;
        msg_type_t      type;
```

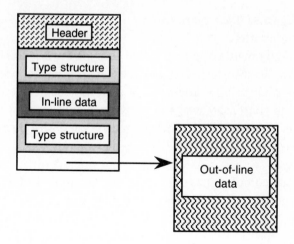

Figure 7.1: IPC Message with Out-of-Line Data

```
union {
        char    bytes[MAXINLINE];
        char    *ptr;
} msg;
};
```

The next two code fragments are intended to work together, similar to the time server example of Chapter 3. In this example we will use in-line data if we are sending less than 128 (MAXINLINE) bytes of data, and out-of-line data otherwise. We could send more data using in-line transfers. However, remember that the maximum size of the message header, all type structures, in-line data, and pointers for out-of-line data can be no more than MSG_SIZE_MAX bytes—Mach defines this constant to be 8192 bytes.

Whether we use in-line or out-of-line data, we will print the fourth byte of the message. The first code fragment shows the receive operation:

```
#include "ooldefs.h"

struct message  msg;
port_name_t     receive_port;

/*
 * Initialize header for receive.  As with in-line data,
 *  only the msg_local_port and msg_size fields need to
 *  be initialized.
 */
```

```
message.hdr.msg_local_port = receive_port;
message.hdr.msg_size = sizeof(struct message);

/*
 * Receive the message.
 */
ret = msg_receive(&message.hdr, MSG_OPTION_NONE, 0);
if (ret != RCV_SUCCESS) {
        mach_error("msg_receive:", ret);
        return;
}

/*
 * Determine if the message contained in-line or out-of-line
 *  data by examining the msg_type_inline field of the 'type'
 *  structure.
 * Print the fourth character.
 */
if (message.type.msg_type_inline)
        putchar(message.msg.bytes[3]);
else
        putchar(*(message.msg.ptr+3));
```

Figure 7.2 illustrates the data's location when using in-line data. Note that the data is contained as part of the message. Figure 7.3 illustrates the data's location when using out-of-line data. In this case, we must dereference the pointer contained in the message body. The kernel initializes the pointer when the **msg_receive** completes.

The code changes required to use out-of-line data are very small. The initialization of the message header is identical to that done in our time server. Our example allows the use of either in-line or out-of-line data. While we could have permitted any valid message size when using in-line

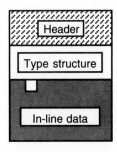

Figure 7.2: The Fourth Byte of In-Line Data

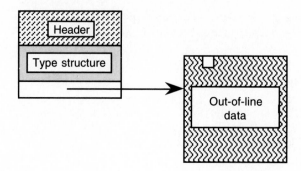

Figure 7.3: The Fourth Byte of Out-of-Line Data

data, our example restricts in-line data to 128 bytes. Out-of-line data is
used for messages larger than 128 bytes.

After receiving the message, the program examines the *msg_type_inline*
field of the type structure to determine if this was in-line or out-of-line data.
Examining the *msg_type_inline* field and following a pointer to extract the
data are the only changes required when receiving out-of-line data.

The next code fragment is the other half of our example. This program
will send data using either in-line or out-of-line data, as appropriate.

```
#include "ooldefs.h"

struct message  msg;
port_name_t     comm_port;
char            *data;
int             msgsize;

/*
 * Allocate memory.  This will hold data
 *  for both in-line and out-of-line cases.
 */
ret = vm_allocate(task_self(), &data, MAXSIZE, TRUE);
if (ret != KERN_SUCCESS) {
        mach_error("vm_allocate:", ret);
        exit(1);
}
/*
 * The following operations would be performed at this
 *  point in the program (but have been omitted here for
 *  brevity):
 *     1) Process data - Fill in newly allocated memory
 *     2) Initialize 'msgsize' variable to indicate length.
```

```
 *      3) Perform netname_look_up to obtain port of 'server'.
 */

/*
 * Initialize all fields of the header which are
 *  not dependent on the type of data being sent.
 */
message.hdr.msg_local_port = PORT_NULL;
message.hdr.msg_remote_port = comm_port;
message.hdr.msg_type = MSG_TYPE_NORMAL;

/*
 * Initialize all fields of the type structure except
 *  for msg_type_inline.
 */
message.type.msg_type_name = MSG_TYPE_CHAR;
message.type.msg_type_size = sizeof(char) * 8;
message.type.msg_type_number = msgsize;
message.type.msg_type_longform = FALSE;
message.type.msg_type_deallocate = FALSE;

if (msgsize <= MAXINLINE) {
        /*
         * In-line data:
         *   msg_simple and msg_type_inline are set to TRUE
         *      to indicate we are not sending out-of-line data.
         *   The msg_size field must have the size of the
         *      header and type fields as well as the
         *      data length.
         *   Move the data from the program's buffer area into
         *      the message structure.
         */
        message.hdr.msg_simple = TRUE;
        message.type.msg_type_inline = TRUE;
        message.hdr.msg_size = sizeof(msg_header_t) +
            sizeof(msg_type_t) + msgsize;
        bcopy(data, message.msg.bytes, msgsize);
} else {
        /*
         * Out-of-line data:
         *   msg_simple and msg_type_inline are set to FALSE
         *      to indicate we are sending out-of-line data.
         *   The msg_size field must have the size of the
         *      header and type fields as well as room for
```

```
 *      a pointer to the data.
 *      Initialize the pointer to the data.
 */
message.hdr.msg_simple = FALSE;
message.type.msg_type_inline = FALSE;
message.hdr.msg_size = sizeof(msg_header_t) +
    sizeof(msg_type_t) + sizeof(char *);
message.msg.ptr = data;
}
```

While this example may seem complex, sending out-of-line data is no more complex than sending in-line data. Sending out-of-line data is one of the operations that requires the *msg_simple* field of the header initialized to FALSE. We will see another use of the *msg_simple* field later in this chapter. Each type structure describing out-of-line data must have its *msg_type_inline* field initialized to FALSE. In-line and out-of-line data may be intermixed in the same IPC message.

The only other change to the program relates to where the data is located. Our example copies the data from a **vm_allocate**'d buffer into the static message body for in-line data, or sets the *msg_send.msg.ptr* field for out-of-line data.

Out-of-line data is an important capability that provides high-performance data transfer capabilities between tasks. As you can see by these examples, out-of-line data is easy to use and should be employed whenever sending more than a page (typically 8192 bytes) of data.

7.2   Message RPC

Many programs send a message and wait for an immediate reply. This is exactly what the client side of our time server example does. Mach provides a more efficient mechanism for this common case with the **msg_rpc()** system call. This system call combines the functionality of both the **msg_send** and **msg_receive** system calls into one. The **msg_rpc** system call provides all of the options available when using the two separate system calls.

```
#define RCVSIZE    (128)        /* Bytes       */
#define TIMEOUT    (50)         /* Milliseconds */

kern_return_t    ret;

ret = msg_rpc(&hdr, SEND_TIMEOUT|RCV_INTERRUPT,
```

```
                RCVSIZE, TIMEOUT, 0);
if (ret != RPC_SUCCESS) {
        mach_error("msg_rpc:", ret);
        exit(1);
}
```

The preceding code fragment shows that the **msg_rpc** system call is
similar in format to the other IPC system calls. The first parameter is a
pointer to a message header. The second parameter contains option specifications. Options are the same as those for the individual **msg_send** and
msg_receive system calls, logically OR'd together. The options in this
example specify a send timeout and permit interrupts during the receive
operation.

The third parameter contains the maximum size that the receive is allowed to accept. Normally this value is contained in the *msg_size* field of
the header. When using **msg_rpc**, the *msg_size* field specifies the size of
the message being sent; hence a separate argument to the system call must
provide the receive size.

The fourth and fifth parameters specify send and receive timeout values
respectively. These are only used when the SEND_TIMEOUT or RCV_TIMEOUT
options, respectively, are used. The preceding example specifies a fifty millisecond timeout on the send. As no receive timeout is desired, the example
uses zero as a "place holder" for the system call. The kernel does not use or
examine the value since the RCV_TIMEOUT option was not used.

The received message overwrites the contents of the buffer that held the
transmitted message. When using out-of-line data with the **msg_rpc** call,
only the data pointer(s) and data are overwritten. Memory regions pointed
to in the original message will not be modified. When using separate system
calls for the send and receive operations, separate buffers may be specified.
Msg_rpc trades off flexibility against using a single system call for a common
series of operations.

Figure 7.4 illustrates the memory utilization during a **msg_rpc** system
call. Before the call, a message points to a single out-of-line data region at
address 0xF0000. After the system call this region is unmodified, but the
header, type structure, and data pointer have been modified. A new out-
of-line memory region, at location 0xA0000, was allocated as a result of the
receive portion of the system call.

Mach returns RPC_SUCCESS at the end of a successful **msg_rpc** system
call. Should the system call fail, the error codes are the same as for the
msg_send and **msg_receive** system calls, as appropriate for the error.

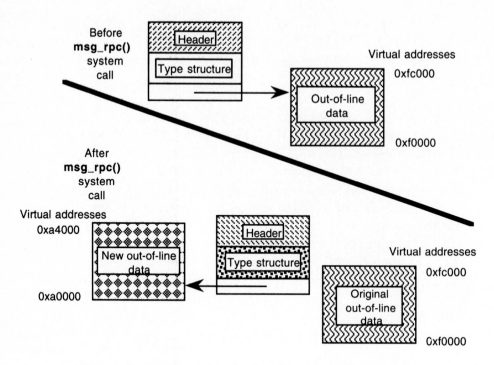

Figure 7.4: Before and after a **msg_rpc()** System Call

Section 3.3.3 contains the complete program listing of a client program
that communicates with our time server. The **process()** function of that
example could be modified to use **msg_rpc** as shown here:

```
process()
{
        msg_return_t           ret;
        union {
                struct request_msg request_msg;
                struct reply_msg    reply_msg;
        } rpcmsg;

        /*
         * Fill in the message header.
         */
        rpcmsg.request_msg.hdr.msg_simple = TRUE;
        rpcmsg.request_msg.hdr.msg_size =
                               sizeof(struct request_msg);
        rpcmsg.request_msg.hdr.msg_type = MSG_TYPE_NORMAL;
        rpcmsg.request_msg.hdr.msg_local_port = cport;
```

```
rpcmsg.request_msg.hdr.msg_remote_port = server_port;
rpcmsg.request_msg.hdr.msg_id = 123;

/*
 * Fill in the type structure.  The request code is
 *  sent as an integer.
 */
rpcmsg.request_msg.type.msg_type_name = MSG_TYPE_INTEGER_32;
rpcmsg.request_msg.type.msg_type_size = sizeof(int) * 8;
rpcmsg.request_msg.type.msg_type_number = 1;
rpcmsg.request_msg.type.msg_type_inline = TRUE;
rpcmsg.request_msg.type.msg_type_longform = FALSE;
rpcmsg.request_msg.type.msg_type_deallocate = FALSE;

/*
 * Specify that we want the time in string form.
 */
rpcmsg.request_msg.request = TS_STRING_FORM;

/*
 * Send the request to the time server and
 *  await the reply.
 */
ret = msg_rpc(&rpcmsg.request_msg.hdr,
            sizeof(struct reply_msg),
            MSG_OPTION_NONE, 0, 0);
if (ret != RPC_SUCCESS) {
        mach_error("msg_rpc:", ret);
        exit(1);
}

printf("Time is: %s\n", rpcmsg.reply_msg.time.ctime);
}
```

As you can see, there are few changes to the program. As **msg_rpc** uses the same buffer for both send and receive, the request and reply structures are declared within a union, thus allowing the two message structures to be declared separately. The next change is to substitute a **msg_rpc** system call for the **msg_send** and **msg_receive** calls. The initialization of the reply message in the original example becomes unnecessary.

We use **msg_rpc** for efficiency. Eliminating an additional system call for this common sequence will improve efficiency and lessen system overhead.

In addition, the nature of the **msg_rpc** call allows the kernel to optimize this operation within the operating system.

7.3   Port Sets

Application programs typically have several ports with similar functions. For example, a server may have a separate port for each client. As Mach does not have an IPC equivalent of the UNIX **select()** system call, the original model for managing ports uses a separate thread for each port, and each thread does a **msg_receive** for a single port. Creating threads requires few system resources compared to a UNIX process,[1] and when a thread blocks pending receipt of a message, it does not consume CPU cycles.

Regardless of the resources a thread requires, many threads could be created to perform similar functions or to perform functions that occur rarely. An alternative is to group ports together into a set that can be the target of a single **msg_receive** operation. Mach version 2.5 has added the ability to group ports into a *port set*. This grouping allows the programmer to issue a single **msg_receive** system call that will read the first available message from any of the ports that are members of the port set.

A port set is created by issuing the **port_set_allocate()** system call, as shown in the following example.

```
task_t              target_task;
port_set_name_t     port_set;
kern_return_t       ret;

ret = port_set_allocate(target_task, &port_set);
if (ret != KERN_SUCCESS) {
        mach_error("port_set_allocate:", ret);
        exit(1);
}
```

This call creates a port set for the specified task. The second parameter to the system call, *port_set*, is a pointer to a variable in which the kernel stores the name of the newly created port set. Two error returns are possible: KERN_INVALID_ARGUMENT and KERN_RESOURCE_SHORTAGE. The former indicates that the task is invalid or the user did not have permission to allocate a port set in that task. The latter indicates that the kernel

---

[1]Resource requirements for threads have been further reduced in Mach 3.

had insufficient memory to allocate the internal data structures required to represent the port set.

Rules concerning the use of port sets include the following:

- Newly allocated ports are not members of a port set.

- Newly allocated port sets are like an empty bucket; no ports are members of the new port set.

- Ports may only belong to one port set at a time.

- Message receive operations are not allowed on an individual port that has been added to a port set.

- The task must have receive rights to a port in order to add that port to a port set.

We must explicitly add ports to a set by invoking the **port_set_add()** system call. Attempting to add a port to a second port set will cause **port_set_add** to return an error.

Ports are removed from a port set under two conditions. The programmer may explicitly remove a port by issuing the **port_set_remove()** system call. Alternatively, ports are automatically removed from a port set when a task transfers a port receive right to another task. Invocations of these calls are demonstrated in the following code fragment.

```
task_t              target_task;
port_set_name_t     port_set;
port_name_t         port;
kern_return_t       ret;

ret = port_set_add(target_task, port_set, port);
if (ret != KERN_SUCCESS) {
        mach_error("port_set_add:", ret);
        exit(1);
}

ret = port_set_remove(target_task, port);
if (ret != KERN_SUCCESS) {
        mach_error("port_set_remove:", ret);
        exit(1);
}
```

The first argument to both system calls names the task containing the port set. For **port_set_add**, both the name of the port set and the port to be added are provided as arguments. **Port_set_remove** does not require the port set as an argument since, as we noted, a port may belong to only one port set at a time.

To use a port set, the programmer can use the name of the port set during a **msg_receive** system call. The receive operation will complete when a message is available on any port within the named port set. Note that the name of a port set may not be used in all the ways a single port name may be used. For example, the name of a port set may not be checked in to the network message server or environment manager in the same way a single port can be.

Error codes from the **port_set_add** and **port_set_remove** system calls are shown in Table 7.1.

Using only the port set capabilities described thus far, it would be the programmer's responsibility to keep track of relationships between ports and port sets. The **port_set_status()** system call shown in the following example simplifies this chore by listing members of a port set.

```
port_set_name_t    port_set;
port_name_array_t parray;
unsigned int       count;

ret = port_set_status(task_self(), port_set, &parray, &count);
if (ret != KERN_SUCCESS) {
        mach_error("port_set_status:", ret);
```

Error Code	Meaning
KERN_NOT_RECEIVER	The specified task (the first argument to each of these functions) does not have receive rights for the named port.
KERN_INVALID_ARGUMENT	One of the function arguments was invalid. For example, **port_set_add** was issued but the user had not yet done a **port_set_allocate**.
KERN_NOT_IN_SET	The port was not a member of the specified port set (**port_set_remove** only).

Table 7.1: Port Set Operation Error Codes

```
        exit(1);
}
```

The first two parameters specify the task and port set, respectively. The third and fourth parameters are addresses of variables to be filled in by the kernel. On successful return, the third parameter, *parray*, will point to an array of port identifiers. The fourth parameter, *count*, will contain the number of ports in the array. Each port that is a member of the port set will be listed in this array. Note that the order in which ports appear in this array does not necessarily coincide with the order in which they were added to the set.

The kernel will allocate memory in the calling task's address space for the array. The space should be deallocated with the **vm_deallocate()** system call when there is no further need for it.

7.4   Kernel Notifications

There are circumstances in which the Mach kernel will send asynchronous messages to a user-level task. These messages are *kernel notification* messages and are typically meant to advise the task of an abnormal condition. The kernel sends these messages to a special per-task notification port, which is automatically allocated when a task is created. If the user deallocates this port, the kernel will never send notification messages to the task.

Because of the important nature of these messages, they are always sent with a message type of MSG_TYPE_EMERGENCY (the *msg_type* field of the header).

The data structure format of these messages, and relevant manifest constants, are contained in the `<mach/notify.h>` header file. This structure, shown next, consists of the message header, a type structure, and a port identifier.

```
typedef struct {
        msg_header_t       notify_header;
        msg_type_t         notify_type;
        port_t             notify_port;
} notification_t;
```

In addition to the standard information contained in the header and type structures, there are two important pieces of information relevant to notification messages. The message identifier (the *msg_id* field of the header) specifies what type of notification is being sent. The possible values for this field are shown in Table 7.2. The second piece of information is the *notify_port* field, which identifies the port to which the notification refers. A task's notification port is obtained through either the **task_notify()** or **task_get_special_port()** functions. The following code fragment demonstrates how a task would wait for a notification message.

```
#include <mach/notify.h>

notification_t  notify;
char            *p;

notify.notify_header.msg_local_port = task_notify();
notify.notify_header.msg_size = sizeof(notification_t);

ret = msg_receive(&notify.notify_header, MSG_OPTION_NONE, 0);
if (ret != KERN_SUCCESS) {
        mach_error("msg_receive:", ret);
        exit(1);
}

switch (notify.notify_header.msg_id) {
        case NOTIFY_PORT_DELETED:
                p =  "PORT_DELETED";
        case NOTIFY_MSG_ACCEPTED:
                p =  "MSG_ACCEPTED";
        case NOTIFY_OWNERSHIP_RIGHTS:
                p =  "OWNERSHIP_RIGHTS";
        case NOTIFY_RECEIVE_RIGHTS:
                p =  "RECEIVE_RIGHTS";
        case NOTIFY_PORT_DESTROYED:
                p =  "PORT_DESTROYED";
}
printf("Notification message received:\n");
printf("\tCause: %s\n", p);
```

The task need not reply to notification messages. The kernel ignores port backlogs, described in Section 7.6, when sending notification messages.

7.5 Header and Type Structure Options

The Mach IPC subsystem was designed to provide programmer flexibility yet not sacrifice performance or force unwanted functionality on common

Code	Meaning
NOTIFY_PORT_DELETED	A port to which the task had some rights, such as send rights, was deleted. The *notify_port* structure member contains the port name of the deleted port.
NOTIFY_MSG_ACCEPTED	The task had successfully issued a **msg_send** or **msg_rpc** system call with the SEND_NOTIFY option. When the target task receives the "forced" message, the kernel sends this notification message with the *notify_port* structure member containing the name of the target port.
NOTIFY_OWNERSHIP_RIGHTS	When a task with the ownership, but not receive right, to a port deallocates a port, this notification is sent to the task with receive rights. This message advises the task that it now has ownership rights to the port named in the *notify_port* structure member.
NOTIFY_RECEIVE_RIGHTS	When a task with the receive, but not ownership, right to a port deallocates that port, this notification is sent to the task with ownership rights. That task now has receive rights to the port named by *notify_port*.
NOTIFY_PORT_DESTROYED	A message indicating that the port has been destroyed is similar to that when a port is deleted. The recipient of this message had some rights to the port named by *notify_port*. This notification message is sent when both the owner and receiver die. This may be a result of two separate tasks terminating, or a single task with both rights terminating.

Table 7.2: Notification Message Types

operations. Providing the flexibility to go beyond the common case is required in many instances. That flexibility makes the programmer's job easier. Mach provides flexibility in the IPC facilities in several ways. Enhanced performance and simplified programming are achieved by limiting the maximum size of a message that can be specified with the type structure. Larger messages may be sent using the *longform* of the type structure described in Section 7.5.1.

One common programming procedure is to send a message and deallocate the memory holding that message. Mach automates this operation with an option in the header structure. These and other features are described in the remainder of this section.

7.5.1   Longform of the Type Structure

In Section 3.2.3 we described the contents of the type structure. The fields of this structure contain a small number of bits, enough to describe the size of most messages. This structure contains a single 32-bit integer and is illustrated in Fig. 7.5. There are cases, however, when we wish to send data larger than can be represented by these bit fields. In these cases we use the *longform* version of the type structure.

The longform version of the type structure uses a full integer (32 bits) to replace the *msg_type_number* field and a "short" integer (16 bits) to replace the *msg_type_name* and *msg_type_size* fields. This is illustrated in Fig. 7.6. In the following example, note the use of a *msg_type_long_t* structure following the header. This structure contains the standard type structure as well as the longforms of the number, size, and name fields. The example shows the use of the longform version of the structure when sending a large message with out-of-line data.

```
#define MSGSIZE    (4*1024*1024)      /* ~4 Million */

/*
 * Structure used to send messages.
 *  Note the long-form declaration.
```

```
┌─────────────────────────────────────┐
│         Standard type structure      │
└─────────────────────────────────────┘
  1 2 3 4...                ... 30 31 32
```

Figure 7.5: Standard Version (Shortform) Type Structure

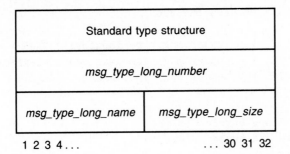

Figure 7.6: Longform Version of the Type Structure

```
 */
struct msg_snd {
        msg_header_t      hdr;
        msg_type_long_t   type;
        char              *ptr;
} msg_snd;
kern_return_t  ret;

ret = vm_allocate(task_self(), &msg_snd.ptr, MSGSIZE, TRUE);
if (ret != KERN_SUCCESS) {
        mach_error("vm_allocate:", ret);
        exit(1);
}
/*
 * Code to process data would go here...
 *     (omitted from example for brevity)
 */
/*
 * The header initialization below is identical for both short
 *   and long forms.
 */
msg_snd.hdr.msg_local_port = PORT_NULL;
msg_snd.hdr.msg_remote_port = comm_port;
msg_snd.hdr.msg_type = MSG_TYPE_NORMAL;
msg_snd.hdr.msg_size = sizeof(struct msg_snd);
msg_snd.hdr.msg_simple = FALSE;


/*
 * msg_type_longform is defined as TRUE
 *
 * Note that the short version of the name, size and
 *   number fields are not filled in -- the
```

```
 *  longform will be used instead.
 */
msg_snd.type.msg_type_header.msg_type_longform = TRUE;
msg_snd.type.msg_type_header.msg_type_deallocate = FALSE;
msg_snd.type.msg_type_header.msg_type_inline = FALSE;

/*
 * Fill in the long version of the
 *   name, size and number fields.
 */
msg_snd.type.msg_type_long_name = MSG_TYPE_CHAR;
msg_snd.type.msg_type_long_size = sizeof(char);
msg_snd.type.msg_type_long_number = MSGSIZE;

msg_send.ptr = data;
```

When using the longform version, the programmer sets the *msg_type_longform* field of the type structure to TRUE. There is no need to initialize the *msg_type_name*, *msg_type_size*, or *msg_type_number* fields, as their alternate longforms will be used. The longform versions of these three fields are part of the *msg_type_long_t* structure declaration.

In this example, only the size of data stored in the *msg_type_number* field was too large for the standard structure. However, all three of the longform variables must be filled in when using the longform of the type structure.

Our example sends 4 MB of data. The standard version of the type structure limits us to 4 K bits of data. Using the longform capability, we can send up to $2^{32} - 1$ data elements, each of which can be $2^{16} - 1$ bits.

7.5.2   Transferring Port Rights

A task may give away port rights to another task. Port rights may be transferred to

- Grant permission for a task to send messages to a specific port

- Have another task "take over" receive operations on a port.

A single port right or combination of send, receive, or ownership rights may be passed to another task. When a task sends a port right, that right is transferred to the Mach kernel and transferred again to the target task.

During this transfer, the kernel holds the port rights and enqueues any messages sent to the port. If the target task terminates before the rights are transferred, the kernel sends receive rights to the task with ownership, or ownership to the task with receive rights, as appropriate. If the receiver and owner have both terminated, the port is deallocated and tasks holding send rights will receive a port deleted (NOTIFY_PORT_DELETED) notification message.

When a task sends either receive or ownership rights, the sending task loses that capability. Send rights remain with the sending task and are given to the target task.

Port rights are transferred by sending an IPC message to a task. The message may be sent to *any* port that a task owns.[2] A task transfers port rights in one of two ways. The first is to specify a port, defined by using a type structure, as a data item in an IPC message. The second method is to send a message and place a port identifier in the *msg_local_port* field of the IPC header. The receiving task automatically obtains send rights to that port. It is recommended, however, that the first mechanism be used and that the *msg_local_port* field only be used for the reply port when using **msg_rpc**.

When sending port rights with a type structure, the *msg_simple* field of the header must be set to FALSE. The *msg_type_name* field of the type structure will specify the type of right being sent. The following code fragment shows how to transfer port send rights:

```
struct msg {
        msg_header_t    hdr;
        msg_type_t      type;
        port_t          port;
} msg;

port_t    dst_port, port;

msg.hdr.msg_simple = FALSE;
msg.hdr.msg_size = sizeof(struct msg);
msg.hdr.msg_type = MSG_TYPE_NORMAL;
msg.hdr.msg_local_port = PORT_NULL;
msg.hdr.msg_remote_port = dst_port;
msg.hdr.msg_id = 456;

msg.type.msg_type_name = MSG_TYPE_PORT;
```

---

[2]You might expect to be able to send a message to the task control port to transfer port rights, but you cannot. When messages are sent to a task control port, the Mach kernel is the recipient of the message, not the task.

Code	Meaning
MSG_TYPE_PORT_OWNERSHIP	Transfers ownership and send rights
MSG_TYPE_PORT_RECEIVE	Transfers receive and send rights
MSG_TYPE_PORT_ALL	Transfers send, receive, and ownership rights
MSG_TYPE_PORT	Transfers send rights

Table 7.3: Definitions for Transferring Port Rights

```
msg.type.msg_type_size = sizeof(port_t) * 8;
msg.type.msg_type_number = 1;
msg.type.msg_type_inline = TRUE;
msg.type.msg_type_longform = FALSE;
msg.type.msg_type_deallocate = FALSE;

msg.port = port;
```

Initialization of the header is similar to that shown elsewhere in this chapter. As already stated, the only change required when sending port rights is for the *msg_simple* field to be set to FALSE.

The *msg_type_name* field of the type structure specifies the type of right being sent. Appropriate values for this field are shown in Table 7.3.

The initialization of the remaining fields is similar to that shown earlier.

7.5.3   Deallocation of Resources

After sending a message with port rights or data, the sending task often no longer needs the data or port that was sent. For example, imagine an environment with a server that accepts IPC messages containing requests for services. For each request the server runs a program that can perform the appropriate service. Different programs would be executed depending on the service requested. This environment is similar to the UNIX inetd server.

After the server passes control to the specialized program, the server no longer needs the port used to communicate with the client. Send rights for the communication port are passed from the server to the specialized program, and the server can now delete its access to the port. The server has handed off all responsibility of communicating with the client to another program and will not respond to the client itself.

This common operation can be optimized by initializing the *msg_type_deallocate* field of the type structure to TRUE. Prior to the message being enqueued, any memory or port rights pointed to in the message will be deallocated. Note that when deallocating memory, this capability is limited to out-of-line data. It is important to note that, because the resource is deallocated *before* the message is enqueued, it is possible to lose data if the message is not enqueued (e.g., because of a kernel resource shortage).

7.6   Port Backlog

The Mach kernel limits the number of messages that may be queued for a port. This limit is termed the port *backlog*. The port backlog is controlled with the **port_set_backlog()** system call and may be examined with **port_status()**.

When a thread sends a message to a port, it must only wait for the kernel to enqueue the message to the target task. If the port backlog is reached, the thread will be suspended until the receiving task has removed messages from the queue. The SEND_NOTIFY option, discussed in Section 3.2.3, describes how to send a single additional message when the port backlog has been reached.

The port backlog could be adjusted to optimize performance. For example, the backlog would be reduced if the processing time per message is long. By reducing the backlog, supplier tasks would not continue to produce messages that would not be acted on for some time. When the sending thread is suspended, CPU resources are available for the receiving thread to continue message processing.

The default backlog for a port is five outstanding messages. This may be changed to any value from one to sixteen. These constants are specified by the operating system and are defined in the file <mach_param.h> by PORT_BACKLOG_DEFAULT and PORT_BACKLOG_MAX, respectively. The following example shows how to set the port backlog to ten for a port.

```
task_t        target_task;
port_t        port;
kern_return_t ret;

ret = port_set_backlog(target_task, port, 10);
```

```
if (ret != KERN_SUCCESS) {
        mach_error("port_set_backlog:", ret);
        exit(1);
}
```

Port_set_backlog operates on a single port. Regardless of the implication in the name, this system call has nothing to do with port sets. Each
member of a port set maintains an independent backlog value.

7.7   Port Status

Applications that monitor or dynamically control their execution need to
obtain information about the ports they are using. For example, a task with
a port whose backlog is increasing may create additional threads to process
incoming requests. Providing this and other information about a port is
accomplished with the **port_status()** system call.

Port_status provides all relevant information concerning a port, including the number of messages currently enqueued, the port backlog, etc. The
system call is issued as

```
port_t            port;
kern_return_t     ret;
port_set_name_t   set;
int               count, backlog;
boolean_t         owner, receiver;

ret = port_status(task_self(), port, &set, &count,
                  &backlog, &owner, &receiver);

if (ret != KERN_SUCCESS) {
        mach_error("port_status:", ret);
        exit(1);
}
```

The first two arguments identify the task and the name of the port. The
remaining five parameters are pointers to local storage, in which the kernel
will return status information. If the port is a member of a port set, *set* will
contain the name of that set, or PORT_NULL otherwise. *Count* and *backlog*
return the number of messages currently enqueued for this port and the
maximum number of messages that may be enqueued, respectively.

The last two parameters are booleans that are TRUE if the task has
ownership and receive rights, respectively. Only the *owner* and *receiver*

variables are meaningful on return if the named task does not have receive rights to the port. The contents of the *set*, *count*, and *backlog* variables are undefined in this case.

7.8   Port Names and Port Rights

In this section we describe several important concepts for dealing with ports. The first is the concept of a *port name*. We have used ports in many programming examples but have only identified them through variables returned from system calls such as **port_allocate** or contained in an IPC message header structure. In this section we learn what a port name is, how to manage port names, and how to manipulate them.

Port rights are one of the most important concepts in the Mach system. Because Mach is a capability-based system, port rights must be sent from one task to another. Each task has the right to perform certain operations on a port. Other operations are not permitted. This section discusses port rights in more detail and discusses how ports are used to identify objects and how to interpose port rights.

7.8.1   Renaming Ports

Each port is known by a unique name. With only two exceptions, any 32-bit integer value may be used as a port name. Those two exceptions are the values represented by the constants PORT_NULL (integer value zero) and PORT_ENABLED (integer value negative one). Port names are unique to each task; task A may know a port by the name 5 while task B may know the same port by the name 32768.

There are circumstances in which a task may wish to rename a port. For example, a program may have a large number of ports, each of which logically represents a data stream. Associated with that data would be a structure that defines the data's status. Rather than having a table that translates a port name to the address of the associated structure, the port can be renamed to a value that represents that address. The translation step becomes unnecessary.

The **port_rename()** system call changes the name by which a port or port set is known to a task. If the new name is already in use, the error code KERN_NAME_EXISTS is returned.

```
task_t          task;
port_name_t     old_name, new_name;
kern_return_t   ret;
struct buffer   buf;

new_name = (port_name_t) buf;
ret = port_rename(task, old_name, new_name);
if (ret != KERN_SUCCESS) {
        mach_error("port_rename:", ret);
        exit(1);
}
```

The first argument, *task*, is the task that contains the port. The second and third arguments specify the current name of the port and the new name of the port, respectively. When the call completes successfully, the constant KERN_SUCCESS is returned. Should the calling task not have permission to change the target task, or if the second argument did not name a valid port, the KERN_INVALID_ARGUMENT error code is returned.

7.8.2   Port Names

We previously described how to obtain information about a particular port by using **port_status**. Obviously this call can only work when the name of each port in the task is known. The **port_names()** system call is available to help keep track of the ports in use.

```
task_t              task;
port_name_array_t   names;
unsigned int        name_count;
port_type_array_t   types;
unsigned int        type_count;
kern_return_t       ret;

ret = port_names(task, &names, &name_count, &types, &type_count);
if (ret != KERN_SUCCESS) {
        mach_error("port_names:", ret);
        exit(1);
}
```

The first argument is the task whose port name space will be examined. All remaining arguments are pointers to local variables that the kernel fills in. The second (*names*) and fourth (*types*) parameters are pointers to arrays that the kernel allocates. These arrays must be freed using **vm_deallocate** when the information is no longer needed.

Definition	Send Rights	Receive Rights	Ownership Rights	Port Set
PORT_TYPE_SEND	X			
PORT_TYPE_RECEIVE		X		
PORT_TYPE_OWN	X		X	
PORT_TYPE_RECEIVE_OWN	X	X	X	
PORT_TYPE_SET				X

Table 7.4: Port Rights

The second argument will point to a newly allocated region of memory containing an array with the name of each port and port set in the task's port name space. Note that ports are not listed in any particular order. The number of entries in this array is returned in the variable that the third parameter points to, *name_count*.

The fourth argument will point to a second newly allocated region of memory, which will contain an array with the *port type* for each port or port set pointed to in the first array. The port type defines a task's rights to a port. The matrix in Table 7.4 describes port types and the associated rights associated with that definition. The number of entries in this array is returned in the variable that the fifth argument points to, *type_count*; this value should always be identical to the value returned in the third argument.

While **port_names** returns the port type for each port a task holds, the type of a single port may be determined with the **port_type()** system call. Both of these calls return KERN_SUCCESS when the call completes successfully or KERN_INVALID_ARGUMENT when the calling task does not have access to the target task or the target task does not have a port with the specified name.

The system call is issued with three arguments, as shown in the following code fragment:

```
task_t         target_task;
port_name_t    name;
port_type_t    returned_type;
kern_return_t  ret;

ret = port_type(target_task, name, &returned_type);
if (ret != KERN_SUCCESS) {
        mach_error("port_type:", ret);
        exit(1);
}
```

The first argument is the task whose port name space is being queried. The second argument is the name of the port being interrogated. The last argument is a pointer to a local variable that will contain the port type. Port types are defined in Table 7.4.

7.8.3   Ports as Objects

In Mach, ports are both a communications channel and a mechanism to reference objects. In Chapter 2 we explained that each task and thread is identified by a port. Tasks and threads are objects. Operations on an object are performed by sending an IPC message to the port that represents that object. Each of the Mach system calls takes a port as one of its arguments that identifies the task on which the system call will operate. That port is managed by the Mach kernel; hence it is the kernel that receives the message. The message contains the system call arguments, and the kernel then performs the requested operation in the target task.

This concept is used throughout the Mach system. Since ports are used as objects, it is important to understand that ports are also protected. The kernel manages and protects ports. In the next section we will look at that protection mechanism.

7.8.4   Interposing Port Rights

Port rights are an important concept that we discussed earlier in this chapter. So far, we have discussed methods by which a task can pass port rights to another task. In this section, we discuss methods for a task to obtain rights to a port directly; that is, without having a task pass the right.

Obtaining a port right without action by the task with that right would normally be considered a security violation. This capability is therefore limited to only those tasks with rights to a task's control port. Typically only the creating task would have such permission. If task A creates task B, then task A would have the right to insert or extract port rights into task B. Task B would not have the capability of manipulating task A, however.

There are four system calls that explicitly insert and extract port rights:

- **port_insert_send()**   • **port_insert_receive()**
- **port_extract_send()**   • **port_extract_receive()**

These calls provide the ability to add or remove send and receive rights for a particular port within a task, and they have several possible uses. They can be used to interpose on the target task's port right. For example, you may be debugging a task and want to intercept all messages it sends to a certain port. To accomplish this, you would extract the task's original send right and insert a new send right (with the same name) for your own port. After examining the intercepted messages, you could then forward them to the intended recipient. Similarly, a task could intercept all messages destined for the target task by manipulating receive rights.

Port_insert_send inserts send rights, while **port_insert_receive** inserts both receive and ownership rights. These two system calls are invoked in an identical manner:

```
task_t        task;
port_t        port;
port_name_t   target;
kern_return_t ret;

ret = port_insert_send(task, port, target);

ret = port_insert_receive(task, port, target);
```

The first parameter (*task*) to both system calls identifies the task into which the right will be inserted. The second argument (*port*) is the port to be inserted. The third argument (*target*) is the name by which the target task may access those port rights. The target name must not identify an existing port. If successful, the constant KERN_SUCCESS is returned; otherwise, one of the error codes shown in Table 7.5 is returned.

Error Code	Meaning
KERN_NAME_EXISTS	The target task already has a right with the same name as the one we are attempting to insert.
KERN_FAILURE	The target task already has rights to the port that the second argument specifies.
KERN_INVALID_ARGUMENT	Either the calling task did not have permission to the target task or the target port name is invalid.

Table 7.5: Port Right Insertion Errors

Port_extract_send removes (extracts) send rights, while **port_extract_receive** removes both receive and ownership rights. These two system calls are also invoked in an identical manner:

```
task_t        task;
port_t        port;
port_name_t   target;
kern_return_t ret;

ret = port_extract_send(task, target, &port);

ret = port_extract_receive(task, target, &port);
```

The first argument names the task from which to extract the right. The second argument is the name by which the task knows the port. The last argument is a pointer to a local variable that will contain the port right. When successful, the task no longer has rights to the port and the constant KERN_SUCCESS is returned. The KERN_INVALID_ARGUMENT error code is returned when the task does not have a port with the appropriate rights or the calling task did not have rights to the target task.

7.9   Forging Ports

We have stated that Mach is a capability-based system and that port rights must be sent from one task to another. However, is it possible to trick the kernel into allowing a task to send an IPC message to a port for which the task does not have send rights?

The answer, of course, is no. But let us convince you with an example. If we create a program that obtains send rights to a port, what is it that the program has actually obtained? It appears as if the program obtains a value, declared as type *port_t*, and sends a message to it by placing that value in the *msg_remote_port* field of a header.

The following program does a port look-up and displays the value received. In our example we presume the program prints the value 0x23B470.

```
main()
{
        kern_return_t    ret;
        netname_name_t   name;
        port_name_t      server_port;
```

```
        strcpy(name, "Server-Port");

        ret = netname_look_up(name_server_port, "*",
                              name, &server_port);

        if (ret != NETNAME_SUCCESS) {
                mach_error("netname look up:", ret);
                exit(1);
        }

        printf("Server Port is: %#x\n", server_port);
}
```

A second program, which attempts to forge send rights to a port, might
then be written as follows:

```
struct msg {
        msg_header_t    hdr;
        msg_type_t      type;
        int             value;
} msg;

port_t   dst_port, port;

main()
{
        msg.hdr.msg_simple = TRUE;
        msg.hdr.msg_size = sizeof(struct msg);
        msg.hdr.msg_type = MSG_TYPE_NORMAL;
        msg.hdr.msg_local_port = PORT_NULL;
        /*
         * Try to forge the destination port.
         */
        msg.hdr.msg_remote_port = 0x23b470;
        msg.hdr.msg_id = 456;

        msg.type.msg_type_name = MSG_TYPE_INTEGER_32;
        msg.type.msg_type_size = sizeof(int) * 8;
        msg.type.msg_type_number = 1;
        msg.type.msg_type_inline = TRUE;
        msg.type.msg_type_longform = FALSE;
        msg.type.msg_type_deallocate = FALSE;

        msg.value = 43;
```

```
            ret = msg_send(&msg.hdr, MSG_OPTION_NONE, 0);
            if (ret != SEND_SUCCESS) {
                    mach_error("msg_send:", ret);
                    exit(1);
            }
    }
```

Running this program yields the following:

```
msg_send: (ipc/send) invalid port
```

Why did we get an error? While the value specified to **msg_send** may have been the correct port name, it is important to remember that the Mach kernel manages port rights. The first program in this example obtained rights to the port from the network message server (netmsgserver). However, using the same value was insufficient to allow another task to send a message to the same port because the kernel never gave send rights to that task.

Ports are not forgeable under Mach. The only way for a task to obtain rights to a port is for a task with those rights to directly provide those rights.

7.10   Name Servers

The port is the basic mechanism for intertask communication in Mach. However, for a task to send a message, it must have send rights to a port. While there are mechanisms to insert and extract port rights (Section 7.8.4), these mechanisms are used only under special circumstances: when one task has rights to the task port of another. Another mechanism must be made available for the more general case. That mechanism makes use of a "third-party" name server.

Mach provides two name servers, the network message server (netmsgserver) and the environment manager (envmgr). We have briefly described these name servers in Chapter 3. In this section we describe these two name servers in more detail.

When a task is created, there are several "special" ports that the task is given send rights to. Details on these ports and their management are provided in Section 2.6.2. Two of these ports communicate with the network message server and environment manager.

7.10.1   Network Message Server

The basis of a distributed computing environment is the ability to send and receive information among the hosts on a network. This ability should not require the user or programmer to know or understand the location of data or hosts. Mach implements such an environment using the network message server (netmsgserver).

The Mach network message server provides several important services to the user of Mach IPC. This server provides both a network-wide ASCII name registration of ports and network transparent transmission of messages.

Applications wishing to provide distributed services could be a database server providing access to data, a file server providing access to remote files, or our time server providing the time of day. As Mach is a relatively new operating system, few of these applications exist today. However, as Mach moves out of the research laboratory through commercial offerings such as OSF/1, such applications will become available.

Applications using the netmsgserver call the **netname_check_in** function to register a port with an ASCII name. **Netname_look_up()** is called by an application program to obtain send rights to the port. The calling sequence for these functions was described in Section 3.3.1. Both functions return NETNAME_SUCCESS when the call successfully completes.

If the **netname_look_up** fails, one of the error codes shown in Table 7.6 is returned.

Additional services that the netmsgserver provides include the ability to remove port registration and obtain the version of the network message server. These capabilities are demonstrated with the following code fragments:

Error Code	Meaning
NAME_NOT_CHECKED_IN	The name was not found. This is an indication that the server has either not been run or has terminated.
NETNAME_NO_SUCH_HOST	The host name specified is unknown.
NETNAME_HOST_NOT_FOUND	The named host could not be reached. The most likely cause is that the host is currently down.

Table 7.6: **Netname_look_up()** Errors

```
#include <mach.h>
#include <servers/netname.h>

netname_name_t name;
port_name_t    port;
kern_return_t  ret;

ret = netname_check_in(name_server_port, name, task_self(), port);
if (ret != NETNAME_SUCCESS) {
        mach_error("netname check in:", ret);
        exit(1);
}

ret = netname_look_up(name_server_port, "*", name, &port);
if (ret != NETNAME_SUCCESS) {
        mach_error("netname look up:", ret);
        exit(1);
}

ret = netname_check_out(name_server_port, name, task_self(), port);
if (ret != NETNAME_SUCCESS) {
        mach_error("netname check out:", ret);
        exit(1);
}

ret = netname_version(name_server_port, name);
if (ret != NETNAME_SUCCESS) {
        mach_error("netname version:", ret);
        exit(1);
}
```

Netname_check_out() removes a name to port mapping. For security reasons, removing this mapping requires that the third parameter, *signature*, be a port to which the caller has send rights. In these code fragments, we use the task port as returned by the function **task_self()**. Using a signature of PORT_NULL disables this security feature—but even trivial programs should leave this enabled.

Netname_version() returns a string with the version of the server. In reality, this is the RCS (Revision Control System) header of one of the source files to the netmsgserver. An example of this string is

```
$Header: nn_procs.c,v 1.21 89/05/02 11:14:54 dpj Exp $
```

In addition to a name-to-port mapping service, the netmsgserver also provides important data conversion functions. Mach runs on a large number of systems, many of which use different data representations. When transferring data between systems, the netmsgserver translates the data to the target system's internal data representation. This operation is done transparently; the application program sees the data in a format appropriate for the computer it is running on.[3]

An important consideration for a distributed computing environment is communications reliability. To ensure that IPC messages are delivered reliably, each message is acknowledged between communicating netmsgservers. These acknowledgments are invisible outside the netmsgservers and, if the application uses remote procedure calls, there are no extra messages being transmitted[4] and hence no performance penalty.

7.10.2   Environment Manager

The environment manager serves a similar role to the netmsgserver: It provides a mapping service between a name and information that the name represents. The environment manager differs from the netmsgserver in two important ways. Whereas the netmsgserver provides a name-mapping service for computers on a network, the information that the environment manager stores is only from applications running on the local system. The environment manager has the ability to provide a name-to-port mapping identical to the netmsgserver. It also provides a name-to-string mapping capability not present in the netmsgserver.

Use of the environment manager is not, however, recommended. This server was written primarily as an example of how to write servers under Mach. We describe the interfaces to the environment manager because, regardless of its original purpose, it has been used as a name server. New applications should use the netmsgserver.

The name-to-port mapping is identical to that available with the netmsgserver, with the exception that the mapping is local. The name is an arbitrary ASCII string of up to eighty characters, including the terminating NULL. The name is declared using the *env_name_t* type definition. The following code fragment shows the function calls to check in, look up, and remove a name.

---

[3]Floating point numbers are not converted.

[4]No extra messages are required because the acknowledgments are piggybacked on return messages.

```
#include <mach.h>
#include <servers/env_mgr.h>

env_name_t      name;
port_name_t     port;
kern_return_t   ret;

ret = env_set_port(environment_port, name, port);
if (ret != KERN_SUCCESS) {
        mach_error("env_set_port:", ret);
        exit(1);
}

ret = env_get_port(environment_port, name, &port);
if (ret != KERN_SUCCESS) {
        mach_error("env_get_port:", ret);
        exit(1);
}

ret = env_del_port(environment_port, name);
if (ret != KERN_SUCCESS) {
        mach_error("env_del_port:", ret);
        exit(1);
}
```

The first argument is the port on which the environment manager will be listening. As with the netmsgserver, each task is given send rights to an environment manager when the task is created. This port is named in the global variable *environment_port*.

The second argument, *name*, is the name by which the port is known. The third argument for **env_set_port()** is the name of the port being registered. **Env_get_port()**'s third argument is the address of the variable where the environment manager will store the port name. Note that **env_del_port()** does not accept a parameter equivalent to the *signature* variable in the netmsgserver's **netname_check_out** call. If the task that checked in the port deletes it, the port will no longer be accessible for future **env_get_port** calls. Other tasks only remove the name to port mapping from the per-task context that the environment manager maintains.

On success, all of these functions return KERN_SUCCESS. The codes in Table 7.7 are returned in case of an error.

The second use of the environment manager provides a name-to-string mapping. This mapping is analogous to UNIX environment variables. In

Code	Meaning
ENV_UNKNOWN_PORT	The port used to communicate with the environment manager does not reference a known environment.
ENV_READ_ONLY	A modification to a read-only environment is being attempted.
ENV_WRONG_VAR_TYPE	The variable name was already in use for a string variable.

Table 7.7: Environment Manager Port Error Codes

fact, this capability was conceived to provide a system-wide equivalent of environment variables. Operations on strings are similar to those for ports. The name of the string, as defined by the *env_name_t* definition, is limited to eighty characters. The string is defined by the *env_value_t* definition, which has a length of 256 characters. The following code fragment shows function calls to check in, look up, and remove a string.

```
#include <mach.h>
#include <servers/env_mgr.h>

port_name_t    port;
env_name_t     name;
env_value_t    value;
kern_return_t  ret;

strcpy(name, "Dog");
strcpy(value, "Beagle");
ret = env_set_string(environment_port, name, value);
if (ret != KERN_SUCCESS) {
        mach_error("env_set_string:", ret);
        exit(1);
}

ret = env_get_string(environment_port, name, value);
if (ret != KERN_SUCCESS) {
        mach_error("env_get_string:", ret);
        exit(1);
} else
        printf("%s=%s\n", name, value);

ret = env_del_string(environment_port, name);
```

Code	Meaning
KERN_SUCCESS	The operation was successful.
ENV_UNKNOWN_PORT	The port used to communicate with the environment manager does not reference a known environment.
ENV_VAR_NOT_FOUND	The name does not yet exist.
ENV_READ_ONLY	A modification to a read-only environment is being attempted.
ENV_WRONG_VAR_TYPE	The variable name was already in use for a port variable.

Table 7.8: Environment Manager String Error Codes

```
if (ret != KERN_SUCCESS) {
        mach_error("env_del_string:", ret);
        exit(1);
}
```

Arguments to these functions are identical to those for ports, except that strings, rather than ports, are checked in and out. Return codes from these functions are described in Table 7.8.

Additional functions are available to examine and manipulate sets of strings and ports. The four functions in this category are invoked as

```
#include <mach.h>
#include <servers/env_mgr.h>

env_name_list    names;
env_str_list     string_vals;
port_array_t     port_vals;
int              name_cnt, pcnt, scnt;

ret = env_list_strings(environment_port, &names, &name_cnt,
                       &string_vals, &scnt);

if (ret != KERN_SUCCESS) {
        mach_error("envmgr list strings:", ret);
        exit(1);
}
```

```
ret = env_list_ports(environment_port, &names, &name_cnt,
                     &port_vals, &pcnt);

if (ret != KERN_SUCCESS) {
        mach_error("envmgr list ports:", ret);
        exit(1);
}
ret = env_set_stlist(environment_port, names, name_cnt,
                     string_vals, scnt);

if (ret != KERN_SUCCESS) {
        mach_error("envmgr set string-list:", ret);
        exit(1);
}

ret = env_set_ptlist(environment_port, names, name_cnt,
                     port_vals, pcnt);

if (ret != KERN_SUCCESS) {
        mach_error("envmgr set port-list:", ret);
        exit(1);
}
```

The **env_list_strings()** and **env_list_ports()** functions return all strings
or ports accessible by the calling task. The first three arguments to both
calls are identical in purpose. As with all environment manager calls, the
first argument names the port on which the environment manager will be
listening. The second argument, *names*, must be an address of a pointer.
Upon successful completion of the call, this variable will point to a newly allocated region of memory that contains the name associated with each string
or port, as appropriate for the call. The number of elements in that region
is returned in a variable that the third argument points to, *name_cnt*.

For the **env_list_strings** call, the fourth parameter is a pointer to a variable (*string_vals*) that will point to a second newly allocated region of memory. That region will contain the string mapping. The number of elements
in that region is returned in the variable that the fifth and final parameter
points to, *scnt*. *Scnt* and *name_cnt* should contain identical values.

The following code fragment displays the invocation of this call and shows
how to print the name-to-string mappings:

```
prstrings()
{
        int             i, cnt, scnt;
        env_str_list    strings;
        env_name_list   names;

        ret = env_list_strings(environment_port, &names,
                        &cnt, &strings, &scnt);

        if (ret != KERN_SUCCESS) {
                mach_error("envmgr list strings", ret);
                exit(1);
        }

        if (cnt != scnt) {
                printf("prstrings: cnt = %d, scnt = %d\n",
                        cnt, scnt);
                return;
        }

        printf("String names:\n");
        for (i=0; i<cnt; i++)
                printf("%2d: %s = %s\n", i, names[i], strings[i]);
}
```

For the **env_list_ports** call, the fourth parameter is a pointer to a variable (*port_vals*) that will point to another newly allocated region of memory. That region will contain the port names of each port named in the *names* array. The number of elements in that region is returned in the variable that the fifth parameter points to, *pcnt*. *Pcnt* and *name_cnt* should contain identical values.

Two additional functions are available to add multiple name-to-port (**env_set_ptlist()**) or name-to-string (**env_set_stlist()**) mappings with a single call. For each function, the second parameter contains the address of an array containing the names to be mapped. The third parameter is an integer specifying the number of elements in the array. The fourth and fifth parameters are similar but specify an array of port names[5] (for

---

[5]The documentation available for the environment manager describes the variable type of *port_vals* incorrectly as *env_str_list*. The declaration shown here of *port_array_t* is correct.

env_set_ptlist) or strings (**env_set_stlist**). The fifth parameter is an integer containing the number of elements in that array. The value that the third and fifth parameters represent should be identical.

7.11   Summary

In this chapter we described a number of important facilities for the advanced IPC user. Out-of-line data represents an important performance optimization that should be used whenever transferring large amounts of data. Port sets allow the programmer to group ports together logically. We also described port names and port rights in additional detail. We closed the chapter with a description of the two name servers available under Mach.

Mach provides more than the simple ability to transfer data between two unrelated tasks. Because the IPC system is capability based, the message queues are protected from unauthorized tasks. Yet the ability to provide tasks with send access to a port has been simplified with easy-to-use name server interfaces.

Flexibility and performance optimizations have been included in the system. The result is a coherent system that provides the functionality to build any application based on a message-passing paradigm.

Chapter 8

Mach Interface Generator (MIG)

Programs using Mach IPC often follow the client/server programming paradigm. In this model, clients request information from a server by sending a message and usually receive data back from a server via another message. In the larger context of the client/server model, setting up and sending messages is a tedious process that does not affect the actual work the client and server perform. Much of this mechanical process is conceptually the same across programs using IPC; only the details differ. To relieve the programmer of much of the burden of those details, Mach provides an IPC interface generator called MIG. MIG takes a specification of a message-passing interface and a procedure call interface and generates appropriate C language code for both client and server programs. The code that MIG generates eliminates the need for the programmer to implement the packing, sending, receiving, and unpacking of IPC messages.

The programmer benefits in several ways by using an interface generator instead of writing the message-passing code manually. The first reason was already stated: The burden of writing that code is relieved. Additionally, generating code via MIG significantly reduces the potential for programming errors because the generated code is already debugged. By using MIG, the programmer is guaranteed that the client and server programs are consistent with each other and "speak" the same specification. MIG reduces the time spent designing and implementing client and server interfaces because a single focal point for that interface exists. If the interface changes or evolves, the implementor only has to change the one file in which the interface is defined. Using MIG allows the programmer to think more abstractly about the program rather than get mired down in the details of message-passing mechanisms.

8.1   MIG Overview

To give a concrete idea of what MIG will do for you, let us revisit the work involved in the Time Server, introduced in Chapter 3, and illustrate which portions MIG subsumes. Refer to the complete Time Server client program in Section 3.3.3, which has a significant amount of code devoted to IPC. Figure 8.1 demonstrates the work MIG performs with respect to message passing. Notice that the new MIG-generated function **get_time()** replaces all the original code dealing with formatting, sending, and receiving messages.

MIG reduces the amount of code you write by accepting as input a user specification file and generating corresponding modules for the client and server programs. MIG converts the defined interface into suitable message-passing functions, hiding the IPC details from the programmer.

The programmer provides MIG with a *specification* file or *definition* file describing IPC-related interfaces. By convention, a MIG specification file-name has a *.defs* extension. When MIG processes the .defs file, it generates three new files, as shown in Fig. 8.2.

1. **User header file:** This file is included in the client code and contains declarations of the routines that the client needs at compilation time.

2. **User interface module:** You compile and link this module into the client program. It contains functions used to transfer messages between the client and server.

1. Look up server's port.	1. Look up server's port.
2. Allocate a reply port.	
3. Set up message to send to server.	
4. Perform the **msg_send()**.	2. Call **get_time()** to get the time from server.
5. Set up to receive reply.	
6. Perform the **msg_receive()**.	
7. Print the time.	3. Print the time.

Figure 8.1: MIG Functionality

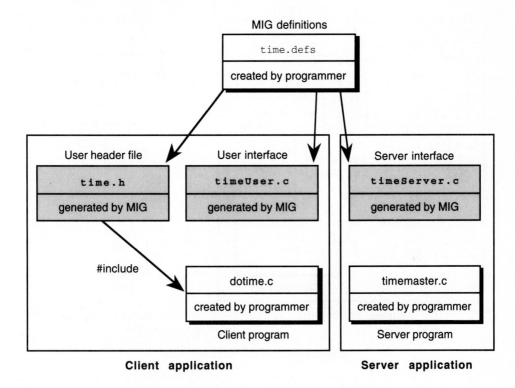

Figure 8.2: MIG File Relationships

3. **Server interface module:** You compile and link into the server program. This module contains code to receive an IPC message and to call the appropriate programmer-supplied function within the server. That function performs the requested operation. This module also contains code to assemble and send reply messages.

Figure 8.2, based on the Time Server, gives a comprehensive picture of the modules that MIG produces and how those modules interact with the client and server programs. In our example, MIG parses `time.defs` to generate three files, `time.h`, `timeUser.c`, and `timeServer.c`. The `time.h` file is the user header file, and the client program dotime.c, includes this header file. The `timeUser.c` file is the user interface module. The programmer compiles and links this module with dotime.c to form the client application. The `timeServer.c` file is the server interface module. Again the programmer compiles and links this module with the server program, timemaster.c, to create the entire server application.

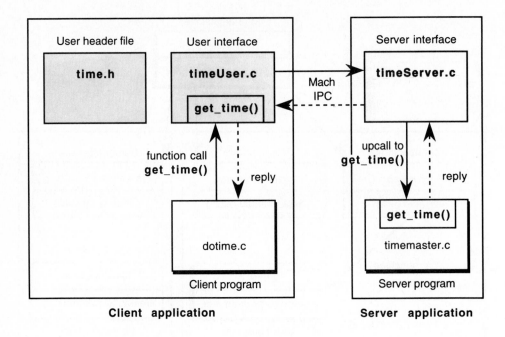

Figure 8.3: MIG Interactions

Figure 8.3 illustrates the interactions between the client and server programs. The generated `timeUser.c` contains the client side code supporting the **get_time** function. The server interface module contains the server side code to make an upcall to the **get_time** function provided in timemaster.c. Notice that in the entire application, there are two functions called **get_time**. The client's version performs message passing and the server's version carries out the real operation. The user interface module and server interface module perform all the message-passing tasks and communicate with each other via IPC. The server program in timemaster.c simply provides the **get_time** function as a subroutine. The client program calls **get_time** as if it were a local subroutine. The MIG modules handle the calls between the client and server in a transparent fashion.

While the calls to **get_time** look like local function calls, both the client and server must know that they communicate via IPC. The server must allocate and register a port to receive messages, and the client must look up that port. Beyond that, the client program's task is trivial, as shown in

Fig. 8.1. The server's general algorithm is

1. Allocate and register a port with the netmsgserver.

2. Call **time_server()**, the MIG-generated server function that waits for incoming requests.

3. Dispatch from **time_server** to the requested server subroutine.

Thus the interaction between the server interface module and timemaster.c requires that timemaster.c know the name of the overall server function, **time_server**, provided by MIG. The **time_server** function decodes the incoming requests and dispatches to the appropriate code in the server program to handle the request. For example, a specification file for a more functionally complete time server may have several interfaces defined, such as **set_time()**, and **get_gmttime()** in addition to **get_time**. The **time_server** function decodes a message, based on its identifier, and calls one of **set_time**, **get_gmttime**, or **get_time**.

Of course the focal point of these modules is the specification file. The user must define an interface that accurately reflects the tasks to be accomplished. Several factors should be considered when defining an interface. These factors correspond to the various components that make up a specification file. The implementor must decide what operations the interface provides, such as the **get_time** function. The programmer must also determine what arguments those operations require. For instance, **get_time** may need a port representing the server, a format identifier, and a data area in which to receive the time from the server. The programmer must also consider what data types these arguments are. Figure 8.4 shows the sections comprising a specification file.

MIG uses a Pascal-style syntax for most of its declarations. This is for historical reasons, since MIG was derived from an earlier program named *MatchMaker* that generated Pascal code. Recall that Pascal uses the ";" as a *separator*, not a terminator. Forgetting this difference can cause some frustrating (yet eventually obvious) problems. However, MIG uses C-style comments (/* ... */) and allows preprocessor macros such as #define.

As Fig. 8.4 illustrates, the specification file contains five different kinds of sections:

1. **Subsystem identifier:** Names the MIG subsystem

2. **Type declarations:** Declares data types for interface parameters

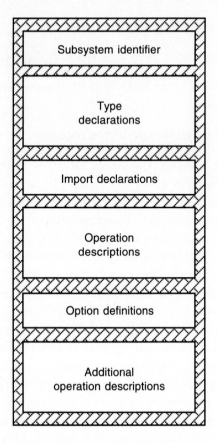

Figure 8.4: Specification File Components

3. **Import declarations:** States include files to be placed in the generated files

4. **Option definitions:** Defines various special-purpose options for MIG

5. **Operation descriptions:** Specifies function call interfaces to server exported operations.

The *import* and *option* sections are optional. The option definitions, since they are directed to MIG itself, may appear throughout the file and affect only subsequent portions of the file.

Since the *type declarations* describe the data types of all arguments to all interfaces, and the *operation descriptions* describe the actual interface itself, these are the most complicated sections of the file. The other sections contain directives for MIG itself to use when building the interface. For the

get_time example, the types of all the arguments (port, integer, and the data area) must be declared for MIG. The interface to the function, showing the order of arguments and describing how they will be used in the program, must also be defined.

In the remainder of this chapter we discuss each of the sections of the specification file in detail. We pay particular attention to the types and operations sections since they comprise the bulk of the work necessary to define an interface to MIG.

8.2 Subsystem Identifier

Each client and server program with related operations is known as a subsystem and must have its own identifier. The syntax to identify the subsystem is

`subsystem system-name message-id-base;`

The *system-name* is an ASCII name designating the subsystem. This name prefixes all of the generated files and is the prefix for the overall server function as well. This name is arbitrary and is user defined. However, the convention is that the subsystem name is the same name as the specification file. Thus in the Time Server example presented earlier, `time.defs` would have a *system-name* of *time* in order to generate `time.h`, `timeUser.c`, `timeServer.c`, and the server function **time_server**. Users should be aware of any limitations (such as filename length) the filesystem may have on their particular system and choose the identifier accordingly.

The *message-id-base* supplies the initial value MIG uses in the *msg_id* field in the header of IPC messages. The server code that MIG generates uses this field as an index to determine which operation a client requested. The first operation specified in the definitions file uses the base integer. Each subsequent operation is numbered sequentially from this base. The implementor selects this integer arbitrarily. One caveat exists relating to this value. MIG implicitly uses *msg_id* values that are incremented by 100 over the original when sending a reply back to a client. If your interface contains more than 100 different functions, the application should be broken into multiple subsystems. In addition, if a server handles multiple interfaces, the identifiers for those interfaces should be disjoint.

Therefore for our Time Server example we declare the subsystem as

`subsystem time 400;`

This identification causes the files shown earlier to be generated and begins with an initial *msg_id* base of 400.

8.3   Type Specifications

MIG does not know about the data types that exist in the C language. Furthermore, it does not know about any complex data types constructed in the user program. The type specifications define the data types that will be used as parameters to calls that the user interface module exports. MIG supports several kinds of type declarations, including

- **Simple types:** a type declaration primitive

- **Structured types:** arrays, structures, and pointers

- **Polymorphic types:** C language unions.

For all complex types defined in the specification file, MIG assumes that the programmer compatibly declares these types in the client and server programs. This assumption is a weakness of MIG, and the programmer should be careful with declarations.

For convenience, Mach supplies two files that contain MIG definitions for the most commonly used types for C programs and Mach programs. By using the `#include` mechanism, you can import type definitions from another file into the specification file. This mechanism is similar to including a header file into a C program. These two files define the basic C and Mach types respectively:

```
#include <mach/std_types.defs>
#include <mach/mach_types.defs>
```

The `std_types.defs` file declares type specifications for standard C types such as `char`, `short`, and `int`. The `mach_types.defs` file declares Mach-related types such as `task_t`, `thread_t` and `vm_offset_t`, and so on.

For our Time Server example, the `port_t` definition comes from the `std_types.defs` file.

8.3.1 Simple Types

The simple type declaration has the following syntax:

`type typename = typedesc;`

The **typename** is any user-specified type, such as *typedefs*, a programmer may declare in the program. The **typedesc** may be

- A single IPC type primitive (e.g., MSG_TYPE_INTEGER_32, MSG_TYPE_CHAR, or MSG_TYPE_PORT). Please refer to Chapter 3 for a complete list of primitives.

- A previously declared **typename**.

- A compound expression consisting of an IPC type primitive followed by a size, in bits, and, optionally, a deallocation flag, all separated by commas and enclosed in parentheses. For example,

$$(\text{MSG\_TYPE\_STRING, 8*26, dealloc})[1]$$

In this example, the string contains 26 8-bit bytes that would automatically be deallocated when communication is complete. We do not recommend that you specify the deallocation flag as part of the type declaration. If deallocation is desired, it is better to specify deallocation as part of the parameter. See Section 8.5 for more details.

All IPC type primitives, with two exceptions, have an implicit size and are suitable as simple type definitions. For example, a MSG_TYPE_INTEGER_16 is always 16 bits long. However, MSG_TYPE_STRING and MSG_TYPE_REAL are variable sized and require a compound expression to specify how big they are.

Examples of simple type declarations include

```
type int = MSG_TYPE_INTEGER_32;
type status_t = int;
type time_string = ( MSG_TYPE_STRING, 8*26 );
type tmp_string = ( MSG_TYPE_STRING, 8*80, dealloc );
```

---

[1]Throughout this chapter we may insert spaces in examples for readability. MIG does not have any such spacing requirements.

The first example illustrates the most basic use of a type declaration and appears in the `<mach/std_types.defs>`, described earlier. The second example demonstrates how to use a previously defined type in a new declaration. The remaining examples show more complicated uses. The *time_string* example shows how we might declare the string that the Time Server returns. The *tmp_string* shows the use of the deallocation flag. Notice that since these last two definitions contain sizes, they must be parenthesized.

8.3.2   Complex Types

MIG supports complex types describing structures, arrays, and pointers. Arrays and structures have the following syntax:

```
type typename = array [ num_elem ] of type-desc;
type typename = struct [ num_elem ] of type-desc;
```

These forms declare an array or structure, respectively, of the specified size of the specified type. The `num_elem` indicates the number of elements and may either be an integer constant or an expression. The `type-desc` describes the type of the components of the array or structure. This type may either be an IPC primitive type, a simple type described in the previous section, or it may be an array or struct type. MIG allows complex type declarations to be recursive.

The difference between using the *array* construct versus the *struct* construct is how they are treated as arguments. An array must correspond to a C language array. The generated MIG code will treat its use as an array and assume it is passed by reference. Special C code is generated for array assignments. On the other hand, MIG assumes that struts are passed by value, and they are treated as C structures in assignments. Unfortunately MIG does not have the capability to support varying fields in C structures. This missing capability is a major problem with MIG. To declare a C structure, you must use the overall size of the structure for its type definition, which you must figure out by hand by totalling the sizes of the different fields in the structure. Portability issues may also be a factor when using structs. All data associated with arrays and structures is passed in-line in the message.

```
type typename = array [ * :  maxsize ] of type-desc;
```

This third form declares an array with a variable length. The maximum size of the array must be specified in `maxsize`. When using this form, MIG

automatically generates an additional parameter in a procedure's arguments
that specifies how much of the array is actually used on each invocation of
the procedure.

Some examples of structures and arrays follow:

```
type int_array = array [ 5 ] of MSG_TYPE_INTEGER_32;
type char_array = array [ * : 4096 ] of char;
type big_info = struct [ 10*5 ] of int;
type some_str = struct [ 10 ] of array [ 50 ] of MSG_TYPE_CHAR;
```

The first example, *int_array*, declares an array of five integers. The second example, *char_array*, declares an array of characters that can be up to
4096 characters long. When a program invokes a routine that uses *char_array*
as an argument, the following argument to that routine would specify a count
of how much of the array is used. The third example, *big_info*, shows how
to declare a structure that contains the equivalent of 50 integers. The last
example, *some_str*, demonstrates that complex types may be recursive.

Suppose you have a large array of data that you would rather not pass
within the body of the message, as the **array** and **struct** types do. The use
of **pointer** types cause MIG to construct messages using out-of-line data.
(Please refer to Section 7.1 for a discussion of out-of-line data.) To define
a pointer type, precede the normal type declaration with the "ˆ" character.
Any simple type, array, or structure may be declared as a pointer type.
However, keep in mind that the data will be passed out of line; therefore
pointers are best used with large amounts of data or variable sizes. For small
amounts of data, it is more efficient to simply pass the data in-line. When
using **pointers** with **arrays** or **structs**, the *size* field may be left blank or
may be a "*". Both styles indicate that the array or structure is of variable
size, and MIG generates an additional parameter immediately following to
contain the size. Some examples of pointer types are

```
type int_ptr = ^ MSG_TYPE_INTEGER_32;
type some_ptr = ^ array [ 10000 ] of int;
type large_char_array = ^ array [] of MSG_TYPE_BYTE;
```

In the first example, *int_ptr* represents a pointer to an integer. An address to this integer would be passed in the message and the contents would
be passed out of line. Since the size of an integer is small, this use of a
pointer construct should be avoided. The second example, *some_ptr*, illustrates how to declare a pointer to a large integer array. The final example,

large_char_array, shows how to declare a variable-sized array passed out
of line. Again, similar to the previous *char_array* example, MIG generates
an additional argument in the interface for the specification of the actual
length of the array.

Certain tradeoffs exist between using in-line, variable-length data and
out-of-line, variable-length data. The programmer needs to anticipate the
typical usage of the application. If the maximum size is less than a page,
efficiency indicates using the in-line form. If the maximum size anticipated is
greater than a page, then a decision based on usage should be made. When
the maximum size is large, but the expected "normal" size will be small
(under a page), then in-line may be the appropriate choice. The developer
must be aware of the efficiency tradeoffs in that gray area and make a decision.

8.3.3   Polymorphic Types

Sometimes programs need a single argument to represent several different
types of data. Polymorphic types handle this case. The syntax for declaring
a polymorphic type is

```
type typename = polymorphic;
```

The aforementioned scenario is similar in concept to C language union
declarations. The nature of the data is determined at run time, and the user
passes the type information as an auxiliary argument to the interface. If an
argument is defined as both polymorphic and variable sized, as described
earlier, the auxiliary type argument precedes the auxiliary count argument.
To use a polymorphic type, simply declare a type as such:

```
type format_t = polymorphic;

simpleroutine send_format( server : port_t;
                           format : format_t );
```

The preceding example illustrates how to use a polymorphic type as an
argument in an interface, **send_format()**. The details of declaring an interface routine are described in Section 8.5. Suffice it to say that **send_format**
expects a *server* port and a *format* as arguments. Suppose the server program expected either a character or an integer as the format. By declaring
format as a polymorphic type, we have to specify its type when **send_format**
is invoked in the client:

```
port_t          server;
kern_return_t ret;

ret = send_format(server, 'x', MSG_TYPE_CHAR);
ret = send_format(server, 42, MSG_TYPE_INTEGER_32);
```

MIG automatically added the third argument, allowing the client to specify the type of the polymorphic second argument. When the client sends a character as the *format* argument, it also sends the MSG_TYPE_CHAR type. Likewise, when it sends an integer as the *format*, the type specified must be MSG_TYPE_INTEGER_32. On the server side, the subroutine that the programmer provides would expect three arguments. The type information is passed to the server so it can properly interpret the *format* argument.

8.3.4   Translation Information

Type translation information is a mechanism by which an argument to an interface can be one type on transmission and a different type on receipt. Use of this mechanism is quite rare and infrequent. We discuss translation information in Section 8.7.

8.4   Import Declarations

Import declarations provide a mechanism for the programmer to specify header files that should be included in the C language client and server modules that MIG generates. The import declarations directly translate into #include statements in the appropriate C module. Do not confuse the import declaration with the #include allowed in the MIG specification file described in Section 8.3.

There are three forms of import declarations. Each form takes a filename that identifies the file to be included in the module. This filename must be a C header file (i.e., <file.h> or "file.h"). The three forms are

```
uimport filename;
simport filename;
import filename;
```

The first two forms, **uimport** and **simport**, signify that the named file should only be included in the user module or the server module, respectively.

The third form, *import*, indicates that the named file should be included in both the user and server modules.

The Time Server example requires a header file that contains the C language *typedef* for the *time_data* polymorphic type described earlier. We want this header file, "`time_server.h`", included in both the server and user modules. Some examples of the use of importing are

```
import   "time_server.h";
import   <cthreads.h>;
uimport  "client_defs.h";
```

The first example causes MIG to generate an `#include "time_server.h"` statement in our files `timeUser.c` and `timeServer.c`. The second example shows a similar import declaration, but using the `<cthreads.h>` file from `/usr/include`. The third example illustrates including a file in only one of the generated modules. Here, `client_defs.h` would only be included in the user module.

8.5   Operation Descriptions

An operation description is a declaration of a subroutine for which MIG creates a stub. It contains the name and all arguments to that subroutine. For every operation declared, MIG creates a function in the client to send a message. For the server, MIG generates a stub that unpacks the message and calls the programmer-provided server code to process the contents of the message. Five different operation types exist, each performing the task differently:

1. `simpleroutine`

2. `routine`

3. `simpleprocedure`

4. `procedure`

5. `function`

In addition to these five types, the keyword `skip` is allowed for operations. This keyword may be used in place of an operation description, and a hole in the message ID numbering results. Use of `skip` allows an implementor

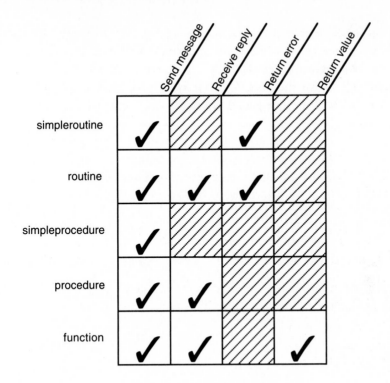

Figure 8.5: MIG Operations

to maintain backward compatibility when interfaces become obsolete. The *msg_id* specified in the **subsystem** declaration is incremented by one for each interface specified. When an interface is removed, the *msg_id* values will adjust unless the **skip** directive appears in the specification file in place of the removed interface.

Figure 8.5 illustrates the differences between the five operations. The **simpleroutine** operation implements asynchronous communication with the server. This operation sends a message to the server but does not expect a reply. The operation returns the value from the **msg_send()** system call.

The **routine** operation implements basic synchronous message passing, as described in the client portion of the Time Server example presented in Chapter 3, using the **msg_rpc()** system call. This operation sends a message to the server and waits for a reply message from the server. Again, the operation returns the value from the system call. We use the **routine** operation to implement the version of the Time Server presented in this chapter.

The `simpleprocedure` and `procedure` operations are very similar to the two `routine` operations. The only difference is that the two procedure operations do not return an error code.

The `function` operation also does not return an error code. This operation returns a value from the server function. This value can be any scalar or structure type.

The syntax for each of the operations is similar. Each takes a name of the subroutine the client program calls and a parameter list describing the arguments to the subroutine. In the case of the `function` operation, a type indicating what kind of value will be returned is also specified. The syntax is

```
operation-type op-name ( parameter-list );
function op-name ( parameter-list ) :  func-type;
```

Each parameter in `parameter-list` may contain an optional specification and an optional deallocation flag. The syntax of the parameters is

```
[specification] var-name :  type [,dealloc-flag ]
```

The optional `specification` may be one of the following:

`in:` The argument is sent to the server.

`out:` The argument is "filled in" by the server.

`inout:` The variable contains a value sent to the server, and the server returns a value in this variable.

`RequestPort:` The port via which the message is sent to the server.

`ReplyPort:` The port to which the server sends replies.

`WaitTime:` The variable specifies a timeout for the IPC call.

`MsgType:` The variable specifies the message type to be used for the message.

The parameter list declarations have the following default settings:

- The first unspecified parameter is assumed to be the `RequestPort` unless the `RequestPort` is already specified.

- If no `ReplyPort` is specified, MIG allocates its own internal reply port to be used for the reply message (if a reply is expected).

- All other unspecified parameters are assumed to be in.

- If no WaitTime is specified, no timeout is used.

- If no MsgType is specified, the message type used is MSG_TYPE_NORMAL and, if **msg_rpc** is used, the type also has MSG_TYPE_RPC set.

All of the possibilities available for the parameter list make that portion of the operation description seem more complicated than it really is. Let us look at a few examples of operation declarations, starting with the Time Server. Given the simple functionality of the Time Server, we only need one interface definition. This operation, **get_time**, requires a reply from the server, and we want any error code indications returned. As such, we declare **get_time** as a routine.

```
routine get_time (
            server_port : port_t;          /* Server port     */
            format      : int;             /* Format to send  */
    out     time        : time_data  );    /* Time from server */
```

In this example, the first argument, *server_port* (obtained from a look-up to the netmsgserver), contains the port to communicate with the server. *Server_port* is implicitly the RequestPort since it is the first argument without an explicit specification. The second argument, *format*, indicates whether we want time returned as an integer or string. The third argument, *time*, as an out parameter, will contain the output from the server. Time is declared to be type *time_data* since it may return different types of values based on format.

Our example actually declares two interfaces for illustrative purposes. The **get_time_num()** returns the time in numeric format, and **get_time_str()** returns the time in string format.

```
routine get_time_num (
            server_port : port_t;
    out     time        : time_num );

routine get_time_str(
            server_port : port_t;
    out     time        : time_str );
```

Some examples to illustrate the use of other declarations follow. All of the examples implicitly pass the RequestPort, *server_port*, as the first argument.

```
/*
 * A function to return the numeric equivalent of a
 * string in the given base.
 */
function string_to_number (
               server_port : port_t;
               base        : int;
               intstr      : string ) : int;
```

This function returns an integer translated from the given string. The *base* parameter indicates to use to convert the string parameter, *intstr*. Since neither *base* nor *intstr* have an explicit specification, both are treated as in arguments.

```
/*
 * A function that notifies the server that this client is
 * exiting with the given code.  Notice the client does not
 * care about the return value of the message, by virtue of
 * using simpleprocedure.
 */
simpleprocedure client_exit (
               server_port : port_t;
               exit_code   : int     );
/*
 * A function that notifies the server that this client is
 * exiting with the given code.  This function specifies
 * a timeout and cares about the return value.
 */
simpleroutine client_exit2 (
               server_port : port_t;
   WaitTime    timout_val  : int;
               exit_code   : int     );
```

These two examples show how a client may notify a server it is exiting with a particular return code. Since both examples do not expect a reply message from the server, they use the "simple" operations. The first exit example, **client_exit()**, illustrates a basic notification scheme. The client simply sends an exit code to the server. By declaring **client_exit** as a `simpleprocedure`, the client does not expect any return value from sending the message. The second exit example, **client_exit2()**, demonstrates a slightly more robust mechanism. Declaring the function as a `simpleroutine` allows the client to determine whether the send was successful. Since the client is interested in the return value from the send, we do not want the client waiting indefinitely just to send the exit code. In this example, therefore, we specify a timeout with the `WaitTime` specification. The *wait_time* argument is the value that will be used as the timeout argument for the **msg_send** call. See Chapter 3 for a full description of using the timeout value.

Since the `simpleprocedure`, `procedure`, and `function` operations do not return error codes, they have another mechanism for handling errors. The user can define an error-handling function using the `error` option, described in Section 8.6.

8.6   Option Declarations

Several option declarations exist to allow global defaults to be defined. When an option appears in a MIG definition file, all subsequent operations are affected until the end of the file or until the option is explicitly turned off. Most of these options are special purpose and have defaults. Typically, most interfaces do not need to change these options.

This list of available options is as follows:

1. `WaitTime, NoWaittime`: Set a reply timeout.

2. `MsgType`: Set the message type.

3. `ServerPrefix`: Specify interface function name prefix for server.

4. `UserPrefix`: Specify interface function name prefix for client.

5. `error`: Designate an error-handling function.

The first option, `WaitTime`, specifies the maximum timeout the client will wait for a reply from the server. For instance, suppose an application contains several operations that all require a timeout of 1000 milliseconds. Rather than specify a parameter for each of those routines, using the `WaitTime` option allows a general timeout to be declared:

```
WaitTime 1000 ;
NoWaitTime ;
```

The first example will specify a timeout of 1000 milliseconds for all operation declarations following that statement. The second use, `NoWaitTime`, demonstrates how to turn off the global option. `NoWaitTime` is the default for this option.

The next option that can also be passed as an argument, `MsgType`, was described briefly earlier. Specifying this option changes the message type for all subsequent operations. The type specified must be one of the values from `<msg_type.h>`. This option is correctly set up by default, and changing its value is discouraged. The default value is `MSG_TYPE_NORMAL`. However, should the application require this option, here is how to use it:

```
MsgType MSG_TYPE_ENCRYPTED ;
MsgType MSG_TYPE_NORMAL ;
```

The first example sets the message types for encryption. The second example resets the `MsgType` option.

In general, operations (such as **get_time**) are called by that name in the client. The server, upon receiving that message, will call its own **get_time** function. Both the client and server use the same name for the function, but the functions do very different things. On the client side, the function will construct and send the message. On the server side, the function will perform the time acquisition. There may be times when it is necessary for the generated MIG functions to have different names in the client and server. This distinction may be necessary when a server can be its own client as well. MIG provides two mechanisms for creating this distinction. A prefix for the server functions can be specified or, conversely, a prefix for the client side can be specified. Only one mechanism is necessary to accomplish the distinction, but they are both provided for completeness. In general, it is suggested that the server side prefix be used since there may be many client programs that call a single server. Therefore only the single server would be affected by the name changes rather than many client programs. For instance, suppose we wanted to distinguish the server side of our **get_time** function:

```
ServerPrefix  Serv_ ;
```

Now the generated server functions call, and expect the server program to provide, a routine named **Serv_get_time()**. However, all client programs would still call **get_time**. For completeness, setting a client side prefix can be done:

```
UserPrefix Client_ ;
```

As you would expect, the client would now invoke the **Client_get_time()** function, but the server would provide **get_time**.

We mentioned earlier that `procedure`, `simpleprocedure`, and `function` do not return an error code from the message calls. The method of designating an error-handling routine is of the form

```
error error_func ;
```

The error function, **error_func()**, in this example would be declared as

```
void error_func(error_code)
kern_return_t error_code;
{
        /*
        * Code to take appropriate action based on error_code.
        */
}
```

If no error function is specified and procedures or a function is used, the default error handler is **MsgError()**. However, given that using the procedures or function circumvents the error returned from the message passing, use this error mechanism (and procedures and functions) with extreme caution.

8.7   Type Translation Information

Information describing translation of type definitions and the possible deallocation of input types (on the server) can be included in a type definition. Optional information further characterizing the declared types may occur after the definition of the type. This information is known as *type translation information.* To understand translating types, consider where a type declared in a MIG file is used by the overall application. There are three places where MIG-defined types map into C language types:

1. On the client side, in the MIG-generated message-passing function

2. On the server side, in the MIG-generated receipt function

3. On the server side, in the user code to perform the request.

Several directives exist in MIG to perform translation and deallocation functions for types:

`CUserType:` The argument will have this type when used on the client side of a message.

270   CHAPTER 8   MACH INTERFACE GENERATOR (MIG)

`CServerType`: The argument will have this type when used by the MIG server code.

`CType`: Both the client and server MIG code will use this type.

`InTran`: Specifies a function that the server code uses to translate the type upon receipt.

`OutTran`: Specifies a function that the server uses to translate the type before returning.

`Destructor`: Specifies a server function to deallocate space used by its input argument.

MIG supports types that change during transmission between the client and server modules. The user specifies what types are allowed, what type is used on the client end, and what is expected on the server end.

```
type my_poly_type = MSG_TYPE_INTEGER_32 | MSG_TYPE_PORT
        CUserType: int
        CServerType: port_t;

type my_int = int
        CUserType : u_long
        CServerType : svr_int;
```

The first example's declaration states that *my_poly_type* will be either of MSG_TYPE_INTEGER_32 type or a MSG_TYPE_PORT type. The `CUserType` and `CServerType` specify that a *my_poly_type* argument will be an integer on the client side and a port on the server side, respectively. The second example says that *myint* is an integer. On the client it is an unsigned long integer, and on the server it is some other defined integer type. The `CType` option specifies the type used on both the client and server:

```
type string = (MSG_TYPE_STRING, 8*80, dealloc)
        CType = line_t;
```

In this example both the client and server will use `string` as a *line_t*.

The `InTran` and `OutTran` functions translate types on the incoming and outgoing sides on the server, respectively. The syntax states the output type of the function, the function name, and the type of an argument to that function.

```
type child_info = struct [ 10*5 ] of int
        InTran : info_t  Child2Info(child_info)
        OutTran: child_info Info2Child(info_t);
```

In this example, the client code would send an argument of type *child_info* in its message. The type that the server code sees is *info_t*. When the message arrives on the server, the **Child2Info()** function is called to convert from the *child_info* type to the *info_t* type. Similarly, when the reply is leaving the server, the **Info2Child()** function is called to convert back, from the *info_t* type to a *child_info* type. The translation functions, **Child2Info()** and **Info2Child()**, automatically map the type appropriately. The MIG code on the server side calls those mapping functions, even though the code must be supplied by the programmer's server program. The programmer must also declare the function definitions for the aforementioned translation functions within the MIG file:

```
info_t Child2Info(ch)
        child_info ch;


child_info Info2Child(info)
        info_t info;
```

The Destructor function can be used to deallocate all or part of the translated variables. The deallocation occurs before the MIG code sends the reply back to the client. As such, only input arguments should be deallocated. Output arguments should not be deallocated before the reply is sent since they are needed for the reply. Alternately, a Destructor function may specify a deallocation routine to release memory after an out-of-line message was received.

```
type child_info = struct [ 10*5 ] of int
        InTran : info_t  Child2Info(child_info)
        OutTran: child_info Info2Child(info_t)
        Destructor: DeallocInfo(info_t);
```

Using the preceding type declaration, the addition of the Destructor directive indicates to deallocate the *info_t* input parameter after the return from the server procedure. Similar to the translation directives, the MIG code calls the deallocation function, **DeallocInfo()**, which the implementor provides. The function definitions must be declared:

```
void DeallocInfo(info)
        info_t info;
```

8.8   Compiling a Specification File

MIG is a wrapper program that calls two other programs to process the file. First MIG calls `cpp` to process comments and preprocessor macros. Then MIG passes the output from the preprocessor to `migcom`, which generates the C files. MIG understands several command line options to control the processing. Any options it does not understand are passed on to `cpp`. The options MIG recognizes are as follows:

`-r`, `-R`: r indicates that MIG will use **msg_rpc**. R tells MIG to use **msg_send** and **msg_receive** pairs. The default is `r`.

`-q`, `-Q`: q suppresses the printing of warning statements. Q causes warnings to be printed. The default is Q.

`-v`, `-V`: r indicates that verbose mode, types, and routines are printed out as they are processed. V indicates silent mode. The default is V.

`-s`, `-S`: s causes a symbol table to be generated in the server module. The `<mig_error.h>` file contains a layout of the symbol table of *mig_symtab_t*. S suppresses the symbol table. The default is S.

`-i`: This flag causes MIG to generate a different user module for each interface defined. This option is useful for building a library. The name given to each file is *routine_name*.c.

`-header` *file* : The flag causes the header file to be named *file*.

`-user` *file* : The flag causes the user module to be named *file*.

`-server` *file* : The flag causes the server module to be named *file*.

To generate the modules, give the desired options and the name of the specification file. For example, to run MIG on our example program,

```
mig -v time.defs
```

8.9   Complete Example

This section contains the complete Time Server example. There are four files comprising the example.

1. MIG definitions file (`time.defs`)

2. Header file (`time_defs.h`)

3. Client program (`dotime.c`)

4. Server program (`timemaster.c`).

The three files that MIG generates, `time.h`, `timeUser.c`, and `timeServer.c`, are reproduced in Appendix A. Since these are generated files, there are no comments in them.

8.9.1 MIG Definitions File

```
/*
 * time.defs.  The MIG specification for the Time Server example.
 */

/*
 * Subsystem definition
 */
subsystem time 400;

/*
 * Type declarations.  First include a standard types file
 * and then declare those specific to this program.
 */
#include <mach/std_types.defs>
#include <mach/mach_types.defs>

type time_str = (MSG_TYPE_STRING, 8*26);
type time_num = MSG_TYPE_INTEGER_32;

/*
 * Import declarations.  These will be #included into the
 * generated files
 */
import "time_defs.h";

/*
 * Operation Descriptions
 *
 * Declare one interface to get the time numerically and one
 * interface to get the time as a string.  Both have the time
```

```
 * returned from the server, and, as such, declare 'time' as
 * an 'out' parameter.
 */
routine get_time_num      (        server_port : port_t;
                  out              time        : time_num );

routine get_time_str      (        server_port : port_t;
                  out              time        : time_str );
```

8.9.2   Header File

```
/*
 * time_defs.h
 *
 * Constants for the server and client programs.
 */

#include <stdio.h>
#include <mach_error.h>
#include <mach/mig_errors.h>

/*
 * String the server port is registered under
 */
#define MIG_TS  "Mig-timeserver"

/*
 * The time formats supported
 */
#define TS_NUMERIC     0
#define TS_STRING      1

/*
 * Data representations
 */
typedef char time_str[26];
typedef int time_num;
```

8.9.3   Client Program

```
/*
 * dotime.c: Client program
```

```
 */

#include "time_defs.h"
#include <mach.h>
#include <servers/netname.h>
#include <mach/port.h>
#include <sys/time.h>

port_name_t server_port;

main(argc, argv)
int argc;
char **argv;
{
        int format;
        kern_return_t ret;
        time_num time_num;
        time_str time_str;

        /*
         * Format of 0 returns numeric time.
         * Format of 1 returns string time.
         */
        if (argc != 2) {
                printf("usage: %s format\n",argv[0]);
                exit(1);
        }

        format = atoi(argv[1]);
        if (format != TS_NUMERIC && format != TS_STRING) {
                printf("%s: illegal format %d\n",argv[0], format);
                exit(1);
        }

        /*
         * Look up the server port using the MIG_TS name.
         * If the lookup fails, the server
         * is not running anywhere on the local network and
         * we will exit.
         */
        ret = netname_look_up(name_server_port, "*",
                              MIG_TS, &server_port);
        if (ret != NETNAME_SUCCESS) {
                mach_error("netname lookup:", ret);
```

```
              exit(1);
      }


      /*
       * Call server to get the time:
       *  Send in the proper type based on format.
       */
      if (format == TS_NUMERIC) {
              ret = get_time_num(server_port, &time_num);
              if (ret != KERN_SUCCESS) {
                      mach_error("get_time_num:",ret);
                      exit(2);
              }
              printf("Time is %d\n",time_num);
      } else {
              ret = get_time_str(server_port, &time_str, &format);
              if (ret != KERN_SUCCESS) {
                      mach_error("get_time_str:",ret);
                      exit(2);
              }
              printf("Time is %s\n",time_str);
      }
}
```

8.9.4   Server Program

```
/*
 * timemaster.c: Server program
 */

#include "time_defs.h"
#include <mach.h>
#include <servers/netname.h>
#include <mach/message.h>
#include <mach/port.h>
#include <sys/time.h>


port_name_t server_port;

/*
 * The server needs to declare a dummy message that will accommodate
 * all types of interfaces it serves.  This message is needed in
 * the msg_send and msg_receive calls.
 */
```

```
typedef char max_time[1024];      /* Maximum message size */

typedef struct dummy_msg {
        msg_header_t    hdr;
        msg_type_t      type;
        max_time        time;
} dummy_msg;


/*
 * The main function simply calls the setup function to
 * perform all the initialization.  Then the server will
 * call 'process,' which does all the work.
 */
main()
{
        setup();
        process();
}


/*
 * Initialization.  This function allocates the server's
 * listening port and also registers the port with the
 * netmsgserver.
 */
setup()
{
        kern_return_t    status;

        /*
         * First allocate the new port.
         */
        status = port_allocate(task_self(), &server_port);
        if (status != KERN_SUCCESS) {
                mach_error("port_allocate:",status);
                exit(1);
        }

        /*
         * Now check in the name.  The local header file
         * contains the definition of MIG_TS, which is
         * the ASCII name both the client and server will use.
         */
        status = netname_check_in(name_server_port, MIG_TS,
```

```
                                task_self(), server_port);
        if (status != NETNAME_SUCCESS) {
                mach_error("netname_check_in:",status);
                exit(1);
        }
}


/*
 * Process requests.  This function is an infinite loop that waits
 * for messages and then processes them.
 */
process()
{
        dummy_msg       req_msg;
        dummy_msg       reply_msg;
        msg_return_t    status;

        while(1) {
                /*
                 * Wait for an incoming message.
                 */
                req_msg.hdr.msg_local_port = server_port;
                req_msg.hdr.msg_size = sizeof(dummy_msg);
                status = msg_receive(&req_msg.hdr,
                                        MSG_OPTION_NONE,
                                        0);
                if (status != RCV_SUCCESS) {
                        mach_error("msg_receive:",status);
                        continue;
                }


                /*
                 * Now feed the message into the server
                 */
                (void) time_server(&req_msg, &reply_msg);

                /*
                 * All done, now send the reply
                 */
                status = msg_send(&reply_msg,
                            MSG_OPTION_NONE,
                            0);
                if (status != SEND_SUCCESS) {
```

```
                                mach_error("msg_send:",status);
                                continue;
                        }
                }
}


/*
 * Function to get the time numerically.  It is called from the
 * time_server function generated by MIG in timeServer.c.
 */
kern_return_t
get_time_num(server, time)
port_t server;
time_num *time;
{
        struct timeval timeofday;

        gettimeofday(&timeofday, 0);
        *time = timeofday.tv_sec;
        return(KERN_SUCCESS);
}


/*
 * Function to get the time as a string.  It is called from the
 * time_server function generated by MIG in timeServer.c.
 */
kern_return_t
get_time_str(server, time)
port_t server;
time_str *time;
{
        struct timeval timeofday;

        gettimeofday(&timeofday, 0);
        strcpy(time, ctime(&timeofday.tv_sec));
        return(KERN_SUCCESS);
}
```

Chapter 9

External Memory Management

9.1 Introduction

Mach provides the unique ability for an application programmer to control virtual memory paging operations traditionally reserved for the operating system. The user can create a *pager* that controls the use of memory within portions of a task's address space. A pager can allow memory to be fully shared for reading and writing between completely unrelated tasks. A pager may even coordinate the use of memory across multiple machines, providing shared virtual memory across a network. The control of paging operations from a user-level task is called *external memory management* (EMM).

A pager assumes responsibility for the mechanics of page-in and page-out operations over a memory region. A page-in operation takes place when a kernel detects a task's attempt to use data residing on a virtual page not currently in memory, a *page fault* (see Section 4.2). Mach forwards the page-in request to the pager responsible for the requested page. The pager fetches the page's data—for instance, from a disk drive. The pager returns the new page of data to the requesting kernel, which in turn inserts the page into the faulting task's address space and resumes executing the task. Pages supplied by a pager to a kernel can be shared among unrelated tasks.

Similarly, a page-out operation takes place when a kernel evicts a *dirty* page from memory. If the page's contents have been modified since its last

281

282   CHAPTER 9   EXTERNAL MEMORY MANAGEMENT

page-in, the page is dirty and its data must be saved in case of future use.
The kernel sends the dirty page to the pager responsible for it. The pager
implements the details of saving the page's contents.

Ordinarily a programmer need never be concerned with managing a task's
address space at the page-in and page-out level of detail. In this regard, Mach
resembles a more traditional operating system, such as UNIX, handling page-
ins and page-outs as well as paging policy invisibly to the user. Mach has
its own *internal* pagers[1] to handle ordinary page-in and page-out requests.
However, unlike UNIX, Mach also permits user-level (also known as *external*)
pagers to manage memory regions. Internal pagers are built into Mach;
external pagers are provided by user-level programs. A task's address space
may have any number of internal or external pagers managing separate pieces
of it.

Mach supports external pagers for several reasons. By providing general
interfaces available to the application programmer, Mach avoids the need to
provide additional, special-purpose memory sharing or paging control features. The user can control memory sharing and paging operations directly.
Main memory may be used as a cache for user-level data objects, such as
databases and files. Rather than force an application to manage static caches
of the object's contents, the entire object can be made available as a range
of pages. The kernel then manages the problem of obtaining the data when
the pages are accessed and saving it when the pages are no longer used.
Examples of uses of external pagers include the following:

File servers: Files may be represented as memory-mapped objects.

Databases: Memory manipulations can be used to construct transactions
    or to map a database into memory.

Hardware devices: Disk drives, graphics buffers, and other devices can
    appear as an area of memory.

Shared memory: A pager can allow memory to be shared fully between
    unrelated tasks on the same machine.

Distributed shared memory: With the aid of an external pager, memory
    may be shared fully across a network of machines.

---

[1]The *default* and *vnode* pagers.

You may recall from Chapter 4 that the basic virtual memory interfaces limit full read/write sharing of memory to tasks related by **fork()** or **task_create** and hence confined to the same machine. In contrast, another feature of the external memory management interfaces allows unrestricted memory sharing.

Mach retains control over *paging policy*, which refers to the rules that guide a kernel when deciding how much physical memory to allocate among competing tasks; when that memory should be reclaimed from one task for use by others; and which pages to reclaim. For example, when selecting pages to reclaim, a kernel's paging policy usually prefers pages from idle tasks over pages from active tasks. Pagers do not participate in policy decisions.

The fundamental abstractions that a pager manipulates are *memory objects* and *pages*. Pages were described in Chapter 4. A memory object contains a range of pages whose properties are controlled by a single pager. A client program can arrange for some or all of a memory object's pages to appear in its address space at arbitrary locations. We call this arrangement *mapping*, or *backing*, a portion of an address space with a memory object. A memory object may represent a hardware device or a software construct, as illustrated in the previous examples.

Separate client tasks running on the same machine and mapping the same memory object physically share that object's pages in memory, although the pages may appear at different virtual addresses in the tasks' address spaces. Unlike clients, which know a page by its virtual address, a pager knows a page by its offset within its memory object. All manipulations by a pager use page offsets, which remain unique even when clients have pages mapped at different virtual addresses. Thus a memory object has its own *offset space* containing its pages. Consider Fig. 9.1. The memory object has two pages, starting at offset 0x1000, mapped into task A, starting at address 0x20000. Similarly, the two memory object pages starting at address 0x2000 are mapped into task B at offset 0x3E000. Moreover, the page at offset 0x2000 in the memory object is shared fully between tasks A and B. Modifications by either task will be visible to the other. The pager managing the memory object refers to the shared page by its offset, 0x2000, which remains unique even though the page has different virtual addresses in tasks A and B. Throughout this chapter, when referring to a page's offset we mean its offset within its memory object and not its virtual address in a task's address space.

In Fig. 9.1, one task's modifications to the shared page's data are visible immediately to the other task sharing the page. Later in this chapter we will

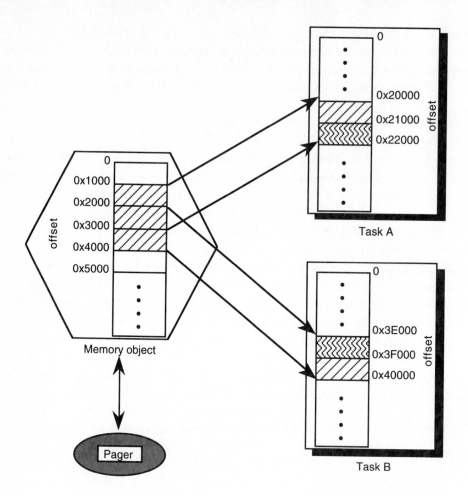

Figure 9.1: Object Offsets versus Task Addresses

consider the problem of sharing memory objects between separate machines (Section 9.14). This facility is sometimes called *distributed shared memory.*

The external memory management interfaces are completely integrated with the virtual memory and interprocess communication facilities. A pager benefits from the same copy-on-write and lazy evaluation techniques under-lying the virtual memory system. From the standpoint of an application, a memory object is represented by a port. Thus Mach's transparent IPC subsystem makes it possible for a pager to run on one machine and manage a memory object on another machine.

To demonstrate the use of the external memory management system calls, we have developed the Secure Memory (SM) pager, which enhances system security. To prevent intruders from gaining unauthorized access to data by stealing or examining secondary storage paging devices (e.g., disk drives), the SM pager encrypts the contents of all memory objects it manages. On a kernel page-out request, the pager encrypts a page before saving it on disk. On a page-in request, the pager reads the page from disk, decrypts it, and then forwards it to the requesting kernel. An SM pager memory object may be *persistent*, meaning that the object outlasts the client that created it and continues to exist after the host is rebooted. A persistent SM memory object remains available until it is explicitly destroyed by a client's request. A memory object managed by SM may be shared between machines.

The demonstration consists of two programs. The SM pager, called sm_pager, creates and manages secure memory objects. The client, named demo_sm, illustrates the use of a secure memory object. The demo_sm program may be invoked in several ways to demonstrate various features of Secure Memory.

While reading the rest of this chapter, you should consult Appendix B, which contains the complete source code for the client and pager programs. As we discuss functions within the programs, you should follow along in the Appendix. We have only sparingly included fragments of the source code in this chapter. We generally do not include portions of the two programs that are self-explanatory or use features already demonstrated elsewhere in this book. We also omit much of the error-checking code and even definitions of otherwise obvious constants for the sake of brevity. You may also wish to refer to other chapters of this text, as the demonstration SM programs draw liberally on many Mach features.

9.2   Overview of Relationships

The external memory management subsystem may initially seem difficult to understand for two reasons. First, three parties interact with each other: a client program, a kernel, and an external pager. The client program is both client to the kernel on its machine and to the pager managing a portion of its address space. Second, unlike other Mach services, nearly all of the external memory management interfaces are asynchronous. A party using one of these asynchronous interfaces does not block during the requested operation. A response to the operation, if any, occurs as a completely separate operation. In fact, there may be multiple responses. This asynchrony can be confusing but provides flexibility and concurrency. Asynchronous operations

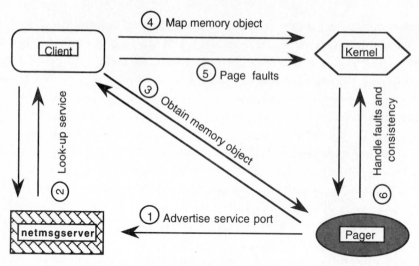

Figure 9.2: Parties to External Memory Management

are limited to the interfaces between kernel and pager, and are not visible to client programs.

Consider the high-level view shown in Fig. 9.2 of the relationships among a client, a kernel, and a pager. In the first step, a pager offers a memory object service by advertising it with some external entity, such as the netmsgserver. A client obtains a port for the service from the netmsgserver in step 2. The client then communicates directly with the pager to obtain a memory object (step 3). In the fourth step, the client asks Mach to map all or part of the memory object into the client's address space. The client then causes page faults as it accesses the newly mapped memory (step 5). To construct the mapping of step 4 and resolve the page faults of step 5, in step 6 the kernel and the pager exchange asynchronous messages.

Figure 9.2 is complex, so we will break it into several pieces and analyze one piece at a time. We begin with a client's view of this process and then move on to pagers and their interactions with kernels. We conclude with a discussion of the problems of sharing memory objects between separate machines.

9.3   Client View of EMM

A task cannot distinguish memory managed by the kernel (with its internal pagers) from memory managed by an external pager. In both cases, memory has protection and inheritance restrictions (e.g., VM_PROT_NONE

or VM_INHERIT_NONE), it may be transferred via **vm_read**, **vm_write**, and
vm_copy, and so on. In fact, a task's address space contains memory objects
before the task begins to execute. Its address space is initially constructed
with one memory object representing the program binary and another object
representing dynamically allocated memory. These memory objects may be
managed by internal or external pagers, invisible to the task itself.

A task may explicitly arrange to map portions of its address space from
a memory object. A memory object appears to a client as a port that
represents the actual memory object, in the same way that ports can be
used to represent tasks or threads. We defer discussion of what messages
are sent over the port and what actions are taken by the program listening
on the port. In the next two sections, we describe the process of obtaining
a memory object and using it to map memory into a task's address space.

9.3.1   Obtaining a Memory Object

Because Mach represents a memory object as a port, there are as many ways
of obtaining memory objects as there are of obtaining ports. For instance, a
pager may register a memory object port with the netmsgserver using a well-
known name. A client need only contact the netmsgserver with the agreed-on
name to obtain the port representing the memory object.

However, directly advertising the memory object this way has the limitation that all clients receive the same memory object port and therefore
map the same object. For a few applications, this behavior may be desirable.
For most applications, such as the Secure Memory service, a pager exercises
greater control over what memory object it provides to a client. Instead
of registering a memory object with the netmsgserver, a pager registers a
service request port. A client looks up the service request port and then obtains a memory object by requesting one directly from the pager. Figure 9.3
illustrates this process for the SM pager.

The SM pager follows the model of advertising a service rather than
directly advertising a memory object (step 1 of Fig. 9.3). A client wishing
to obtain an SM memory object first obtains the SM service port from the
netmsgserver (step 2) and then contacts the SM pager directly (step 3). This
level of indirection permits a pager to decide which memory object to provide
to a client. The memory object returned to the client might be private and
created from scratch, or might be reactivated from a region already created
and stored on disk, or even might be shared with another client.

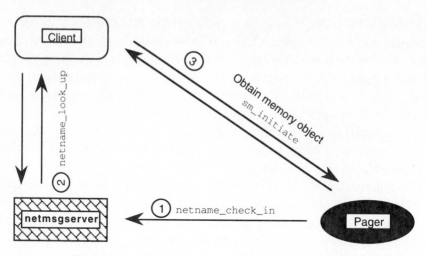

Figure 9.3: Obtaining a Memory Object Port

In the SM example, after obtaining the SM service port from the netmsgserver a client calls **sm_initiate()** to obtain a memory object. The MIG definitions for this operation are as follows (refer to Appendix B for the complete text of this file):

```
type sm_status_t =      int;
type sm_key_t =         int;
type sm_identifier =    array [SM_IDENTIFIER_LENGTH] of char;

routine sm_initiate(
                pager_port:     port_t;
                identifier:     sm_identifier;
                crypt_key:      sm_key_t;
                create:         boolean_t;
        out     response:       sm_status_t;
        out     sm_obj:         memory_object_t);
```

The *pager_port* variable in **sm_initiate()** is the Secure Memory port advertised by the pager. An SM object is identified by an ASCII name, so the client supplies a name in *identifier*. Each object also has its own encryption key (*crypt_key*). For simplicity, the key is implemented as an integer and not as a readable ASCII string. The client also indicates whether the object should be newly created, by setting *create* to TRUE; otherwise the client expects that the object already exists. We will explain how the SM pager handles this request in a later section. The results of the operation are contained in *response*, indicating whether *sm_initiate* succeeded, and *sm_obj*, containing the memory object on success. Our sample client, demo_sm, uses code similar to the following to obtain a memory object. Comments, error checking, and some variable initializations have been omitted for brevity.

```
typedef int      sm_status_t;
#define SM_INIT_GRANTED      1
#define SM_INIT_NO_REGION    2


port_t           sm_pager;
memory_object_t  sm_object;
sm_status_t      response;
kern_return_t    status;

status = netname_look_up(name_server_port, "",
                         "secure_memory", &sm_pager);

status = sm_initiate(sm_pager, "client:memory_region", 631118,
                     TRUE, &response, &sm_object);
```

The demo_sm client locates the SM pager by looking up the port associated with the well-known name, *secure_memory*. In this code fragment, the look-up only involves the local machine's netmsgserver because an empty host name was specified. Using the SM pager port, demo_sm requests the creation of a new SM object by setting the *create* argument to TRUE. The new object is called *client:memory_region* and is encrypted with the key *631118*. If the pager succeeds in creating the requested object, *response* is set to SM_INIT_GRANTED and *sm_object* contains the new memory object. It should not surprise you that the *memory_object_t* typedef used for *sm_object* ultimately becomes a *port_t*. However, it is more convenient to think of the returned entity as a memory object rather than as a port representing a memory object.

9.3.2 Mapping a Memory Object

Once a client task has obtained a memory object, it uses the **vm_map()** system call to obtain access to portions of the memory object (see Fig. 9.4). The Mach kernel performs the necessary bookkeeping to map the memory object into a client's address space. If necessary, the kernel communicates with the memory object's pager to initialize it. We will discuss the pager's responsibilities in Section 9.5. This communication and initialization sequence is invisible to the client. The result is a range of the client's address space mapped from the memory object.

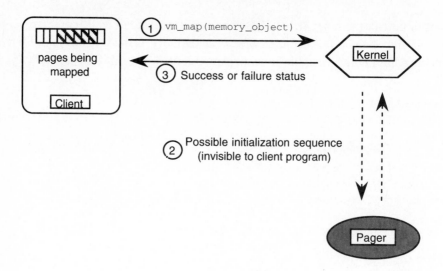

Figure 9.4: Mapping from a Memory Object

You can think of **vm_map** analogously to **vm_allocate**. Whereas **vm_allocate** supplies temporary memory managed by the Mach kernel, **vm_map** supplies memory managed by an external pager. However, unlike **vm_allocate**, clients using **vm_map** on the same memory object obtain shared access to the object's pages. Thus tasks may fully share memory through the **vm_map** interface. The **vm_map** interface is as follows:

```
task_t          target_task;
vm_offset_t     address;        /* in/out */
vm_size_t       size;
vm_offset_t     mask;
boolean_t       anywhere;
memory_object_t memory_object;
vm_offset_t     offset;
boolean_t       copy;
vm_prot_t       cur_protection;
vm_prot_t       max_protection;
vm_inherit_t    inheritance;
kern_return_t   status;

status = vm_map(target_task, &address, size, mask, anywhere,
            memory_object, offset, copy, cur_protection,
            max_protection, inheritance);
```

Argument	Type	Compare With
target_task	*task_t*	**vm_allocate**
address	*vm_offset_t* *	**vm_allocate**
size	*vm_size_t*	**vm_allocate**
mask	*vm_offset_t*	See text
anywhere	*boolean_t*	Similar to **vm_allocate**
memory_object	*memory_object_t*	See text
offset	*vm_offset_t*	See text
copy	*boolean_t*	See text
cur_protection	*vm_prot_t*	**vm_protect**
max_protection	*vm_prot_t*	**vm_protect**
inheritance	*vm_inherit_t*	**vm_inherit**

Table 9.1: **vm_map** Arguments Compared to Other System Calls

```
if (status != KERN_SUCCESS)
        mach_error("vm_map", status);
```

While the sheer number of arguments to **vm_map** (eleven) may appear daunting, in fact they are easy to understand. Most of the arguments behave in the same fashion as arguments to **vm_allocate**, **vm_protect**, or **vm_inherit**. By examining Table 9.1, you will find that **vm_map** uses only four arguments that have not been seen before in other virtual memory system calls.

The *target_task* argument specifies the task whose address space will be affected by **vm_map**. Frequently this argument is **task_self()**, so the memory being mapped appears in the calling task's address space. With another task port, however, **vm_map** can be used to modify the address space of any other task, just like **vm_allocate**.

The *address* argument must be a pointer to a variable of type *vm_offset_t*, in which Mach returns the location of the newly mapped memory within the task's address space. Setting the boolean *anywhere* argument to TRUE causes the kernel to map the memory object into the first sufficiently large portion of the task's address space. With **vm_allocate**, Mach begins the search at the beginning of the task's address space, making initialization of *address* unnecessary. However, with **vm_map**, the kernel starts its search at the

location specified by *address*, so you must initialize *address* before calling
vm_map. Failing to initialize *address* is a common bug. The rules by which
the kernel selects a portion of the address space are modified by the value
of the *mask* argument, discussed later.

When *anywhere* is FALSE, *address* must contain the address at which
the object is to be mapped. If the memory object cannot be mapped at
that address, the kernel returns an error to the calling task. In this respect,
vm_map also resembles **vm_allocate**.

The third argument, *size*, indicates how much memory should be mapped,
in bytes. As with other Mach virtual memory calls, the kernel adjusts *size*
and truncates *address* as needed to specify a memory region consisting of
an integral number of pages. It is worth remembering that you can use the
vm_page_size variable to construct an appropriately aligned request to avoid
depending on the kernel's behavior.

The *mask*, *memory_object*, *offset*, and *copy* arguments to **vm_map** perform functions with no exact counterpart in the earlier virtual memory system calls. The *mask* restricts the kernel's allocation algorithm when the
kernel searches the task's address space for a contiguous region for the new
mapping. (This search happens when *anywhere* is set to TRUE.) Normally
the kernel searches for a page-aligned portion of the task's address space
that is both free and large enough to contain the requested allocation. However, for each bit set in *mask*, the kernel ignores addresses that have the
corresponding bit set. Using *mask* allows an application to specify its own
alignment restriction for the allocated memory. For instance, specifying a
mask of 0x3FFFFF forces memory to be aligned on a four-megabyte boundary.

The *memory_object* argument specifies the object to be mapped into the
affected task's address space. As already noted, in practice a *memory_object*
is a port. The kernel uses this port to contact the external pager responsible for this object, as described in the next section. Using the special-case
value of MEMORY_OBJECT_NULL as the *memory_object* causes the kernel to
allocate zero-filled memory. The kernel then manages the memory itself,
without involving an external pager. In this case, the basic behavior of
vm_map becomes similar to that of **vm_allocate**, with the two provisos
that *anywhere* behaves slightly differently and that **vm_map** also incorporates the functionality of **vm_protect** and **vm_inherit**.

The *offset*, in conjunction with the *size* argument described earlier, indicates which portion of the memory object should be mapped into the
affected task's address space. Recall from Section 9.1 that a memory object
has its own offset space distinct from the address space of any task. The *size*

argument indicates how much memory to map. The *address* argument specifies the destination of that memory within the task's address space. The *offset* indicates the source of that memory within the memory object's offset space.

The *copy* argument is a boolean variable that, when TRUE, means that pages should be mapped copy-on-write from the memory object rather than fully managed by the object's pager. When the target task uses a page, the kernel fetches it from the pager and makes a private copy for the application's use. Changes that the task makes to the page are not sent back to the external pager. Instead, when the task exits the changes are lost. Similarly, changes made by other tasks to pages in the memory object are not visible in the pages appearing in the target task's address space. Once obtained, these private pages are managed by the kernel, without further recourse to the pager that initially supplies them.

Beware that the copy caused by setting *copy* to TRUE occurs when a page is first modified and *not* at the time of the **vm_map** call. For example, consider **vm_copy**. All pages operated on by **vm_copy** are copied by the call itself. Even though lazy evaluation and copy-on-write techniques defer physical page copies until a future time, the contents of the copied memory are guaranteed to be the values existing at the time **vm_copy** was called. In contrast, when using **vm_map** the contents of a page can be changed by some other application until the task modifies the page, thus forcing the kernel's copy-on-write logic to copy the page.

When set to FALSE, the *copy* argument specifies that memory mapped into the target task's address space is managed fully by the memory object's pager. Changes that the task makes to this memory are communicated back to the pager. Changes that other tasks make to the memory object's pages are visible in the target task's address space, if the tasks are on the same machine. When tasks share a memory object between machines, it is not automatically the case that modifications made on one machine are visible to a task on another. (See Section 9.14 for a discussion of this problem.) In most cases, you want the pager to be fully responsible for the memory object, so typically you set *copy* to FALSE when invoking **vm_map**.

The last three arguments, *cur_protection*, *max_protection*, and *inheritance* specify initial virtual memory protection and inheritance values. These values are identical to the values used in **vm_protect** and **vm_inherit**. Unlike the separate **vm_allocate**, **vm_protect**, and **vm_inherit** calls, all of these values can be specified simultaneously as part of a **vm_map** call. If you wish, you can always use **vm_protect** and **vm_inherit** to change the

Error Code	Meaning
KERN_SUCCESS	The **vm_map** call succeeded.
KERN_INVALID_ADDRESS	An impossible *address* was specified when *anywhere* was set to FALSE. The address probably was not page aligned.
KERN_INVALID_ARGUMENT	One or more of the arguments to **vm_map** was illegal.
KERN_NO_SPACE	The address space of the task operated on by **vm_map** did not have sufficient contiguous free memory for the requested allocation. If you set *anywhere* to FALSE and supplied a specific *address*, the actual free region may not be large enough to accommodate your request. Note that specifying an unduly restrictive memory alignment *mask* argument can also cause **vm_map** to fail even when the address space appears to contain sufficient memory.
SEND_INVALID_PORT	This error may be returned if the task argument was invalid *or* if *memory_object* was invalid.

Table 9.2: Error Codes that **vm_map** Returns

settings on any memory region, including any memory made available by **vm_map**. Mach includes these arguments in the **vm_map** interface to reduce the number of system calls required to set up a memory region with all of its attributes.

While **vm_map** can fail in several ways, the most pernicious case arises from invoking the system call with a port that does not represent a memory object. The Mach kernel has no way to check whether the task holding a port's receive right is an external pager. Thus the **vm_map** may hang. Another thread attempting to access the supposedly mapped memory may hang, too, or fail with a memory exception. In addition to these deferred problems, Table 9.2 lists the error codes **vm_map** may return directly.

One other behavior unique to **vm_map** must be described. The system call can be used to map the same pages more than once into a single address

space. These pages are fully shared, so a modification to any instance of a
page is visible instantly in all other instances. The exception to this rule is
using **vm_map** on MEMORY_OBJECT_NULL, which yields discrete instances
of zero-filled memory. Mapping the same pages multiple times in the same
address space may have an occasional use.

In our SM example, the actual **vm_map** invocation in the client appears
as follows. This code executes after the client has successfully obtained a
memory object from the SM pager. The **vm_map** call uses the *sm_object*
returned from **sm_initiate**.

```
#define MAX_REGION_PAGES          20
#define MY_REGION_SIZE            (vm_page_size * MAX_REGION_PAGES)

kern_return_t    status;

address = 0;
status = vm_map(task_self(), &address, MY_REGION_SIZE, 0,
          TRUE, sm_object, 0, FALSE, VM_PROT_ALL,
          VM_PROT_ALL, VM_INHERIT_DEFAULT);
```

Our client requests the first twenty pages of its SM object. The client allows the kernel to choose an appropriate location anywhere in the client's
address space for the newly mapped memory, with the search starting at
address 0. The client imposes no alignment restrictions on the memory region in addition to those restrictions that the kernel imposes. Therefore the
resulting region is page aligned. Further, the client specifies that all possible
protections should be set on this memory, with default inheritance properties. Because the client sets the *copy* argument to FALSE, changes that
the client makes to the pages mapped from this object are shared with any
other clients mapping the object. Changes are also communicated back to
the pager.

9.3.3   Accessing Mapped Memory

We pointed out previously that memory obtained from a memory object can
be used in the same way as memory obtained directly from the operating
system. To illustrate this point, the demo_sm client copies its command line
arguments into the area that the **vm_map** call mapped previously. The
address variable, returned by **vm_map**, points to this area.

```
/* text points into the argv array */
while (text < &argv[argc])
        (void) strcat ((char *) address, *text++);
```

You can see that demo_sm treats *address* as it would any other pointer into memory. Before the **vm_map** call, the memory at that location would have been invalid. Now this memory can be read and written in the usual way, as demonstrated by **strcat**. The string concatenation function first reads through the character string that *address* specifies to find the terminating NULL and then writes the characters from *text* at the end of the string.

This example depends on a subtle property of the SM object. The first time a page is mapped—one that has never before been modified—the page must be filled with zeroes. Otherwise the **strcat** function behaves unexpectedly. It reads through the page, and possibly even off the page, trying to find a terminating NULL for the string that *address* points to. Because the SM pager always returns zero-fill memory, the example works correctly. However, a pager can implement unexpected or even undesirable semantics. Care should be taken to write pagers that implement semantics consistent with standard Mach features.

9.4   Pager Overview

The SM pager is loosely organized into three pieces. The first piece is concerned with program initialization, registering the SM service with the netmsgserver, and initiating and destroying connections with clients. It is also concerned with the various support routines that other parts of the pager require. Most of this functionality is standard and does not need discussion. Of this piece, we will discuss only those portions that are unique to implementing a pager or that deal with initiating a client connection for the SM pager in particular.

The second piece of the pager implements the external memory management operations that handle the page-in and page-out requests that a Mach kernel sends. We will discuss these kernel requests, expected responses from the pager, sample code, and issues that arise in an implementation. The heart of the pager is the EMM module.

The third piece of the pager implements distributed shared memory (DSM). The EMM routines can exist without the DSM module, although in that case memory may be shared reliably only by tasks executing on the same machine. Tasks executing on separate machines can map separate SM objects without any problem. With the addition of the DSM module, tasks executing anywhere in a network can reliably share SM objects.

The SM pager deploys several threads. The initial thread that starts the program is responsible for initialization, for creating the additional threads, and for waiting for the other threads to terminate. One of these additional threads monitors the service port the pager registered with the netmsgserver. This thread processes the **sm_initiate** requests sent by clients, which we will discuss in detail in the next section.

The remaining threads, called memory_object_ths, handle the EMM messages that Mach kernels send. These threads carry out the requested operations and when necessary generate responses. Except for the assignment of memory objects to threads (discussed in Section 9.13.2), there is nothing interesting about these threads. We usually do not bother referring to these threads when discussing EMM operations; you should only keep in mind that these threads exist to carry out the operations. Multithreading a pager is not mandatory but is very convenient and offers the opportunity for concurrency (e.g., overlapping page-in or page-out requests to disk) or parallelism (simultaneously executing threads).

9.5 Pager View of the Initial Connection

Upon receiving an **sm_initiate** request from a client, the SM pager must determine whether the requested object exists or can be created. If the request passes this test, the pager creates an internal data structure to manage the memory object and sends a port representing the memory object back to the client. The SM pager also creates files to store the object's pages when they are not in use (see Fig. 9.5).

A pager maintains an internal data structure for each object it manages. The SM pager's per-object data structure, called an *sm_object*, includes these fields (see sm_pager.h):

```
typedef struct sm_object {
        unsigned int            refcount;
        char                    backing_file[MAX_FILE_NAME];
        int                     backing_fd;
        char                    page_map_file[MAX_FILE_MAP_NAME];
        int                     page_map_fd;
        char                    page_map[MAX_PAGES_BYTES];
} sm_object;
```

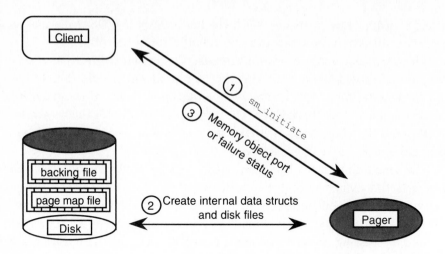

Figure 9.5: SM Pager Creates Memory Object

When creating an object, the SM pager creates two files for it on disk. The names of these files are stored in *backing_file* and *page_map_file*. The first file, *backing_file*, contains all of the object's pages. Initially this file is empty. Because this file is retained even when the SM pager exits or the system reboots, an SM object is persistent. The second file, *page_map_file*, contains a map indicating which pages in the backing file are valid. An *sm_object* also includes open file descriptors, *backing_fd* and *page_map_fd*, for both files.

The SM pager also creates an empty page map in memory. The map is implemented as an array of bits, one bit for each page in the object. Each bit is initially set to FALSE to indicate that there is no valid page in the backing file. The pager sets a map bit to TRUE whenever it saves a page in the backing file. Eventually the map is stored in the page map file when the object is no longer used.

The reference count, *refcount*, tracks the number of users of the *sm_object*. When a client requests an object already in use, the *refcount* is incremented to account for the additional user. If a client stops using an object, the *refcount* is decremented. If the count reaches zero, the object is no longer in use. At that time, the page map is written back to the page map file, both backing and page map files are closed, and the *sm_object* can be deallocated.

In response to the **sm_initiate** request, the pager also creates a port representing the new memory object (see the following code fragment). This

port, *memory_object_port*, is returned to the client so the client may use
vm_map on it to map memory from the object.

```
status = port_allocate(task_self(), &memory_object_port);
status = port_rename(task_self(), memory_object_port,
                     (port_name_t) obj);
```

For convenience, we give the port a new name within the pager's port name
space. The new name is the address of the newly allocated *sm_object*, called
obj in this example. The port name and the address of the *sm_object* are
identical. When a future request arrives on the port, the pager locates the
associated *sm_object* by casting the port name into a pointer to the *sm_object*.
An alternative to renaming a memory object port is using a look-up table
to locate a pager's internal data structure based on the port name.

After Mach receives a memory object port in a **vm_map** call, it may send
EMM requests over the port to the pager. The pager must be prepared to
receive and process each request. In the SM pager, a memory_object_th handles these requests. The pager can have more than one memory_object_th
to improve performance, but each object is assigned to only one thread.
Therefore the pager maintains an array of port sets, one port set for each
memory_object_th. Each memory_object_th monitors its assigned port set
from the array.

```
port_set_name_t memory_object_set[MAX_OBJ_THREADS];
```

```
status = port_set_add(task_self(), memory_object_set[next_thread++],
                      (port_name_t) obj);
```

After allocating the new *sm_object* and its port, we add the port to one of
the port sets. The *next_thread* variable cycles through the port set array, so
object handling is balanced across each available memory_object_th.

For an object that already has a backing file and page map file on disk,
the SM pager creates an *sm_object* based on the existing information. The
initialization of the *sm_object* is similar to the foregoing, including creating
and returning a *memory_object_port*. For an object that already has an
sm_object initialized in memory, the pager simply increments the *sm_object*'s
reference count and returns the existing *memory_object_port* to the client.
Once the client has the port, it may call **vm_map** to gain access to the
object's pages and thus begin paging operations.

9.5.1   EMM Message Processing

Many EMM operations are invoked as *upcalls* from a kernel to a pager. The opposite of a task invoking a service from Mach, in an upcall a kernel sends a message to a pager requesting that the pager perform an operation on behalf of that kernel. In practice, a kernel sends a message to the pager, which uses a MIG stub to interpret it, which in turn calls one of the pager's external memory management routines. In some instances, a pager replies with a message back to the requesting kernel. In other cases, a pager generates its own requests of a kernel. Both kernel requests and pager responses are asynchronous.

Since a Mach kernel requests operations to be carried out by a pager, a pager is built around a message processing loop that awaits a request from a memory object port and invokes the appropriate routine. The SM pager uses the following code as its message processing loop.

```
sm_object_server(memory_object_set)
port_set_name_t         memory_object_set;
{
        msg_header_t    *request = (msg_header_t *) request_buf;
        death_pill_t    *reply = (death_pill_t *) reply_buf;
        msg_return_t    mr;
        boolean_t       valid;

        for (;;) {
                request->msg_local_port = memory_object_set;
                request->msg_size = sizeof(request_buf);
                status = msg_receive(request, MSG_OPTION_NONE, 0);

                valid = memory_object_server(request, &reply->Head);
                if (valid == FALSE) {
                        printf("%s:  ignored foreign request %d\n",
                                Me, request->msg_id);
                        continue;
                }

                if ((reply->Head.msg_remote_port != PORT_NULL) &&
                    (reply->RetCode != MIG_NO_REPLY)) {
                        printf("%s:  replying with id %d???\n",
                                Me, reply->Head.msg_id);
                        status = msg_send(reply,MSG_OPTION_NONE,0);
                }
        }
}
```

Each `memory_object_th` enters this loop to handle messages arriving on its port set. Once a message is received, it is passed off to **memory_object_server()**. This function comes from `libmach.a`, the standard Mach library. **Memory_object_server** examines an incoming message and, based on its message ID, invokes one of the pager's memory object functions. (Refer to Chapter 8 for a discussion of MIG demultiplexing functions.) Also, although the kernel should never send a message that does not belong to the EMM subsystem, we defensively detect such a message by checking for a return value of FALSE from **memory_object_server**.

Finally, although it is a good idea when processing messages with MIG to be prepared to send a reply, we never expect to have to send one because the external memory management interfaces between kernel and pager execute asynchronously. Neither kernel threads nor pager threads expect immediate replies to their messages. The individual memory object routines that the pager implements should return KERN_SUCCESS.[2]

9.6   EMM Interfaces

The `sm_pager` demonstrates most of the external memory management interfaces that Mach provides. These are the same interfaces that OSF/1 Release 1.0 provides. We will trace these operations in the order that a pager might encounter them as it handles a memory object from creation to destruction.

Mach also provides EMM interfaces reserved for trusted pagers that can assume responsibility for paging out the memory of the operating system itself. These interfaces find very limited and cautious use among operating system designers. Mach 3.0 and OSF/1 Release 1.1 include additional interfaces and modifications to the Mach 2.0 interfaces. All of these interfaces lie beyond the scope of this chapter.

9.7   Memory Object Initialization

When a client sends a **vm_map** request on a memory object, the kernel handling the request checks whether it has already mapped the object. If

---

[2]The return code is not checked in Mach 2.5. However, in Mach 3.0 most of this message loop is replaced by a library routine that *does* check return codes. If the return code is FALSE, in Mach 3.0 all out-of-line data and ports in the message will be deallocated and the message destroyed. To make a Mach 2.5 pager more easily portable to Mach 3.0, adhere to the convention of returning KERN_SUCCESS.

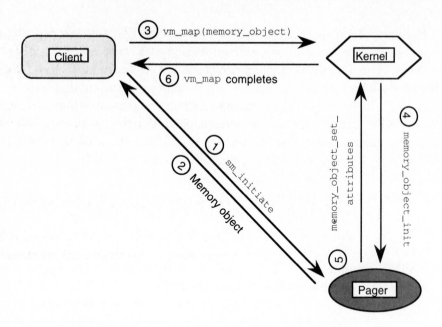

Figure 9.6: A Kernel Uses an Object for the First Time

so, the kernel completes the **vm_map** request immediately. However, if the kernel has never mapped the object, it notifies the object's pager that the object is being mapped. The kernel does not complete the **vm_map** call until the pager processes the initialization notification. This notification takes place by using the **memory_object_init()** upcall from the kernel to the pager (see Fig. 9.6).

Because clients on different machines can request mappings for the same object, the pager must be supplied with necessary information specific to each kernel that knows about the object. A kernel mapping a memory object does not send any more requests about the object until the pager indicates to that kernel that it is ready for them. We postpone discussion of the pager's response to **memory_object_init** until the next section. The **memory_object_init** interface has this form:

```
kern_return_t                                    /* UPCALL */
memory_object_init(memory_object, memory_control,
                memory_object_name, memory_object_page_size)
memory_object_t       memory_object;
memory_object_control_t memory_control;
memory_object_name_t   memory_object_name;
vm_size_t              memory_object_page_size;
```

```
{
        /*
         *        Code to implement memory_object_init
         *        in the pager goes here.
         */
}
```

We have written this interface example differently from the style followed for Mach system calls in this book because **memory_object_init**
is an upcall rather than a system call. In this case, a kernel sends a
memory_object_init message to a pager, which uses **memory_object_
server** to decode the message and call **memory_object_init**. The developer
of a pager must write code to implement the details of **memory_object_init**,
which are specific to each pager. We will develop code fragments that implement the Secure Memory pager's version of **memory_object_init**. Consult
Appendix B for the entire routine.

The *memory_object* is a port representing a memory object that the
pager manages. The pager originally created this port. A kernel calling
memory_object_init supplies the *memory_object* argument so the pager
can identify the memory object to manipulate. In the SM pager, this port
is created and returned to a client during an **sm_initiate** operation. Every
memory management upcall from a kernel to a pager includes *memory_object*.
If a pager gives the same object port to clients on different machines, the
pager will receive the same *memory_object* argument as part of each kernel's
upcalls.

The *memory_control* argument differentiates requests that different kernels generate. It is the port a pager uses to send requests or replies to a kernel. Because the EMM interfaces are asynchronous, it is not always the case
that a pager generates a reply for each request that a kernel sends. This port
is unique for each kernel mapping the same object. Like *memory_object*, this
argument is included with every EMM upcall. By remembering this port, a
pager can distinguish between requests that different Mach kernels generate
for the same memory object.

The *memory_object_name* argument is a port name unique to each kernel
mapping a memory object. The *memory_object_name* identifies the memory region in a **vm_region()** call. When calling **vm_region**, a region in
a task's address space can be identified as a mapping from a particular
memory object by matching **vm_region**'s *object_name* return value against
memory_object_name.

The last argument, *memory_object_page_size*, contains the mapping kernel's page size, in bytes. The page size may differ from one kernel to another. A pager must remember the page size of each kernel mapping an object because all requests and responses to a kernel must specify a page-aligned, integral number of pages relative to the *mapping* kernel's page size. Carrying out operations in terms of a pager's native page size does not work if the mapping kernel's page size is larger than the native page size. A kernel silently ignores or incorrectly handles pager messages specifying short or unaligned pages.

In the SM pager, **memory_object_init** saves the information that the mapping kernel supplies in the following data structure:

```
typedef struct kernel {
        memory_object_name_t      name;
        vm_size_t                 page_size;
} kernel;
```

In our example, we record the name of the memory region and the calling kernel's page size. The SM pager does not use either of these variables. The *name* only has use in conjunction with **vm_region()** calls, which our pager does not perform. Moreover, to simplify its code, the SM pager implementation assumes that all kernels mapping SM objects have identical page sizes. The pager uses the *kernel* data structure only as an identifier to record which kernels map an object. The following sample code is based on the **memory_object_init** routine in sm_pager:

```
kern_return_t
memory_object_init(memory_object, memory_control,
                   memory_object_name, memory_object_page_size)
memory_object_t          memory_object;
memory_object_control_t  memory_control;
memory_object_name_t     memory_object_name;
vm_size_t                memory_object_page_size;
{
        sm_object      *obj;
        kernel         *kern;

        obj = (sm_object *) memory_object;

        kern = (kernel *) malloc(sizeof(kernel));

        kern->name = memory_object_name;
```

```
        kern->page_size = memory_object_page_size;

        status = port_rename(task_self(), memory_control,
                             (port_name_t) kern);
}
```

After allocating and initializing the *kern* structure, the *memory_control* port
is renamed using the address of the new data structure as the port's new
name. This renaming is similar to the renaming of the *memory_object*
done in **sm_initiate**. Renaming is not necessary, only convenient for the
pager. In the next section, we describe how a pager responds to a kernel's
memory_object_init.

9.8   Memory Object Attributes

Each kernel that maps a memory object stores a set of attributes for that
object. These attributes include a flag indicating whether the object can
accept further paging requests and values specifying caching and copying
strategies for the object. Keep in mind, however, that attributes are specific
to an individual kernel. When multiple kernels map the same object, each
kernel has its own set of attributes for the object.

9.8.1   Setting Attributes

A pager uses the **memory_object_set_attributes()** system call to set a
kernel's attributes for a memory object. A pager normally sets an object's
attributes once, in response to **memory_object_init** (see Fig. 9.6). The
memory_object_set_attributes call takes this form:

```
kern_return_t                   status;
memory_object_control_t         memory_control;
boolean_t                       object_ready;
boolean_t                       may_cache_object;
memory_object_copy_strategy_t   copy_strategy;

status = memory_object_set_attributes(memory_control, object_ready,
                                      may_cache_object,
                                      copy_strategy);
if (status != KERN_SUCCESS)
        mach_error("memory_object_set_attributes", status);
```

The *memory_control* argument is the same as the *memory_control* passed to **memory_object_init**. This port serves two purposes. First, it directs a pager's responses to the correct kernel. Second, from the standpoint of the kernel mapping the object, *memory_control* uniquely identifies the object to manipulate.

The three memory object attributes a pager may set are readiness (*object_ready*), cachability (*may_cache_object*), and copying strategy (*copy_strategy*). Before a kernel sends a **memory_object_init** upcall to a pager, it initializes the object's *object_ready* attribute to FALSE; this causes the kernel to delay sending further paging requests to the pager until it has a chance to handle the **memory_object_init** and respond. A pager sets *object_ready* to TRUE to advise a kernel it is ready to accept paging requests.

A memory object that is not cachable is evicted from memory when a kernel detects that it no longer has any users. Its clean pages are reclaimed, its dirty pages are sent back to its pager, and its pager is told that the kernel no longer uses the object. Making an object cachable allows a kernel to retain the object even though it has no users and as long as the kernel has sufficient memory. For instance, a database might mark its objects cachable. After the database program exits, a subsequent invocation using the same objects may benefit because the objects' pages may still be in memory. Typically *may_cache_object* should be set to TRUE, marking an object cachable.

Mach has three strategies for copying memory regions backed by external memory objects. Copies happen during **fork()**, **task_create()**, **vm_copy**, and other virtual memory-related calls by a task mapping an object. These strategies are as follows:

MEMORY_OBJECT_COPY_NONE: The kernel should do nothing special when copying any of the object's pages. Lazy-evaluation and copy-on-write techniques will not be used. The pages will be copied immediately.

MEMORY_OBJECT_COPY_CALL: The kernel notifies the pager (via the **memory_object_copy()** upcall) before copying any of the object's pages, so the pager can decide how pages are copied.

MEMORY_OBJECT_COPY_DELAY: The kernel may use its normal copy-on-write strategies, minimizing system overhead. However, the pager must guarantee not to modify data that the kernel caches.

Typically a pager specifies MEMORY_OBJECT_COPY_DELAY, which permits the greatest efficiency for a kernel. Only a pager that modifies memory that

has been sent to a kernel should use MEMORY_OBJECT_COPY_NONE. Avoid
using MEMORY_OBJECT_COPY_CALL, as at the time of this writing there are
no implementations of Mach 2.5 or Mach 3.0 that implement it correctly.
Since MEMORY_OBJECT_COPY_CALL does not work, we do not document the
memory_object_copy upcall in this chapter. The **memory_object_copy**
function will never be invoked because its only use depends on MEMORY-
OBJECT_COPY_CALL.

Having created the data structures necessary to maintain a memory object, **sm_pager** informs the calling kernel that the pager is ready to accept
further requests. The last piece of code in the **memory_object_init** operation as implemented by **sm_pager** is

```
(void) memory_object_set_attributes((memory_object_control_t)
                                 kern, TRUE, FALSE,
                                 MEMORY_OBJECT_COPY_DELAY);
```

```
return(KERN_SUCCESS);
```

In other words, **sm_pager** indicates to the kernel mapping the memory object that the pager is ready to accept new paging operations by setting
object_ready to TRUE. The pager forbids the kernel from caching pages after
the object is unmapped by setting *may_cache_object* to FALSE, and it sets
copy_strategy to MEMORY_OBJECT_COPY_DELAY to permit the kernel to use
its normal copy-on-write strategies on the object's pages. Note that **sm_pager**
sets *may_cache_object* to FALSE only for pedagogical purposes. A kernel will
evict an SM object when the object has no more users, which causes the
memory_object_terminate() upcall of Section 9.12.

You might also observe that, having used **memory_object_set_**
attributes, the **sm_pager**'s implementation of **memory_object_init** has no
further work to do so it terminates by returning KERN_SUCCESS to its caller.
In fact, any return value would do. As we explained earlier in the chapter,
the return values from the EMM upcalls are ignored in Mach 2.5. In Mach
3.0 the return values matter, so you should make a habit of explicitly returning KERN_SUCCESS from external memory management upcalls. There
is no way for **memory_object_init** to inform a kernel of a failure. Once a
memory object has been made available, it is presumed to be valid for use.

We conclude our discussion of **memory_object_set_attributes** by emphasizing that a memory object's attributes should be set once, in response
to **memory_object_init**. Trying to change the attributes later may only
confuse the kernel in its handling of the memory object. For instance, trying

to stop paging activity on an object by setting *object_ready* to FALSE does not produce the desired result. There is a better way for a pager to shut down a memory object (see Section 9.12.2). Set an object's attributes once and leave them alone while a kernel has the object mapped.

9.8.2   Retrieving Attributes

Memory object attributes may be retrieved using the **memory_object_get_attributes()** system call. This call synchronously retrieves the attribute settings stored by the kernel mapping the memory object.

```
kern_return_t                    status;
memory_object_control_t          memory_control;
boolean_t                        object_ready;
boolean_t                        may_cache_object;
memory_object_copy_strategy_t    copy_strategy;

status = memory_object_get_attributes(memory_control,
                            &object_ready,
                            &may_cache_object,
                            &copy_strategy);
if (status != KERN_SUCCESS)
        mach_error("memory_object_get_attributes", status);
```

The arguments to **memory_object_get_attributes** parallel those of **memory_object_set_attributes**. The *memory_control* argument, unique for each memory object, indicates which kernel mapping the memory object will be interrogated. The **memory_object_get_attributes** call returns its results immediately, not through an asynchronous message.

9.9   Page Fault Handling

After successfully calling **vm_map**, a client program may access the newly mapped memory object. If a client attempts to use a page of the object that is not in memory, the client's kernel transforms the resulting page into a request sent to the object's pager. The pager takes responsibility for supplying the requested data or returning an error. The page fault upcall from kernel to pager is **memory_object_data_request()**, one of the most important EMM interfaces.

Consider Fig. 9.7. The client generates a page fault in step 1 that turns into a **memory_object_data_request** from the kernel to the pager in step

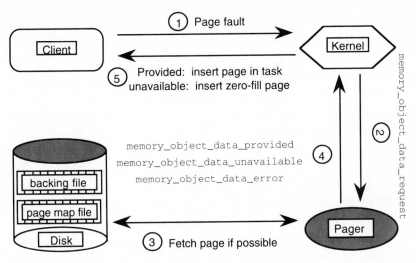

Figure 9.7: Page Fault Resolution

2. In step 3, the pager selects and uses one of three EMM interfaces to reply to the kernel's **memory_object_data_request**. We will discuss these interfaces one by one, as well as the process the SM pager follows when handling **memory_object_data_request**.

The **memory_object_data_request** upcall has the following form:

```
kern_return_t                                     /* UPCALL */
memory_object_data_request(memory_object, memory_control,
                    offset, length, desired_access)
memory_object_t         memory_object;
memory_object_control_t memory_control;
vm_offset_t             offset;
vm_size_t               length;
vm_prot_t               desired_access;
{
      /*
      *      Code to implement memory_object_data_request
      *      in the pager goes here.
      */
}
```

The first parameter, *memory_object*, specifies the object for which data is requested. The pager's response should be sent via the port indicated in the second parameter, *memory_control*. The *offset* and *length* parameters collectively designate the requested region of the memory object. This region is page aligned and an integral number of pages in length, in terms

of the page size of the requesting kernel. In current implementations of
Mach, the requested region consists of only one page.[3] However, you should
write a pager to handle multiple-page requests rather than relying on this
implementation-dependent assumption. Finally, the *desired_access* parameter informs the pager of the needed access to the requested pages. This
parameter consists of one or more of the protection values VM_PROT_READ,
VM_PROT_WRITE, and VM_PROT_EXECUTE.

A pager can respond to **memory_object_data_request** in one of three
ways. First, it may supply the requested data. This case is typical. Second, a
pager may indicate that the region is valid but that there is no data available
for it. This case arises when using a page in an object for the first time,
possibly so a client can initialize the page with data. Third, a pager may
indicate that the request cannot be fulfilled due to an error. A pager also
has the implicit option of not responding at all. This behavior is malicious:
Client threads suspended while waiting for the page fault to complete will
never resume. A well-behaved pager should use one of these three methods
(discussed next in detail) to satisfy a **memory_object_data_request**.

9.9.1   Supplying the Data

A pager normally responds to **memory_object_data_request** by fetching
the requested page(s) and sending them back to the kernel. The pager has
complete control over this process. Perhaps the pager stores its pages on disk,
or on tape, or fetches them over a network. The pager could even create the
data from scratch. In the case of sm_pager, pages are stored in an encrypted
form on disk. Regardless of the method, the pager obtains the data and
returns it to the requesting kernel with **memory_object_data_provided()**:

```
kern_return_t                  status;
memory_object_control_t        memory_control;
vm_offset_t                    offset;
pointer_t                      data;
int                            data_count;
vm_prot_t                      lock_value;

status = memory_object_data_provided(memory_control, offset, data,
                                      data_count, lock_value);
if (status != KERN_SUCCESS)
        mach_error("memory_object_data_provided", status);
```

---

[3]OSF/1 Release 1.1, and possibly versions of Mach 3.0 available after the publication
of this book, may send multiple-page requests.

memory_control is the port on which the kernel listens for responses from the pager. The data that the pager supplies will be inserted in the memory object at *offset*, which in most instances will be the same value sent by the kernel in **memory_object_data_request**. This value must be page aligned with respect to the page size of the kernel receiving the data.

It is possible for a pager to return data to a kernel using several **memory_object_data_provided** calls in place of one, given that each call returns page-aligned, page-multiple pieces of data. This situation can arise if a request is so large that it has to be handled in pieces. In this case, *offset* must still be page aligned although it might not have the same value sent to **memory_object_data_request**. Whenever possible, the best solution is to return all requested data in a single **memory_object_data_provided** call.

The *data* argument points to the data to be sent. Technically, unlike *offset*, the *data* pointer need not be page aligned. However, some versions of Mach have bugs and cannot correctly handle a *data* pointer that does not point to a page boundary. Moreover, Mach may be able to handle the operation more efficiently if the data are aligned. Therefore we recommend storing the data to be sent on a page boundary. The companion parameter, *data_count*, indicates the length of the data and must be a multiple of the page size. In particular, *data_count* must be a multiple of the page size of the kernel receiving the data.

Sending back data in units of the pager's machine's page size may not work correctly. This situation arises when a **memory_object_data_request** is sufficiently large that a pager must handle it in pieces, resulting in multiple **memory_object_data_provided** calls. If the receiving kernel's page size is larger than the pager's page size, the data may not appear to be integral pages to the receiving kernel. Mach ignores EMM calls that do not specify integral pages, or adjusts the calls in ways that may produce undesirable results. For instance, Mach might drop portions of the data to yield integral pages, which might then be inserted at the wrong offset from the standpoint of the pager. The moral of the story is to return data in integral pages with respect to the page size of the receiving kernel.

A pager uses the last argument to **memory_object_data_provided**, *lock_value*, to indicate restrictions on accessing the data. A **memory_object_data_request** upcall includes a *desired_access* parameter specifying the permissions needed for the requested memory. By setting *lock_value*, a pager informs a kernel of the access that the kernel may grant to clients mapping the memory object. Unlike a protection value used in **vm_protect**, which grants the specified permissions, *lock_value* denies the specified permissions. Setting *lock_value* to (VM_PROT_EXECUTE|VM_PROT_WRITE), for example, forbids the receiving kernel from granting write or execute access to the supplied pages. The memory therefore would be treated as read-only.

A pager might return data with less than full access but typically will return data with at least the access originally sought in **memory_object_data_request**. Otherwise the receiving kernel will respond with a request for expanded access to the region, as described in Section 9.11. Generally it is a good idea to return data with precisely the access specified in the original **memory_object_data_request** call.

9.9.2   Valid Region, No Data

A pager may receive a **memory_object_data_request** upcall for a region within the memory object that is valid but has no associated data yet. A pager can detect this condition and use **memory_object_data_provided** to return memory full of zeroes to the requesting kernel. Alternately, by using **memory_object_data_unavailable()**, a pager causes a kernel to create zero-filled pages for that region. The **memory_object_data_unavailable** call differs from returning zeroes with **memory_object_data_provided** in two important ways. First, the **memory_object_data_unavailable** call is more efficient than returning a page of zeroes. Mach has special code that optimizes the use of zero-filled pages. Second, **memory_object_data unavailable** grants all possible access to the region, not just the access that the requesting kernel originally specified in **memory_object_data_request**. When using **memory_object_data_provided**, access can be limited to just that sought by **memory_object_data_request**. You must be careful of this semantic when choosing **memory_object_data_unavailable** over **memory_object_data_provided**. The **memory_object_data_unavailable** call is very simple:

```
kern_return_t                   status;
memory_object_control_t         memory_control;
vm_offset_t                     offset;
vm_size_t                       size;

status = memory_object_data_unavailable(memory_control,
                                        offset, size);
if (status != KERN_SUCCESS)
        mach_error("memory_object_data_unavailable", status);
```

Memory_control is the port on which the kernel expects to receive replies from the pager. The *offset* and *size* parameters specify the region that will receive zero-filled memory. These arguments should specify an aligned range of pages. As with **memory_object_data_provided**, specifying an unaligned range yields incorrect results.

9.9.3   Paging Error

If a page cannot be supplied due to an error of some kind (for instance, an unrecoverable disk error), then the pager may use **memory_object_data_error()** to notify the requesting kernel that the desired memory will not be forthcoming. This call looks like

```
kern_return_t               status;
memory_object_control_t     memory_control;
vm_offset_t                 offset;
vm_size_t                   size;
kern_return_t               reason;

status = memory_object_data_error(memory_control, offset,
                                  size, reason);
if (status != KERN_SUCCESS)
        mach_error("memory_object_data_error", status);
```

You should supply the same *memory_control* argument to **memory_object_data_error** that was received by **memory_object_data_request**. As with the request upcall, *offset* and *size* designate the region provoking the error.

The *reason* argument can be set to any value you prefer to provide information to the application about the source of the error. The application can detect the error code if it has an exception handler. In Mach 2.5, you can use a kernel error code such as KERN_MEMORY_ERROR, which means that the data could not be returned on this request but might in fact be accessible in the future. However, this practice is not portable. In Mach 3.0, user-supplied error codes are limited to values not including the kernel error code range.[4] You should always use pager-specific error codes that do not conflict with the kernel's error codes. The SM pager uses these error codes:

---

[4]Coming soon in a Mach 3.0 release. In the meantime, avoid using the kernel's error codes.

```
#define SM_ERROR_OFFSET        (err_local|err_sub(77)|1)
#define SM_ERROR_SEEK          (err_local|err_sub(77)|2)
#define SM_ERROR_READ          (err_local|err_sub(77)|3)
```

The choice of 77 as the subsystem identifier for the SM pager is entirely arbitrary. The error code macros are defined in mach/error.h.

Unfortunately, existing Mach implementations are broken with respect to propagating *reason* back to the program that originally took the page fault. If the application catches the exception, it may receive the same exception code (e.g., KERN_MEMORY_FAILURE, indicating that the access will *never* succeed) regardless of the reason that the pager specified. This problem is fixed in later versions of Mach 3.0 but not in Mach 2.5.

9.9.4   memory_object_data_request Example

Given the material we have covered in discussing **memory_object_data_request** and the various responses to it, consider the following example based on sm_pager. Our example resolves a **memory_object_data_request** by fetching the requested data from disk, decrypting it, and returning it to the requesting kernel. The SM pager only supports kernels that request one page at a time, although it could easily be generalized to handle arbitrarily long requests. We break the example into several smaller pieces for ease of presentation. Declarations accompany each fragment rather than being declared at the beginning of the routine, as they would be in real code. Some declarations are omitted.

In the first code fragment, the pager locates the *sm_object* and *kernel* data structures based on the *memory_object* and *memory_control* ports. This translation is done simply by casting the variables into pointers of the appropriate type. Some variable declarations and error checking have been removed from this example.

```
kern_return_t
memory_object_data_request(memory_object, memory_control,
                           offset, length, desired_access)
memory_object_t        memory_object;
memory_object_control_t memory_control;
vm_offset_t            offset;
vm_size_t              length;
vm_prot_t              desired_access;
{
        sm_object      *obj;
```

```
kernel          *kern;

obj = (sm_object *) memory_object;
kern = (kernel *) memory_control;

len = (int) length;
off = (int) offset;

if (!PAGE_IN_MAP(obj->page_map, off / vm_page_size)) {
        (void)memory_object_data_unavailable(memory_control,
                                              offset, length);
        return(KERN_SUCCESS);
}
```

After obtaining the *sm_object*, sm_pager determines whether the requested data exist by consulting the page map. The page map has a bit set for each of the object's pages present in its backing file. If no valid data has ever been established for the page, sm_pager uses **memory_object_data_unavailable** to inform the requesting kernel that it should use zero-fill memory for the requested region.

In the next code fragment, sm_pager has already determined that the requested page exists in the backing file. The pager allocates a temporary buffer and uses the UNIX **lseek()** and **read()** system calls to fetch the requested data from the backing file. If the **read** fails, the sm_pager branches to an error handler, which we describe in a subsequent code fragment. The pager must also decrypt the retrieved data because, as we will see in Section 9.10, the pages were encrypted when they were stored in the backing file. The encryption and decryption routines are assumed to work *in place*; that is, the length of the data does not change after encryption or decryption.

```
kern_return_t   reason;
char            *buffer;

(void) vm_allocate(mytask, (vm_address_t) &buffer,
                   MAX_BUFFER_SIZE, TRUE);
(void) lseek(obj->backing_fd, (off_t) off, L_SET);
if ((r = read(obj->backing_fd, buffer, len)) < 0) {
        perror("memory_object_data_request:  read");
        reason = SM_ERROR_READ;
        goto request_data_error;
}

sm_decrypt(buffer, r, obj->crypt_key);
```

At the conclusion of a successful **memory_object_data_request**, the pager returns the requested data via **memory_object_data_provided**. By negating *desired_access*, the resulting *lock_value* denies only those protections not requested. In other words, the pager grants exactly those permissions sought in the **memory_object_data_request** upcall.

```
vm_prot_t        lock_value;

lock_value = (~desired_access) & VM_PROT_ALL;
(void) memory_object_data_provided(memory_control,
                        offset, (pointer_t) buffer,
                        (int) length, lock_value);
return(KERN_SUCCESS);
```

The final code fragment illustrates the error case for **memory_object_data_request**. If sm_pager encounters an error condition such as a **read** failure, it returns an error to the requesting kernel. In a previous code fragment, *reason* was set to SM_ERROR_READ. This code is returned to the requesting kernel through **memory_object_data_error**.

```
request_data_error:
        (void) memory_object_data_error(memory_control, offset,
                                length, reason);
        return(KERN_SUCCESS);
```

9.10   Page-Out Handling

What happens when a kernel needs to reclaim memory, to make way for some other application or memory object? A kernel may immediately reclaim and reuse any pages that have not been modified since they were originally provided by an object's pager. A future request for one of these pages will be satisfied by sending the pager a **memory_object_data_request** upcall again. However, this procedure does not suffice for a modified page. A modified page must be sent back to the pager from whence it came (see Fig. 9.8). The kernel removes the modified page from the address spaces of all clients using it, so the page cannot be used again without first taking a page fault. Then the kernel sends the page to the object's pager via **memory_object_data_write()**. The pager then decides what to do with it. Usually the pager stores the page on disk. In our example, the SM pager first encrypts a dirty page and then stores it in the object's backing file. Finally the pager deallocates the page so the kernel can reclaim memory.

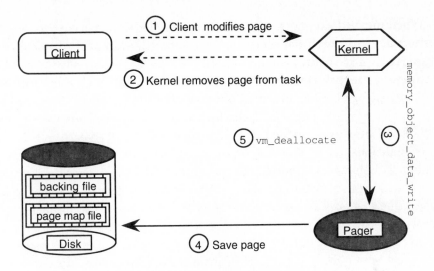

Figure 9.8: Page-Out Handling

A kernel sends a range of dirty pages to a pager through the
memory_object_data_write interface:

```
kern_return_t                                    /* UPCALL */
memory_object_data_write(memory_object, memory_control,
                         offset, data, data_count)
memory_object_t          memory_object;
memory_object_control_t memory_control;
vm_offset_t              offset;
pointer_t                data;
unsigned int             data_count;
{
        /*
        *       Code to implement memory_object_data_write
        *       in the pager goes here.
        */
}
```

The *memory_object* and *memory_control* arguments to this upcall have the
same meaning as in other upcalls. The *offset* argument indicates the location
of the page range within the memory object. The last two arguments, *data*
and *data_count*, specify the modified pages that the kernel sent. These pages
arrived as out-of-line memory in the **memory_object_data_write** message.
This region will be aligned on a page boundary and will be a multiple of the
page size in length.

When finished saving the supplied pages, a pager is expected to respond to **memory_object_data_write** by using **vm_deallocate()** to deallocate those pages. You might have expected to use an EMM interface to respond to **memory_object_data_write**, but **vm_deallocate** is all that is needed. By deallocating the memory from the pager's address space, the kernel can reclaim the physical pages it needs for other purposes. Thus the eventual response to **memory_object_data_write** is **vm_deallocate**.

A malicious pager can ignore **memory_object_data_write** requests. While this behavior is undesirable, eventually Mach compensates by using one of its internal pagers to page-out the pages that were sent to the malicious pager. There is no way for a user-level pager to exhaust system memory by ignoring **memory_object_data_write**. However, a pager that ignores page-out requests probably fails to handle correctly page-in requests for pages that were paged-out. Such a pager is of little use to its clients. In addition, a well-written pager should handle page-out efficiently to maximize system throughput and minimize the time required for clients to use the pager's memory objects.

9.10.1   memory_object_data_write Example

The following example illustrates the actions of sm_pager when handling a kernel's page-out request.

```
kern_return_t
memory_object_data_write(memory_object, memory_control,
                         offset, data, data_count)
memory_object_t          memory_object;
memory_object_control_t memory_control;
vm_offset_t              offset;
pointer_t                data;
unsigned int             data_count;
{
        sm_object         *obj;

        obj = (sm_object *) memory_object;

        sm_encrypt((char *) data, data_count, obj->crypt_key);

        (void) lseek(obj->backing_fd, (off_t) offset, L_SET);
        (void) write(obj->backing_fd, (char *) data, data_count);

        MARK_PAGE_IN_MAP(obj->page_map,
```

```
                    ((int) offset) / vm_page_size);

    (void) vm_deallocate(mytask, data, (vm_size_t) data_count);

    return(KERN_SUCCESS);
}
```

First the pager converts the *memory_object* into a pointer to the pager's internal data structure, an *sm_object*. Then the pager encrypts the page and sends it to the *sm_object*'s backing file. In the sm_pager, we assume that the encrypted form of the data takes up the same amount of space as the original data. The pager also updates the page map to reflect that the page starting at address *offset* in the object has valid data stored in the backing file. Finally, sm_pager uses **vm_deallocate** to free the data that the kernel sent.

9.11   Page Protection Faults and Consistency

Once a kernel has obtained pages from a pager, protection restrictions may still prevent a client program from accessing data it has mapped. A kernel must have some way to indicate to a pager its need for less restrictive access, and there must be a way for a pager to respond to this request. Furthermore, there must be a method whereby a pager can force a kernel to send back modified pages or completely relinquish a memory object's pages. This ability is a prerequisite for a pager to provide consistency between different clients or even different kernels mapping the same memory object.

9.11.1   memory_object_data_unlock

A kernel's request for increased permission on a page is sent to a pager via **memory_object_data_unlock()**. If a page does not exist at all in memory, a kernel uses **memory_object_data_request**; but when a page exists without sufficient permission to complete handling, a fault **memory_object_data_unlock** is used instead. A fault for increased permission, when the page already exists, is called a *protection fault* instead of a page fault. The **memory_object_data_unlock** interface is

```
kern_return_t                                          /* UPCALL */
memory_object_data_unlock(memory_object, memory_control,
                          offset, length, desired_access)
```

```
memory_object_t          memory_object;
memory_object_control_t memory_control;
vm_offset_t              offset;
vm_size_t                length;
vm_prot_t                desired_access;
{
      /*
      *      Code to implement memory_object_data_unlock
      *      in the pager goes here.
      */
}
```

The *memory_object*, *memory_control*, *offset*, and *length* arguments all have
the meanings you have come to expect from the other external memory
management interfaces. The *offset* and *length* arguments collectively specify an aligned range of pages. Like **memory_object_data_request**, the
desired_access argument indicates the access the kernel requires to the region.

9.11.2   memory_object_lock_request

A pager responds to a **memory_object_data_unlock** message with
memory_object_lock_request, setting a new value for the region's permissions.   Besides resolving protection faults, **memory_object_lock_
request** is used for page consistency operations. Through **memory_object_
lock_request**, a pager can force a kernel to send back an object's dirty pages
or even completely relinquish pages. This additional functionality makes the
memory_object_lock_request interface somewhat complex.

```
kern_return_t                status;
memory_object_control_t      memory_control;
vm_offset_t                  offset;
vm_size_t                    size;
boolean_t                    should_clean;
boolean_t                    should_flush;
vm_prot_t                    lock_value;
port_t                       reply_to;

status = memory_object_lock_request(memory_control, offset, size,
                              should_clean, should_flush,
                              lock_value, reply_to);
if (status != KERN_SUCCESS)
      mach_error("memory_object_lock_request", status);
```

The *memory_control*, *offset*, *size*, and *lock_value* arguments have the same meanings as in other EMM calls. As with other EMM calls, the *offset* and *size* arguments must designate an integral page range. The *lock_value* parameter indicates which access permissions are forbidden on the indicated region. The *lock_value* works the same way in **memory_object_lock_request** as it does in **memory_object_data_provided**. A new lock value replaces the previous lock value for a region.

The three new arguments, *should_clean*, *should_flush*, and *reply_to* all have uses for consistency control, as mentioned at the beginning of this section. These variables permit a pager to control pages that have already been sent to a kernel. Setting *should_clean* to TRUE causes the kernel targeted by **memory_object_lock_request** to scan the specified range for dirty pages. All dirty pages found in that range will be sent back to the pager, asynchronously, through **memory_object_data_write**. However, unlike a page-out initiated by the kernel, the kernel keeps a now-clean copy of these pages and the pages remain mapped into client address spaces, marked read-only. A client attempting to modify a clean page will cause a protection fault.

Setting *should_flush* to TRUE invalidates all pages in the specified range. Mappings of those pages are removed from clients' address spaces. The data are flushed and any modifications are lost. By setting both *should_flush* and *should_clean*, a pager can force a kernel to send back dirty pages and flush them from all address spaces including the kernel's. A client's subsequent attempt to access a flushed page will cause a page fault.

The last argument, *reply_to*, is a port that the kernel can use to send a completion message to the pager. (We describe the EMM interface for the completion in the next section.) In some cases, a pager must be sure that a kernel has completed a clean and/or flush operation before continuing with new paging operations. By specifying *reply_to*, a pager can force a kernel to send a message when the clean and/or flush operations complete. A pager can also force a completion message when setting a new *lock_value* on a page range, although this combination may not be useful. Setting *reply_to* to PORT_NULL disables the completion message.

Setting *reply_to* to PORT_NULL is one common use of **memory_object_lock_request**. Another common technique is setting *reply_to* to the port of the memory object itself. By using the memory object port, the completion message will arrive in order after any **memory_object_data_write** upcalls caused by dirty pages. This ordering eliminates the need for additional synchronization logic in the pager.

If you request multiple actions in a single **memory_object_lock_ request**, Mach carries them out in the following order:

1. Restrict access based on *lock_value*.

2. Clean pages if *should_clean* is TRUE.

3. Flush pages if *should_flush* is TRUE.

4. Send completion reply, if *reply_to* is not PORT_NULL.

The ordering is important to eliminate races and to avoid losing modified pages. Furthermore, the ability to trigger these operations as part of the same **memory_object_lock_request** provides a guarantee of atomicity. Consider trying to perform separate clean and flush operations. A pager could send two requests, the first to clean pages and the second to flush them. (Reversing the order of these operations is undesirable because then the flush operation can eliminate modified pages.) However, between the first and second requests it is possible for clients to modify pages in the mapped object. The flush request therefore could cause modified pages to be lost.

The ability to specify cleaning and flushing separately has uses. For instance, a database application might checkpoint its objects by occasionally issuing a **memory_object_lock_request** with *should_clean* set to TRUE. The application would receive a copy of all dirty pages, which could then be sent to disk. Flushing can be useful when an application needs to be certain that Mach no longer has any copies of read-only pages. Because a kernel can reclaim read-only pages at any time without notifying a pager, there must be a way for a pager to guarantee that a kernel has none of an object's pages. By issuing **memory_object_lock_request** with *should_flush* set to TRUE, an application can force a kernel to rid itself of any read-only pages for an object.

Unfortunately, the Mach EMM interfaces make no provision for an otherwise useful ability. There is no easy way to enforce read-only memory through EMM. When a protection fault for write access occurs, a kernel with a read-only page will send a **memory_object_data_unlock** request to the pager responsible for that page. The **memory_object_data_error** interface is oriented toward fatal errors wherein the data are not available at all. However, there is no other way to inform a kernel that the access attempt should fail even though the data are present. A pager should always be prepared to grant read/write access to its objects.

9.11.3 memory_object_lock_completed

After completing a **memory_object_lock_request** with a valid *reply_to* port, the kernel sends a **memory_object_lock_completed** upcall to the pager. This upcall takes the following form:

```
kern_return_t                                       /* UPCALL */
memory_object_lock_completed(memory_object, memory_control,
                             offset, length)
memory_object_t        memory_object;
memory_object_control_t memory_control;
vm_offset_t            offset;
vm_size_t              length;
{
        /*
         *      Code to implement memory_object_lock_completed
         *      in the pager goes here.
         */
}
```

The **memory_object_lock_completed** upcall includes sufficient information to identify the memory object in question and the kernel operating on it (*memory_object* and *memory_control*). Because clean and/or flush requests can be carried out concurrently against different regions in a memory object, the completion upcall also includes the *offset* and *length* arguments that a pager can use to match against its outstanding **memory_object_lock_request** operations. Tracking the outstanding requests and matching up the replies may require additional logic in a pager.

9.11.4 memory_object_data_unlock() Example

The following simple example demonstrates a use of **memory_object_data_unlock** and **memory_object_lock_request**. On taking any kind of protection fault, a kernel will invoke **memory_object_data_unlock**. The following implementation grants all requests by negating the desired access and using the result as *lock_value*. For instance, a request for full access would set *lock_value* to VM_PROT_NONE, thus allowing all access.

```
kern_return_t
memory_object_data_unlock(memory_object, memory_control,
                          offset, length, desired_access)
memory_object_t        memory_object;
```

```
memory_object_control_t memory_control;
vm_offset_t              offset;
vm_size_t                length;
vm_prot_t                desired_access;
{
        vm_prot_t       lock_value;
        kern_return_t   status;

        lock_value = (~desired_access) & VM_PROT_ALL;

        status = memory_object_lock_request(memory_control,
                                    offset, length, FALSE,
                                    FALSE, lock_value,
                                    PORT_NULL);

        return(KERN_SUCCESS);
}
```

There is no reason to wait for a response to this **memory-object_lock_request**. The operation does not specify either cleaning or flushing, just the setting of *lock_value*. Often it is not important for a pager to know precisely when a kernel grants increased access to a page. Usually a

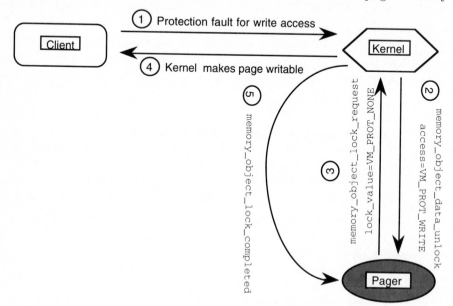

Figure 9.9: Protection Fault Handling

pager only needs to know that it has sent a **memory_object_lock_request** granting the increased access in the first place.

Figure 9.9 illustrates the sequence of events when satisfying a **memory_object_lock_request**. The client takes a protection fault for write access on a read-only page in step 1. In step 2, the fault is converted into a **memory_object_data_unlock** with *desired_access* including VM_PROT_WRITE. The pager responds in step 3 with **memory_object_lock_request**, granting the sought-after access. The pager could also set up the *reply_to* port for this operation, in which case the pager will eventually receive a completion message. The kernel receives the **memory_object_lock_request** message from the page and gives write access to the faulting client task. Finally, if a completion message was requested, in step 5 the kernel sends **memory_object_lock_completed** back to the pager.

9.12   Shutting Down a Memory Object

When a kernel has no more users of a memory object, it may decide to relinquish access to the object. This decision results in one of two ways. If the object was initialized by **memory_object_set_attributes** with *may_cache_object* set to FALSE, a kernel will relinquish its access as soon as there are no more users of a memory object. If *may_cache_object* was set to TRUE, a kernel will only relinquish access to an object when memory is full and the object's memory is needed for some other purpose.

9.12.1   memory_object_terminate()

A kernel relinquishes access to an object by notifying the object's pager through the **memory_object_terminate()** interface. This upcall has the following form:

```
kern_return_t                               /* UPCALL */
memory_object_terminate(memory_object, memory_control,
                        memory_object_name)
memory_object_t        memory_object;
memory_object_control_t memory_control;
memory_object_name_t    memory_object_name;
{
        /*
        *       Code to implement memory_object_terminate
```

```
 *        in the pager goes here.
 */
}
```

The *memory_object*, *memory_control*, and *memory_object_name* parameters are identical to those of **memory_object_init**.   They are passed to **memory_object_terminate** so a pager may identify the object that is being terminated and the kernel that is terminating it.

The kernel neither waits for nor expects a reply to **memory_object_terminate**. As soon as a kernel sends **memory_object_terminate**, it has completely deallocated all of its data structures relating to the memory object and reclaimed all of the object's pages. Any pages that were dirty were sent to the pager through **memory_object_data_write**. By the time a pager enters **memory_object_terminate**, all it must do is take care of any of its own state that must be shut down. For example, the SM pager forces any pending I/O through to the disk via **fsync()**, writes the *sm_object*'s page map out to disk, and deallocates the *memory_control* and *memory_object_name* ports associated with the kernel that terminated the object. The **memory_object_terminate** code from sm_pager looks like this:

```
kern_return_t
memory_object_terminate(memory_object, memory_control,
                        memory_object_name)
memory_object_t         memory_object;
memory_object_control_t memory_control;
memory_object_name_t    memory_object_name;
{
        sm_object       *obj;
        kernel          *kern;
        kern_return_t   status;
        char            error_buffer[BUFSIZ];

        obj = (sm_object *) memory_object;
        kern = (kernel *) memory_control;

        (void) fsync(obj->backing_fd);

        (void) lseek(obj->page_map_fd, (off_t) 0, L_SET);
        (void) write(obj->page_map_fd, obj->page_map,
                    (int) MAX_PAGES_BYTES);
        (void) fsync(obj->page_map_fd);
```

```
        status = port_deallocate(mytask, memory_control);
        status = port_deallocate(mytask, memory_object_name);

        (void) free((char *) kern);

        return(KERN_SUCCESS);
}
```

In addition to flushing its data back to disk, **sm_pager** also takes this opportunity to deallocate the *kern* data structure that had been dynamically allocated in **memory_object_init**. As with all EMM routines in a pager, this one, too, returns KERN_SUCCESS.

9.12.2   memory_object_destroy()

If a pager must force a kernel to relinquish a memory object, Mach provides the **memory_object_destroy()** call. This call indicates to a kernel that an object should be terminated immediately. A kernel receiving this command halts paging and EMM activity on the specified object and ultimately returns a **memory_object_terminate** message to its pager.

If an object might have important modified data, a pager should issue a **memory_object_lock_request** call before invoking **memory_object_destroy()**. By calling **memory_object_lock_request** with *lock_value* set to VM_PROT_ALL and *should_clean* set to TRUE, a pager can obtain all modified data while prohibiting new modifications. In this case, a pager should also use *reply_to* to force a **memory_object_lock_completed** message when the kernel has finished sending back modified data. If a pager does not wait for a completion message, it risks losing modified data by sending **memory_object_destroy** before all page-outs complete.

The **memory_object_destroy** interface is

```
memory_object_control_t        memory_control;
kern_return_t                  reason;

status = memory_object_destroy(memory_control, reason);
if (status != KERN_SUCCESS)
        mach_error("memory_object_lock_request", status);
```

The *memory_control* port specifies which object to terminate. The *reason* variable indicates why the object must be destroyed. However, this value is ignored in Mach 2.5.

9.13   Races and Other Topics

Mach 2.5 has two notable races in its EMM interfaces: the *init/terminate* race and the *page-in/page-out* race. These races affect the way a pager is structured when running on Mach 2.5. When implementing a pager, both races should be considered and prevented. Newer versions of Mach eliminate one or both races but may require restructuring a pager's code.

9.13.1   Terminate versus Init

The init/terminate race results from a bug in the Mach 2.5 kernel. On occasion, a pager may receive two **memory_object_init** requests in a row *before* receiving the **memory_object_terminate** request that matches the first **memory_object_init**. Unfortunately, it is possible for a Mach kernel to begin the process of terminating an object and then reactivate it before sending the **memory_object_terminate** message. The following statements illustrate the problem.

1. The kernel issues **memory_object_init** for the first use of the object.

2. The pager receives **memory_object_init** and initializes the object.

3. The kernel detects no more users of the object and begins deallocating its data structures.

4. A client maps the object while the kernel is still cleaning up. The kernel immediately issues another **memory_object_init**.

5. The pager receives the second **memory_object_init** call.

6. At the end of the kernel's termination sequence, still in progress, the kernel issues **memory_object_terminate**.

7. The pager receives the first **memory_object_terminate**.

At the end of this sequence, the object is still active and in use. If the pager acts on the **memory_object_terminate**, it will deallocate the object while a kernel still uses it. Paging requests will follow and the pager will not be prepared to deal with them.

This race may be detected by introducing checks in **memory_object_init** and **memory_object_terminate**. In **memory_object_init**, maintain a linked list or similar data structure of kernels known to be using an object.

If a kernel is already on the list, an init/terminate race has been discovered. At this point, the pager can implement two alternatives. First, it can allocate new data structures for the object so that the old data structures can be consumed by **memory_object_terminate**. Second, it can reuse the object's old data structures.

In **memory_object_terminate**, introduce a check to see whether the object really should be terminated. This check might be based on a reference count, or a flag that indicates that an init/terminate race is in progress. Alternately, if **memory_object_init** allocates new object data structures, **memory_object_terminate** may not need any additional logic. It simply disposes of the old data structures.

This kernel bug has been eliminated from later versions of Mach 3.0 but not from standard Mach 2.5 or OSF/1 Release 1.0. This bug may have been eliminated from OSF/1 Release 1.1.

9.13.2   Page-In versus Page-Out

The second important race pits page-in requests against page-out requests. A kernel assumes that a page-out has taken place as soon as it sends a **memory_object_data_write** message to the page's pager. However, assume the pager is multithreaded and more than one thread can handle EMM requests for the same object. The thread handling the **memory_object_data_write** request can be delayed in arbitrary ways. It can be rescheduled by the kernel, or wait on a lock, or otherwise take longer to execute than expected. In the meantime, if the kernel needs the same page again, it will issue a **memory_object_data_request**. By our assumptions, another thread in the pager can handle this message while the **memory_object_data_write** thread is still running. In fact, it is possible for the pager to satisfy the **memory_object_data_request** before becoming aware of the pending **memory_object_data_write**. The kernel thus receives stale data, losing the modifications to the page it just paged-out.

There is no way to eliminate this race when multiple threads can handle paging messages for the same object. A thread handling **memory_object_data_write** can be suspended or delayed immediately after **msg_receive()** takes a **memory_object_data_write** message off the object's port. The race must be eliminated by allowing only one thread to handle EMM operations for a given object. A pager may still be multithreaded by using multiple threads to handle paging requests for multiple objects, as long as an object is assigned to the same thread while the object exists. This is why sm_pager is multithreaded but assigns an object permanently to one thread.

9.14   Distributed Shared Memory

We conclude with a discussion of distributed shared memory (DSM) and its implications for external memory managers. As we have stated repeatedly, a memory object can be used by multiple machines simultaneously. This feature is one of the major benefits of EMM. Clients scattered around a network as well as clients sharing the same machine can have the same view of shared memory.

It is easy to make a memory object available to any machine that wants to use it. One way is to register a pager with the netmsgserver, which can respond to look-up requests from any machine on the local area network. Unfortunately, the EMM interfaces by themselves do not provide a consistent view of shared memory. Consider Fig. 9.10. This example corresponds to the situation in which the sm_pager is built without DSM support. Any pager that grants access to its objects' pages without remembering what kernels are using those objects will suffer similar problems. Kernel A acquires a writable page in steps 1 and 2, modifying it in step 3. Meanwhile, in step 4 kernel B attempts to acquire the same page for read access. Because the pager does not track ownership of its pages, it grants kernel B's request immediately in step 5. Kernel B's clients now have a stale copy of the page

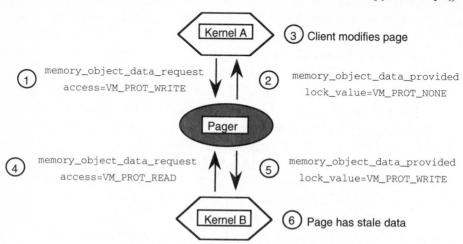

Figure 9.10: A Page Coherency Problem

because their copy of the page does not include the modifications made in step 3. Kernel A eventually sends the modified page back to the pager in step 7, but by then the damage has been done. In fact, the damage could be made worse: If kernel B subsequently modifies its page, the page-out from kernel B will overwrite the results of the page-out from kernel A.

Maintaining a predictable view of memory across machines is called page *consistency* or page *coherency*. If a pager implements *full* coherency, data modified by one machine will be immediately visible to all other machines sharing the page. Alternately, a pager may implement *loose* coherency, in which page updates are deferred until absolutely needed or until triggered by a special mechanism. For instance, the use of a special hardware lock instruction might trigger a page coherency mechanism. As long as all clients used lock instructions appropriately, memory would appear consistent. Only clients failing to use lock instructions as they should might see inconsistent values in shared memory. A pager that implements *no* coherency may lose some or all modifications to data made by separate machines as in Fig. 9.10.

The major issue in page coherency is handling writable pages. Read-only pages cannot be modified, so their use does not pose a threat to the integrity of memory. However, when one client has write access to a page that another is reading, or when two clients both have write access to a page, a coherent pager must have a way to prevent inconsistent results.

One popular scheme for maintaining page coherency is *multiple-readers/ single-writer*. With this protocol, memory integrity can be guaranteed. The key is this: Only one kernel at a time ever has a copy of a writable page. Before write access on a page can be given to another kernel, the kernel already writing the page must relinquish its access. Even if a kernel attempts to acquire a page for read access, the kernel with write access (if any) must relinquish the page. Only multiple readers are allowed to use a page at the same time.

Figure 9.11 illustrates a portion of the multiple-readers/single-writer coherency protocol. Begin by assuming that kernels A and B both have read-only copies of the same page. This is legal because no other kernels have copies of the page and neither the clients of kernel A nor the clients of kernel B can modify the page without first requesting increased access from the pager. At some point in time, a third kernel, C, requests write access to the page (step 1). Before the pager can grant kernel C's request, it must revoke the outstanding copies of the page from kernels A and B. The pager uses **memory_object_lock_request** to flush the page from each kernel that has

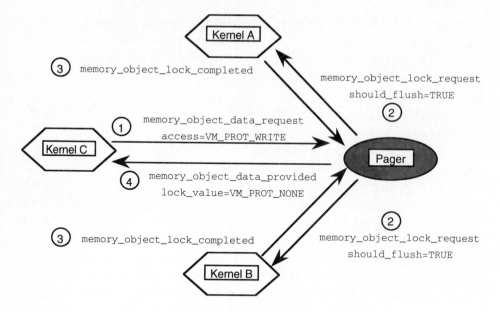

Figure 9.11: Page Transition from Read to Write

a copy (step 2). The page does not have to be cleaned because it is read-only. One **memory_object_lock_request** message must be sent to each kernel. Because the EMM interfaces are asynchronous, the pager can send both **memory_object_lock_request** messages right away. The pager uses **memory_object_lock_request**'s *reply_to* port to cause a completion message. If the pager did not wait for completion messages from the two kernels, it would be possible for a client of kernel C to modify the page while a client of kernel A or B was still examining a (stale) copy of the page. After kernels A and B respond in step 3, the pager at last allows kernel C write access to the page in step 4. The properties of the coherency protocol have been preserved and only a single writer now has access to the page.

The sm_dsm.c module of the sm_pager implements a multiple-reader/single-writer page coherency protocol for the SM pager. A few hooks from the EMM routines feed state information into the distributed shared memory module. Otherwise the DSM module is largely standalone. In fact, sm_pager can be built entirely without distributed shared memory. The sample programs can be read without considering the implications of DSM simply by ignoring all code under #ifdef DSM.

9.15   EMM Interface Summary

Table 9.3 summarizes the EMM interfaces discussed in this chapter. The table's *Caller* field distinguishes among three cases. When *Caller* is *Client*, the operation is invoked by a client program on a memory object. When *Caller* is *Kernel*, the operation is a request from a kernel to a pager. Finally, when *Caller* is *Pager*, the interface is used by an external pager to respond to a kernel request or to initiate a kernel action.

Operation	Caller
memory_object_data_error	Pager
memory_object_data_provided	Pager
memory_object_data_request	Kernel
memory_object_data_unavailable	Pager
memory_object_data_unlock	Kernel
memory_object_data_write	Kernel
memory_object_destroy	Pager
memory_object_get_attributes	Pager
memory_object_init	Kernel
memory_object_lock_completed	Kernel
memory_object_lock_request	Pager
memory_object_set_attributes	Pager
memory_object_terminate	Kernel
memory_object_copy	Kernel
vm_map	Client

Table 9.3: Callers of EMM Interfaces

Chapter 10

OSF/1 P Threads

In recent years, several organizations have developed UNIX packages for handling threads. Examples include Brown Threads from Brown University, SunOS Lightweight Processes (LWP) from Sun Microsystems, Inc., CMA Threads from Digital Equipment Corporation, and the C Threads package from Carnegie Mellon University. Each of these implementations defines its own set of (incompatible) interfaces.

With so many different sets of interfaces, porting multithreaded applications from system to system was difficult. To address this problem, the POSIX standards activities of the Institute of Electrical and Electronics Engineers Computer Society (IEEE CS) are defining a common set of interfaces for working with threads. This draft POSIX threads standard (known colloquially as the *P Threads* standard), P1003.4a, is one of the series of open systems standards promulgated by the IEEE CS.

One of the first implementations of this emerging standard is the P Threads library supplied as part of the OSF/1 operating system. The OSF/1 P Threads library corresponds to Draft 4 of P1003.4a. It reflects some changes that appear in Draft 5, where they do not conflict with Draft 4.

The P Threads library is built on the Mach kernel's task and thread facilities. P Threads provides a portable way of accessing these Mach task and thread calls in OSF/1. This is important, because not all system vendors may include these kernel interfaces in their own OSF/1 products. Using the P Threads interfaces presented in this chapter provides a portable approach for developing multithreaded OSF/1 applications.[1]

---

[1] The P Threads implementation described here corresponds to Release 1.1 of the OSF/1 operating system.

In addition to improved application portability, using P Threads provides the same advantages as C Threads:

1. There is no need for the machine-dependent code required when using the Mach kernel's task and thread calls directly.

2. Synchronization facilities are provided that facilitate multithreaded application design.

3. The P Threads interfaces are simpler than the kernel task and thread interfaces.

As with C Threads, using the OSF/1 P Threads package allows your application to automatically take advantage of multiple CPUs on multiprocessor systems.

The remainder of this chapter introduces P Threads as a standard application programming interface (API) for multithreaded applications. If you already know about the Mach C Threads library described in Chapter 5, many of the P Threads interfaces are familiar to you. We begin our tour with a brief overview of the basic calls in the P Threads library. Next we discuss several areas in which P Threads and C Threads differ. These include mechanisms specific to P Threads, such as per-thread error handling, thread cancellation, and the use of signals. After contrasting the two packages, we present two example programs from previous chapters, implemented using P Threads.

10.1   Basic P Threads Calls

Many of the C Threads concepts presented in Chapter 5 also apply to P Threads. This section presents the P Threads calls corresponding to these common concepts. Table 10.4 summarizes the similarities and differences between the P Threads and C Threads calls.

The naming convention that P1003.4a uses helps in learning these calls: All pthread-related functions specified in P1003.4a begin with *pthread_* (for instance, **pthread_create**). Those functions specific to a particular data object then include the name of the object. For example, you initialize a *mutex object* (see Section 10.1.5) with the call **pthread_mutex_init**.

The calls presented in this section follow the convention in the P Threads standard that 0 is returned on success and -1 on failure. More information on errors is given in Section 10.3.

10.1.1   Creating and Terminating Pthreads

A *pthread* is a flow of control, an executing computation, within a UNIX process.[2] As with C Threads, there can be many pthreads within a process, all sharing the resources (VM, file descriptors, IPC Ports, etc.) of the process. Some systems may achieve this effect by implementing P Threads via a user-mode scheduler that executes one of a process's pthreads at a time. OSF/1 implements P Threads by using Mach kernel threads, so there is true concurrency.

You create and start a new pthread using the **pthread_create()** call:

```
int            status;
pthread_t      thread;
pthread_attr_t attr;
void           *arg;
void           *start_routine();

status = pthread_create(&thread, attr, start_routine, arg);
if (status == -1) {
        perror("pthread_create");
        exit(1);
}
```

The caller of **pthread_create** supplies a location in which Mach stores the pthread ID, *thread*, a set of attributes for the new pthread, *attr*, and an initial routine, *start_routine*, invoked with the single argument *arg* specified in the **pthread_create** call. Specifying the constant pthread_attr_default for *attr* indicates that a default set of attributes is to be used. Section 10.1.2 discusses attributes in more detail.

The **pthread_create** call can fail due to either system resource shortages or invalid arguments. Table 10.1 lists these situations and the corresponding error codes.

When a pthread completes its work, it should execute the **pthread_exit()** call. This call does not return; it terminates the calling pthread. An implicit **pthread_exit** call occurs when a pthread returns from its initial function, *start_routine*, with the function's return value employed as the pthread's exit status. An explicit call to **pthread_exit** allows terminating the pthread and setting the exit status from any point in the program:

---

[2]A UNIX process in OSF/1 is implemented as a Mach task with additional UNIX-specific information. In this chapter we refer to process rather than task for consistency with the terminology used in P1003.4a.

Error Code	Meaning
EAGAIN	The system lacks the resources necessary to create another thread. The new thread cannot be created without exceeding the system-imposed limit on the total number of threads allowed for each user.
ENOMEM	There is not enough memory to create the thread. This is not a temporary condition.
EINVAL	The value that the thread or *attr* parameter specifies is invalid.

Table 10.1: **pthread_create** Error Codes

```
void pthread_exit();
void *exit_status;

pthread_exit(exit_status);
```

10.1.2   Pthread Attributes

A *pthread attributes object* determines various characteristics of the pthread to be created. Currently the only item that may be specified in OSF/1 P Threads is the minimum stack size to be used. To obtain a new attributes object, allocate space for the object, and then issue the **pthread_attr_create()** call to initialize it. You then set the minimum stack length with the function **pthread_attr_setstacksize()**:

```
int             status;
pthread_attr_t attr;
long            stacksize = 8192;   /* An example stack size value */

status = pthread_attr_create(&attr);
if (status == -1) {
        perror("pthread_attr_create");
        exit(1);
}
status = pthread_attr_setstacksize(&attr, stacksize);
if (status == -1) {
        perror("pthread_attr_setstacksize");
        exit(1);
}
```

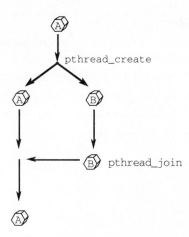

Figure 10.1: The **pthread_join** Operation Waits for Another Pthread

In this code fragment, the attributes object *attr* has been allocated on the stack. You cannot use *attr* when creating new pthreads until you initialize it by calling **pthread_attr_create**. The P Threads library sets *errno* to ENOMEM if there is not enough memory, or to EINVAL if the value that *attr* specified is invalid.

Once you have initialized the new attributes object, *attr*, you store a new stack size in it using **pthread_attr_setstacksize**. Then you specify *attr* in subsequent calls to **pthread_create** in order to create pthreads with your customized stack size.

The *stacksize* parameter to **pthread_attr_setstacksize** is specified in units of bytes. The appropriate stack size is specific to each architecture. You should normally use the default stack size, unless in practice you find that your application exceeds its stack. The only error from the function **pthread_attr_setstacksize** occurs if an invalid argument is supplied, in which case *errno* is set to EINVAL.

10.1.3   Waiting for Pthreads

One or more pthreads may wait for another pthread to terminate by using **pthread_join()** (see Fig. 10.1):

```
int       status;
pthread_t thread;
void      *exit_status;

status = pthread_join(thread, &exit_status);
```

Error Code	Meaning
EINVAL	The value that the thread parameter specified is invalid.
ESRCH	The value that the thread parameter specified does not refer to an existing thread.
EDEADLK	A deadlock condition was detected: The target thread is the calling thread.

Table 10.2: **pthread_join** Error Codes

```
if (status == -1) {
        perror("pthread_join");
        exit(1);
}
```

The **pthread_join()** call is similar to the join operation in the C Threads library. As in C Threads, multiple pthreads may wait for the target pthread, *thread*, to terminate. The exit status from *thread* is made available to the caller of **pthread_join** in *exit_status*. If *thread* has already terminated, **pthread_join** sets *exit_status* and returns immediately without blocking. Table 10.2 lists the possible error codes **pthread_join** returns.

10.1.4   Detaching Pthreads

The P Threads library must retain information about pthreads even after they have terminated. For example, the exit status may be required to satisfy a subsequent **pthread_join** call. You can optimize the operation of P Threads by providing advice that allows the library to release its records about a given pthread using the **pthread_detach()** function as follows:

```
int        status;
pthread_t thread;

status = pthread_detach(thread);
```

Detaching pthreads that will not be joined allows the P Threads library to release its internal information about those pthreads. This practice is similar to closing files that will no longer be accessed, and it indirectly results in better performance for your application (less paging, faster access to internal P Threads library data, and so on). Detaching unneeded pthreads also lessens the likelihood that future **pthread_create** calls will fail due to resource shortage.

10.1.5   Synchronization Facilities

The OSF/1 P Threads implementation provides synchronization calls similar to those of the Mach C Threads library. These comprise operations on the same synchronization abstractions used in C Threads: *mutex* objects for short duration mutual exclusion, and *condition variables* for event notification.

Mutual Exclusion

You generally work with mutexes in P Threads the same way as in C Threads. The three central mutex operations lock, unlock, and test the locked state of a specified mutex: **pthread_mutex_lock()**, **pthread_mutex_unlock()**, and **pthread_mutex_trylock()**.

Setup and cleanup of mutexes is somewhat different, however. P1003.4a specifies the calls **pthread_mutex_init()** to create a mutex object and **pthread_mutex_destroy()** to destroy a mutex object when it is no longer needed. Note that there is no P Threads analog for the C Threads calls to allocate and release mutex objects (**mutex_alloc** and **mutex_free**). In P Threads, allocating space for mutexes is your responsibility, as is disposing of the space after the mutex has been destroyed.

Working with Mutexes

You prepare a previously allocated mutex for use as follows:

```
int                  status;
pthread_mutex_t      nascent_mutex;
pthread_mutexattr_t mattr;

status = pthread_mutex_init(&nascent_mutex, mattr);
if (status == -1) {
        perror("pthread_mutex_init");
        exit(1);
}
```

The *mattr* parameter specifies a *mutex attributes object*. Use the constant pthread_mutexattr_default to request a default set of characteristics. In the OSF/1 implementation of P Threads, no attributes are defined for mutex objects, so conventional usage would specify this constant.

The P Threads library returns zero in *status* if the fields of the mutex, *nascent_mutex*, are successfully initialized. The only possible error is an invalid argument. In this case, the library returns -1 and stores EINVAL in *errno*.

Although OSF/1 does not support attributes for mutexes, other P Threads implementations may implement such attributes. For completeness, here are the calls to create and delete attribute objects for mutexes:

```
int                     status;
pthread_mutexattr_t *mattr;

status = pthread_mutexattr_create(&mattr);
if (status == -1) {
        perror("pthread_mutexattr_create");
        exit(1);
}

status = pthread_mutexattr_delete(&mattr);
if (status == -1) {
        perror("pthread_mutexattr_delete");
        exit(1);
}
```

Note that these calls allocate and free storage. The **pthread_mutexattr_create** call allocates and initializes the fields of an existing mutex attributes object, and the **pthread_mutexattr_delete** call releases the storage for a mutex attributes object. If *mattr* is invalid, both calls set *errno* to EINVAL. In addition, the **pthread_mutexattr_create** call sets *errno* to ENOMEM if there is insufficient memory to create the attributes object.

You advise the P Threads library that a mutex is no longer needed using the **pthread_mutex_destroy** call as follows:

```
int                status;
pthread_mutex_t unneeded_mutex;

status = pthread_mutex_destroy(&unneeded_mutex);
if (status == -1) {
        perror("pthread_mutex_destroy");
        exit(1);
}
```

If *unneeded_mutex* is invalid, the P Threads library sets *errno* to EINVAL. Note that *unneeded_mutex* must be unlocked when the **pthread_mutex_destroy** call is performed. Otherwise the library returns -1 in *status*, does not mark the mutex as invalid, and sets *errno* to EBUSY.

You lock an unlocked mutex as follows:

```
int             status;
pthread_mutex_t unlocked_mutex;

status = pthread_mutex_lock(&unlocked_mutex);
if (status == -1) {
        perror("pthread_mutex_lock");
        exit(1);
}
```

Two errors are possible. If *unlocked_mutex* is invalid, the P Threads library stores EINVAL in *errno*. If the calling pthread already locked *unlocked_mutex*, the library stores EDEADLK in *errno*.

You unlock a locked mutex as follows:

```
int             status;
pthread_mutex_t locked_mutex;

status = pthread_mutex_unlock(&locked_mutex);
if (status == -1) {
        perror("pthread_mutex_unlock");
        exit(1);
}
```

Again, two errors are possible. If *locked_mutex* is invalid, the P Threads library stores EINVAL in *errno*. If *locked_mutex* is not already locked, the library stores EPERM in *errno*.

The **pthread_mutex_trylock** call deviates a bit from the usual P Threads convention regarding return codes. The value -1 indicates an error as usual. The value zero, however, means that *mutex* is already locked. If *mutex* is not locked, the **pthread_mutex_trylock** call locks it and returns a status value of 1. Here is the calling sequence:

```
int             status;
pthread_mutex_t mutex;

status = pthread_mutex_trylock(&mutex);
if (status == -1) {
        perror("pthread_mutex_trylock");
        exit(1);
}
```

The only error condition is an invalid *mutex* argument, indicated by the code
EINVAL stored in *errno*.

To summarize our discussion of mutexes, here is the typical sequence you
use to create, lock, unlock, and destroy a mutex object:

```
/*
 * Allocate space for the mutex lock
 */
pthread_mutex_t lock;

/*
 * Create and acquire the lock.
 */
pthread_mutex_init(&lock, pthread_mutexattr_default);
pthread_mutex_lock(&lock);
/*
 * Code to manipulate the resource protected
 * by the mutex goes here
 *
 */
/*
 * After all the work is done, we release the lock.
 */
pthread_mutex_unlock(&lock);

/*
 * The lock is no longer needed, release it.
 */
pthread_mutex_destroy(&lock);
```

Note that the **pthread_mutex_init** call may allocate resources internally
when creating the mutex. Such resources must be released when the mutex
is no longer needed by performing the **pthread_mutex_destroy** call.

Using Condition Variables

The concepts involved in using P Threads condition variables are identical
to those described in the C Threads chapter. Here we briefly present the
calling sequences and mechanics of using the corresponding P Threads calls.

You create a P Threads condition variable with the **pthread_cond_init()**
call:

```
pthread_cond_t     new_cond;
pthread_condattr_t cattr;

status = pthread_cond_init(&new_cond, cattr);
if (status == -1) {
        perror("pthread_cond_init");
        exit(1);
}
```

As with mutexes, you allocate storage for the condition variable *new_cond*.
You then call **pthread_cond_init** to initialize the condition variable.
The *cattr* parameter specifies a *condition attributes object*. The constant
pthread_condattr_default initializes *new_cond* with a default set of attributes.
If either *new_cond* or *cattr* is invalid, *errno* is set to EINVAL.

OSF/1 does not currently define any attributes for condition variables.
Other P Threads implementations may include condition variable attributes,
however. For portability, OSF/1 includes the **pthread_condattr_create()**
call to allocate and initialize a condition variable attributes object:

```
pthread_condattr_t *nascent_cattr;

status = pthread_condattr_create(&nascent_cattr);
if (status == -1) {
        perror("pthread_condattr_create");
        exit(1);
}
```

If successful, **pthread_condattr_create** stores the address of the new attributes object in *nascent_cattr* and returns 0 in *status*. The value -1 is returned on either of the two possible errors: If *nascent_cattr* is invalid, *errno*
is set to EINVAL; if there is insufficient memory to create a new attributes
object, *errno* is set to ENOMEM.

When a condition attributes object is no longer needed, it should be
released with the **pthread_condattr_delete()** call:

```
pthread_condattr_t *unneeded_cattr;

status = pthread_condattr_delete(&unneeded_cattr);
if (status == -1) {
        perror("pthread_condattr_delete");
        exit(1);
}
```

The **pthread_condattr_delete** call frees the storage used for the attributes object. The only error possible occurs if you specify an invalid attributes object. In this case the P Threads library sets *errno* to EINVAL.

Once you no longer have any use for a condition variable, you destroy it using the **pthread_cond_destroy()** call. Note that no thread can be waiting on the condition variable when you destroy it. Here is the calling sequence for **pthread_cond_destroy**:

```
pthread_cond_t unneeded_cond;

status = pthread_cond_destroy(&unneeded_cond);
if (status == -1) {
        perror("pthread_cond_destroy");
        exit(1);
}
```

This call marks *unneeded_cond* as no longer valid and releases any resources allocated when the condition variable was created. If an invalid parameter is supplied for *unneeded_cond*, the P Threads library sets *errno* to EINVAL. If a thread is currently executing a **pthread_cond_wait()** or **pthread_cond_timedwait()** call on *unneeded_cond*, the library sets *errno* to EBUSY.

To awaken a pthread waiting on a condition variable, you issue the **pthread_cond_signal()** call, or the **pthread_cond_broadcast()** call, to awaken all waiting pthreads:

```
pthread_cond_t a_cond;

status = pthread_cond_signal(&a_cond);
if (status == -1) {
        perror("pthread_cond_signal");
        exit(1);
}

status = pthread_cond_broadcast(&a_cond);
if (status == -1) {
        perror("pthread_cond_broadcast");
        exit(1);
}
```

If no pthread is waiting on condition variable *a_cond*, the **pthread_cond_signal** or **pthread_cond_broadcast** call has no effect. If one pthread is waiting, it is awakened. If multiple pthreads are waiting, **pthread_cond_signal** wakes exactly one of them (which one is undefined), and **pthread_cond_broadcast** awakens them all. The only error occurs if you specify an invalid condition variable, in which case *errno* is set to EINVAL.

Pthreads wait on condition variables by performing the **pthread_cond_wait()** call:

```
boolean_t       some_condition;
pthread_cond_t  cond;
pthread_mutex_t mutex;

pthread_mutex_lock(&mutex);
while (!some_condition) {
        status = pthread_cond_wait(&cond, &mutex);
        if (status == -1) {
                perror("pthread_cond_wait");
                exit(1);
        }
}
/*
 * some_condition is known to be TRUE here,
 * take the appropriate action
 */
pthread_mutex_unlock(&mutex);
```

The **pthread_cond_wait** call atomically unlocks *mutex* and then blocks the calling pthread (inside the **pthread_cond_wait** call) until another pthread signals condition *cond*. Once awakened (still inside the **pthread_cond_wait** call), the calling pthread attempts to lock *mutex*, waiting if necessary. When the **pthread_cond_wait** call completes, the calling pthread knows that *cond* has been signaled and that *mutex* is locked.

It is important to note several fine points concerning the **pthread_cond_wait** call. First, *mutex* must already be locked when **pthread_cond_wait** is called. Second, if more than one pthread is waiting when *cond* is signaled, at least one of them is awakened (which one is not defined). Finally, you typically associate *cond* with some condition in your application, as indicated by, for instance, *some_condition* in the sample fragment. There is an inherent race between the completion of the **pthread_cond_wait** call and the next statement, during which the condition you were waiting for may no longer hold. Be sure to check again that the condition still obtains on exiting the **pthread_cond_wait** call; this is why the sample code shows a `while` loop.

The P Threads library incorporates a facility to limit waiting on a condition variable to a specific time interval. To perform such a timed wait on a condition variable, you supply a locked mutex, a condition variable, and a time period in nanoseconds to the **pthread_cond_timedwait()** call as follows:

```
struct timespec abstime;
pthread_cond_t  a_cond;
pthread_mutex_t a_mutex;
int             status;

status = pthread_cond_timedwait(&cond, &mutex, &abstime);
if (status == -1) {
        perror("pthread_cond_timedwait");
        exit(1);
}
```

As with **pthread_cond_wait**, the mutex *a_mutex* is atomically unlocked and the calling pthread waits for another pthread to signal *a_cond*. If the condition is signaled before the specified time expires, *a_mutex* is relocked and the **pthread_cond_timedwait** call completes. If the specified time interval elapses before the *a_cond* is signaled, the **pthread_cond_timedwait** call completes with *a_mutex* locked, returning the status code EAGAIN. Code EINVAL is returned if any of the three parameters are invalid. If the pthread issuing the **pthread_cond_wait** call has not locked *a_mutex*, code EDEADLK is returned.

10.1.6   Who Am I?

A pthread obtains its own identifier with the **pthread_self()** call:

```
pthread_t my_id;

my_id = pthread_self();
```

For maximum portability, you should not assume that pthread identifiers are any particular size or underlying data type. Instead treat pthread identifiers as opaque data types. To determine if two pthread identifiers represent the same pthread, use the **pthread_equal()** call as follows:

```
pthread_t an_id;
pthread_t another_id;
int       status;

status = pthread_equal(an_id, another_id);
```

The **pthread_equal** call returns a nonzero value in *status* if *an_id* and *another_id* represent the same pthread. Zero (0) is returned if the two identifiers represent different pthreads. Note that this behavior is an exception to the usual convention in which zero represents success and -1 represents failure.

10.1.7   Yielding the Processor

OSF/1 P Threads takes advantage of the Mach kernel's threads facility to implement pthreads. This scheme provides true concurrency—without placing any particular design requirements on your application. On multiprocessor machines, each pthread is automatically scheduled and executed independently of other pthreads.

However, other versions of the P Threads standard may be implemented to simulate multiple threads without kernel assistance. In these implementations, the deadlock condition known as *starvation* can occur. Starvation happens·on single-CPU systems when one pthread does not relinquish the processor (for example, because it is executing a continuous loop); other runnable pthreads then cannot execute. The solution is to give up the processor; this is the purpose of the **pthread_yield()** call:

```
pthread_yield();
```

The **pthread_yield** function advises the scheduler that it may run another pthread in preference to the pthread issuing the **pthread_yield** call (see Fig. 10.2). If no other thread can be run, the calling thread continues to execute.

You should consider the possibility of starvation in designing your application and include **pthread_yield** calls as needed. On OSF/1, this approach may increase concurrency. If there are more pthreads than processors on your machine, using **pthread_yield** gives waiting pthreads an opportunity to run. Even more importantly, this approach ensures that your application functions correctly even if run on a non-OSF/1 system with a P Threads implementation based on simulated concurrency.

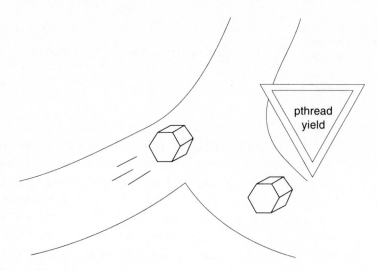

Figure 10.2: **pthread_yield** Permits Another Pthread to Make Progress

The P1003.4a standard includes a number of additional scheduler-related interfaces, primarily intended for real-time systems. These calls are not part of the OSF/1 P Threads implementation.

10.1.8   Pthread-Specific Data

All pthreads in a process share the same virtual memory. Any pthread in a process can thus access all information stored in the process's address space. To handle data specific to a pthread, you could establish a convention that places the information for each pthread at a predetermined place in the address space. Each pthread would by convention look only in its assigned area for its own data. The disadvantage of this design is that you have to manage the storage yourself. For instance, you might access a pthread's data via a hash table based on the pthread identifier.

For convenience, P Threads defines a portable mechansim for associating information with individual pthreads. This per-pthread data is keyed for easy retrieval. You create a key and then advise the P Threads library of the key/pthread/data association:

```
pthread_key_t a_key;
void          *destructor_routine();
int           status;
void          *value;
```

```
status = pthread_keycreate(&a_key, destructor_routine);
if (status == -1) {
        perror("pthread_keycreate");
        exit(1);
}
status = pthread_setspecific(a_key, value);
if (status == -1) {
        perror("pthread_setspecific");
        exit(1);
}

destructor_routine(arg)
void *arg;
{
/*
 * Dispose of per-thread storage here
 */
}
```

The **pthread_keycreate()** call establishes a new key for later use in storing and retrieving per-pthread information. The same key value may be used by multiple pthreads, and each pthread can associate different data with it. You would typically use a pointer to a block of dynamically allocated storage as the data associated with a key. To make it easier to dispose of such dynamic storage, you can optionally specify a function, *destructor_routine*, when creating the key. You supply this function, which is invoked automatically when the pthread terminates by calling **pthread_exit**, either implicitly or explicitly. The function *destructor_routine* is called with the current value associated with the key as its argument and should release the dynamically allocated storage. If the **pthread_keycreate** call succeeds, zero (0) is returned. Otherwise -1 is returned, and *errno* contains one of the error codes listed in Table 10.3.

Error Code	Meaning
EINVAL	The value specified for the key is invalid.
ENOMEM	There is a permanent resource shortage.
EAGAIN	There is currently not enough memory to create the key.

Table 10.3: **pthread_keycreate** Error Codes

P Threads Call	C Threads Call	Comments
	cthread_init	You do not need to initialize the P Threads library.
pthread_create	cthread_fork	C Threads does not permit setting attributes.
pthread_exit	cthread_exit	
pthread_attr_create		There is no analogous function in C Threads.
pthread_attr_setstacksize		C Threads does not allow setting stack sizes.
pthread_join	cthread_join	
pthread_detach	cthread_detach	
pthread_mutex_lock	mutex_lock	
pthread_mutex_unlock	mutex_unlock	
pthread_mutex_trylock	mutex_try_lock	
pthread_mutex_init	mutex_alloc	
pthread_mutex_destroy	mutex_free	
	mutex_init	
	mutex_clear	
pthread_cond_wait	condition_wait	
pthread_cond_signal	condition_signal	
pthread_cond_broadcast	condition_broadcast	
pthread_cond_timedwait		C Threads does not include a way to perform a timed wait.
pthread_cond_init	condition_init	
pthread_cond_destroy		
pthread_self	cthread_self	

Table 10.4: Comparison of P Threads and C Threads Calls

P Threads Call	C Threads Call	Comments
pthread_equal		C Threads does not include a call for comparing thread IDs.
pthread_yield	**cthread_yield**	
pthread_keycreate		C Threads does not use keys for per-thread data.
pthread_setspecific	**cthread_set_data**	
pthread_getspecific	**cthread_data**	
pthread_setcancel		No cancellation mechanism exists in C Threads.
pthread_testcancel		
pthread_setasynccancel		
pthread_cancel		
pthread_cleanup_push		C Threads has no provision for executing clean-up routines.
pthread_cleanup_pop		
sigwait		C Threads does not include signal handling facilities.
flockfile		C Threads was not intended to handle synchronization of I/O calls.
funlockfile		

Table 10.4   *Continued*

The **pthread_setspecific()** call stores the association between the data (*value*) and a key (*a_key*). Zero (0) is returned in *status* if the association is successfully recorded. Supplying an invalid key causes -1 to be stored in *status* and *errno* to be set to EINVAL.

You issue the **pthread_getspecific()** call to retrieve data associated with a particular key:

```
pthread_t a_key;
void      *retrieved_value;
int       status;

status = pthread_getspecific(a_key, &retrieved_value);
```

The **pthread_getspecific** call retrieves the data (*value*) currently associated with *a_key* in the calling pthread. If an invalid key is supplied, EINVAL is stored in *errno* and -1 is returned. Otherwise 0 is returned.

The routines described here roughly correspond to the C Threads library functions **cthread_set_data** and **cthread_data**.

10.2   Advanced P Threads Topics

The calls presented in the previous section represent the features common to both C Threads and P Threads. Although the details of the calling sequences differ, the concepts and usage of these calls are similar for both threads libraries.

The P1003.4a standard specifies a number of additional P Threads operations beyond those already covered. These concepts and the associated calls have no counterpart in the C Threads library. These areas comprise cancellation, cleanup on termination, signal handling differences, and the treatment of errors.

10.2.1   Pthread Cancellation

The P Threads package provides a facility for cleanly stopping the execution of a pthread. This *cancellation* mechanism allows a pthread to request termination of another pthread in the same process. You issue the **pthread_cancel()** call to make such a *cancellation request*.

Pthreads may specify cleanup processing that occurs when they are terminated due to a cancellation request. Pthreads can also hold cancellation requests pending by setting a pthread's *cancelability state*.[3] Without this ability, applications would have to be designed in such a way that unexpected pthread termination could occur at any time. The ability to choose *cancellation points* (explicit places in your program where termination may occur) removes this stringent design requirement.

Cancelability

When a cancellation request is issued, there are three possible effects on the target pthread:

1. The cancellation request is held until the target pthread permits handling it.

2. The target pthread terminates when it reaches the next predetermined cancellation point.

3. The target pthread terminates immediately.

Pthreads may specify which of these actions they prefer and may change the preferred action at any time. By default, cancellation requests are held pending until a cancellation point is reached.

The P Threads library associates these three actions with two per-pthread cancelability states: *general cancelability* and *asynchronous cancelability*. Loosely speaking, general cancelability indicates whether or not cancellation requests for a pthread are held pending or performed. By default, general cancelability is enabled, meaning that cancellation requests can be performed.

Practical applications require more precise control of external termination requests than general cancelability alone provides. For instance, if a pthread in your application must execute two related disk write operations to complete a transaction, you would not allow the pthread to be canceled between the two write actions. For this reason, cancellation requests are normally handled only when explicit cancellation points (CPs) are reached. This design provides a way to protect critical sections from unwanted termination while allowing cancellation where appropriate.

---

[3]Since the completion of OSF/1 Release 1.1, there have been changes in the P Threads P1003.4a standard. For instance, Draft 6 now uses the term *interruptibility state* instead of cancelability state. There are also several changes in the details of the related P Threads calls (e.g., **pthread_setintr**) to set a pthread's interruptibility. This section describes the calls implemented in OSF/1 Release 1.1.

What are these explicit cancellation points in your application? There are four situations in which a pthread can be canceled:

1. When a **pthread_cond_wait** or **pthread_cond_timedwait** call is executed

2. When waiting for another pthread with the **pthread_join** call

3. When general cancelability is enabled with the **pthread_setcancel** call

4. When the **pthread_testcancel** call is performed.

Working with Cancelability States

You normally design your application such that pthreads can be canceled only at cancellation points. Permitting cancellation at any time can cause failures that are difficult to track down and correct. For example, consider a pthread that allocates a block of dynamic memory:

```
char *my_data = NULL;

my_data = malloc(MY_DATA_SIZE);
```

A method of automatically releasing such storage when the pthread terminates is addressed in Section 10.2.2. For now, we only need to know that a *cleanup routine* executes code to release the storage when the pthread terminates:

```
void *
my_cleanup_routine()
{
        free(my_data);
}
```

Consider what happens if another pthread initiates a request to cancel this pthread *after* **malloc** has allocated the storage but *before* the address of the allocated memory has been stored in *my_data*. In this case we certainly cannot allow the cleanup routine to use *my_data* to release the storage; it still contains NULL. Of course, **my_cleanup_routine** could carefully check for NULL before returning the memory. But the storage *has* been allocated, and it should be returned. To address this kind of dilemma, cancellation requests

General Cancelability	Asynchronous Cancelability	Requests Are:
Enabled	Enabled	Performed
Enabled	Disabled	Held until CP
Disabled	Enabled	Held
Disabled	Disabled	Held

Table 10.5: Cancelability States

are not usually handled immediately. Instead they are held pending until a safe cancellation point is reached.

Although you typically want to postpone acting on cancellation requests until a cancellation point, there are situations in which this scheme is not the best approach. For example, if a pthread performs a lengthy computation in which there are no critical sections, it may be safe to process cancellation requests during the calculations. The benefit of this scheme is that you avoid a long period during which a pthread cannot be canceled.

To permit handling cancellation requests immediately, you can set a pthread's asynchronous cancelability state. If asynchronous cancelability is enabled, cancellation requests may be processed at any time. If asynchronous cancelability is disabled, cancellation requests are processed at the next cancellation point. By default, asynchronous cancelability is disabled. Be sure that your code is amenable to sudden interruptions before you enable asynchronous cancelability. Note that a pthread's asynchronous cancelability state is immaterial if general cancelability is disabled. Table 10.5 summarizes the handling of cancellation requests for all combinations of cancellation states.

The P Threads library remembers pending cancellation requests and acts on them as soon as it becomes possible. For example, suppose that a pthread has disabled general cancelability. If you issue a cancellation request for this pthread, the request is held pending because general cancelability is disabled. When general cancelability is later enabled, the pthread will be terminated.

P Threads Cancellation Calls

To enable or disable the general cancelability of a pthread, you issue the **pthread_setcancel()** call:

```
int new_state;
int old_state;
```

```
old_state = pthread_setcancel(new_state);
if (old_state == -1) {
        perror("pthread_setcancel");
        exit(1);
}
```

A successful **pthread_setcancel** call changes the calling pthread's general cancelability as specified by *new_state* and returns the previous cancelability in *old_state*. Otherwise -1 is returned in *old_state* and *errno* is set to indicate the error. The only possible error is EINVAL, returned if the *new_state* parameter is not one of the two constants CANCEL_ON (enable general cancelability) or CANCEL_OFF (disable general cancelability).

To set the asynchronous cancelability of a pthread, execute the call **pthread_setasynccancel()**:

```
int old_state;
int new_state;

old_state = pthread_setasynccancel(new_state);
if (old_state == -1) {
        perror("pthread_setcancel");
        exit(1);
}
```

The calling pthread's asynchronous cancelability state is changed to *new_state*, and the previous state is stored in *old_state*. The *new_state* parameter must be one of the two constants CANCEL_ON (enable asynchronous cancelability) or CANCEL_OFF (disable asynchronous cancelability). Otherwise, -1 is returned and *errno* is set to EINVAL.

To cancel a pthread, use the **pthread_cancel()** call:

```
pthread_t a_thread;
int       status;

status = pthread_cancel(a_thread);
if (status == -1) {
        perror("pthread_cancel");
        exit(1);
}
```

To indicate a cancellation point in your program, you issue the call **pthread_testcancel()** as follows:

$\vdots$

```
pthread_testcancel();    /* Safe to cancel here */
```

$\vdots$

If a cancellation request has been received when the **pthread_testcancel** call is issued, and general cancelability is enabled, the pthread is terminated.

10.2.2   Cleanup Routines

Canceled pthreads may have allocated resources prior to their termination. Typically you want to design your application in such a way that these resources can be returned at pthread cancellation time. For instance, there may be open files, virtual memory, IPC ports, or other resources that are no longer needed. If the pthread that originally requested such resources is canceled, these items should be deallocated.

The system maintains a list of *cleanup routines* for each pthread to facilitate this housekeeping. These routines are part of the application, and you design them to take whatever actions are appropriate for your program at pthread cancellation time. You place each cleanup routine on the pthread's list of cleanup routines using the **pthread_cleanup_push()** call:

```
void *my_cleanup_routine();
void *arg;

pthread_cleanup_push(my_cleanup_routine, arg);
```

Functions are removed from the list of routines using the P Threads function **pthread_cleanup_pop()**:

```
int execute_flag;

pthread_cleanup_pop(execute_flag);
```

Note that neither call returns a status code. The only action of the **pthread_cleanup_push** call is to push the specified function (*my_cleanup_routine*) onto the stack of cleanup routines for the executing pthread. Once this call completes, several situations cause *my_cleanup_routine* and any previously pushed routines to be removed from the stack and invoked:

- The pthread exits (i.e., **pthread_exit** is executed).

- The pthread acts on a cancellation request.

- **pthread_cleanup_pop** is called with a nonzero argument.

Executing **pthread_cleanup_pop** with an argument of zero (0) removes only the top function from the stack of cleanup routines but does not execute the popped function.

10.2.3   P Threads and Signals

P Threads facilitate designing the signal handling portion of your application. By using a new approach to dealing with signals, you can structure your program more cleanly, avoiding some of the difficulties of traditional UNIX signal handlers. In this section we first explore the problems attendant to signal handlers. Then we describe the **sigwait** call, which allows a more convenient strategy for processing signals in multithreaded programs.

Traditional UNIX signal handlers require that you explicitly prevent signals from occurring at "inconvenient" times. For example, a disk file might be inconsistent if only one of two related write operations completes. Good programming practice would suggest disallowing signals prior to starting the first write operation, until the second write had finished successfully. Otherwise an interrupt signal could be delivered between the two output operations. Of course, you can code your application to respond to every possible signal appropriately. The difficulty with this approach is that the "appropriate" action differs at each point in the program. Let us look at how P Threads avoids this dilemma entirely.

Instead of abruptly interrupting an executing program, it would be much more convenient if asynchronous signals could be turned into synchronous notifications. The OSF/1 P Threads library provides the **sigwait()** call for just this purpose. This call blocks the pthread that issues it until one of several signals arrives. Here is the calling sequence:

```
int      status;
sigset_t *setp;

status = sigwait(setp);
```

The set of signals *setp* is constructed using macros defined in the header file `<signal.h>`. Note that these macros modify *setp* (for instance, by adding a

Macro	Usage
sigemptyset(setp)	Clear all signals in signal set *setp*
sigfillset(setp)	Enable all signals in signal set *setp*
sigaddset(setp, S)	Add signal *S* to signal set *setp*
sigdelset(setp, S)	Remove signal *S* from signal set *setp*
sigismember(setp, S)	Return TRUE if signal *S* is in set *setp*
sigsetdiff(setp, set)	Return signals not in *set* in *setp*
sigsetsum(setp, set)	Add signals in *set* to *setp*
sigfirstset(setp)	Return first signal in signal set *setp*
siganyset(setp)	Return TRUE if *setp* contains any signals

Table 10.6: Cancelability States

specified signal to the set). (We use the term *signal* here in the traditional UNIX sense; for example, SIGTERM, SIGUSR1, etc.) Table 10.6 lists these macros.

Typical usage of **sigwait** would be to dedicate one pthread in your application to accept signals by executing the **sigwait** call. Other pthreads would not need to block signals at inconvenient times. Instead the pthread accepting signals would record the occurrence of a signal, and other pthreads in the program would query this record to determine if a signal had been received.

10.3 Pthread Error Reporting

The traditional UNIX mechanism for reporting errors employs the global variable *errno*. UNIX calls store a status code in *errno*, which the application then checks to determine whether the call succeeded or failed.

Unfortunately, this scheme is not suitable for multithreaded applications. Consider an application with two pthreads, Pthread A and Pthread B. Pthread A makes a call, like **read**. Pthread B then makes a call, perhaps a **write**. (For this example, the specific calls are irrelevant.) Pthread A stores the status code from the **read** in the global variable *errno*, and then before Pthread A can check the code, Pthread B overwrites that value with the status from the **write** operation.

To address this problem, the IEEE CS P Threads standard specifies that returned status codes must be maintained on a per-thread basis. In the

previous example, this means that Pthread A would store the result of the
read call, and Pthread B would store the result of the **write** call. When
either pthread checked the value of *errno*, each would see only the status
from the last call executed *by that pthread*. To cause this behavior your
application must include the header file `<errno.h>`. The effect is achieved
by turning the reference to the global variable *errno* into a function call that
retrieves the per-pthread value.

10.4   Two Example P Threads Programs

In this section we present two sample P Threads programs. The first is the
multithreaded matrix multiplication program, mmat, from Chapter 2. The
P Threads version, pmat, illustrates the advantages of using a threads library
like P Threads compared to calling the Mach kernel interfaces directly. Program pmat is much simpler than mmat and contains no machine-specific
code.

The second example program demonstrates the similarities between
C Threads and P Threads. We convert the Text Search example of Chapter 5 from C Threads to P Threads. For both examples, we list the steps
needed to transform the original program into the P Threads version.

A P Threads Version of Program mmat

Changing the mmat program of Chapter 2 to use P Threads is easy. Just a
few simple modifications are needed in these areas:

1. Use of `<pthread.h>` and `<errno.h>`

2. Use of **pthread_create** (without machine-specific code)

3. Changes in pthread termination.

No changes are required to the header file `"mat.h"` or to the matrix printing
routine **matrix_print** in file matprt.c. We list these files here for completeness:

```
/*
 * mat.h - Common definitions for programs smat, mmat
 */

#define N 3
```

```
#define P 4
#define M 5

/*
 * matprt.c - Print matrices for smat, mmat programs
 */

#include "mat.h"

extern int mat_1[N][P], mat_2[P][M], result[N][M];

void
matrix_print()
{
        int i, j;

        printf("mat_1:\n");
        for (i=0; i < N; i++) {
                for (j=0; j < P; j++)
                        printf("%4d ", mat_1[i][j]);
                putchar('\n');
        }

        printf("mat_2:\n");
        for (i=0; i < P; i++) {
                for (j=0; j < M; j++)
                        printf("%4d ", mat_2[i][j]);
                putchar('\n');
        }

        printf("result:\n");
        for (i=0; i < N; i++) {
                for (j=0; j < M; j++)
                        printf("%4d ", result[i][j]);
                putchar('\n');
        }
}
```

Here is the complete program using P Threads:

```
/*
 * Program pmat - Multithreaded Matrix Multiply using Pthreads
 */
```

```
#include <pthread.h>
#include <stddef.h>
#include <stdlib.h>
#include <stdio.h>
#include <mach.h>
#include <errno.h>
#include "mat.h"

int mat_1[N][P] = {{1, 2, 3, 4},
                   {5, 6, 7, 8},
                   {9, 0, 1, 2}};

int mat_2[P][M] = {{3, 4, 5, 6, 7},
                   {8, 9, 0, 1, 2},
                   {3, 4, 5, 6, 7},
                   {8, 9, 0, 1, 2}};

int result[N][M];

#define THREAD_NOT_DONE 0
#define THREAD_DONE     1
#define NTHREADS 8

int threads[NTHREADS];

main()
{
        matrix_multiply();      /* Multiply the matrices   */
        matrix_print();         /* Print the result matrix */
        exit(0);
}

/*
 * Create & start NTHREADS pthreads
 * to multiply matrices mat_1 * mat_2
 */
matrix_multiply()
{
        int thread_num;

        for (thread_num = 0; thread_num < NTHREADS; thread_num++) {
                threads[thread_num] = THREAD_NOT_DONE;
                thread_fork(thread_num);
        }
```

```
                wait_for_threads();
}

void thread_multiply();

/*
 * Create, setup, and start a thread
 */
thread_fork(thread_num)
int thread_num;
{
        int         status;
        pthread_t th;

        status = pthread_create(&th,
                               pthread_attr_default,
                               (void *)thread_multiply,
                               (void *)thread_num);
        if (status != ESUCCESS) {
                perror("pthread_create");
                exit(1);
        }
}

/*
 * Compute one result matrix element
 */
compute_element(i, j)
int i, j;
{
        int l, element;

        element = 0;
        for (l=0; l < P; l++)
                element += mat_1[i][l] * mat_2[l][j];
        return(element);
}

/*
 * Do one thread's multiplications
 */
void
thread_multiply(thread_num)
int thread_num;
```

```
{
        int status;
        int i, j;

        for (i=0; i < N; i++) {
                for (j=thread_num; j < M; j += NTHREADS)
                        result[i][j] = compute_element(i, j);
        }

        threads[thread_num] = THREAD_DONE;
        (void) pthread_exit(0);
}

/*
 * Poll until all threads are done
 */
wait_for_threads()
{
        int thread_num;

        for (thread_num = 0; thread_num < NTHREADS; thread_num++) {
                while (threads[thread_num] == THREAD_NOT_DONE)
                        sleep(1);
        }
}
```

This straightforward conversion of our original mmat program shows how
the use of the P Threads library simplifies writing multithreaded applications. In particular, the machine-dependent code is no longer needed. We
can simplify the pmat program even more, however, by replacing the "manual" synchronization in the **wait_for_threads** routine with its P Threads
equivalent.

The P Threads library provides a routine that performs precisely the
function of **wait_for_threads**. The **pthread_join** operation can be used to
determine that each pthread has completed and the individual pthreads no
longer need to set the THREAD_DONE completion flag manually. Here are
the specific changes required:

1. Remove the definitions of THREAD_NOT_DONE and THREAD_DONE.

2. Change the *threads* array to be of type *thread_t*.

3. Remove the line of code performed by each pthread to initialize its
   entry in the *threads* array with THREAD_NOT_DONE.

4. Modify the **pthread_create** call to store the pthread ID directly into the pthread's entry in the *threads* array.

5. Remove the code performed by each pthread to set the THREAD_DONE flag.

6. Change the **wait_for_threads** function to loop over the *threads* array and perform a **pthread_join** call on each pthread.

There are no changes needed to the files "mat.h" and matprt.c. Here is the modified version of program pmat:

```
/*
 * Program pmat - Multithreaded Matrix Multiply using Pthreads
 *                (modified to use pthread_join to wait for threads)
 */

#include <pthread.h>
#include <stddef.h>
#include <stdlib.h>
#include <stdio.h>
#include <mach.h>
#include <errno.h>
#include "mat.h"

int mat_1[N][P] = {{1, 2, 3, 4},
                   {5, 6, 7, 8},
                   {9, 0, 1, 2}};

int mat_2[P][M] = {{3, 4, 5, 6, 7},
                   {8, 9, 0, 1, 2},
                   {3, 4, 5, 6, 7},
                   {8, 9, 0, 1, 2}};

int result[N][M];

#define NTHREADS 8

pthread_t threads[NTHREADS];

main()
{
        matrix_multiply();      /* Multiply the matrices   */
        matrix_print();         /* Print the result matrix */
```

```
        exit(0);
}

/*
 * Create & start NTHREADS pthreads
 * to multiply matrices mat_1 * mat_2
 */
matrix_multiply()
{
        int thread_num;

        for (thread_num = 0; thread_num < NTHREADS; thread_num++) {
                thread_fork(thread_num);
        }
        wait_for_threads();
}

void thread_multiply();

/*
 * Create, setup, and start a thread
 */
thread_fork(thread_num)
int thread_num;
{
        int        status;

        status = pthread_create(&threads[thread_num],
                                pthread_attr_default,
                                (void *)thread_multiply,
                                (void *)thread_num);
        if (status != ESUCCESS) {
                perror("pthread_create");
                exit(1);
        }
}

/*
 * Compute one result matrix element
 */
compute_element(i, j)
int i, j;
{
        int l, element;
```

```
        element = 0;
        for (l=0; l < P; l++)
                element += mat_1[i][l] * mat_2[l][j];
        return(element);
}


/*
 * Do one thread's multiplications
 */
void
thread_multiply(thread_num)
int thread_num;
{
        int status;
        int i, j;

        for (i=0; i < N; i++) {
                for (j=thread_num; j < M; j += NTHREADS)
                        result[i][j] = compute_element(i, j);
        }
        (void) pthread_exit(0);
}


/*
 * Poll until all threads are done
 */
wait_for_threads()
{
        int thread_num;
        void *exit_status;

        for (thread_num = 0; thread_num < NTHREADS; thread_num++) {
                (void) pthread_join(threads[thread_num],
                                        &exit_status);
        }
}
```

A P Threads Version of the Text Search Program

The steps needed to convert a C Threads program to P Threads are almost mechanical. Here are the changes to the Text Search program to use P Threads:

- In **main**:

  1. Declare *status* (a variable to hold the return status from the P Threads calls).

  2. Change the type of variable *thread* from *cthread_t* to *pthread_t*.

  3. Remove the dynamic allocation of mutexes and the condition variable. They are now statically allocated. Also add calls to initialize them.

  4. Remove the library initialization call **cthread_init**.

  5. Change **cthread_fork** to **pthread_create**, and add a check for failure. (The **cthread_fork** call returns no errors, so no check was needed in the C Threads version.)

  6. Translate the C Threads mutex and condition variable calls into the equivalent P Threads calls.

  7. Remove the code to free the mutexes and condition variables.

- In function **search**:

  1. Typecast the **search** function to agree with the definition of **pthread_create**. For the same reason, change the argument type.

  2. Translate the mutex calls to the corresponding P Threads names.

- In function **search_file**, once again translate the mutex calls to the corresponding P Threads names.

Here is the result of applying these changes:

```
/*
 * Program psearch - "grep-like" program using Pthreads
 */

#include <pthread.h>
#include <stddef.h>
#include <stdlib.h>
#include <stdio.h>
#include <mach.h>
#include <errno.h>

#define          PARENT          "parent"
```

```
#define          MAXNTH          20

char *str;              /* string to search for */
char **files;           /* files to be searched */
int  th_count;          /* number of files      */

pthread_mutex_t   file_lock;   /* lock for index        */
pthread_mutex_t   print_lock;  /* lock for output       */
pthread_mutex_t   count_lock;  /* lock for thread count */

pthread_cond_t    th_cond;   /* condition for exiting threads */

static void *search();

extern char *getenv();
extern char *index();

main(argc, argv)
int  argc;
char **argv;
{
        int      i, status;
        char     *parallel;
        pthread_t thread;

        /*
         * For this example, we require at least one file
         */
        if (argc < 3) {
                usage(argv[0]);
                exit(1);
        }
        str = argv[1];
        argc -= 2;
        files = &argv[2];
        if ((parallel = getenv("PARALLEL")) == NULL)
                th_count = 1;
        else
                th_count = atoi(parallel);
        th_count = (th_count > MAXNTH) ? MAXNTH : th_count;
        /*
         * If there are fewer files than potential threads,
         * only create as many threads as needed.
         */
```

```
if (argc < th_count)
        th_count = argc;

/*
 * Initialize mutex locks and condition variables.
 */
pthread_mutex_init(&file_lock, pthread_mutexattr_default);
pthread_mutex_init(&print_lock, pthread_mutexattr_default);
pthread_mutex_init(&count_lock, pthread_mutexattr_default);
pthread_cond_init(&th_cond, pthread_condattr_default);

/*
 * Fork off all the child threads
 */
for (i = 1; i < th_count; i++) {
        status = pthread_create(&thread,
                                pthread_attr_default,
                                (void *)search,
                                (void *)0);
        if (status != ESUCCESS) {
                perror("pthread_create");
                exit(1);
        }
        pthread_detach(&thread);
}

/*
 * Parent thread does work too
 */
search( PARENT );

/*
 * Wait for all child threads to finish
 */
pthread_mutex_lock(&count_lock);
while (th_count != 0) {
        pthread_cond_wait(&th_cond, &count_lock);
}
pthread_mutex_unlock(&count_lock);

exit(0);
}

/*
```

```
* Search all the files for the string.  If we
* are a child thread (parent_flag == NULL),
* then signal the condition.
*/

static void *
search(parent_flag)
void *parent_flag;
{
        char *cur_file;

        pthread_mutex_lock(&file_lock);
        while (*files != NULL) {
                cur_file = *files++;
                pthread_mutex_unlock(&file_lock);
                (void) search_file(cur_file);
                pthread_mutex_lock(&file_lock);
        }
        pthread_mutex_unlock(&file_lock);

        pthread_mutex_lock(&count_lock);
        th_count--;
        pthread_mutex_unlock(&count_lock);
        if (parent_flag != (char *)PARENT) {
                /*
                 * We are a child thread
                 */
                pthread_cond_signal(&th_cond);
                pthread_exit(0);
        }

}

/*
 * Search the given file for the string.  For each line that matches,
 * print it out
 */
search_file(file)
char *file;
{
        FILE *fp;
        int match_found;
        char *line[BUFSIZ];
        char *p, *p1;
```

```
        char *s, *s1;

        if ((fp = fopen(file, "r")) == NULL) {
                perror(file);
                return(1);
        }

        while (fgets(line, BUFSIZ, fp) != NULL) {
                s = str;
                match_found = 0;
                p = line;
                while ((p = index(p, *s)) && !match_found) {
                        if (strncmp(p, str, strlen(str)) == 0)
                                match_found = 1;
                        p++;
                }
                if (match_found) {
                        pthread_mutex_lock(&print_lock);
                        printf("%s: %s",file, line);
                        pthread_mutex_unlock(&print_lock);
                }
        }
        fclose(fp);
        return(0);

}

usage(prog)
char *prog;
{
        printf("usage: %s str file1 file2 ...\n",prog);
}
```

10.5   Using Reentrant Libraries

In Section 2.2.4 we noted that library routines like **malloc** are not always thread-safe, which means that the code is not *reentrant*. That is, if two threads should execute such a routine simultaneously, the results are indeterminate because of the need to synchronize access to shared data.

To address this problem, POSIX 1003.4a specifies thread-safe versions of many C library (libc) functions. In some cases, only the underlying implementation of a function differs for the thread-safe version. For other routines, the interface is inherently unusable in a multithreaded environment. For these functions, P1003.4a specifies alternative interfaces. These reentrant versions of the routines have the same name as the original function, with _r appended to the end of the name (for example, **gmtime_r**).

For those non-reentrant routines that use global static data, the corresponding _r version passes the data across the interface. With these reentrant functions, the calling pthread saves the data across subsequent calls, rather than the function itself storing the data in static storage. An example of such a (not reentrant) function is **strtok**. You typically call **strtok** repeatedly to obtain tokens from a string, and the **strtok** function itself keeps track of the last string position with data stored in static memory. The reentrant version of this routine, **strtok_r**, instead passes the string position across the interface.

The design of some libc functions requires sharing static data across multiple calls. For example, the stdio calls use static buffers. In these situations, you must explicitly provide synchronization around calls to these routines to ensure correct operation in a multithreaded environment. The **flockfile()** and **funlockfile()** functions perform this synchronization for stdio calls. Their calling sequences are straightforward:

```
#include <stdio.h>
FILE *fp;

void flockfile(fp);
void funlockfile(fp);
```

A pthread executing the **flockfile** call gains exclusive access to the specified *FILE* object. That pthread may issue subsequent **flockfile** calls, so pairs of **flockfile/funlockfile** calls may be nested. Once one pthread has executed the **flockfile** call, other pthreads executing the **flockfile** call will block until the first pthread calls **funlockfile**.

Let us look at some examples to clarify these ideas. Assume an application contains these functions:

```
FILE *debug_file;

/*
 * log_event:
 *    1) lock debug file
 *    2) Seek to the end of the file and
 *    3) Write the date & time
```

```
 *   4) unlock the file.
 */
log_event(datetime)
char *datetime;
{
        flockfile(debug_file);
        fseek(debug_file, 0, SEEK_SET(2));
        fprintf(debug_file, "%s", datetime);
        funlockfile(debug_file);
}


do_something(today)
char *today;
{
        /*
         * Code to do work goes here
         */

        /*
         * Log the 'noteworthy' event.
         */
        log_event(today);
}


/*
 * update_debug_file_hdr
 * parameters: Name of application subsystem (component)
 *             date & time
 *  1) lock debug file
 *  2) move to start of file
 *  3) write name
 *  4) call log_event
 *  5) unlock debug file
 */
update_debug_file_hdr(component, today)
char *component;
char *today;
{
        flockfile(debug_file);
        fseek(debug_file, 0, SEEK_SET(0));
        fprintf(debug_file, "%s", component);
        log_event(today);
        funlockfile(debug_file);
}
```

If Pthread A calls **do-something**, it will lock debug_file. If Pthread B now calls **do-something**, Pthread B will block when it, too, tries to lock debug_file.

Now suppose that Pthread A calls **update-debug-file-hdr**, locking debug_file. If Pthread B then calls **do-something**, Pthread B blocks when it, too, tries to lock debug_file. But what happens when Pthread A, having locked the file and performed the **fseek** and **fprintf**, calls **log-event**? Function **log-event** will also try to lock debug_file. But this lock attempt will *not* cause Pthread A to block, since the **flockfile** calls can be nested. This nesting property allows the use of **flockfile** and **funlockfile** calls in subroutines without concern about their previous use in upper-level routines. The ability to nest these calls is important, since you cannot easily tell if library routines you invoke use **flockfile** and **funlockfile** internally.

The UNIX calls **getc** and **putc** update a global pointer to a stdio buffer. Thus these calls must synchronize their access to the pointer in a multi-threaded environment. P1003.4a specifies exactly this behavior. Of course, this internal synchronization does not prevent multiple pthreads from using these calls, causing incorrect results. For instance, if two pthreads issue several **putc** calls on the same I/O stream, the output will contain characters from the two pthreads intermixed—probably not what you intended. To avoid such garbled output, you should bracket sequences of **getc** or **putc** calls with calls to **flockfile/funlockfile**.

Performance is another reason for using the **flockfile** and **funlockfile** calls. If you issue **getc** or **putc** calls frequently, the overhead of the synchronization may be significant. In this case, you can instead perform your own synchronization and invoke the **getc-unlocked** and **putc-unlocked** calls. There are also corresponding **getchar-unlocked** and **putchar-unlocked** calls. Here is a simple example showing how you might use these calls:

```
flockfile(stdout);        /* Lock the stdout stream       */
putchar_unlocked('1');    /*** Only 1 pthread can execute */
putchar_unlocked('2');    /*** this code (with ***) at a  */
printf("3456789\n");      /*** time for stdout            */
funlockfile(stdout);      /* Unlock the stdout stream     */
```

This code sequence serializes the execution of the output statements, so only one thread at a time will perform them. The example is simple, but this approach would perform better than relying on the internal locking of **putchar** if there were many such calls.

setkey_r	encrypt_r	crypt_r
ctime_r	localtime_r	asctime_r
gmtime_r	dirname_r	getdiskbyname_r
drand48_r	erand48_r	lrand48_r
mrand48_r	srand48_r	seed48_r
lcong48_r	nrand48_r	jrand48_r
ecvt_r	fcvt_r	getfsent_r
setfsent_r	getfsspec_r	getfsfile_r
endfsent_r	getdate_r	fgetgrent_r
getgrent_r	setgrent_r	getgrgid_r
endgrent_r	getgrnam_r	gethostbyname_r
gethostbyaddr_r	getlogin_r	getmntinfo_r
getnetent_r	setnetent_r	getnetbyaddr_r
endnetent_r	getnetbyname_r	fgetpwent_r
getpwent_r	setpwent_r	endpwent_r
getpwnam_r	getpwuid_r	getservent_r
setservent_r	getservbyname_r	endservent_r
getservbyport_r	getttyent_r	setttyent_r
endttyent_r	getttynam_r	getusershell_r
getutent_r	getutid_r	getutline_r
pututline_r	setutent_r	endutent_r
getprotoent_r	setprotoent_r	getprotobynumber_r
endprotoent_r	getprotobyname_r	hcreate_r
hdestroy_r	hsearch_r	l64a_r
linkntoa_r	nsntoa_r	ptsname_r
rand_r	srandom_r	random_r
initstate_r	setstate_r	readdir_r
recomp_r	reexec_r	hostalias_r
ssignal_r	gsignal_r	strerror_r
strtok_r	syslog_r	openlog_r
closelog_r	setlogmask_r	ttyname_r
wcstok_r		

Table 10.7: OSF/1 libc_r Functions

OSF/1 provides a version of the standard C library containing thread-safe versions of many functions. This reentrant variant of the library, libc_r, should be used with applications that employ P Threads. Table 10.7 lists the functions supplied in the OSF/1 libc_r library.

Chapter 11

Mach Programming

Most of this book describes the key technical features of Mach and demonstrates how to use the interfaces (system calls) to the kernel. This chapter deals with the more general topic of how to work within the environment Mach provides and make the best use of that environment.

Mach is compatible with 4.3BSD so a programmer familiar with that environment will have little trouble working with Mach. However, Mach is not 4.3BSD. The UNIX environment layered on top of Mach contains a few differences from a native 4.3BSD system. While there are not many differences, a programmer must be aware of them.

Many of these differences arise due to Mach's affinity for multiprocessor systems. The advent of such systems has increased the use of multithreading. Multithreaded applications require a different problem-solving approach from that used for single-threaded processes, as exists under UNIX. While most UNIX system and library calls will work in a multithreaded environment, there are precautions a programmer must take. Mach also offers features whose use may not be obvious without prior experience in a multithreaded environment.

We begin this chapter with a discussion of how UNIX memory management and signal management differ between native 4.3BSD and Mach. We then discuss how a programmer might use multiple threads of control within an application to increase performance through concurrency. In this chapter we emphasize the practical aspects of multithreading a program in contrast to the mechanical issues, such as the appropriate parameters to system calls, described earlier.

379

11.1   Memory Management

In Chapter 4 we described the features and benefits of Mach's memory management subsystem. This subsystem is both more robust and more flexible than many memory management systems. This is evidenced by capabilities such as external memory management. However, regardless of the capabilities of this system, what is important to a UNIX programmer are the differences between UNIX and Mach memory management which may cause UNIX programs to fail.

There are two common failure scenarios:

1. A working UNIX program fails when run under Mach, and

2. A program written using both UNIX and Mach primitives unexpectedly fails.

In this section we describe both forms of problems and suggest solutions.

11.1.1   Why a UNIX Program Might Fail under Mach

The likelihood of problems when writing or porting a UNIX program to Mach that does not use Mach-specific functionality may not be obvious. However, there *could* be problems when mixing UNIX and Mach primitives in the same program. Indeed there are, and we discuss those problems later in this chapter. A few incompatibilities exist from a native 4.3BSD system, and a programmer porting UNIX applications to Mach must understand these.

Stack Incompatibilities

One important concern relates to program stacks. A UNIX program run under Mach has its stack size determined when the program begins execution.[1] Conversely, many UNIX systems allocate a small stack at program initialization and grow the stack as needed. The stack may grow as long as the stack resource limit and available memory allow. Allocating memory only for stack pages currently in use increases efficiency. Flexibility is increased by allowing the stack to grow when needed, as long as memory is available.

This optimization is not necessary under Mach, as lazy evaluation provides a similar result. Hence the reason Mach does not allow UNIX program

---

[1] A program written for Mach does not have this limitation, as there are mechanisms (such as catching an exception and using **vm_allocate** to obtain additional stack pages) available to the Mach programmer to avoid this problem.

stacks to grow is not for efficiency reasons, but because Mach treats all memory regions, including the stack, identically. While UNIX has special regions for code, data, and bss, recall that Mach treats all regions (and pages) of memory equally. To provide certain pages, such as the stack, with the unique attribute that the region may dynamically grow would undermine the foundation on which Mach was built.

The kernel determines the stack size from the stack resource limit set with the UNIX **setrlimit()** system call. Hence if the stack is too small, the program will receive a SIGSEGV signal (segmentation violation) during a stack access. In such a case you should increase the stack limit. However, do not be tempted simply to "unlimit" the stack size. Many Mach implementations try to allocate the entire virtual address space for the stack, and the program will not run.

/dev/kmem **Incompatibilities**

Another common problem when porting UNIX programs centers around the use of the special file **/dev/kmem**. A number of UNIX programs open this file to obtain system parameters and status of the running system. A more portable mechanism to obtain such information has not yet been developed for UNIX. When porting programs to different systems, recompiling those programs that open **/dev/kmem** is expected due to data structure changes. It is important to remember, however, that Mach is not a native 4.3BSD system. There are two problems that may arise from using **/dev/kmem**:

1. Kernel data structures may be different than a 4.3BSD system, and

2. There is no guarantee that UNIX data structures, even those that are present, are used or updated.

Data structure differences may cause an existing program not to compile— referenced fields may not be present. While this may require program changes, at least the programmer is directed quickly to the problem area. These are the easy problems to fix.

Even if the program does compile, there are numerous fields that Mach ignores. For example, a useful piece of information is the current amount of memory a program is using. UNIX maintains this value in the *p_rssize* field of the per-process *proc* structure. This field is present in a Mach kernel; however, the field is never updated.[2] As we will describe shortly, Mach

---

[2]This field has been removed in OSF/1.

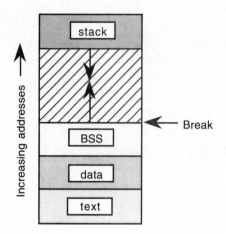

Figure 11.1: UNIX Memory Model

provides several mechanisms to obtain information on a task—none of which require knowledge of kernel data structures.

While it is possible to write programs that use /dev/kmem under Mach, it is not recommended. We have already seen how Mach provides more mechanisms than UNIX to obtain information about the system in a portable way. For example, the user may find

- A task's virtual memory usage information with **vm_region**

- Port information with **port_status**

- A task's virtual and resident memory sizes and scheduling data with **task_info**.

By using these system calls, a Mach programmer should never need to use /dev/kmem.

11.1.2   Mixing UNIX and Mach

Recall from Chapter 4 that UNIX provides a simple memory model, as shown in Fig. 11.1. Mach does not constrain a program to operate under such a model. Program text, data, and stack may reside at any location within a program's virtual address space. Remembering this, let us consider the incompatibility of mixing UNIX and Mach memory management primitives.

A UNIX program that allocates memory typically uses the **malloc()** library function. **Malloc** uses the **sbrk()** and **brk()** system calls to increase

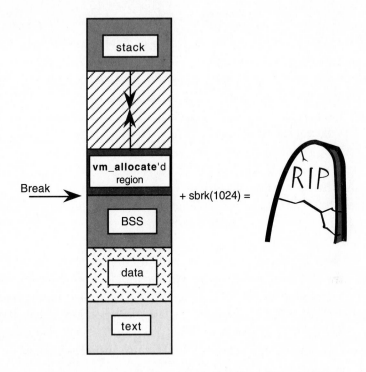

Figure 11.2: UNIX and Mach Do Not Always Mix

memory available to the program by extending the break point, the demarcation between allocated and unallocated memory.[3] Conversely, a Mach program uses **vm_allocate**, which may allocate any free page in a program's address space.

Problems may occur when a program uses both memory allocation mechanisms, **sbrk** and **vm_allocate** (Fig. 11.2). Consider the consequences if the result of a **vm_allocate** call were to allocate memory directly after the break point. Subsequent calls to **sbrk** could not succeed. The call only succeeds when there are enough virtually contiguous pages following the break point to satisfy the **sbrk** request.[4]

There are two mechanisms a programmer may use to resolve this incompatibility. One alternative uses **vm_allocate**'s ability to allocate memory at a programmer-specified address. Using this facility, the programmer could

---

[3] A program may, of course, invoke these system calls directly rather than using **malloc**.

[4] OSF/1 Release 1.1 has modified the Mach memory allocation heuristics such that it attempts to avoid allocating memory in the UNIX heap. This feature reduces, but does not eliminate, the problem.

allocate memory well above the break point and below the stack. Unfortunately this technique requires nonportable code changes as well as increased program complexity.

A better alternative employs a version of **malloc** that uses Mach memory management calls rather than UNIX calls. In this way a UNIX interface is preserved, thus retaining code portability. While this approach is only effective if the program does not directly issue **sbrk** system calls, most programs do use **malloc**. Hence this is the most practical approach to the problem.

You need not rush to implement a new version of **malloc**. The C Threads library contains a version of **malloc** that uses **vm_allocate**. The **malloc** function within the standard C language library (libc) of OSF/1 is not thread-safe; however, a thread-safe version is part of the P Threads library (libpthreads).

While this discussion has focused on mixing memory *allocation* calls, analogous problems exist when mixing memory *deallocation* calls. Mach allows the **vm_deallocate** system call to deallocate a memory segment allocated with UNIX **sbrk**. However, the UNIX portion of the kernel does not know about the deallocation. The program is then likely to fail in an unexpected manner. Hence you should only use **vm_deallocate** on memory obtained via Mach system calls.

Finally we should note that resource limits set through **setrlimit** have no effect on Mach system calls that allocate memory.[5] One implication is that the memory usage statistics obtained through UNIX commands such as ps may be inaccurate if Mach memory management calls are used. While both Mach and UNIX functionality are present within the operating system, and both work as they should within their respective domains, there has been no effort to integrate their functionality; this integration was never intended in the design of the system.

11.2   Signals

Signals are a common part of UNIX programs. In this section we examine the use of signals in a Mach program. As you will see, the problem is not that UNIX signals behave differently under Mach. The problem is that the semantics of the signal delivery mechanism have never been defined for a multithreaded environment (UNIX or Mach). Inconsistency, and hence

---

[5]OSF/1's implementation of **setrlimit** does limit memory obtained through Mach system calls.

unexpected results, are encountered when using signals in a multithreaded Mach task. In a single-threaded task, signals behave identically as they do under 4.3BSD.

UNIX programmers have used signals to solve a variety of problems. For example, prior to the inclusion of sockets in 4.1cBSD, or message operations in System V, a common use of signals was to implement a simple interprocess communication mechanism. Extensive use of signals in UNIX programs requires that a programmer understand any incompatibilities between UNIX and Mach signal handling.

To examine this problem, let us consider the desired behavior and then look at the behavior provided by Mach and one of its derivatives, OSF/1.

We begin our discussion with two representative signals:

SIGINT: *Interrupt*—The program was interrupted. Typically, a user typed Control-C on the keyboard.

SIGSEGV: *Segmentation Violation*—Indicates an attempt to access an invalid memory location.

Consider SIGINT, the *interrupt* signal. If a programmer has not established a *signal handler*,[6] a function, the program receiving the signal will terminate; otherwise the signal handler is called. Most often the signal handler terminates the current operation and either allows the user to continue working or terminates the program after, for example, all files are appropriately written to disk.

Under Mach, SIGINT sent to a multithreaded task is delivered to *any* thread. It is not possible to determine which thread receives the signal; hence this is termed an *asynchronous* signal (see Fig. 11.3). If the signal is repeatedly sent to the task, different threads may receive the signal each time. It would be desirable to have a single thread designated to receive the signal, thus increasing program modularity and predictability. Centralizing signal handling also provides for ease of program maintenance.

To see the value of this predictability, consider the result of a user repeatedly typing Control-C on the keyboard during the execution of a multithreaded task. Most likely, several threads will be sent a SIGINT signal. Each of them will then attempt to terminate the current operation. In a program such as a database where a multistep transaction is the "current operation," it may be difficult to synchronize these operations. Conversely,

---

[6]Signal handlers are often referred to as *interrupt* handlers.

One thread will be randomly selected to
process an asynchronous signal.

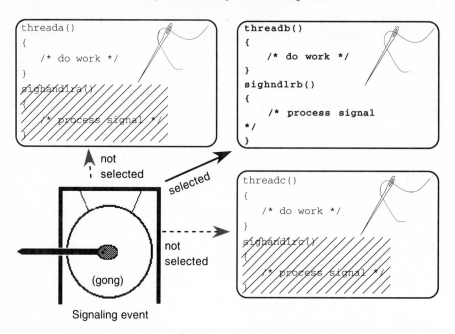

Figure 11.3: Asynchronous Signals

if only a single thread were to handle such a signal, synchronization would
be simplified.

Recognizing this deficiency, OSF/1 Release 1.1 changed signal semantics
such that the first thread in a task will receive asynchronous signals. The first
thread may be identified as the thread that executes the function **main()**
within a C program.

Unlike SIGINT, not all signals should be delivered to a single identified
thread. A class of signals termed *synchronous* is more appropriately delivered to the thread that caused the signal to be generated (see Fig. 11.4). For
example, SIGSEGV is signaled when an invalid memory location is accessed.
The thread making the invalid reference is signaled and allowed to correct
the problem. The faulting thread cannot continue until the problem is cor-
rected. It is therefore appropriate for this thread to correct its own error by
receiving the signal and acting on it.

For simplicity, our discussion of signals has ignored the fact that a signal may be sent from a variety of sources. For example, our discussion of
SIGSEGV presumes that the program made an illegal memory reference and

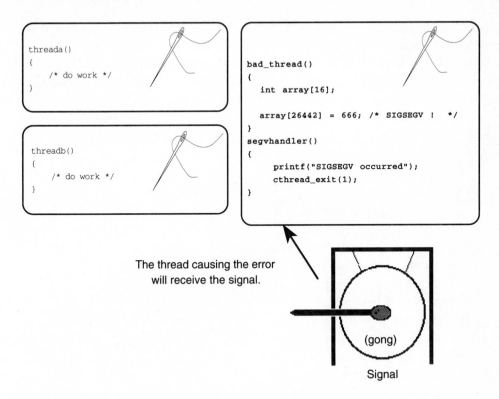

Figure 11.4: Synchronous Signals

the operating system generated the signal. A thread, from either the same or a different task, could issue the **kill()** system call to send a SIGSEGV signal to a task.

To be more precise about synchronous and asynchronous signals, we must examine the *source* of a signal. Without knowing the source, it is impossible to determine if a signal will be delivered synchronously or asynchronously. Signals, regardless of which one, are always delivered asynchronously when generated by system calls such as **kill** or **killpg**. Signals generated by the operating system as a result of a thread's action, such as SIGSEGV when an invalid memory location is accessed, shall be delivered synchronously. In the remainder of this section, our discussion of synchronous signals assumes that the signal is generated by the operating system as a result of a thread's action.

You may see the similarity between synchronous signals and exceptions as discussed in Chapter 6. Indeed, synchronous signals and exceptions are analogous mechanisms that allow a program to take corrective action in the case of an error. When an error occurs, the Mach kernel determines if an exception notification port has been established. If not, as would be the case with a UNIX program running under Mach, a synchronous signal is generated. If an exception port has been established, an exception notification message is delivered rather than the corresponding UNIX signal. For example, attempting to access an invalid memory location results in either

Event	Exception	Signal
Error accessing memory. Memory location is either not mapped into the task's virtual address space, or a protection error (i.e., attempting to write to read-only memory) occurred.	EXC_BAD_ACCESS	SIGSEGV or SIGBUS
Instruction execution error. An illegal or undefined instruction was attempted, or an operand of a legal instruction was invalid. A privileged instruction may have been attempted in user mode.	EXC_BAD_INSTRUCTION	SIGILL
Arithmetic error. Various errors, including arithmetic overflow or underflow and divide by zero.	EXC_ARITHMETIC	SIGFPE
Emulation trap. Executing an instruction that requires software emulation. Typically such an instruction is substituted for a floating point instruction on systems without floating point hardware.	EXC_EMULATION	SIGEMT
Breakpoint instruction. A breakpoint instruction was encountered, or the CPU was in "single-step" mode.	EXC_BREAKPOINT	SIGTRAP

Table 11.1: Events in Exception and Signal Mapping

an EXC_BAD_ACCESS message or a SIGSEGV signal. Table 11.1 lists each exception, the event that generates that exception, and the UNIX signal that results if an exception handler has not been established.

There are several advantages of using the exception notification mechanism. This mechanism provides

- More information than a signal. This information can help diagnose a problem more readily.

- A common interface, Mach IPC, which may be used for all communication with the task.

- The elimination of asynchronous signals. Exception notification messages are delivered in lieu of signals.

The synchronous signals that Mach defines are

• SIGILL	• SIGTRAP
• SIGEMT	• SIGFPE
• SIGBUS	• SIGSEGV
• SIGSYS	• SIGPIPE

As you can see, writing a multithreaded program must be done with careful attention to signal semantics. You must pay careful attention to both your own code and, perhaps unexpectedly, to the C language library (libc).

Several libc functions use signals. A multithreaded program using these functions may not work correctly due to race conditions within the library. Table 11.2 lists libc functions and the signals they use for both Mach and OSF/1. One example is **sleep()**; the **sleep** library function traditionally uses SIGALRM, the *alarm clock* signal, to wake the suspended program.

To work around this problem, we can write a new version of **sleep** that does not use signals. Recall from Chapter 3 that a timeout may be specified for both send and receive operations. By issuing a **msg_receive()** system call with a timeout, we can provide functionality similar to the **sleep** library function. In fact, where **sleep** only provides one-second resolution, Mach provides millisecond resolution.[7]

---

[7]While the IPC interface permits a programmer to specify a timeout measured in milliseconds, there is no guarantee that the system provides a timeout granularity that fine. Often the system's real-time clock provides 100-millisecond resolution. Rescheduling latency may also be nondeterministic. Relying on short timeouts is not recommended.

Function	Signal(s)
abort()	SIGABRT
getpass()	SIGINT
pclose()	SIGINT
	SIGQUIT
	SIGHUP
rcmd()	SIGURG
syslog()	SIGINT
	SIGQUIT
system()	SIGINT
	SIGQUIT

Table 11.2: libc Functions that Manipulate Signals

The following code fragment provides functionality similar to the **sleep** function in libc but uses Mach IPC system calls.[8]

```
#include <mach.h>
#include <mach/message.h>
#include <mach/port.h>
#include <cthreads.h>

static port_name_t  timeout_port;

/*
 * SLEEP: Emulate 'sleep' library function.
 *
 * Issue msg_receive against a port whose only use is for
 *  this function.  Timeout value provides length of delay.
 *
 * Return code: 0 on success (timeout); -1 otherwise.
 */
sleep(seconds)
int      seconds;
{
        msg_return_t    ret;
        msg_header_t    hdr;
```

---

[8]If the **msg_receive** call is interrupted, the return value from our implementation of **sleep** does not conform to POSIX P1003.4 (remaining time).

```
        /*
         * Initialize 'sleep' functionality (if necessary).
         */
        if(sleep_init() != 0)
                return(-1);

        hdr.msg_local_port = timeout_port;
        hdr.msg_size = sizeof(hdr);

        ret = msg_receive(&hdr, RCV_TIMEOUT, seconds*1000);
        return( (ret == RCV_TIMED_OUT) ? 0 : -1 );
}

/*
 * Initialize 'sleep' functionality.
 */
sleep_init()
{
        static mutex_t sleep_lock = mutex_alloc();
        static int     sleep_initialized;
        kern_return_t  ret;

        mutex_lock(sleep_lock);
        if ( sleep_initialized ) {
                mutex_unlock(sleep_lock);
                return(0);
        }

        /*
         * Allocate the timeout port.
         */
        ret = port_allocate(task_self(), &timeout_port);
        if (ret != KERN_SUCCESS) {
                mutex_unlock(sleep_lock);
                mach_error("port_allocate:", ret);
                return(-1);
        }
        sleep_initialized++;
        mutex_unlock(sleep_lock);
        return(0);
}
```

During initialization the function allocates a port for use by **msg_receive**.
For each invocation the IPC header structure is initialized and a **msg_receive**

system call is executed. This port is unknown to any other task; we do not register the port with a name server. Hence only the task executing this function could send a message to the port. A message will therefore never be enqueued to this port and the **msg_receive** call will timeout as we desired. When it does, the sleep function returns a zero (0) to indicate success.

Each thread executing this function will execute its own **msg_receive** system call; hence multiple threads may simultaneously call **sleep** and not interfere with each other.

11.3   Library Interaction

We said that there are only a few problems using existing UNIX programs on a Mach system. However, obstacles may arise when multithreading a UNIX application. The UNIX libraries, such as libc, may not work correctly in a multithreaded application.

The library code was written many years ago, long before threads became common. There was no need to consider simultaneous access to data. One outcome was the use of global data within many library functions. This data may be corrupted by simultaneous access by multiple threads within a task. For example, the **ctime** function returns a pointer to a static data area. A function that calls **ctime** cannot guarantee the validity of this data; another thread may have made a simultaneous call, thus overwriting the global data area.

This problem is pervasive throughout the UNIX libraries. Simultaneous calls to **printf()** may produce garbled messages, functions to read the password and group files (**getpwent()** and **getgrent()**) may produce unpredictable results, and so on. Surrounding calls to these functions with locks is tedious and error prone and produces code that is difficult to read. At best, you can hide much of this detail by writing functions that acquire a lock, call a library function, and release the lock.

In recent years vendors have begun to recognize the necessity of providing libraries that are safe for multithreaded applications. OSF/1 provides a version of libc with appropriate locking. If you are unfortunate enough to have a system without a thread-safe version of these libraries, be aware that you may have to place locks in your multithreaded code.

11.4   Using Threads

Multithreaded tasks allow for greater performance and modularity. However, an inappropriate use of threads may lead to a *loss* of performance and modularity. To take best advantage of an environment with multiple threads, a programmer must learn a few new techniques.

In this section we describe some of the techniques a programmer may use to divide an application into multiple threads of control. We rely on the background from several other chapters (including Chapter 2, "Tasks and Threads," and Chapter 5, "C Threads") that described some of the differences and techniques of working in a multithreaded environment. As with most other types of programming where there are many ways of solving the same problem, there are many methods of using multiple threads. The techniques we provide here are built from our experience and are intended to provide a foundation for your own programs.

The classic programming model that we all learned is depicted in Fig. 11.5. We take that simple model and multithread it, demonstrating techniques a programmer may apply when developing a multithreaded application.

The first approach to multithreading this program would be to create a thread for each segment, *input, processing,* and *output.* Often these three segments are separate, with the exception that they communicate with each other. A code segment is a good candidate for a separate thread when

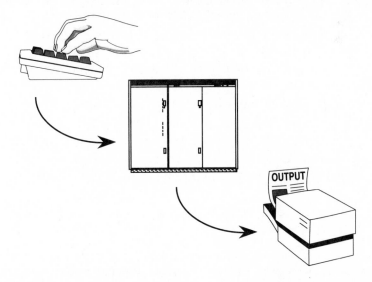

Figure 11.5: Simple Program Model: Input, Processing, Output

- The problem it solves is well defined

- The segment has clear boundaries

- There is relatively little interaction between this and other portions of the program.

Our simple model has three segments that are clearly well defined and suitable for multithreading. Input processing does not share any functionality with either data processing or output. Hence we do not have to worry about interdependency of data. In other words, we presume that, other than data directly passed to or from the preceding or following segment, there is no shared data. Since each segment *does* communicate with other segments, we must provide a synchronized mechanism of transferring data between segments.

When examining a program to determine the need for synchronization, we can consider that need in terms of *producers* and *consumers* of data. Whenever data are passed between a producer thread and a consumer thread, that data exchange must be synchronized. In our model we may consider the input thread as a producer of data for the processing thread. Similarly, the processing thread is a consumer of data from the input thread. There are several mechanisms to synchronize data transfer.

One possibility would be to use Mach IPC. For example, we could create a port to which the input thread sends data for receipt by the processing thread. This would be a good approach if, at some time in the future, we were interested in placing each thread in a separate task perhaps running those tasks on separate computers. Otherwise there is no reason to suffer the overhead of using Mach IPC rather than shared memory.

We will use a locked data queue as the data interface between threads and a condition/wait mechanism to signal the consumer thread that data are available. A locked data queue is often the best approach for intratask data protection. Locks are easy to use, are often provided in system libraries (so you do not have to write new mechanisms yourself), and can be very efficient.[9]

The C Threads library **mutex_lock** and **mutex_unlock** functions provide locks to protect data. In addition, **condition_signal** and **condition_**

---

[9]There are often several types of locks. Spin locks, mutual exclusion locks, and read/write locks are the most common. Each has advantages over the others. A complete description of these locks is beyond the scope of this book; however, the reader should be aware that not all locks are equivalent.

wait functions will provide synchronization between threads. The functions and techniques to implement this approach were used earlier in this book. The next issue to solve is how best to partition the program into individual threads.

Analysis and a good understanding of the program are absolutely essential. For example, analysis may show a bottleneck in the processing section, in which case additional processing threads could be created to keep up with the input thread. In analyzing a multithreaded application, it is important to determine

- Which program segments are a bottleneck (all threads performing that function are constantly busy),

- If there are any locks that are held for long periods of time. Such locks become bottlenecks when threads cannot acquire them.

- How the computer system affects program performance. For example, creating more threads than there are processors may not increase performance when the threads are running CPU-intensive code.

Tools to analyze and debug multithreaded programs have not reached the quality and sophistication as those available for traditional single-threaded environments. For example, lock packages may not provide a means of measuring lock contention, and function profiling (e.g., UNIX **gprof**) may not work correctly with multithreaded programs. While a programmer working on a multithreaded application is often left to his or her own devices, new tools are becoming available.

If we design the interthread interfaces such that each thread is independent of the other, we can easily create additional threads to increase throughput. A large application may have many threads. Ten or twenty would not be unusual. For a very large application on a large multiprocessor, there may be hundreds of threads. Because there may be a large number of threads, *thread management* often becomes an important consideration. We can divide thread management into three basic approaches:

1. Create a new thread each time new work arrives.

2. Create a constant number of threads, each of which is dispatched to work on a specific problem. A thread may work on a different program segment each time the thread is dispatched.

3. Create a number of threads, each with a particular purpose.

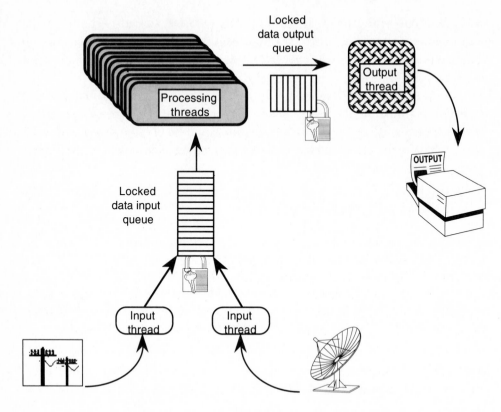

Figure 11.6: A Multithreaded Application

The advantage of creating a thread for each new work item is that there are no unnecessary threads. This dynamic allocation of threads may be advantageous in an environment with a small amount of memory. Thread resources, such as the thread stack within the application and data structures within the kernel, would be free for other uses. The disadvantage is the performance penalty of repeatedly creating and destroying threads.

The second approach, creating a fixed number of threads, prevents an application from consuming more resources than desired. By limiting the number of threads and dispatching them to work on whatever problem needs solving, the programmer knows the maximum number of threads that may be active at any one time. The programmer may desire this behavior to prevent excessive memory utilization and processor thrashing between executing threads. As with too many processes running in a UNIX environment, too many threads may cause a *decrease* in performance if they are all competing for insufficient resources at the same time.

One difficulty occurs when all threads happen to be in the same part of
the program at the same time (e.g., all threads performing processing while
none are available for input). If the input stream is from a network or other
source not capable of extensive buffering, data may be lost.

The final approach creates a number of threads for each segment of the
program. The programmer may determine that, for example, two input
threads, twelve processing threads, and a single output thread provide the
proper ratio (Fig. 11.6). This technique ensures that all segments of the program have threads available. Threads are created at program initialization,
hence the cost of repeatedly creating and destroying threads is eliminated.

The last approach is the one we recommend, although the others are often
appropriate for particular application environments. While thread creation
under Mach is a fast operation, faster than creating a process under UNIX,
repeatedly creating and destroying threads is not recommended. Regardless
of how fast this operation is, it is still wasteful of resources to do so.[10]

Creating a pool of threads may cause segments of the program to be
"starved" for processing time. Hence finding the right ratio and determining
the total number of threads from available resources provides the best overall
solution.

11.4.1   Multiplexing I/O with Threads

Let us turn now to a classic problem under UNIX and see how using
multiple threads alleviates that problem. A large program may process data
associated with multiple file descriptors. For example, a server may have
multiple network connections, each represented by a single file descriptor.
Data arrival, from the server's perspective, occurs randomly. The server
may block waiting for data to become available on one descriptor while data
is already available from another.

Several solutions to this problem have been implemented. A program
could perform polled I/O by using nonblocking I/O on each file descriptor.[11]
This is inefficient, but it does work. A more elegant approach is the **select()**
system call introduced in 4.2BSD. This call allows the program to block until
data is available on one or more file descriptors specified in the system call.

While the **select** call represents a good approach for a single-threaded
environment, it is not optimal in a multithreaded environment. The problem arises when data is simultaneously available from more than one file

---

[10]The C Threads library caches threads to avoid the cost of thread creation.

[11]This is accomplished with the **fcntl()** system call with a flag of FNDELAY.

descriptor. A single thread needing to read data from several file descriptors will be serialized when it reads from one file descriptor, then the next, and so on. However, under UNIX there is no alternative but to read sequentially from each file descriptor.

The alternative available under Mach is to create a single thread for each file descriptor being read. The thread may block waiting for data, but if so we are not delaying input from other descriptors. When data becomes simultaneously available from multiple file descriptors, we are able to read the data in parallel. Once the data is read, the thread could, for example, insert the data on a queue (with the appropriate locking, of course) for a processing thread to handle. The advantages of this approach include

- Increased modularity. It is easy to define which functions process data from which file descriptor.

- Increased performance. Performance could be enhanced, as data would be read from multiple file descriptors simultaneously.

Enhancing program performance is the largest advantage of writing multithreaded applications. On a multiprocessor, separate threads may truly execute in parallel. A well-modularized program may acheive near-linear speed-up when using a multiprocessor. Performance improvements of that magnitude are rarely, if ever, possible without multiple threads. Even on a uniprocessor, performance is often enhanced by using multiple threads.

Most programs are balanced between I/O operations and CPU operations. If the program executes an I/O operation (for example, a read from tape) the program will be delayed until the read operation completes. If the program is single threaded, the program can make no progress until the read operation completes. Hence even on a uniprocessor, multiple threads would allow overlapped CPU and I/O operations, significantly increasing program performance.

11.4.2   Debugging a Multithreaded Program

Many assert that multithreaded programs are difficult to write. Bugs in a multithreaded program are more difficult to find than bugs in a single-threaded program. There can be no argument that this is true.

Debugging a single-threaded program for correctness is (relatively) easy. You enter a debugger, execute the next line of code, and determine if the results are correct. If so, you repeat the process until you find an error.

While the error may require more than fixing a single line of code, it is generally not difficult to find the problem. In a multithreaded program you cannot follow this procedure.

A multithreaded program has, by its nature, more than one thread running at the same time. The hardest problems to find are those stemming from thread interaction. When you start to look for the bug, the question is, What do I look for? A good starting point for most programs is looking for unlocked global data.

The problem probably lies with multiple threads each attempting to read or write global data without mediated access to that data. If your program fails, begin by examining each piece of global data. The first question to ask is, Could there be more than one thread that touches that data? If so, examine each use of that data and ensure that a lock mediates access to the data. This simple procedure will find many of your problems.

11.4.3   Implicitly Shared Data

Previously we described the necessity of using locks to protect shared data. Memory is shared by all threads in a task and hence must be protected against simultaneous modifications. Such explicit sharing of data is obvious. However, a task's address space is not the only memory that a task uses. There are also per-task data structures within the operating system that all threads in a task *implicitly* share.

While the operating system will protect these structures against corruption by multiple threads, the content of those structures must be coordinated between running threads. Let us look at one such structure.

For each UNIX process, the operating system maintains the *current working directory*. A program may issue the UNIX **chdir()** system call to change the current working directory. The operating system maintains this information on a per-task basis. Thus if two threads issue the **chdir** system call with different directory names, the directory from the second thread to execute **chdir** overwrites the directory name from the first thread.

How might this affect the design of a program? Consider a program such as find that searches a directory hierarchy for files with a particular set of attributes. Each time find encounters a subdirectory, it issues a **chdir** call and recursively continues the search. An attempt to multithread this program could prove difficult. Different threads operating in different portions of the directory hierarchy would each need to work relative to a different current working directory. As the operating system maintains the directory

Data	Manipulated by
Signal information. This includes the action to take when a signal occurs, the set of masked signals, and the stack to use for the signal handler.	**signal, sigblock, sigpause, sigsuspend, sigsetmask, sigstack, sigvec**
The root directory.	**chroot**
The current working directory.	**chdir, fchdir**
User and group IDs.	**setgid, setuid setegid, seteuid setrgid, setruid**
Interval timers. The three timers are for real time, process virtual time, and a profiling timer. Each issues a signal when the timer expires.	**setitimer**
Resource limits. These include CPU time, file size, stack size, etc.	**setrlimit**
Open file information.	**read, write, lseek**

Table 11.3: Per-Task Data that the Operating System Maintains

information, an approach that did not have multiple threads requiring a different directory would have to be implemented. Each thread could use the full path name of the file rather than work relative to the current directory. However, this is significantly slower than working relative to the current working directory.

The operating system maintains other information that may affect the way a multithreaded program is implemented. The information of interest to most programmers is described in Table 11.3.

As shown in Table 11.3, open file descriptors are also maintained on a per-task basis. The current offset within a file, the starting location for the next **read** or **write**, is also shared.[12] Consider a program in which multiple threads operate on the same open file.

---

[12]An equivalent problem exists in C library functions such as **fseek()** and **fwrite()**. The P Threads library provided with OSF/1 deals with this problem by providing the **flockfile()** and **funlockfile()** functions for the user to lock data. The library also provides

Because multiple threads may issue **lseek()** system calls, an **lseek** followed by a **read** may not read from the expected location. Two alternatives are available to solve this problem:

1. Acquire a lock before each **lseek** and release that lock after the accompanying **read** or **write**.

2. Restrict I/O operations for each open file to a single thread.

Using a lock clearly solves this problem. However, there may be *implicit* **lseek**s within the file. For example

```
int     fid1;
char    buf1[1024], buf2[1024];
struct mutex fid1lock;

mutex_lock(&fid1lock);
lseek(fid1, offset, 0);
write(fid1, buf1, 1024);    /* Will work   */
mutex_unlock(&fid1lock);
write(fid1, buf2, 1024);    /* May not work */
```

The second **write** call may not have written the data contiguously after the first write. Another thread may have performed an **lseek** or done an I/O prior to the second write.

One approach that does not require the use of a lock limits all I/O operations for a particular file descriptor to a single thread. No lock need be used, as no other thread attempts to perform I/O to the file. Greater modularity is achieved by isolating operations to a particular thread. However, this technique has a performance tradeoff. While holding a lock across an I/O operation may cause other threads to wait for a significant amount of time, using a single thread may cause a bottleneck.

Neither approach provides an optimal solution in all cases. The programmer must be aware of the problems and choose a solution appropriate to the application.

11.5 Summary

In this chapter we have described the differences a programmer familiar with a 4.3BSD environment may encounter when moving to Mach. Most UNIX

---

thread-safe versions of functions that confirm to POSIX P1003.4a. The use of this library is defined in Section 10.5.

programs will run unmodified under Mach. There are, however, a few cases (such as when a program uses /dev/kmem) when a UNIX program will not run correctly.

Multithreading a program poses particular problems. The semantics of UNIX system and library calls have not been defined for a multithreaded environment. For example, we saw how signals may not work as expected in a multithreaded task.

Finally, we provided some insight into multithreading an application.

Appendix A

MIG Generated Files

This appendix contains the three files that MIG generates for the Time Server example.

A.1   time.h

```
#ifndef _time
#define _time

/* Module time */

#include <mach/kern_return.h>
#if (defined(__STDC__)||defined(c_plusplus))||defined(LINTLIBRARY)
#include <mach/port.h>
#include <mach/message.h>
#endif

#ifndef mig_external
#define mig_external extern
#endif

mig_external void init_time
```

```
#if    (defined(__STDC__) || defined(c_plusplus))
    (port_t rep-port);
#else
    ();
#endif
#include <mach/std_types.h>
#include <mach/mach_types.h>
#include "time_defs.h"

/* Routine get_time_num */
mig_external kern_return_t get_time_num
#if    defined(LINTLIBRARY)
    (server_port, time)
        port_t server_port;
        time_num *time;
{ return get_time_num(server_port, time); }
#else
#if    (defined(__STDC__) || defined(c_plusplus))
(
        port_t server_port,
        time_num *time
);
```

```
#else
        ();
#endif
#endif

/* Routine get_time_str */
mig_external kern_return_t get_time_str
#if     defined(LINTLIBRARY)
    (server_port, time)
        port_t server_port;
        time_str time;
{ return get_time_str(server_port, time); }
#else
#if     (defined(__STDC__) || defined(c_plusplus))
(
        port_t server_port,
        time_str time
);
#else
        ();
#endif
#endif

#endif _time
```

A.2   timeUser.c

```
#include "time.h"
#include <mach/message.h>
#include <mach/mach_types.h>
#include <mach/mig_errors.h>
#include <mach/msg_type.h>
#if !defined(KERNEL) && !defined(MIG_NO_STRINGS)
#include <strings.h>
```

```
#endif
/* LINTLIBRARY */

extern port_t mig_get_reply_port();
extern void mig_dealloc_reply_port();

#ifndef mig_internal
#define mig_internal    static
#endif

#ifndef TypeCheck
#define TypeCheck 1
#endif

#ifndef UseExternRCSId
#ifdef hc
#define UseExternRCSId          1
#endif
#endif

#ifndef UseStaticMsgType
#if     !defined(hc) || defined(__STDC__)
#define UseStaticMsgType        1
#endif
#endif

#define msg_request_port        msg_remote_port
#define msg_reply_port          msg_local_port

mig_external void init_time
#if     (defined(__STDC__) || defined(c_plusplus))
        (port_t rep_port)
#else
        (rep_port)
        port_t rep_port;
```

```
#endif
{
#ifdef    lint
    rep-port++;
#endif
}

/* Routine get_time_num */
mig_external kern_return_t get_time_num
#if (defined(__STDC__) || defined(c_plusplus))
(
    port_t server_port,
    time_num *time
)
#else
    (server-port, time)
    port_t server_port;
    time_num *time;
#endif
{

typedef struct {
    msg_header_t Head;
} Request;

typedef struct {
    msg_header_t Head;
    msg_type_t RetCodeType;
    kern_return_t RetCode;
    msg_type_t timeType;
    time_num time;
} Reply;

union {
    Request In;
    Reply Out;
};
```

```
} Mess;

register Request *InP = &Mess.In;
register Reply *OutP = &Mess.Out;

msg_return_t msg_result;

#if TypeCheck
boolean_t msg_simple;
#endif TypeCheck

unsigned int msg_size = 24;

#if UseStaticMsgType
static msg_type_t RetCodeCheck = {
    /* msg_type_name = */       MSG_TYPE_INTEGER_32,
    /* msg_type_size = */       32,
    /* msg_type_number = */     1,
    /* msg_type_inline = */     TRUE,
    /* msg_type_longform = */   FALSE,
    /* msg_type_deallocate = */ FALSE,
    /* msg_type_unused = */ 0
};
#endif UseStaticMsgType

#if UseStaticMsgType
static msg_type_t timeCheck = {
    /* msg_type_name = */       MSG_TYPE_INTEGER_32,
    /* msg_type_size = */       32,
    /* msg_type_number = */     1,
    /* msg_type_inline = */     TRUE,
    /* msg_type_longform = */   FALSE,
    /* msg_type_deallocate = */ FALSE,
    /* msg_type_unused = */ 0
};
```

```
#endif	UseStaticMsgType

	InP->Head.msg_simple = TRUE;
	InP->Head.msg_size = msg_size;
	InP->Head.msg_type = MSG_TYPE_NORMAL | MSG_TYPE_RPC;
	InP->Head.msg_request_port = server_port;
	InP->Head.msg_reply_port = mig_get_reply_port();
	InP->Head.msg_id = 400;

	msg_result = msg_rpc(&InP->Head, MSG_OPTION_NONE,
			sizeof(Reply), 0, 0);
	if (msg_result != RPC_SUCCESS) {
		if (msg_result == RCV_INVALID_PORT)
			mig_dealloc_reply_port();
		return msg_result;
	}

#if	TypeCheck
	msg_size = OutP->Head.msg.size;
	msg_simple = OutP->Head.msg.simple;
#endif	TypeCheck

	if (OutP->Head.msg_id != 500)
		return MIG_REPLY_MISMATCH;

#if	TypeCheck
	if (((msg_size != 40) || (msg_simple != TRUE)) &&
	  ((msg_size != sizeof(death_pill_t)) ||
	  (msg_simple != TRUE)) ||
	  (OutP->RetCode == KERN_SUCCESS)))
		return MIG_TYPE_ERROR;
#endif	TypeCheck

#if	TypeCheck
#if	UseStaticMsgType
	if (*(int *)&OutP->RetCodeType != *(int *)&RetCodeCheck)
#else	UseStaticMsgType
	if ((OutP->RetCodeType.msg_type_inline != TRUE) ||
	    (OutP->RetCodeType.msg_type_longform != FALSE) ||
	    (OutP->RetCodeType.msg_type_name !=
				MSG_TYPE_INTEGER_32) ||
	    (OutP->RetCodeType.msg_type_number != 1) ||
	    (OutP->RetCodeType.msg_type_size != 32))
#endif	UseStaticMsgType
		return MIG_TYPE_ERROR;
#endif	TypeCheck

	if (OutP->RetCode != KERN_SUCCESS)
		return OutP->RetCode;

#if	TypeCheck
#if	UseStaticMsgType
	if (* (int *) &OutP->timeType != * (int *) &timeCheck)
#else	UseStaticMsgType
	if ((OutP->timeType.msg_type_inline != TRUE) ||
	    (OutP->timeType.msg_type_longform != FALSE) ||
	    (OutP->timeType.msg_type_name !=
				MSG_TYPE_INTEGER_32) ||
	    (OutP->timeType.msg_type_number != 1) ||
	    (OutP->timeType.msg_type_size != 32))
#endif	UseStaticMsgType
		return MIG_TYPE_ERROR;
#endif	TypeCheck

	*time /* time */ = /* *time */ OutP->time;

	return OutP->RetCode;
}

/* Routine get_time_str */
```

```
mig_external kern_return_t get_time_str
#if (defined(__STDC__) || defined(c_plusplus))
(
    port_t server_port,
    time_str time
)
#else
(
    server_port, time)
    port_t server_port;
    time_str time;
#endif
{
    typedef struct {
        msg_header_t Head;
    } Request;

    typedef struct {
        msg_header_t Head;
        msg_type_t RetCodeType;
        kern_return_t RetCode;
        msg_type_t timeType;
        time_str time;
        char timePad[2];
    } Reply;

    union {
        Request In;
        Reply Out;
    } Mess;

    register Request *InP = &Mess.In;
    register Reply *OutP = &Mess.Out;
    msg_return_t msg_result;

#if TypeCheck
    boolean_t msg_simple;
#endif TypeCheck

    unsigned int msg_size = 24;

#if UseStaticMsgType
    static msg_type_t RetCodeCheck = {
        /* msg_type_name = */       MSG_TYPE_INTEGER_32,
        /* msg_type_size = */       32,
        /* msg_type_number = */     1,
        /* msg_type_inline = */     TRUE,
        /* msg_type_longform = */   FALSE,
        /* msg_type_deallocate = */ FALSE,
        /* msg_type_unused = */ 0
    };
#endif UseStaticMsgType

#if UseStaticMsgType
    static msg_type_t timeCheck = {
        /* msg_type_name = */       MSG_TYPE_STRING,
        /* msg_type_size = */       208,
        /* msg_type_number = */     1,
        /* msg_type_inline = */     TRUE,
        /* msg_type_longform = */   FALSE,
        /* msg_type_deallocate = */ FALSE,
        /* msg_type_unused = */ 0
    };
#endif UseStaticMsgType

    InP->Head.msg_simple = TRUE;
    InP->Head.msg_size = msg_size;
    InP->Head.msg_type = MSG_TYPE_NORMAL | MSG_TYPE_RPC;
    InP->Head.msg_request_port = server_port;
    InP->Head.msg_reply_port = mig_get_reply_port();
```

```
    InP->Head.msg_id = 401;

    msg_result = msg_rpc(&InP->Head, MSG_OPTION_NONE,
                         sizeof(Reply), 0, 0);
    if (msg_result != RPC_SUCCESS) {
        if (msg_result == RCV_INVALID_PORT)
            mig_dealloc_reply_port();
        return msg_result;
    }

#if     TypeCheck
    msg_size = OutP->Head.msg_size;
    msg_simple = OutP->Head.msg_simple;
#endif  TypeCheck

    if (OutP->Head.msg_id != 501)
        return MIG_REPLY_MISMATCH;

#if     TypeCheck
    if (((msg_size != 64) || (msg_simple != TRUE)) &&
        ((msg_size != sizeof(death_pill_t)) ||
         (msg_simple != TRUE) ||
         (OutP->RetCode == KERN_SUCCESS)))
        return MIG_TYPE_ERROR;
#endif  TypeCheck

#if     TypeCheck
#if     UseStaticMsgType
    if (*(int *)&OutP->RetCodeType != *(int *)&RetCodeCheck)
#else   UseStaticMsgType
    if ((OutP->RetCodeType.msg_type_inline != TRUE) ||
        (OutP->RetCodeType.msg_type_longform != FALSE) ||
        (OutP->RetCodeType.msg_type_name !=
                        MSG_TYPE_INTEGER_32) ||
        (OutP->RetCodeType.msg_type_number != 1) ||
        (OutP->RetCodeType.msg_type_size != 32))
#endif  UseStaticMsgType
        return MIG_TYPE_ERROR;
#endif  TypeCheck

    if (OutP->RetCode != KERN_SUCCESS)
        return OutP->RetCode;

#if     TypeCheck
#if     UseStaticMsgType
    if (*(int *)&OutP->timeType != *(int *)&timeCheck)
#else   UseStaticMsgType
    if ((OutP->timeType.msg_type_inline != TRUE) ||
        (OutP->timeType.msg_type_longform != FALSE) ||
        (OutP->timeType.msg_type_name != MSG_TYPE_STRING) ||
        (OutP->timeType.msg_type_number != 1) ||
        (OutP->timeType.msg_type_size != 208))
#endif  UseStaticMsgType
        return MIG_TYPE_ERROR;
#endif  TypeCheck

    (void) mig_strncpy(time /* time */,
                       /* time */ OutP->time, 26);
    time /* time */[25] = '\0';

    return OutP->RetCode;
}
```

A.3   timeServer.c

```
/* Module time */

#define EXPORT_BOOLEAN
#include <mach/boolean.h>
```

```
#include <mach/message.h>
#include <mach/mig_errors.h>

#ifndef mig_internal
#define mig_internal    static
#endif

#ifndef TypeCheck
#define TypeCheck 1
#endif

#ifndef UseExternRCSId
#ifdef  hc
#define UseExternRCSId  1
#endif
#endif

#ifndef UseStaticMsgType
#if     !defined(hc) || defined(__STDC__)
#define UseStaticMsgType  1
#endif
#endif

/* Due to pcc compiler bug, cannot use void */
#if (defined(__STDC__) || defined(c_plusplus)) || defined(hc)
#define novalue void
#else
#define novalue int
#endif

#define msg_request_port    msg_local_port
#define msg_reply_port      msg_remote_port
#include <mach/std_types.h>
#include <mach/mach_types.h>
#include "time_defs.h"


/* Routine get_time_num */
mig_internal novalue _Xget_time_num
#if (defined(__STDC__) || defined(c_plusplus))
    (msg_header_t *InHeadP, msg_header_t *OutHeadP)
#else
    (InHeadP, OutHeadP)
        msg_header_t *InHeadP, *OutHeadP;
#endif
{
    typedef struct {
        msg_header_t Head;
    } Request;

    typedef struct {
        msg_header_t Head;
        msg_type_t RetCodeType;
        kern_return_t RetCode;
        msg_type_t timeType;
        time_num time;
    } Reply;

    register Request *InP = (Request *) InHeadP;
    register Reply *OutP = (Reply *) OutHeadP;
    extern kern_return_t get_time_num
#if (defined(__STDC__) || defined(c_plusplus))
    (port_t server_port, time_num *time);
#else
    ();
#endif
#if TypeCheck
    boolean_t msg_simple;
#endif  TypeCheck
```

```
        unsigned int msg_size;

#if     UseStaticMsgType
        static msg_type_t timeType = {
                /* msg_type_name = */       MSG_TYPE_INTEGER_32,
                /* msg_type_size = */       32,
                /* msg_type_number = */     1,
                /* msg_type_inline = */     TRUE,
                /* msg_type_longform = */   FALSE,
                /* msg_type_deallocate = */ FALSE,
                /* msg_type_unused = */     0
        };
#endif  UseStaticMsgType

#if     TypeCheck
        msg_size = InOP->Head.msg_size;
        msg_simple = InOP->Head.msg_simple;
        if ((msg_size != 24) || (msg_simple != TRUE))
                { OutP->RetCode = MIG_BAD_ARGUMENTS; return; }
#endif  TypeCheck

        OutP->RetCode =
                get_time_num(InOP->Head.msg_request_port,
                             &OutP->time);

#ifdef  label_punt0
#undef  label_punt0
punt0:
#endif  label_punt0
        if (OutP->RetCode != KERN_SUCCESS)
                return;

        msg_size = 40;

#if     UseStaticMsgType
        OutP->timeType = timeType;
#else   UseStaticMsgType
        OutP->timeType.msg_type_name = MSG_TYPE_INTEGER_32;
        OutP->timeType.msg_type_size = 32;
        OutP->timeType.msg_type_number = 1;
        OutP->timeType.msg_type_inline = TRUE;
        OutP->timeType.msg_type_longform = FALSE;
        OutP->timeType.msg_type_deallocate = FALSE;
        OutP->timeType.msg_type_unused = 0;
#endif  UseStaticMsgType

        OutP->Head.msg_simple = TRUE;
        OutP->Head.msg_size = msg_size;
}

/* Routine get_time_str */
mig_internal novalue _Xget_time_str
#if     (defined(__STDC__) || defined(c_plusplus))
        (msg_header_t *InHeadP, msg_header_t *OutHeadP)
#else
        (InHeadP, OutHeadP)
        msg_header_t *InHeadP, *OutHeadP;
#endif
{
        typedef struct {
                msg_header_t Head;
        } Request;

        typedef struct {
                msg_header_t Head;
                msg_type_t RetCodeType;
                kern_return_t RetCode;
                msg_type_t timeType;
                time_str time;
                char timePad[2];
        } Reply;
```

```c
	register Request *InOp = (Request *) InHeadP;
	register Reply *OutP = (Reply *) OutHeadP;
	extern kern_return_t get_time_str
#if	(defined(__STDC__) || defined(c_plusplus))
		(port_t server_port, time_str time);
#else
		();
#endif

#if	TypeCheck
	boolean_t msg_simple;
#endif	TypeCheck

#if	UseStaticMsgType
	static msg_type_t timeType = {
		/* msg_type_name = */		MSG_TYPE_STRING,
		/* msg_type_size = */		208,
		/* msg_type_number = */		1,
		/* msg_type_inline = */		TRUE,
		/* msg_type_longform = */	FALSE,
		/* msg_type_deallocate = */	FALSE,
		/* msg_type_unused = */ 0
	};
#endif	UseStaticMsgType

	unsigned int msg_size;

#if	TypeCheck
	msg_size = InOp->Head.msg_size;
	msg_simple = InOp->Head.msg_simple;
	if ((msg_size != 24) || (msg_simple != TRUE))
		{ OutP->RetCode = MIG_BAD_ARGUMENTS; return; }
#endif	TypeCheck

	OutP->RetCode =
		get_time_str(InOp->Head.msg_request_port,
			OutP->time);
#ifdef	label_punt0
#undef	label_punt0
#endif
punt0:
	if (OutP->RetCode != KERN_SUCCESS)
		return;

#if	UseStaticMsgType
	OutP->timeType = timeType;
#else	UseStaticMsgType
	OutP->timeType.msg_type_name = MSG_TYPE_STRING;
	OutP->timeType.msg_type_size = 208;
	OutP->timeType.msg_type_number = 1;
	OutP->timeType.msg_type_inline = TRUE;
	OutP->timeType.msg_type_longform = FALSE;
	OutP->timeType.msg_type_deallocate = FALSE;
	OutP->timeType.msg_type_unused = 0;
#endif	UseStaticMsgType

#if	UseStaticMsgType
	msg_size = 64;
#endif
	OutP->Head.msg_simple = TRUE;
	OutP->Head.msg_size = msg_size;
}

boolean_t time_server
#if	(defined(__STDC__) || defined(c_plusplus))
	(msg_header_t *InHeadP, msg_header_t *OutHeadP)
#else
	(InHeadP, OutHeadP)
	msg_header_t *InHeadP, *OutHeadP;
#endif
{
```

```
{
    register msg_header_t *InP = InHeadP;
    register death_pill_t *OutP = (death_pill_t *)OutHeadP;

#if UseStaticMsgType
    static msg_type_t RetCodeType = {
        /* msg_type_name = */       MSG_TYPE_INTEGER_32,
        /* msg_type_size = */       32,
        /* msg_type_number = */     1,
        /* msg_type_inline = */     TRUE,
        /* msg_type_longform = */   FALSE,
        /* msg_type_deallocate = */ FALSE,
        /* msg_type_unused = */     0
    };
#endif UseStaticMsgType

    OutP->Head.msg_simple = TRUE;
    OutP->Head.msg_size = sizeof *OutP;
    OutP->Head.msg_type = InP->msg_type;
    OutP->Head.msg_local_port = PORT_NULL;
    OutP->Head.msg_remote_port = InP->msg_reply_port;
    OutP->Head.msg_id = InP->msg_id + 100;

#if UseStaticMsgType
    OutP->RetCodeType = RetCodeType;
#else UseStaticMsgType
    OutP->RetCodeType.msg_type_name = MSG_TYPE_INTEGER_32;
    OutP->RetCodeType.msg_type_size = 32;
    OutP->RetCodeType.msg_type_number = 1;
    OutP->RetCodeType.msg_type_inline = TRUE;
    OutP->RetCodeType.msg_type_longform = FALSE;
    OutP->RetCodeType.msg_type_deallocate = FALSE;
    OutP->RetCodeType.msg_type_unused = 0;
#endif UseStaticMsgType
    OutP->RetCode = MIG_BAD_ID;


    if ((InP->msg_id > 401) || (InP->msg_id < 400))
        return FALSE;
    else {
#if (defined(__STDC__) || defined(c_plusplus))
        typedef novalue (*SERVER_STUB_PROC)
            (msg_header_t *, msg_header_t *);
#else
            ();
#endif
        static SERVER_STUB_PROC routines[] = {
            _Xget_time_num,
            _Xget_time_str,
        };

        if (routines[InP->msg_id - 400])
            (routines[InP->msg_id - 400])
                (InP, &OutP->Head);
        else
            return FALSE;
    }
    return TRUE;
}
```

Appendix B

EMM Example

This appendix contains the complete source code for the programming example developed in Chapter 9, "External Memory Management." The Secure Memory service includes a pager and a sample client application. We present the `Makefile` and common definition files first, followed by the source code for sm_pager, and conclude with the client program, demo_sm. For simplicity, the pager does not support multipage operations.

B.1 Reading the Programs

The various modules of **sm_pager** have been thoroughly documented and are structured to be easily readable. In particular, the reader may examine the external memory management interfaces, in `sm_emm.c`, without worrying about the modifications necessary to support distributed shared memory. The hooks for DSM are very small and may be ignored safely.

The reader interested in pursuing distributed shared memory will find that nearly all of the logic implementing the **sm_pager**'s DSM protocol is confined to `sm_dsm.c`. The hooks into the DSM protocol from the EMM routines are limited to upcalls from the kernel to the pager: **memory_object_data_request**, **memory_object_data_unlock**, and so on. Nearly all of the EMM code is identical between the DSM and non-DSM versions of sm_pager. Be wary, however; distributed shared memory is tricky and the protocol may still have bugs.

The demonstration program, demo_sm, has the virtue of being small and should be straightforward. It concentrates on command line parsing and setting options for calls to **vm_map**. It has several ways of accessing a

413

memory object, including one designed specifically to illustrate distributed shared memory between two or more machines (`loopsource/loopsink`).

Do not despair if these programs seem large. In fact, there may be more comments than program. The programs use a lot of already familiar Mach and UNIX features.

B.2   Running the Programs

Before running these programs, make sure the `netmsgserver` is running on the machine where `sm_pager` will run and on all machines where `demo_sm` will run. The directory where `sm_pager` runs must have a subdirectory, called **Paging**, to contain the paging files established for SM objects. To execute the sample programs, simply run the pager in the background. Then invoke `demo_sm` with one of the arguments `create`, `append`, `display`, or `loopsource` or `loopsink`. Both `create` and `append` require additional text on the command line, which will be added to the contents of the memory region. Consult the source for `demo_sm` for additional options. A simple run might look like this:

```
% ./sm_pager &
% ./demo_sm create "hello, world" " here is some"
% ./demo_sm append " sample text\!"
% ./demo_sm display
./demo_sm:  object contents, page=0:
        "hello, world here is some sample text!"
```

For a demonstration of distributed shared memory, run `sm_pager` on one machine. Run two copies of `demo_sm`, the first on the same machine as `sm_pager`. Invoke these programs as

```
% ./sm_pager &
% ./demo_sm loopsource &
```

The `loopsource` option causes `demo_sm` to enter an infinite loop writing an ASCII character every second into a page in the memory object. On another machine, run a second copy of `demo_sm`, as follows:

```
% ./demo_sm host=machine1 loopsink
```

For *machine1*, substitute the name of the machine running `sm_pager`. The `host` option tells `demo_sm` to look for the SM paging service on a machine other than the one running `demo_sm`. The `loopsink` option causes `demo_sm` to enter a loop repetitively examining a page in the memory object. Whenever the contents of the page changes, `demo_sm` prints out the new version.

Thus, one machine is writing into the object and another is reading from it, demonstrating distributed shared memory. Sample output from the demo_sm reading memory looks like this:

```
% ./demo_sm host=machine1 loopsink
./demo_sm:  watching memory contents:
found:   ABCD
found:   ABCDE
found:   ABCDEF
found:   ABCDEFG
found:   ABCDEFGH
found:   ABCDEFGHI
```

Be sure that the machines you use for the distributed shared memory demonstration have the same page size. For simplicity, the pager assumes that all machines running sm_pager and demo_sm have identical page sizes.

B.3 Makefile

```
# Simple Makefile for SM pager and client
# (sm_pager and demo_sm).
#
# Three major compilation options:  -DDSM builds a pager capable
# of supporting distributed shared memory.  This is the default.
#
# Use CFLAGS_OSF1_1 instead of CFLAGS_25 to build a pager that
# runs under OSF/1 Release 1.1.  CFLAGS_25 supports Mach 2.5 and
# OSF/1 Release 1.0.
#
# The pager and client can also be built using Pthreads in place
# of C threads.
#

CLIENT_OBJS    =    smUser.o demo_sm.o common_funcs.o
SMS_OBJS       =    smServer.o common_funcs.o \
                    sm_emm.o sm_pager.o sm_dsm.o \
                    sm_encryption.o
PROGRAMS       =    demo_sm sm_pager
MIG_MISC       =    sm.h smServer.c smUser.c

LIBS_25        =    -lthreads -lmach
LIBS_OSF1_1    =    -lpthreads -lmach -lc_r

CFLAGS_COM     =    -DDSM -DDEBUG -g
CFLAGS_25      =    ${CFLAGS_COM}
OSF1_1A        =    -DUSE_PTHREADS -DOSF1_1 -D_BSD
OSF1_1B        =    -noshrlib
CFLAGS_OSF1_1  =    ${OSF1_1A} ${OSF1_1B} \
                    ${CFLAGS_COM}

CFLAGS         =    ${CFLAGS_25}

LIBS           =    ${LIBS_25}
#CFLAGS        =    ${CFLAGS_OSF1_1}
#LIBS          =    ${LIBS_OSF1_1}

all:            ${PROGRAMS}

clean:          ${RM} -f ${CLIENT_OBJS} ${SMS_OBJS} ${PROGRAMS} \
                ${MIG_MISC}

${MIG_MISC}:    sm.defs
                mig sm.defs

demo_sm:        ${CLIENT_OBJS}
                ${CC} -o demo_sm ${CFLAGS} ${CLIENT_OBJS} ${LIBS}

sm_pager:       ${SMS_OBJS}
                ${CC} -o sm_pager ${CFLAGS} ${SMS_OBJS} ${LIBS}

sm_emm.o sm_pager.o:                 sm_pager.h
sm_dsm.o common_funcs.o:             sm_pager.h
demo_sm.o sm_encryption.o:           sm_pager.h
demo_sm.o sm_encryption.o:           sm_decls.h
```

B.4 sm.defs

```
/*
 *      sm.defs:  MIG definitions for the exported
 *      Secure Memory operations.
 */

#include <mach/std_types.defs>
#include <mach/mach_types.defs>
```

```
#define SM_IDENTIFIER_LEN        80

subsystem sm 631118;

import "sm_decls.h";

type sm_status_t =      int;
type sm_key_t =         int;
type sm_identifier =    array [SM_IDENTIFIER_LEN] of char;

/*
 *      Request creation of a new memory object or attachment to
 *      an existing memory object.  An object is identified by
 *      the combination of its name and its encryption key.
 *
 *      The SM pager responds with a status code; if that code
 *      is SM_INIT_GRANTED, then sm_obj contains a port_name_t
 *      representing the memory object created or attached on
 *      behalf of the client.
 *
 *      Identifier names the sought-after object and crypt_key
 *      contains its encryption key.  The trace option causes
 *      the pager to print out messages about its actions.
 */
routine sm_initiate(
                pager_port:     port_t;
                identifier:     sm_identifier;
                crypt_key:      sm_key_t;
                create:         boolean_t;
                trace:          boolean_t;
        out     response:       sm_status_t;
        out     sm_obj:         memory_object_t);

/*
 *      The termination request informs the SM pager that the
 *      client no longer requires access to the indicated SM
 *      object.  If deallocate is TRUE, the object will be
 *      deleted from backing store when it has no more users.
 */
routine sm_terminate(
                pager_port:     port_t;
                sm_obj:         memory_object_t;
                deallocate:     boolean_t;
        out     response:       sm_status_t);
```

B.5 sm_decls.h

```
#ifndef _SM_DECLS_H_
#define _SM_DECLS_H_

/*
 *  sm_decls.h:
 *
 *  Common types and definitions for the Secure Memory
 *  pager and its clients.
 */

#include <mach/message.h>

/*
 *      Convenient short-hand.
 */
#define mytask          task_self()

/*
 *      Name by which a client may find the SM pager.
 */
#define SECURE_MEMORY_PAGER     "secure_memory"
```

```
/*
 *      Maximum length of the name a client may use to
 *      identify a memory region, including terminating null.
 */
#define SM_IDENTIFIER_LEN       80
typedef char            sm_identifier[SM_IDENTIFIER_LEN];

/*
 *      Status codes communicated from pager to client.
 */
#define SM_INIT_GRANTED         1
#define SM_INIT_NO_OBJECT       2
#define SM_INIT_OBJECT_EXISTS   3
#define SM_INIT_CLEAN_SHUTDOWN  4
#define SM_INIT_ERROR           5
typedef int             sm_status_t;

/*
 *      The nature of an encryption key.
 */
typedef int             sm_key_t;

#endif /* _SM_DECLS_H_ */
```

B.6 sm_pager.h

```
#ifndef _SM_PAGER_H_
#define _SM_PAGER_H_

/*
 * sm_pager.h:
 *      Definitions of important pager data structures.
 */

#include <mach/error.h>
#include "sm_decls.h"

/*
 *      File names are formed by concatenating the name supplied
 *      by a client program with the ASCII representation of the
 *      client's password modulo 26 and scaled into the
 *      character set [A..Z]. A period is used to separate the
 *      components of the resulting file name.  Thus if a client
 *      supplied the name "foo" and the password 55, the
 *      resulting file name is "foo.C".
 *
 *      MAX_FILE_NAME is larger than SM_IDENTIFIER_LEN to
 *      account for the SUBDIR string prefixed to
 *      the identifier.
 *
 *      MAP_SUFFIX is the string to add to the end of the file
 *      name to form the name of the page-map file.
 *      MAX_FILE_MAP_NAME is the size of this file name.
 */
#define SUBDIR                  "./Paging/"
#define MAP_SUFFIX              ".dir"
#define MAX_FILE_NAME           (SM_IDENTIFIER_LEN+11)
#define MAX_FILE_MAP_NAME       (MAX_FILE_NAME + \
                                 sizeof(MAP_SUFFIX))

/*
 *      Declare maximum buffer size handled by pager.  The pager
 *      is not prepared to handle requests larger than this
 *      value.  There is no good reason for this limit other
 *      than as a simplifying assumption.
 */
#define MAX_BUFFER_SIZE         (16 * 1024)
```

```
/*
 *      Maximum size of a memory object handled by this pager.
 *      This limit exists only to size the page_map array,
 *      defined later. For convenience, this array is static,
 *      hence the limit on an object's size.  By defining the
 *      maximum size as a number of pages, the limit will be
 *      machine dependent -- on an individual machine's page
 *      size.  For instance, on a computer with a 4K page size,
 *      an SM object cannot exceed 134,217,728 bytes.
 */
#define MAX_PAGES          32768
#define NPPB               (8)
#define MAX_PAGES_BYTES    (MAX_PAGES/NPPB)

/*
 *      NPPB is the number of pages represented per byte.
 */

/*
 *      Queue definitions.
 */
#define QFIRST(q)    (q)->q_next
#define QNEXT(q)     (q)->q_next
#define QPREV(q)     (q)->q_prev
#define QLAST(q)     ((qelem *) &(q)->q_next)
#define QEMPTY(q)    (QFIRST(q) == QLAST(q))

typedef struct qelem {
    struct qelem    *q_next;
    struct qelem    *q_prev;
} qelem;

/*
 *      Information retained by pager for each kernel managing
 *      an SM object, including its name (really a port) and its
 *      page size.  The structure implicitly records the memory
 *      object's control port, as well; the name of the control
```

```
 *      port is the same as the address of the kernel structure.
#ifdef DSM
 *      Keep track of init and terminate requests to detect the
 *      infamous Mach 2.5 init/init/terminate race.
#endif
 */

#define KERNEL_SIZE      (sizeof(kernel))
#define KERNEL_NULL      ((kernel *) 0)
typedef struct kernel {
memory_object_name_t          name;
vm_size_t                     page_size;
#ifdef DSM
unsigned int                  init_count;
unsigned int                  terminate_count;
#endif
} kernel;

/*
 *      Data structure containing all the information we need to
 *      know about a memory object.  Besides the queue links
 *      linking all objects together, an instance of an
 *      sm_object requires:
 *          - reference count of object's uses
 *          - the name of the region's paging file
 *          - paging file's open file descriptor
 *          - encryption key for region's data
 *          - name of region's page_map file
 *          - page_map file's open file descriptor
 *          - the page_map itself
 *          - identifier of thread managing this object
 *          - trace variable, enables printfs for this obj
 *
#ifdef DSM
 *          - a queue of entries for each page in memory
#endif
 *
```

```
*    The page_map tracks the presence of memory object pages
*    on disk.  A page that has never been written to disk
*    will have a page_map entry of zero.  By examining this
*    entry on a page-in request, the pager can determine that
*    the data have never before existed and respond with
*    zero-fill memory.  The page_map is a statically
*    allocated bit array for convenience, which places an
*    upper bound on the size of a memory object that can be
*    handled by this pager (MAX_PAGES).
*/
#ifdef DSM
/*
*    The pages qelem is the header for a queue of page
*    entries that track the locations and protections of
*    pages that have been handed from the SM pager to
*    requesting kernels.  These entries are used to coordinate
*    memory shared across machines.  Rather than a queue,
*    with average access time O(n) or at best O(n/2), a
*    production pager might use a faster method, such as a
*    hashing scheme.
*/
#endif

#define SMO_NULL              ((sm_object *) 0)
typedef struct sm_object {
    qelem          obj_links;
    unsigned int   refcount;
    char           backing_file[MAX_FILE_NAME];
    int            backing_fd;
    sm_key_t       crypt_key;
    char           page_map_file[MAX_FILE_MAP_NAME];
    int            page_map_fd;
    char           page_map[MAX_PAGES_BYTES];
    int            thread_index;
    boolean_t      trace;
#ifdef DSM
    qelem          pages;
#endif
} sm_object;

/*
*    Error codes returned by pager on paging failures.
*    Choice of error subsystem number (77) is arbitrary.
*/

#define SM_ERROR_NONE      (err_local|err_sub(77)|0)
#define SM_ERROR_OFFSET    (err_local|err_sub(77)|1)
#define SM_ERROR_SEEK      (err_local|err_sub(77)|2)
#define SM_ERROR_READ      (err_local|err_sub(77)|3)
#define SM_ERROR_FAILURE   (err_local|err_sub(77)|4)

/*
*    Miscellaneous debugging assertions.
*/

#ifdef assert
#undef assert
#endif

#ifdef DEBUG
#define assert(e) if (!(e)) assfail(__FILE__, __LINE__, "e")
#else
#define assert(e)
#endif

#endif /* _SM_PAGER_H_ */
```

B.7 sm_pager.c

```
/*
* sm_pager.c:
*    Demonstrate external memory management by providing a
```

```
/*
 *  "secure memory" service.  This pager encrypts all such
 *  memory before writing it out to disk and automatically
 *  decrypts it before returning it to a client.
 *
 *  Secure memory regions are named and persist across
 *  invocations of a client program.  Thus secure memory can
 *  be reused and it may be shared (fully read/write) by
 *  more than one client.
 *
 *  Once created, an SM object persists until a client
 *  explicitly requests that it be destroyed.
 */

#include <stdio.h>
#include <mach.h>
#include <mach/mig-errors.h>
#include <servers/netname.h>
#ifdef  USE_PTHREADS
#include <pthread.h>
#else
#include <cthreads.h>
#endif
#include <fcntl.h>
#include "sm.h"
#include "sm-pager.h"

#ifdef   USE_PTHREADS
#define  thread_t pthread_t
#else
#define  thread_t cthread_t
#endif

/*
 *  Default mode for creating paging files.
 */
#define PAGING_FILE_MODE       0666

/*
 *  Queue of objects known to the pager and macros to
 *  manipulate the queue.
 *
 *  The object queue must be locked for safety.  The queue
 *  potentially is used from multiple threads.  The
 *  pager_connection_loop adds objects to the queue and
 *  possibly removes them from the queue in sm_terminate.
 *  However, it is also possible for memory object threads
 *  to remove objects from the queue via sm_object_unref.
 */

qelem                       obj_queue;
#define OBFIRST(q)          ((sm_object *) QFIRST(q))
#define OBLAST(q)           ((sm_object *) QLAST(q))
#define OBNEXT(q)           ((sm_object *) QNEXT(q))
#ifdef   USE_PTHREADS
pthread_mutex_t             qlock;
#define OBJ_QUEUE_LOCK_INIT()  (void)pthread_mutex_init(&qlock,\
                                      pthread_mutexattr_default)
#define OBJ_QUEUE_LOCK()       (void)pthread_mutex_lock(&qlock)
#define OBJ_QUEUE_UNLOCK()     (void)pthread_mutex_unlock(&qlock)
#else
struct mutex                qlock;
#define OBJ_QUEUE_LOCK_INIT()  mutex_init(&qlock)
#define OBJ_QUEUE_LOCK()       mutex_lock(&qlock)
#define OBJ_QUEUE_UNLOCK()     mutex_unlock(&qlock)
#endif

/*
 *  The pager has a number of threads devoted to servicing
 *  memory object requests from the kernel.  As an object is
 *  created, it is assigned to one of these threads by the
```

```c
*      connection thread, pager_connect_th.  Each
*      memory_object_th has its own port set containing memory
*      object ports.
*
*      An object will be managed by the same thread throughout
*      its existence.  By only allowing one thread to service
*      an object, we eliminate page-in/page-out races with the
*      kernel.  A page-in request can immediately follow a
*      page-out request; if two threads each handled one of
*      these requests, there is no way to guarantee that the
*      page-out would be handled before the page-in.  The
*      page-in could receive stale data.  With only one thread,
*      the page-out will always be handled before the page-in.
*/

#define MAX_OBJ_THREADS      5
port_set_name_t memory_object_set[MAX_OBJ_THREADS];

char     *Me;

void     pager_connection_loop();
void     sm_object_ref(), sm_object_unref();
void     service_register(), service_unregister();
void     allocate_ports(), deallocate_ports();
extern void sm_object_server();
extern void fatal();
extern void kchk();
extern void mchk();
extern char *malloc(), *strcpy();

main(argc, argv)
int     argc;
char    *argv[];
{
     port_name_t      sm_request_port;
     port_name_t      signature;
     thread_t         pager_connect_th;
     int              n;
     thread_t         memory_object_th[MAX_OBJ_THREADS];
#ifdef USE_PTHREADS
     int              st;
     void             *exit_status;
#endif

     Me = argv[0];

     if (argc != 1) {
          printf("usage:  %s\n", Me);
          exit(1);
     }

     /*
      *      1.  Allocate ports for
      *              - pager to advertise in netmsgserver
      *              - signature port for netmsgserver
      *              - port set for all memory objects
      *                we will manage
      */
     allocate_ports(&sm_request_port, &signature,
                    memory_object_set, MAX_OBJ_THREADS);

     /*
      *      2.  Initialize memory object data structures.
      */
     queue_init(&obj_queue);
     OBJ_QUEUE_LOCK_INIT();

     /*
      *      3.  Register this service with the netmsgserver.
      */
```

```
service_register(SECURE_MEMORY_PAGER,
        sm_request_port, signature);

/*
 *      4.  The pager connect thread processes initial
 *          connection requests from clients.
 */

#ifdef USE_PTHREADS
if (pthread_create(&pager_connect_th,
            pthread_attr_default,
            pager_connection_loop,
            (void *) sm_request_port) < 0) {
    perror("pthread_create");
    fatal("pager_connect_th");
}

#else
pager_connect_th = cthread_fork(pager_connection_loop,
            sm_request_port);

#endif

/*
 *      5.  The memory_object_th threads handle all
 *          requests from Mach kernels concerning memory
 *          objects managed by this pager. They each enter
 *          sm_object_server with their own port set.
 */

#ifdef USE_PTHREADS
for (n = 0; n < MAX_OBJ_THREADS; ++n) {
    st = pthread_create(&memory_object_th[n],
            pthread_attr_default,
            sm_object_server,
            (void *)memory_object_set[n]);
    if (st < 0) {
        perror("pthread_create");
        fatal("memory_object_th");
    }

#else
    }

    memory_object_th[n] =
            cthread_fork(sm_object_server,
            memory_object_set[n]);

#endif
}

#ifdef USE_PTHREADS
for (n = 0; n < MAX_OBJ_THREADS; ++n)
    if (pthread_join(memory_object_th[n],
            &exit_status) < 0) {
        perror("pthread_join");
        fatal("memory_object_th");
    }

#else
for (n = 0; n < MAX_OBJ_THREADS; ++n)
    (void) cthread_join(memory_object_th[n]);

#endif

/*
 *      6.  Wait for all services to terminate.
 */

if (pthread_join(pager_connect_th, &exit_status) < 0) {
    perror("pthread_join");
    fatal("pager_connect_th");
}

#else
    (void) cthread_join(pager_connect_th);

#endif

/*
 *      7.  Clean up and exit.
 */

service_unregister(SECURE_MEMORY_PAGER, signature);
deallocate_ports(sm_request_port, signature,
        memory_object_set, MAX_OBJ_THREADS);

exit(0);
```

```c
}

/*
 *	The thread entering pager_connection_loop waits for and
 *	processes connection requests from clients.  This
 *	functionality has been separated from the primary
 *	memory object management functionality because setting
 *	up the initial connection can be done in many different
 *	ways that have little bearing on subsequent memory
 *	object management.
 */
void
pager_connection_loop(sm_request_port)
port_name_t		sm_request_port;
{
	port_set_name_t	pager_connect_set;
	port_name_t		reply_port;
	int				request_buf[MSG_SIZE_MAX/sizeof(int)];
	int				reply_buf[MSG_SIZE_MAX/sizeof(int)];
	msg_header_t	*request = (msg_header_t *) request_buf;
	death_pill_t	*reply = (death_pill_t *) reply_buf;
	msg_return_t	mr;
	kern_return_t	kr;

	/*
	 *	1.  Allocate a port set to contain the request
	 *		port for establishing initial client/pager
	 *		connections, along with some other ports.
	 *		Add sm_request_port.
	 */

	kr = port_set_allocate(mytask, &pager_connect_set);
	kchk(kr, "port_set_allocate",
		"unable to allocate init_pager_set");

	kr = port_set_add(mytask, pager_connect_set,
					sm_request_port);
	kchk(kr, "port_set_add", "adding sm_request_port");

	/*
	 *	2.  Add this task's notification port to the
	 *		pager_connect_set.  It is more convenient to
	 *		do a single receive on both the sm_request
	 *		and notification ports instead of inventing
	 *		a separate thread just for handling
	 *		notifications.
	 */

	kr = port_set_add(mytask, pager_connect_set,
					task_notify());
	kchk(kr, "port_set_add",
		"notify port to pager_connect");

	for (;;) {
		/*
		 *	3.  Listen for requests to create a new
		 *		memory object.
		 */

		request->msg_local_port = pager_connect_set;
		request->msg_size = sizeof(request_buf);
		mr = msg_receive(request, MSG_OPTION_NONE, 0);
		mchk(mr, "msg_receive", "pager_connect_set");

		/*
		 *	4.  Ignore notifications about the
		 *		destruction of ports to which we have
		 *		send rights.  A client sends us a port
		 *		on which to reply to its requests; MIG
		 *		never deallocates the port.  We
		 *		deallocate the port anyway, after
		 *		sending any reply, but the client could
```

```
	 *	terminate prematurely and still cause a
	 *	notification to be sent.
	 */
	if (request->msg_local_port == task_notify())
		continue;

	/*
	 *	5.	Decode and handle the request.
	 *		This stub is generated by MIG.
	 */
	if (sm_server(request, &reply->Head) == FALSE) {
		printf("%s: unknown SM request %d\n",
			Me, request->msg_id);
		continue;
	}

	/*
	 *	6.	If a reply is needed, send one.
	 */
	reply_port = reply->Head.msg_remote_port;
	if ((reply_port != PORT_NULL) &&
		(reply->RetCode != MIG_NO_REPLY)) {
		mr = msg_send(reply,MSG_OPTION_NONE,0);
		mchk(mr, "msg_send",
			"can't respond to client init");
	}

	/*
	 *	7.	Deallocate the reply port to avoid
	 *		cluttering up pager's port name space
	 *		and to avoid port death notifications.
	 */
	if (reply_port != PORT_NULL) {
		kr = port_deallocate(mytask,reply_port);
		kchk(kr,"port_deallocate","MIG reply");
	}
}
}

/*
 *	Initiate a connection between client and pager.  The
 *	client requests a memory object and, if appropriate, the
 *	pager returns a port to the client that can be used to
 *	map the object into its address space.  This function is
 *	called from sm_server(), a stub created by MIG and
 *	invoked by the pager from the init-pager thread.  Refer
 *	to sm_defs for a discussion of the arguments to
 *	sm_initiate.
 */

kern_return_t
sm_initiate(port, identifier, crypt_key, create, trace,
		response, sm_obj)
	port_t			port;
	char			*identifier;
	sm_key_t		crypt_key;
	boolean_t		create;
	boolean_t		trace;
	sm_status_t		*response;
	memory_object_t *sm_obj;
{
	sm_object		*obj;
	port_name_t		memory_object_port;
	kern_return_t	kr;
	char			backing_file_name[MAX_FILE_NAME];
	char			page_map_file_name[MAX_FILE_MAP_NAME];
	int			backing_fd;
	int			page_map_fd;
	int			oflags;
	static int		next_thread = 0;
```

```
crypt_key = crypt_key % 26;
(void) sprintf(backing_file_name, "%s/%s.%c",
            SUBDIR, identifier, crypt_key + 'A');
(void) sprintf(page_map_file_name, "%s/%s",
            backing_file_name, MAP_SUFFIX);
```

```
/*
 *    1.  Convert the encryption key to a more easily
 *    usable form and create the backing file name.
 *    Also construct the name of the page_map file.
 */
```

```
/*
 *    2.  Search cache of existing objects to
 *    determine whether the client's proposed
 *    object exists.
 */
OBJ_QUEUE_LOCK();
for (obj = OBFIRST(&obj-queue);
    obj != OBLAST(&obj-queue);
    obj = OBNEXT(&obj->obj_links))
    if (obj->crypt_key == crypt_key &&
        !strcmp(obj->backing_file,backing_file_name))
        break;
```

```
/*
 *    3.  Hit in cache.  If the request was to create
 *    an object, reject it.  Otherwise grant access to
 *    this object and increase its reference count to
 *    account for an additional user.
 */
if (obj != OBLAST(&obj-queue)) {
    if (create == TRUE)
        *response = SM_INIT_OBJECT_EXISTS;
    else {
```

```
        sm_object_ref(obj);
        *sm_obj = (memory_object_t) obj;
        *response = SM_INIT_GRANTED;
    }
    OBJ_QUEUE_UNLOCK();
    return(KERN_SUCCESS);
}
OBJ_QUEUE_UNLOCK();
```

```
/*
 *    4.  If the memory object has not already been
 *    cached, determine whether a paging file for the
 *    object already exists on disk.  If the client
 *    specified create == TRUE, the initiation attempt
 *    should fail if the file already exists.  On the
 *    other hand, if create == FALSE, the client may
 *    be trying to attach to a persistent memory obj.
 */
if (create == TRUE)
    oflags = O_CREAT|O_EXCL|O_RDWR;
else
    oflags = O_RDWR;

if ((backing_fd = open(backing_file_name, oflags,
                    PAGING_FILE_MODE)) < 0) {
    if (create == TRUE)
        *response = SM_INIT_OBJECT_EXISTS;
    else
        *response = SM_INIT_NO_OBJECT;
    return(KERN_SUCCESS);
}
```

```
/*
 *    5.  Also open the region's page_map file,
 *    creating it if it does not already exist.
```

```c
 *	We really do not expect this call to fail.
 */
if ((page_map_fd = open(page_map_file_name,
				O_CREAT|O_RDWR,
				PAGING_FILE_MODE)) < 0) {
	*response = SM_INIT_ERROR;
	(void) close(backing_fd);
	return(KERN_SUCCESS);
}

/*
 *	6.  A paging file existed or was created for
 *	the client's memory object.  Initialize the
 *	necessary internal data structures.
 *	First, allocate the sm_object required for
 *	internal bookkeeping.
 */
if ((obj=(sm_object *)malloc(sizeof(*obj)))==SMO_NULL)
	fatal("malloc unable to create new memory obj");

/*
 *	7.  Allocate a port to give the client.  This
 *	port represents the memory object.  The client
 *	will pass the port to the kernel in a vm_map
 *	call; the kernel will then send us EMM requests
 *	over this port.
 */
kr = port_allocate(mytask, &memory_object_port);
kchk(kr, "port_allocate", "new memory_object_port");

/*
 *	8.  Rather than using the kernel's default name
 *	for this port, use a more convenient name.  We
 *	set the name of the port to be the address of
 *	the sm_object we just allocated.
 */
kr = port_rename(mytask, memory_object_port,
				(port_name_t) obj);
kchk(kr, "port_rename", "renaming memory_object_port");

/*
 *	9.  Finally, add the new port to one of the sets
 *	of ports listened to by one of the memory_object
 *	threads.   Perform simple load balancing by
 *	stepping through the array each time.  N.B.  The
 *	new port is now named "obj" and
 *	not memory_object_port.  Even though "obj" is a
 *	pointer to a data structure we just allocated,
 *	it is also the name of a port.
 */
kr = port_set_add(mytask,
				memory_object_set[next_thread++],
				(port_name_t) obj);
kchk(kr, "port_set_add", "adding new memory object");

if (next_thread >= MAX_OBJ_THREADS)
	next_thread = 0;

/*
 *	10.  Initialize the state of the structure
 *	representing the new memory object.  We remember
 *	the name of the backing file, its open file
 *	descriptor, and the encryption key.  The paging
 *	area will be retained on disk for future access
 *	even after all clients currently using it exit,
 *	unless sm_terminate is called with
 *	deallocate=TRUE.
 *
 *	Set the reference count to one because we are
 *	about to hand a port back to the client that can
 *	be used to find this memory object.
```

```
         */
(void) strcpy(obj->backing_file, backing_file_name);
(void) strcpy(obj->page_map_file, page_map_file_name);
        obj->trace = trace;
        obj->crypt_key = crypt_key;
        obj->backing_fd = backing_fd;
        obj->refcount = 1;
        obj->page_map_fd = page_map_fd;
        obj->thread_index = next_thread - 1;
#ifdef DSM
        queue_init(&obj->pages);
#endif

        /*
         * 11.  If the object is brand new, initialize the
         * page_map by filling it with zeroes (indicating
         * page not present); otherwise fetch the page_map
         * from its file.
         */
        if (create == TRUE) {
            bzero(obj->page_map, (int) MAX_PAGES_BYTES);
        } else {
            if (read(page_map_fd, obj->page_map,
                (int) MAX_PAGES_BYTES) < 0) {
                perror("read page_map_fd");
                exit(1);
            }
        }

        /*
         * 12.  Insert the new sm_object into the cache.
         * Note:  If there were more than one
         * pager_connection_loop thread, there would be
         * a race between two connection threads creating
         * the same new object.  Both look in the cache,
         * see it is not there, and insert it.  Either
         * another cache check must be inserted here or
         * the lock must be held from look-up until
         * insertion.
         */
        OBJ_QUEUE_LOCK();
        insque(&obj->obj_links, &obj_queue);
        OBJ_QUEUE_UNLOCK();

        /*
         * 13.  Return a favorable response, including the
         * new memory object port, to the client.
         */
        *response = SM_INIT_GRANTED;
        *sm_obj = (memory_object_t) obj;
        return(KERN_SUCCESS);
}

/*
 * Sever the connection between pager and client for this
 * SM object.  Free up resources.  All we need to do is
 * unlink any files if deallocate=TRUE.  When we decrement
 * the object's reference count, if there are no more
 * users the remaining cleanup will happen right away.
 * Otherwise the object can continue to be used by current
 * clients until they all relinquish their access, at which
 * point the object will be closed out.
 */
kern_return_t
sm_terminate(port, sm_obj, deallocate, response)
        port_t          port;
        memory_object_t sm_obj;
        boolean_t       deallocate;
        sm_status_t     *response;
```

```
{
    sm_object    *obj;
    char         error_buffer[BUFSIZ];

    /*
     *  1.  Use sm_obj to find pager's internal
     *      data structure.
     */
    obj = (sm_object *) sm_obj;

    if (deallocate == TRUE) {
        if (unlink(obj->backing_file) < 0) {
            perror("unlink backing file");
            (void) sprintf(error_buffer,
                          "sm_terminate: %s\n",
                          obj->backing_file);
            fatal(error_buffer);
        }

        if (unlink(obj->page_map_file) < 0) {
            perror("unlink page map file");
            (void) sprintf(error_buffer,
                          "sm_terminate: %s\n",
                          obj->page_map_file);
            fatal(error_buffer);
        }
    }

    /*
     *  Unfortunately, we cannot deallocate the sm_obj
     *  port here because it might still be in use by
     *  other clients.  We are trusting the client not
     *  to use the port in a vm_map call before calling
     *  back with another sm_initiate request.
     *  Otherwise the pager's object reference counts
     *  can become confused.
     */
```

```
    */
    /*
     *  Delete client's hold on the object.
     */
    sm_object_unref(obj);

    *response = SM_CLEAN_SHUTDOWN;
    return(KERN_SUCCESS);
}

/*
 *  Record an increase in an SM object's users.
 */
void
sm_object_ref(obj)
sm_object    *obj;
{
    obj->refcount++;
}

/*
 *  Decrease the number of users of an SM object.  If the
 *  count falls to zero, the structure may be reclaimed.
 */
void
sm_object_unref(obj)
sm_object    *obj;
{
    kern_return_t   kr;
    char            error_buffer[BUFSIZ];

    /*
```

```
*       Decrement the object's reference count.  If the
*       count falls to zero, remove it from the queue
*       while still holding the lock.  With the object
*       no longer on the queue, it cannot be found in
*       sm_initiate.  There will be no races with
*       another thread trying to reactivate the object;
*       the actions taken in this routine are all
*       harmless with regard to that race.
*/
OBJ_QUEUE_LOCK();
obj->refcount--;
if (obj->refcount > 0) {
    OBJ_QUEUE_UNLOCK();
    return;
}
remque(obj);
OBJ_QUEUE_UNLOCK();

/*
*       No users of the object currently exist.  Close
*       the backing and page map files.  If a client
*       called sm_terminate with deallocate=TRUE, the
*       kernel will free up disk space now.
*/
if (close(obj->backing_fd) < 0) {
    perror("close");
    (void) sprintf(error_buffer,
            "sm_object_unref:  %s\n",
            obj->backing_file);
    fatal(error_buffer);
}
if (close(obj->page_map_fd) < 0) {
    perror("close2");
    (void) sprintf(error_buffer,
            "sm_object_unref:  %s\n",
            obj->page_map_file);
    fatal(error_buffer);
}

/*
*       We no longer have a need for the object port.
*/
kr = port_deallocate(mytask, (port_name_t) obj);
kchk(kr, "port_deallocate", "sm_terminate");

/*
*       Reclaim the object.
*/
(void) free((char *) obj);
}

/*
*       Allocate important initial ports.
*/
void
allocate_ports(pager_request_port,signature_port,object_set,len)
port_name_t     *pager_request_port;
port_name_t     *signature_port;
port_set_name_t object_set[];
int             len;
{
    kern_return_t   kr;
    int             n;

/*
*       Allocate a port for incoming service requests.
*       Clients will contact the netmsgserver with the
*       name of our service and will in return receive
*       a send right to this port.
*/
```

```
	*/
	kr = port_allocate(mytask, pager_request_port);
	kchk(kr, "port_allocate","can't allocate service port");

	/*
	 *	Allocate a port solely for use as a signature
	 *	for netname_check_in.  Only a program that has
	 *	the signature port can then delete the name.
	 */
	kr = port_allocate(mytask, signature_port);
	kchk(kr, "port_allocate", "can't allocate signature");

	/*
	 *	Allocate a port set for each thread for all its
	 *	memory object ports.
	 */
	for (n = 0; n < len; ++n) {
		kr = port_set_allocate(mytask, &object_set[n]);
		kchk(kr, "port_set_allocate",
			"can't allocate object_set");
	}
}

/*
 *	Deallocate important, well-known ports.
 */
void
deallocate_ports(pager_request_port, signature_port,
		object_set, len)
port_name_t	pager_request_port;
port_name_t	signature_port;
port_set_name_t	object_set[];
{
	kern_return_t	kr;
	int		n;

	kr = port_deallocate(mytask, pager_request_port);
	kchk(kr, "port_deallocate",
		"unable to deallocate pager's request_port");

	kr = port_deallocate(mytask, signature_port);
	kchk(kr, "port_deallocate",
		"unable to deallocate signature port");

	for (n = 0; n < len; ++n) {
		kr = port_set_deallocate(mytask, object_set[n]);
		kchk(kr, "port_set_deallocate",
			"unable to deallocate object set");
	}
}

/*
 *	Advertise the service we offer with the netmsgserver.
 *	Clients will look up our service by name and use the
 *	port we provide to contact the pager.
 */
void
service_register(service_name, service_port, signature)
char		*service_name;
port_name_t	service_port;
port_name_t	signature;
{
	kern_return_t	kr;
	char		error_buffer[BUFSIZ];

	kr = netname_check_in(name_server_port, service_name,
			signature, service_port);
	if (kr != NETNAME_SUCCESS) {
```

```c
        mach_error("netname_check_in", kr);
        (void) sprintf(error_buffer,"can't register %s",
                       service_name);
        fatal(error_buffer);
    }
}

/*
 *    Remove our service advertisement from the netmsgserver.
 */
void
service_unregister(service_name, signature)
char            *service_name;
port_name_t     signature;
{
    kern_return_t   kr;
    char            error_buffer[BUFSIZ];

    kr = netname_check_out(name_server_port, service_name,
                           signature);
    if (kr != NETNAME_SUCCESS) {
        mach_error("netname_check_out", kr);
        (void) sprintf(error_buffer,
                       "can't unregister %s",
                       service_name);
        fatal(error_buffer);
    }
}
```

B.8 sm_emm.c

```c
/*
 *  sm_emm.c:
 *       External memory management functions.
 *
 *    This file has two major compilation options.  Building
 *    with DSM defined includes hooks in the EMM routines to
 *    to call into the distributed shared memory coherency
 *    routines.  Memory can be shared between multiple
 *    machines.
 *
 *    The second option is OSF1.1, which provides the small
 *    modifications necessary to run the pager under OSF/1.1.
 *    The EMM interfaces are slightly different in OSF/1.1.
 *    However, under OSF/1.0 the EMM interfaces are identical
 *    to Mach 2.5.
 */

#include <mach.h>
#include <mach/message.h>
#include <mach/mig_errors.h>
#include <mach/notify.h>
#include <stdio.h>
#include <sys/types.h>
#include <sys/stat.h>
#include <sys/file.h>
#include "sm_pager.h"

extern void      sm_encrypt(), sm_decrypt(), fatal();
extern void      sm_object_ref(), sm_object_unref();
extern void      mchk(), kchk();
extern off_t     lseek();
extern char *    malloc();

#define XOFF     ((vm_offset_t) -1)
#define XLEN     ((vm_size_t) -1)
#define XPROT    ((vm_prot_t) -1)
void             trace();
```

```
#ifdef DSM
/*
 *	Information this module must know from the dsm coherency
 *	module.  Normally there would be a much closer coupling
 *	between these modules.  However, for pedagogical reasons
 *	we have concealed coherency issues as much as possible
 *	from the mainstream EMM code.
 */

extern boolean_t	dsm_init();
extern boolean_t	dsm_terminate();
extern boolean_t	dsm_data_request();
extern boolean_t	dsm_data_unlock();
extern boolean_t	dsm_data_write();
#endif

/*
 *	Page map manipulations.  Check for page presence by
 *	examining the bit representing the page in the map.
 *	Mark a page present by setting that bit.
 */

#define PAGE_IN_MAP(map,page)					\
	(map[(page) / NPPB] & (1 << ((page) % NPPB)))
#define MARK_PAGE_IN_MAP(map,page)				\
	(map[(page) / NPPB] |= (1 << ((page) % NPPB)))

/*
 *	Main memory object pager loop.  Wait for incoming
 *	messages on any of the ports in the memory_object_set.
 *	When one arrives, dispatch to the needed subroutine and
 *	send whatever reply is required.
 */

extern char		*Me;


void
sm_object_server(memory_object_set)
port_set_name_t		memory_object_set;
{
	int			request_buf[MSG_SIZE_MAX/sizeof(int)];
	int			reply_buf[MSG_SIZE_MAX/sizeof(int)];
	msg_header_t		*request = (msg_header_t *) request_buf;
	death_pill_t		*reply = (death_pill_t *) reply_buf;
	msg_return_t		mr;
	boolean_t		valid;

	for (;;) {
		request->msg_local_port = memory_object_set;
		request->msg_size = sizeof(request_buf);
		mr = msg_receive(request, MSG_OPTION_NONE, 0);
		mchk(mr, "msg_receive",
			"message error on memory object set");

		/*
		 *	If the message ID matches one of the
		 *	memory object operations, the library
		 *	function memory_object_server (generated
		 *	by MIG) will dispatch to the requested
		 *	subroutine.
		 *
		 *	Otherwise just ignore the message.
		 */

		valid = memory_object_server(request,
			&reply->Head);
		if (valid == FALSE) {
			printf("%s: ignored request %d\n",
				Me, request->msg_id);
			continue;
		}
```

}

```c
	/*
	 *	If a reply is needed, send one.
	 *	However, because the EMM interfaces
	 *	are asynchronous, we do not really
	 *	expect to generate a reply.
	 */
	if ((reply->Head.msg_remote_port != PORT_NULL) &&
	    (reply->RetCode != MIG_NO_REPLY)) {
		printf("%s: replying with id %d???\n",
			Me, reply->Head.msg_id);

		mr = msg_send(reply, MSG_OPTION_NONE,0);
		mchk(mr, "msg_send","failed emm reply");
	}

}

/*
 * The first time a Mach kernel receives a request from
 * a client to map a Secure Memory object, the kernel
 * sends a memory_object_init request to the pager.  One
 * such memory_object_init request will be sent for each
 * newly used memory object.
 *
 * The memory_object_init request contains the following:
 * - the port representing the memory object
 * - a port for use when the SM pager has to
 *   request an action by the kernel on any of the
 *   object's pages
 * - a port representing the object's name, as
 *   revealed in vm_region calls
 * - the page size of the kernel mapping
 *   the object.
 *
 * To simplify the implementation, we only accept init
 *	requests from kernels whose page sizes match the native
 *	page size.
 */
kern_return_t
memory_object_init(memory_object, memory_control,
			memory_object_name, memory_object_page_size)
memory_object_t		memory_object;
memory_object_control_t	memory_control;
memory_object_name_t	memory_object_name;
vm_size_t		memory_object_page_size;
{
	sm_object	*obj;
	kernel		*kern;
	kern_return_t	kr;

	/*
	 *	1.  Use memory_object to find pager's internal
	 *	data structure.
	 */
	obj = (sm_object *) memory_object;

	/*
	 *	2.  Reject page sizes that do not match the
	 *	native page size.  A production pager would
	 *	handle varying page sizes, but for ease the SM
	 *	pager does not.
	 */
	if (memory_object_page_size != vm_page_size) {
		printf("%s: rejected kernel, page size %d\n",
			Me, (int) memory_object_page_size);
		return(KERN_SUCCESS);
	}

#ifdef DSM
	/*
```

```
	*	Detect init/init/terminate races.  An init
	*	request arrived before we saw the previous
	*	terminate request due to a Mach 2.5 bug.
	*	In this case, we continue to use the existing
	*	kern structure.  This race does not exist in
	*	Mach 3.0 or OSF/1 Release 1.1.
	*/
	if (dsm_init(memory_object, memory_control) == TRUE) {
		sm_object_ref(obj);
		(void)memory_object_set_attributes(memory_control,
						TRUE, FALSE,
						MEMORY_OBJECT_COPY_DELAY);

		return(KERN_SUCCESS);
	}

#endif

	/*
	 * 3.  Allocate a data structure to save
	 *     information specific to the kernel mapping
	 *     the memory object.
	 */
	if ((kern=(kernel *)malloc(KERNEL_SIZE)) == KERNEL_NULL)
		fatal("m_o_init:  unable to create new kernel");
	trace(obj), "m_o_init", kern, XOFF, XLEN, XPROT);

	/*
	 * 4.  By renaming the control port, finding the
	 *     newly allocated data structure again will simply
	 *     be a matter of casting the name of the control
	 *     port into a memory address.
	 */
	kr=port_rename(mytask,memory_control,(port_name_t)kern);
	kchk(kr, "port_rename", "renaming kernel control port");

	/*
	 * 5.  Record the relevant, per-kernel information
	 *     necessary to manage the mapping of this memory
	 *     object.
	 */
	kern->name = memory_object_name;
	kern->page_size = memory_object_page_size;

#ifdef DSM
	kern->init_count = 1;
	kern->terminate_count = 0;
#endif

	/*
	 * 6.  Record one more use of the memory object.
	 *     We will not deallocate the memory object until
	 *     all kernels that know about the object have
	 *     terminated their use of it and the port we first
	 *     handed out is destroyed.  This use accounts for
	 *     the object being mapped.
	 */
	sm_object_ref(obj);

	/*
	 * 7.  The old name for the port on which to
	 *     respond to the kernel, memory_control, no
	 *     longer works because we renamed the port.
	 *     Use the new name.
	 *
	 *     By setting the second parameter, object_ready,
	 *     to TRUE, we permit the kernel to begin paging
	 *     operations on this memory object.
	 */
#ifdef OSF1_1
	/*
	 *     The OSF/1 1.0 EMM interfaces match Mach 2.5.
```

```c
#else
        *       In OSF/1 Release 1.1, the EMM interfaces have
        *       a few differences from Mach 2.5.   Argument #4
        *       (before the copy strategy), when set to TRUE,
        *       informs the kernel that the pager will use
        *       memory_object_data_write_completed (also new
        *       in OSF/1) to indicate it has completed a
        *       memory_object_data_write (i.e., a page-out).
        *       The kernel will not start a data-request on
        *       the same page until it sees the write_completed,
        *       thus eliminating the page-in/page-out race.
        *
        *       The last argument specifies the cluster size.
        *       The kernel will group together pages and perform
        *       multipage data_request and data_write operations
        *       for efficiency.  We set the cluster size to the
        *       page size to limit operations to one page.  An
        *       OSF/1 kernel might still make multipage
        *       data_write requests -- but usually will not for
        *       the SM pager because there is only one page
        *       written back from a lock-request at a time.
        *       However, an OSF/1 kernel might still choose to
        *       page-out adjacent writable pages from an SM
        *       object at the same time.  The real solution:
        *       Production pagers should be able to handle
        *       multipage requests.
        */
        kr=memory_object_set_attributes((memory_object_control_t)
                               kern, TRUE, FALSE,
                               FALSE,
                               MEMORY_OBJECT_COPY_DELAY,
                               vm_page_size);
#else
        kr=memory_object_set_attributes((memory_object_control_t)
                               kern, TRUE, FALSE,
                               MEMORY_OBJECT_COPY_DELAY);
#endif
        kchk(kr, "memory_object_set_attributes", "");

        return(KERN_SUCCESS);
}

/*
 *      A kernel that had mapped one of the SM pager's objects
 *      no longer has any valid mappings.  Service to that
 *      kernel can be terminated.  Force any pending I/O through
 *      to the disk.  Tear down this object's "kernel"
 *      structure.  The entire sm_object structure will be
 *      reclaimed when its reference count falls to zero.
 */
kern_return_t
memory_object_terminate(memory_object, memory_control,
                        memory_object_name)
memory_object_t         memory_object;
memory_object_control_t memory_control;
memory_object_name_t    memory_object_name;
{
        sm_object       *obj;
        kernel          *kern;
        kern_return_t   kr;
        char            error_buffer[BUFSIZ];

        /*
         *      1.  Convert ports to internal data structures.
         */
        obj = (sm_object *) memory_object;
        kern = (kernel *) memory_control;

        trace(obj, "m_o_terminate", kern, XOFF, XLEN, XPROT);
```

```c
#ifdef DSM
	/*
	 *	Distributed shared memory.  Inform the dsm
	 *	module that the kernel, kern, has stopped using
	 *	obj.  If dsm detects an init/init/terminate
	 *	race, the only responsibility of this routine is
	 *	to decrement the reference count on the object.
	 *	The rest of this code will be executed on the
	 *	final terminate.
	 */
	if (dsm_terminate(obj, kern) == TRUE) {
		assert(obj->refcount > 1);
		sm_object_unref(obj);
	}
#endif

	/*
	 *	2.	Force any pending I/O to disk.
	 */
	if (fsync(obj->backing_fd) < 0) {
		perror("fsync");
		(void)sprintf(error_buffer,"m_o_terminate: %s\n",
			obj->backing_file);
		fatal(error_buffer);
	}

	/*
	 *	3.	Save the page_map.  We really do not expect
	 *		the lseek operation to fail.  Nor do we make
	 *		provision for the write operation to fail, which
	 *		could happen the first time an object is created
	 *		and has never before had a page map or on an I/O
	 *		error.
	 */
	if (lseek(obj->page_map_fd, (off_t) 0, L_SET) < 0)
		perror("m_o_terminate: lseek");
	if (write(obj->page_map_fd, obj->page_map,
			(int) MAX_PAGES_BYTES) < 0)
		perror("m_o_terminate: write page_map");
	if (fsync(obj->page_map_fd) < 0) {
		perror("fsync page_map_fd");
		printf("%s: m_o_terminate:  %s\n", Me,
			obj->page_map_file);
	}

	/*
	 *	4.	Clean up the pager task's port name space.
	 */
	kr = port_deallocate(mytask, memory_object_name);
	kchk(kr, "port_deallocate", "m_o_terminate memory_control");
	kchk(kr, "port_deallocate", "m_o_terminate m_o_name");

	(void) free((char *) kern);

	/*
	 *	The object is no longer mapped.
	 */
	sm_object_unref(obj);
}

	return(KERN_SUCCESS);
}

/*
 *	Because MEMORY_OBJECT_COPY_CALL does not work in Mach
 *	2.5, we expect never to receive this request.
 */
kern_return_t
```

```
memory_object_copy(old_memory_object, old_memory_control,
                   offset, length, new_memory_object)
memory_object_t         old_memory_object;
memory_object_control_t old_memory_control;
vm_offset_t             offset;
vm_size_t               length;
memory_object_t         new_memory_object;
{
    trace((sm_object *) old_memory_object, "m_o_copy",
          (kernel *)old_memory_control,offset,length,XPROT);
    fatal("memory_object_copy: shouldn't be called");
}

/*
 * Process page fault request from a kernel on one of the
 * memory objects managed by sm_pager. By fiat, the SM
 * pager only handles single-page requests, with the page
 * size identical to the native machine's page size. In a
 * production pager, there would be extra code to handle
 * multipage requests and different page sizes.
 */
kern_return_t
memory_object_data_request(memory_object, memory_control,
                           offset, length, desired_access)
memory_object_t         memory_object;
memory_object_control_t memory_control;
vm_offset_t             offset;
vm_size_t               length;
vm_prot_t               desired_access;
{
    sm_object     *obj;
    kernel        *kern;
    vm_prot_t     lock_value;
    kern_return_t kr, reason;
    char          *buffer;
    int           off, len, r;

    assert(length == vm_page_size);

    /*
     * 1. Convert ports to internal data structures.
     */
    obj = (sm_object *) memory_object;
    kern = (kernel *) memory_control;

    trace(obj, "m_o_data_request", kern, offset,
          length, desired_access);

    /*
     * 2. Determine whether the requested data lies
     *    beyond the maximum size of an SM object. This
     *    limit is an artifact of the page_map, which
     *    could be re-implemented to remove the maximum
     *    size limit. We are unlikely to approach this
     *    limit for this example.
     */
    if (offset > MAX_PAGES * vm_page_size) {
        reason = SM_ERROR_OFFSET;
        goto request_data_error;
    }
#ifdef DSM
    /*
     * Distributed shared memory. If the dsm module
     * must take over, there is no work left to do.
     */
    if (dsm_data_request(obj, kern, offset,
                         desired_access) == TRUE)
        return(KERN_SUCCESS);
```

```
#endif

    len = (int) length;
    off = (int) offset;
    lock_value = (~desired_access) & VM_PROT_ALL;

    /*
     *     Allocate a buffer for the data.
     */
    kr = vm_allocate(mytask, (vm_address_t) &buffer,
                     MAX_BUFFER_SIZE, TRUE);

    /*
     *  3.  Examine the page_map to determine whether
     *  the requested page exists on disk.  If not, use
     *  memory_object_data_unavailable to indicate that
     *  the kernel should supply zero-fill memory.
     */
    if (!PAGE_IN_MAP(obj->page_map, off / vm_page_size)) {

#ifndef DSM
        kr=memory_object_data_unavailable(memory_control,
                                          offset, length);
        kchk(kr, "memory_object_data_unavailable",
                 "no data in paging file");

#else
        /*
         *  Even if the desired_access did not
         *  specify VM_PROT_WRITE, data_unavailable
         *  grants all permissions to the returned
         *  memory.  But we told the dsm module the
         *  access specified to data_request by the
         *  kernel.  Using data_unavailable can lead
         *  to the SM pager thinking the data has
         *  been supplied read-only while the kernel
         *  actually has a writable copy.  We could
         *  fix this problem by detecting this case
         *  and telling the dsm module to assume
         *  write access.
         */
        (void) bzero(buffer, (int) length);
        kr = memory_object_data_provided(memory_control,
                            offset, (pointer_t) buffer,
                            (int) length, lock_value);
        kchk(kr, "memory_object_data_provided", "bzero");

        (void)vm_deallocate(mytask, (vm_address_t)buffer,
                            MAX_BUFFER_SIZE);
#endif

        return(KERN_SUCCESS);
    }

    /*
     *  4.  Fetch the data from the disk.  On any kind
     *  of error, give up on the entire request.
     */
    if (lseek(obj->backing_fd, (off_t) off, L_SET) < 0) {
        perror("m_o_data_request: lseek");
        reason = SM_ERROR_SEEK;
        goto request_data_error;
    }

    if ((r = read(obj->backing_fd, buffer, len)) < 0) {
        perror("m_o_data_request: read");
        reason = SM_ERROR_READ;
        goto request_data_error;
    }

    if (r != vm_page_size)
        fatal("m_o_data_request:  not a page?");

    /*
     *  5.  The data stored in the disk file were
     *  encrypted to preserve security in case someone
```

439

```
/*
 * Handle page-out requests from a kernel.  The page
 * supplied by the kernel should be encrypted, written to
 * disk, and then flushed from the pager's address space.
 * A production pager should also handle multipage
 * requests, varying page sizes.
 */
kern_return_t
memory_object_data_write(memory_object, memory_control,
                         offset, data, data_count)
memory_object_t         memory_object;
memory_object_control_t memory_control;
vm_offset_t             offset;
pointer_t               data;
unsigned int            data_count;
{
    sm_object      *obj;
    kernel         *kern;

    assert (data_count == (unsigned int) vm_page_size);

    /*
     * 1.  Convert ports to internal data structures.
     */
    obj = (sm_object *) memory_object;
    kern = (kernel *) memory_control;

    trace(obj, "m_o_data_write", kern, offset,
          (vm_size_t) data_count, XPROT);

#ifdef DSM
    /*
     * Inform dsm module of this page-out.  We expect
     * dsm always to tell us to continue the page-out.
     */
```

```
     * steals the disk drives.  The data must be
     * decrypted before passing them to the requestor.
     */
    sm_decrypt(buffer, (unsigned int) r, obj->crypt_key);

    /*
     * 6.  Send the region to the kernel that took the
     * page fault.  That kernel will take care of
     * making it available to any and all clients
     * needing it on that machine.
     */
    kr = memory_object_data_provided(memory_control,
                     offset, (pointer_t) buffer,
                     (int) length, lock_value);
    kchk(kr, "memory_object_data_provided", "");

    (void) vm_deallocate(mytask, (vm_address_t) buffer,
                MAX_BUFFER_SIZE);
    return(KERN_SUCCESS);

    /*
     * 7.  Common error exit path.  Indicate to the
     * requesting kernel that the page range cannot be
     * supplied in any form.
     */
request_data_error:
    kr = memory_object_data_error(memory_control, offset,
                     length, reason);
    kchk(kr, "memory_object_data_error", "data_request");
    (void) vm_deallocate(mytask, (vm_address_t) buffer,
                MAX_BUFFER_SIZE);
    return(KERN_SUCCESS);
}
```

```
#endif

    if (dsm_data_write(obj, kern, offset) == TRUE)
        fatal("memory_object_data_write: dsm");

/*
 *  2.  The SM pager guarantees security of its data
 *      by encrypting it all before writing it to disk.
 */
    sm_encrypt((char *) data, (unsigned int) data_count,
        obj->crypt_key);

/*
 *  3.  Write data back to this memory object's
 *      paging file.  A failure here is quite awkward.
 *      There is no thread in the kernel waiting for a
 *      page-in and so there is no one to pay attention
 *      if we responded with m_o_data_error.  In a
 *      production pager, we might make page_map an
 *      array of state variables, not just bits,
 *      permitting us to keep our own record of the
 *      page-out failure.  For the SM pager we will just
 *      deallocate the data and complain.
 */
    if ((lseek(obj->backing_fd, (off_t) offset, L_SET) < 0)
     || (write(obj->backing_fd, (char *) data,
            (int) data_count) < 0)) {
        perror("m_o_data_write: lseek or write!");
        (void) vm_deallocate(mytask, data,
            (vm_size_t) data_count);
        return(KERN_SUCCESS);
    }

/*
 *  4.  Update page_map to record the fact that we
 *      have paged-out data for this region.
 */
    MARK_PAGE_IN_MAP(obj->page_map,
        ((int) offset) / vm_page_size);

/*
 *  5.  Having written the data to disk, there is no
 *      need to keep it in memory.  Flushing it from the
 *      pager's address space allows the kernel to free
 *      up physical pages.
 */
    (void) vm_deallocate(mytask,data,(vm_size_t)data_count);

}

    return(KERN_SUCCESS);

/*
 *  A kernel requests more access to a page than originally
 *  granted by the pager.  Typically the page was first
 *  returned with read access and now the kernel requires
 *  write access.  In a production pager, this routine would
 *  also handle multipage requests and varying page sizes.
 */

kern_return_t
memory_object_data_unlock(memory_object, memory_control,
            offset, length, desired_access)
    memory_object_t         memory_object;
    memory_object_control_t memory_control;
    vm_offset_t             offset;
    vm_size_t               length;
    vm_prot_t               desired_access;
{
    sm_object       *obj;
    kernel          *kern;
    vm_prot_t       lock_value;
```

```
    kern_return_t   kr;

    assert(length == vm_page_size);

    /*
     * 1.  Convert ports to internal data structures.
     */
    obj = (sm_object *) memory_object;
    kern = (kernel *) memory_control;

    trace(obj, "m_o_data_unlock", kern, offset,
          length, desired_access);

#ifdef DSM
    /*
     * Inform dsm of the desired access.  It is
     * possible that, before access can be granted for
     * this kernel, access by other kernels must be
     * revoked.  In that case, the dsm module takes
     * over and there is no more work to be done here.
     */
    if (dsm_data_unlock(obj, kern, offset,
                        desired_access) == TRUE)
        return(KERN_SUCCESS);

#endif

    /*
     * 2.  Return precisely the desired access.  There
     *     is no need to clean or flush the page or wait
     *     for a reply.
     */
    lock_value = (~desired_access) & VM_PROT_ALL;
    kr = memory_object_lock_request(memory_control,
                        offset, length, FALSE,
                        FALSE, lock_value,
```

```
                                        PORT_NULL);
    kchk(kr, "memory_object_lock_request", "");

    return(KERN_SUCCESS);
}

/*
 * In some cases, a pager needs to know when a lock_request
 * operation completes.  The kernel sends a message for
 * this operation to signal the completion.  The dsm module
 * depends heavily on lock_completed messages.
 */
kern_return_t
memory_object_lock_completed(memory_object, memory_control,
                             offset, length)
    memory_object_t      memory_object;
    memory_object_control_t memory_control;
    vm_offset_t          offset;
    vm_size_t            length;
{
    sm_object    *obj;
    kernel       *kern;

    assert(length == vm_page_size);

    /*
     * 1.  Convert ports to internal data structures.
     *     Nothing to do for our sample pager.
     */
    obj = (sm_object *) memory_object;
    kern = (kernel *) memory_control;

    trace(obj, "m_o_lock_completed", kern, offset,
          length, XPROT);
```

```
#ifdef DSM
        /*
         *  Inform dsm of the lock_completed event.  Dsm may
         *  then grant this page to another kernel.
         */
        (void) dsm_lock_completed(obj, kern, offset);
#endif

        return(KERN_SUCCESS);
}

#ifdef OSF1_1
/*
 *  The OSF/1 Release 1.1 EMM interfaces require this
 *  additional operation.  The kernel uses this interface
 *  to inform the pager that a memory_object_data_supply
 *  has completed.  The data_supply operation is not
 *  part of Mach 2.5 but is very similar to data_provided.
 */
kern_return_t
memory_object_supply_completed(memory_object, memory_control,
                offset, length, result, error_offset)
memory_object_t         memory_object;
memory_object_control_t memory_control;
vm_offset_t             offset;
vm_size_t               length;
kern_return_t           result;
vm_offset_t             error_offset;
{
        trace((sm_object_t*)memory_object,
                "m_o_supply_completed",
                (kernel *) memory_control, offset, length, XPROT);
        fatal("memory_object_supply_completed: invoked");
```

```
}
#endif

/*
 *  If an object has trace enabled, printed messages
 *  tracking the progress of page faults for this object.
 */
static void
trace(obj, fnname, kern, offset, length, desired_access)
sm_object       *obj;
char            *fnname;
kernel          *kern;
vm_offset_t     offset;
vm_size_t       length;
vm_prot_t       desired_access;
{
        if (obj->trace == FALSE)
                return;
        printf("==> %s(obj=%#x, kern=%#x", fnname, obj, kern);
        if (offset != XOFF)
                printf(", off=%#x", offset);
#if     0
        /*
         *  Do not bother printing out length; it will
         *  always be vm_page_size in this implementation.
         */
        if (length != XLEN)
                printf(", len=%#x", length);
#endif
        if (desired_access != XPROT) {
                printf(", acc=");
                if (desired_access & VM_PROT_READ)
                        putchar('R');
                if (desired_access & VM_PROT_WRITE)
```

```c
        putchar('W');
    if (desired_access & VM_PROT_EXECUTE)
        putchar('X');

    printf("\n");
}
```

B.9   sm_dsm.c

```c
#ifdef DSM
/*
 * sm_dsm.c:  perform memory coherency operations for
 * distributed shared memory.
 *
 * The coherency module assumes all operations take place
 * on one page at a time and all pages have the same size.
 * Additional logic could eliminate these assumptions.
 */

#include <mach.h>
#include "sm_pager.h"

/*
 * The policy implemented by this module is single-writer,
 * multiple-readers.  Page-in and page-out actions are
 * handled in sm_emm.c, which uses hooks into this module
 * to determine the needed actions.
 *
 * At any instant, a page can be in one of the following
 * states:
 *
 *   - not in memory anywhere
 *   - any number of read-only copies may exist
 *       simultaneously on any number of machines
 *   - one page may be writable by one machine,
 *               with no other copies existing elsewhere
 *
 * When a request for access to a page arrives at the SM
 * pager, the following actions may occur:
 *   - page not in memory anywhere
 *       o Grant requested access
 *   - page in memory, read-only
 *       o If desired access is read, grant access
 *       o If desired access is write
 *           - Flush all outstanding copies
 *           - Grant access
 *
 *   - page in memory, writable
 *       o Clean and flush writable page,
 *           causing page-out
 *       o Grant access (which ultimately uses
 *           the paged-out copy of the page)
 *
 * This policy can lead to page thrashing, especially when
 * two writers compete for access to the same page.  In a
 * production pager, this problem might be resolved by
 * adding a time quantum to each page, so when access is
 * granted to a page for a kernel it will remain with that
 * kernel long enough for useful work to be done.  We
 * do not worry about thrashing in the sample SM pager.
 */

/*
 * The reader structure tracks a kernel that has read
 * access to a particular page.  Obviously, there may be
 * many kernels with read access to the same page.
 */
#define READER_NULL    ((reader *) 0)
#define RDFIRST(q)     ((reader *) QFIRST(q))
#define RDNEXT(q)      ((reader *) QNEXT(q))
#define RDLAST(q)      ((reader *) QLAST(q))
```

```c
typedef struct reader {
    qelem       rdq;            /* queue links */
    kernel      *kern;          /*kernel using page*/
    vm_prot_t   protection;/*actual prot on pg*/
} reader;

/*
 * Pending operations.  Only data_request and data_unlock
 * can be pended.  We always immediately handle init,
 * terminate, data_write, and lock_completed messages.
 */
#define PEND_NULL           ((pending_op *) 0)

#define QPFIRST(q)          ((pending_op *) QFIRST(q))
#define QPNEXT(q)           ((pending_op *) QNEXT(q))
#define QPLAST(q)           ((pending_op *) QLAST(q))

#define OP_NONE             0
#define OP_DATA_REQUEST     1
#define OP_DATA_UNLOCK      2

typedef struct pending_op {
    qelem        opsq;          /* queue links */
    unsigned int operation;     /* pending op */
    kernel       *kern;         /* pended kernel */
    vm_prot_t    access;        /* desired prot */
} pending_op;

/*
 * The page structure records the users of pages handed out
 * to kernels.  Consistency actions take place based on the
 * desired use of a page relative to the current uses of a
 * page.  Pages are always tracked in terms of the native
 *      page size of the Mach kernel running the SM pager.
 */
#define PGFIRST(q)          ((page *) QFIRST(q))
#define PGNEXT(q)           ((page *) QNEXT(q))
#define PGLAST(q)           ((page *) QLAST(q))

#define PSTATE_NONE         0
#define PSTATE_READERS      1
#define PSTATE_WRITER       2
#define PSTATE_CHANGING     3

#define PAGE_NULL           ((struct page *) 0)

typedef struct page {
    qelem        pageq;         /* queue links */
    vm_offset_t  offset;        /* offset into obj */
    unsigned int state;         /* consistency */
    qelem        readers;       /* kerns reading pg */
    int          read_count;/* number of rdrs */
    kernel       *writer;       /* writer of page */
    qelem        ops;           /* pending page ops */
} page;

extern char     *malloc();
extern void     kchk();
void            pending_op_execute();

/*
 * Search for the page at the specified offset in object.
 * Returns PAGE_NULL if we have no entry for this page.
 */
page *
page_lookup(obj, offset)
```

```
sm_object      *obj;
vm_offset_t    offset;
{
    page       *p;

    for (p = PGFIRST(&obj->pages); p != PGLAST(&obj->pages);
         p = PGNEXT(&p->pageq))
        if (p->offset == offset)
            return(p);

    return(PAGE_NULL);
}

/*
 * Make a new page for the specified (object,offset).
 * Assumes that the page does not already exist.
 */
page *
page_create(object, offset)
sm_object      *object;
vm_offset_t    offset;
{
    page       *p;

    p = (page *) malloc(sizeof(*p));
    assert(p != PAGE_NULL);
    p->offset = offset;
    queue_init(&p->readers);
    p->read_count = 0;
    p->writer = KERNEL_NULL;
    queue_init(&p->ops);
    p->state = PSTATE_NONE;
    insque(&p->pageq, &object->pages);
    return(p);
}
```

```
/*
 * Remove a page from an object and free associated memory.
 */
void
page_remove(p)
page       *p;
{
    remque(&p->pageq);
    (void) free((char *) p);
}

/*
 * Check whether a page entry is still in use.
 */
boolean_t
page_in_use(p)
page       *p;
{
    if (p->state == PSTATE_WRITER ||
        p->state == PSTATE_CHANGING ||
        p->read_count > 0 ||
        !QEMPTY(&p->ops))
        return(TRUE);
    return(FALSE);
}

/*
 * Search for an entry on the page's readers queue that
 * matches the desired kernel.
 */
reader *
```

```
page *
kernel *
{
    reader *r;

    for (r = RDFIRST(&p->readers); r != RDLAST(&p->readers);
         r = RDNEXT(&r->rdq))
        if (r->kern == kern)
            return(r);

    return(READER_NULL);
}

/*
 *      Add the specified kernel to the page's queue of readers.
 *      The entry may exist already.  This case arises when the
 *      requesting kernel had a copy of the page earlier, threw
 *      it away, and now needs the page again.  If an entry
 *      already exists, update its protection to the new value.
 */
void
page_reader_add(p, kern, access)
    page      *p;
    kernel    *kern;
    vm_prot_t access;
{
    reader  *r;

    assert(!(access & VM_PROT_WRITE));

    r = page_reader_lookup(p, kern);
    if (r != READER_NULL) {
        r->protection = access;
        return;
    }
```

```
                                No reader entry exists.  Create one.
 */
r = (reader *) malloc(sizeof(*r));
assert(r != READER_NULL);
r->kern = kern;
r->protection = access;
insque(&r->rdq, &p->readers);
p->read_count++;
}

/*
 *      Remove a reader from a page.  Free up storage.
 */
void
page_reader_delete(p, r)
    page    *p;
    reader  *r;
{
    assert(p->state == PSTATE_READERS ||
           p->state == PSTATE_CHANGING);
    assert(p->read_count > 0);

    remque(&r->rdq);
    p->read_count--;
}

/*
 *      Create a pending operation structure.
 */
pending_op *
```

```
pending_op_create(operation, kern, access)
unsigned int    operation;
kernel          *kern;
vm_prot_t       access;
{
        pending_op      *op;

        op = (pending_op *) malloc(sizeof(*op));
        assert(op != PEND_NULL);
        op->operation = operation;
        op->kern = kern;
        op->access = access;
        return(op);
}

/*
 *      Add an operation to the pending queue for this page.
 */
void
page_pending_add(p, operation, kern, access)
page            *p;
unsigned int    operation;
kernel          *kern;
vm_prot_t       access;
{
        pending_op      *op;

        op = pending_op_create(operation, kern, access);
        insque(&op->opsq, &p->ops);
}

/*
 *      Add an operation to the pending queue for this page.
 *      However, insert the op at the front of the queue.
 */
void
page_pending_add_front(p, operation, kern, access)
page            *p;
unsigned int    operation;
kernel          *kern;
vm_prot_t       access;
{
        pending_op      *op;

        op = pending_op_create(operation, kern, access);
        op->opsq.q_next = (qelem *) &p->ops.q_next;
        op->opsq.q_prev = p->ops.q_prev;
        p->ops.q_prev->q_next = (qelem *) &op->opsq.q_next;
        p->ops.q_prev = (qelem *) &op->opsq.q_next;
}

/*
 *      Return the oldest pending operation.
 */
pending_op *
page_pending_next(p)
page            *p;
{
        return((pending_op*) p->ops.q_prev);
}

/*
 *      Delete the specified pending operation from the page's
 *      pending operation queue.  Reclaim storage.
 */
void
```

```
page_pending_delete(p, op)
page            *p;
pending_op      *op;
{
    assert(QPREV(&op->ops) == (qelem *) &op->opsq.q_next);
    remque(&op->opsq);
    (void) free((char *) op);
}

/*
 *  Update the page state to reflect the access granted
 *  to this kernel for this page.
 */
void
page_access_grant(p, kern, access)
page            *p;
kernel          *kern;
vm_prot_t       access;
{
    if (access & VM_PROT_WRITE) {
        p->writer = kern;
        p->state = PSTATE_WRITER;
    } else {
        page_reader_add(p, kern, access);
        p->state = PSTATE_READERS;
    }
}

/*
 *  Migrate a page from read-only mode to write mode.  This
 *  change may require revoking access to the page by
 *  kernels that have it mapped for reading.
 */
```

```
boolean_t
page_read_to_write(obj, operation, p, kern, access)
sm_object          *obj;
unsigned int       operation;
page               *p;
kernel             *kern;
vm_prot_t          access;
{
    memory_object_control_t kern.mem_ctl;
    kern.return_t      kr;
    reader             *r;
                       *next;

    assert(p->state == PSTATE_READERS);
    assert(p->read_count > 0 && !QEMPTY(&p->readers));
    assert(p->writer == KERNEL_NULL);

    /*
     *  Optimize special case:  Only one copy of
     *  the page exists; kernel owning it is
     *  upgrading to write.
     */
    if (p->read_count==1&&RDFIRST(&p->readers)->kern==kern) {
        page_reader_delete(p, RDFIRST(&p->readers));
        p->writer = kern;
        p->state = PSTATE_WRITER;
        return(FALSE);
    }

    /*
     *  Force kernels with read access to the page
     *  to flush their copies of the page.  The only
     *  exception:  If the kernel attempting to gain
     *  write access already has read access, let it
     *  "keep" the page by not sending it a flush.
     */
```

```
*       (But delete its readers' entry now.)  The kernel
*       may have reclaimed the page invisibly but
*       presumably in that case operation ==
*       OP_DATA_REQUEST.
*/
p->state = PSTATE_CHANGING;
for (r = RDFIRST(&p->readers); r!=RDLAST(&p->readers);){
    next = RDNEXT(&r->rdq);
    if (r->kern == kern) {
        page_reader_delete(p, r);
        r = next;
        continue;
    }

    kern_mem_ctl = (memory_object_control_t)r->kern;
    kr = memory_object_lock_request(kern_mem_ctl,
                                    p->offset,
                                    vm_page_size,
                                    FALSE, TRUE,
                                    VM_PROT_ALL,
                                    (port_t) obj);

    kchk(kr, "memory_object_lock_request",
         "page_read_to_write");

    r = next;
}

/*
*       Now we must wait for the replies to the series
*       of lock_request operations we initiated.  As
*       each reply comes back, dsm_lock_completed
*       removes a reader from the readers queue.
*       Eventually, dsm_lock_completed determines that
*       no more readers exist and grants access to the
*       page.  At that time, dsm_lock_completed needs to
*       know what operation to respond to (data_unlock
*       or data_request) and what access to grant.  So
*       save this operation on the *front* of the
*       pending queue for dsm_lock_completed.
*/
page_pending_add_front(p, operation, kern, access);

/*
*       The caller should not take further action.
*       Supplying the requested page and access is now
*       the responsibility of the dsm module.
*/
return(TRUE);

}

/*
*       Revoke outstanding write access so we may pass the page
*       to the requestor.  The new requestor may be seeking read
*       or write access.  Use memory_object_lock_request to
*       force the kernel that currently has the page to page it
*       out and flush it from memory.  When we see the
*       lock_completed message, we will pass the page on to the
*       new requestor.
*
*       Clearly there is a potential optimization for the read
*       case:  We could use lock_request with should_clean=TRUE,
*       should_flush=FALSE, and lock_value=VM_PROT_WRITE to
*       cause the kernel currently writing the page to clean it
*       in place and downgrade its access to read-only.
*/
boolean_t
page_write_revoke(obj, operation, p, kern, access)
sm_object        *obj;
unsigned int     operation;
page             *p;
kernel           *kern;
```

```
vm_prot_t      access;
{
    memory_object_control_t mem_ctl;
    kern_return_t           kr;

    assert(p->state == PSTATE_WRITER);
    assert(p->read_count == 0 && QEMPTY(&p->readers));
    assert(p->writer != KERNEL_NULL && p->writer != kern);

    p->state = PSTATE_CHANGING;
    mem_ctl = (memory_object_control_t) p->writer;
    kr = memory_object_lock_request(mem_ctl,
                                    p->offset,
                                    vm_page_size,
                                    TRUE, TRUE,
                                    VM_PROT_ALL,
                                    (port_t) obj);

    kchk(kr, "memory_object_lock_request",
             "page_write_to_write");

    page_pending_add_front(p, operation, kern, access);

    return(TRUE);
}
```

```
 *      can be devised.
 */
boolean_t
dsm_init(memory_object, memory_control)
memory_object_t         memory_object;
memory_object_control_t memory_control;
{
    kernel          *kern;

    if ((unsigned int) memory_control < 0x1000)
        return(FALSE);
    kern = (kernel *) memory_control;
    assert(kern->page_size == vm_page_size);
    kern->init_count++;
    return(TRUE);
}

/*
 *      When a kernel shuts down its use of an object, clean up
 *      outstanding state for that kernel. We might still have
 *      readable page entries because the kernel can invisibly
 *      flush read-only pages. There should be no writable
 *      pages owned by the kernel terminating the object.
 */
boolean_t
dsm_terminate(obj, kern)
sm_object      *obj;
kernel         *kern;
{
    page    *p, *pnext;
    reader  *r, *rnext;

    /*
     *      1.  Detect init/init/terminate races. An init
```

```
/*
 *      Detect init/init/terminate races on an object. Cheat:
 *      Unrenamed ports are assumed to have small integer values;
 *      renamed ports are believed to have larger values. A
 *      renamed port is a sign that the object has already been
 *      through memory_object_init at least once. Increase the
 *      init_count so the termination routines do the right
 *      thing and return TRUE, causing the caller to abort
 *      memory_object_init processing. A more reliable check
```

```
*    has been seen before the terminate matching the
*    last init.  In this case, we want to avoid
*    freeing up page reader structures because we
*    might destroy readers added by paging operations
*    that took place between the second init request
*    and this terminate request.  The worst that will
*    happen is that we believe the kernel has read
*    access to more pages than it really does.
*    Eventually, this situation will correct itself
*    through page revocations or the next terminate.
*/
assert(kern->terminate_count <= kern->init_count);
kern->terminate_count++;
if (kern->terminate_count < kern->init_count)
    return(TRUE);

/*
*    On a legitimate terminate request, remove
*    any outstanding page reader entries because
*    we know the kernel in question has reclaimed
*    those pages.
*/
for (p = PGFIRST(&obj->pages); p!=PGLAST(&obj->pages);){
    assert(p->writer != kern);
    r = RDFIRST(&p->readers);
    while (r != RDLAST(&p->readers)) {
        rnext = RDNEXT(&r->rdq);
        if (r->kern == kern)
            page_reader_delete(p, r);
        r = rnext;
    }
    pnext = PGNEXT(&p->pageq);
    if (page_in_use(p) == FALSE)
        page_remove(p);
    p = pnext;
```

```
    }
    return(FALSE);
}

/*
*    Examine the current state of a page and take the
*    necessary actions to maintain coherency with respect to
*    handling the incoming request.
*
*    If this function returns FALSE, the caller is allowed to
*    proceed with the proposed action.  As the caller is
*    memory_object_data_request or memory_object_data_unlock,
*    the next action will be to satisfy a page-in request or
*    grant access to a page.
*
*    If this function returns TRUE, then all further action
*    will be driven from the dsm module.  The caller should
*    simply give up and go back to the incoming message loop.
*
*    From the standpoint of maintaining page coherency,
*    a request for execute access is the same as a
*    read request.
*/
boolean_t
dsm_request(obj, op, kern, offset, access)
    sm_object      *obj;
    unsigned int    op;
    kernel         *kern;
    vm_offset_t     offset;
    vm_prot_t       access;
{
    page           *p;
    /*
```

```
	/*
	 *	Look for the page.  If an entry does not
	 *	already exist, create one.
	 */
	if ((p = page_lookup(obj, offset)) == PAGE_NULL)
		p = page_create(obj, offset);

	/*
	 *	If the page has no readers or writer, we can
	 *	grant the access desired by the requesting
	 *	kernel.  This case arises in two ways:
	 *
	 *	1.  The page has not been used before.
	 *	2.  Coherency page transfers.
	 */
	if (p->state == PSTATE_NONE) {
		page_access_grant(p, kern, access);
		return(FALSE);
	}

	/*
	 *	If the page is in the middle of changing
	 *	its state, then incoming requests must be
	 *	deferred until the state change completes.
	 */
	if (p->state == PSTATE_CHANGING) {
		page_pending_add(p, op, kern, access);
		return(TRUE);
	}

	/*
	 *	If the page is in multiple-readers mode,
	 *	allow this request if it is also for read;
	 *	add the requesting kernel to the readers queue.
	 *	Otherwise initiate the process of flushing
	 *	the existing read-only pages to make way for
	 *	the writer.
	 */
	if (p->state == PSTATE_READERS) {
		if ((access & VM_PROT_WRITE) == 0) {
			/*
			 *	We may already believe the kernel
			 *	has read access.  A kernel can
			 *	reclaim a read-only page without
			 *	notifying the pager and then send
			 *	another request for it.  This
			 *	case handled by page_reader_add.
			 */
			page_reader_add(p, kern, access);
			return(FALSE);
		}
		return(page_read_to_write(obj, op,
					p, kern,access));
	}

	/*
	 *	The page is currently writable so it must be
	 *	revoked from the kernel that owns it before this
	 *	request can be granted.  The access sought can
	 *	be READ or WRITE.
	 */
	assert(p->state == PSTATE_WRITER);
	return(page_write_revoke(obj, op, p, kern, access));
}

/*
 *	Catch memory_object_data_request, pass to common routine.
 */
boolean_t
dsm_data_request(obj, kern, offset, access)
	sm_object		*obj;
```

```
kernel       *kern;
vm_offset_t   offset;
vm_prot_t     access;
{
    dsm_request(obj, OP_DATA_REQUEST, kern, offset, access);
}

/*
 * Catch memory_object_lock_request, pass to common routine.
 */
boolean_t
dsm_data_unlock(obj, kern, offset, access)
sm_object    *obj;
kernel       *kern;
vm_offset_t   offset;
vm_prot_t     access;
{
    dsm_request(obj, OP_DATA_UNLOCK, kern, offset, access);
}

/*
 * Take necessary action on a page-out.
 */
boolean_t
dsm_data_write(obj, kern, offset)
sm_object    *obj;
kernel       *kern;
vm_offset_t   offset;
{
    page    *p;

    p = page_lookup(obj, offset);
```

```
    assert(p != PAGE_NULL);
    assert(p->read_count == 0 && QEMPTY(&p->readers));
    assert(p->state == PSTATE_CHANGING ||
           p->state == PSTATE_WRITER);
    assert(p->writer == kern);

    if (p->state == PSTATE_WRITER) {
        p->state = PSTATE_NONE;
        p->writer = KERNEL_NULL;
    }

    if (page_in_use(p) == FALSE)
        page_remove(p);

    return(FALSE);
}

/*
 * On lock completion, pass page on to next user.
 */
boolean_t
dsm_lock_completed(obj, kern, offset)
sm_object    *obj;
kernel       *kern;
vm_offset_t   offset;
{
    reader    *r;
    page      *p;

    p = page_lookup(obj, offset);
    assert(p != PAGE_NULL);
    assert(p->state == PSTATE_CHANGING);
    assert(!QEMPTY(&p->ops));
```

```
        /*
         *  If p->writer matches this kernel, then we are
         *  revoking write access in order to hand the page
         *  to some other kernel.  Otherwise we are
         *  revoking read access.
         */
        if (p->writer == kern) {
                p->state = PSTATE_NONE;
                p->writer = KERNEL_NULL;
        } else {
                r = page_reader_lookup(p, kern);
                assert(r != READER_NULL);
                page_reader_delete(p, r);
                if (p->read_count == 0)
                        p->state = PSTATE_NONE;
        }

        /*
         *  We cannot do anything else until the page state
         *  becomes PSTATE_NONE, indicating that all pending
         *  lock_requests have been carried out.
         */
        if (p->state != PSTATE_NONE)
                return(TRUE);

        /*
         *  The original request that caused the coherency
         *  actions was left on the front of the pending
         *  operations queue.  Now that the page has reached
         *  a stable state, execute the request.
         */
        pending_op_execute(obj, p, (pending_op*)QPREV(&p->ops));

        /*
         *  Now process any pending ops starting from the
         *  front of the queue until the state of the object
         *  becomes PSTATE_CHANGING or the queue is
         *  exhausted.  In a production pager, this would be
         *  a bad idea because it could lead to thrashing.
         *  Instead, a time quantum would be assigned to the
         *  page and ops would be deferred until the quantum
         *  expired.
         */
        while (p->state != PSTATE_CHANGING && !QEMPTY(&p->ops))
                pending_op_execute(obj, p, (pending_op *)
                        QNEXT(&p->ops));

        return(TRUE);
}

/*
 *  Execute the specified pending operation.  Reclaim memory.
 *  We invoke memory_object_data_request or ...lock_request,
 *  which then jumps back into the dsm module at dsm_request.
 *  The desired page was made available before calling this
 *  routine, so when we get back to dsm_request the request
 *  will be satisfied immediately.
 */
void
pending_op_execute(obj, p, op)
        sm_object               *obj;
        page                    *p;
        pending_op              *op;
{
        memory_object_t         mem_obj;
        memory_object_control_t mem_ctl;
        vm_offset_t             offset;
        vm_prot_t               access;
        unsigned int            opcode;
```

455

```
mem_obj = (memory_object_t) obj;
mem_ctl = (memory_object_control_t) op->kern;
offset = p->offset;
access = op->access;
opcode = op->operation;
remque(&op->opsq.q_next);
(void) free((char *) op);


assert(opcode==OP_DATA_REQUEST||opcode==OP_DATA_UNLOCK);
if (opcode == OP_DATA_REQUEST)
        (void) memory_object_data_request(mem_obj,
                                mem_ctl, offset,
                                vm_page_size, access);

    else
        (void) memory_object_data_unlock(mem_obj,
                                mem_ctl, offset,
                                vm_page_size, access);
}
#endif   /* DSM */
```

B.10 sm_encryption.c

```
/*
 * sm_encryption.c:
 *      Encryption support for Secure Memory.
 *
 *      The encryption routines provided herein are a simple
 *      substitution cipher, using the user-supplied key to
 *      shift characters within the machine's character set.
 *
 *      Depending on the addition and subtraction operators to
 *      "wrap around" from the end of the character set back to
 *      the beginning may be machine dependent.
 */

#include "sm_decls.h"

#ifndef u_int
typedef unsigned int u_int;
#endif

/*
 *      Encrypt buffer.
 */
void
sm_encrypt(buf, length, password)
    char            *buf;
    unsigned int    length;
    sm_key_t        password;
{
    char    *cp;

    for (cp = buf; cp < buf + length; ++cp)
        *cp = *cp + (char) password;
}

/*
 *      Decrypt buffer.
 */
void
sm_decrypt(buf, len, password)
    char            *buf;
    unsigned int    len;
    sm_key_t        password;
{
```

```
        char    *cp;

        for (cp = buf; cp < buf + len; ++cp)
                *cp = *cp - (char) password;
}
```

B.11   common_funcs.c

```
/*
 *      common_funcs.c:
 *              Handy functions.
 *
 *      These functions happen to be shared between client
 *      and pager programs for this application.  We share
 *      these routines out of convenience rather than necessity.
 */

#include <mach.h>
#include <mach/message.h>
#include <mach/notify.h>
#include <mach/mig_errors.h>
#include <mach/exception.h>
#include <stdio.h>
#include "sm-pager.h"

/*
 *      Print last message and terminate program.  We use fatal
 *      entirely too often in the SM pager.  A production pager
 *      work harder to avoid or recover from errors.
 */
void
fatal(message)
char    *message;
{
        extern char     *Me;

        printf("%s: %s\n", Me, message);
        exit(1);
}

/*
 *      Check the return code from a Mach system call.  In the
 *      event of a failure, describe the problem and terminate
 *      the program.  A production pager is more robust.
 */
void
kchk(kr, syscall, description)
kern_return_t   kr;
char            *syscall;
char            *description;
{
        char    error_buffer[BUFSIZ];

        if (kr == KERN_SUCCESS)
                return;

        mach_error(syscall, kr);
        (void)sprintf(error_buffer, "\toperation affected: %s",
                        description);
        fatal(error_buffer);
}

/*
 *      Check the return code from a Mach message primitive.  In
 *      case of a failure, describe the problem and terminate
 *      the program.  A more robust pager might not terminate.
 */
```

```
/*
 *    N.B.  In practice RCV_SUCCESS == SEND_SUCCESS == 0.
 */
void
mchk(mr, syscall, description)
msg_return_t    mr;
char            *syscall;
char            *description;
{
    char    error_buffer[BUFSIZ];

    if (mr == RCV_SUCCESS || mr == SEND_SUCCESS)
        return;

    mach_error(syscall, mr);
    (void) sprintf(error_buffer, "operation affected:  %s",
                   description);
    fatal(error_buffer);
}

/*
 *    exception_handler:  Catch exceptions on a task or thread
 *    exception port.  This routine "consumes" a thread:  It
 *    should be called via cthread_fork and will never return.
 *    This code is generic:  It will catch all exceptions and
 *    forward them to catch_exception_raise.
 */
void
exception_handler(exception_port)
port_name_t     exception_port;
{
    int             exc_buf[MSG_SIZE_MAX/sizeof(int)];
    int             reply_buf[MSG_SIZE_MAX/sizeof(int)];
    msg_header_t    *exception = (msg_header_t *) exc_buf;
    death_pill_t    *reply = (death_pill_t *) reply_buf;
    msg_return_t    mr;
    extern char     *Me;

    for (;;) {
        exception->msg_local_port = exception_port;
        exception->msg_size = sizeof(exc_buf);

        mr = msg_receive(exception, MSG_OPTION_NONE, 0);
        mchk(mr, "msg_receive", "exception port");

        if (exc_server(exception, &reply->Head)==FALSE){
            printf("weird request %d on exc port\n",
                   exception->msg_id);
            continue;
        }

        /*
         *    If a reply is needed, send one.
         */
        if ((reply->Head.msg_remote_port != PORT_NULL)
            && (reply->Head.RetCode != MIG_NO_REPLY)) {
            printf("%s:  replying with id %d\n",
                   Me, reply->Head.msg_id);
            mr = msg_send(reply, MSG_OPTION_NONE,0);
            mchk(mr, "msg_send", "exception reply");
        }
    }
}

/*
 *    Handle an incoming exception.  For the sample SM pager
 *    and the demo_sm client, print out a message about the
 *    exception but make no attempt to correct the problem.
 */
```

```
catch_exception_raise (port,thread,task,exception,code,subcode)
port_name_t    port;
thread_t       thread;
task_t         task;
int            exception;
int            code;
int            subcode;
{
    printf("exception %d code %d subcode %d\n", exception,
        code, subcode);
    mach_exception("exception received", exception,
        code, subcode);
    return(TRUE);
}

/*
 * Queue support.  Initialize queue header.  Forward and
 * backward pointers should both point to the header.
 */
queue_init(q)
    qelem    *q;
{
    q->q_next = q->q_prev = (qelem *) &q->q_next;
}

/*
 * Translate an SM response code into something readable.
 */
void
sm_response_to_string(response, result)
    sm_status_t    response;
    char           **result;
{
    switch (response) {
    case SM_INIT_GRANTED:
        *result = "init granted";
        break;
    case SM_INIT_NO_OBJECT:
        *result = "doesn't exist";
        break;
    case SM_INIT_OBJECT_EXISTS:
        *result = "already exists";
        break;
    case SM_CLEAN_SHUTDOWN:
        *result = "clean shutdown";
        break;
    case SM_INIT_ERROR:
        *result = "-- unexpected SM pager error --";
        break;
    default:
        *result = "-- weird response from SM pager --";
        break;
    }
}

#ifdef DEBUG
/*
 * Assertion failure.  The condition in the assert
 * macro evaluated to false, resulting in a call here.
 * Print out the file, line number, and assertion; then die.
 */
assfail(file, line, e)
    char           *file;
    unsigned int   line;
    char           *e;
{
    printf("file %s, line %d: %s\n", file, line, e);
    fatal("assertion failure");
```

```
}
#endif
```

B.12   demo_sm.c

```
/*
 *    demo_sm.c:  Demonstrate the use of externally managed
 *    memory by a client program.
 *
 *    The client requires the use of a persistent region of
 *    memory that will be stored "securely" on disk.  The
 *    pager guarantees security by encrypting the memory on
 *    its way to disk and decrypting it when handing the
 *    memory back to the client.
 *
 *    The client stores text supplied on the command line in
 *    the secure region for future examination.
 */

#include <mach.h>
#include <mach/memory_object.h>
#ifdef  USE_PTHREADS
#include <pthread.h>
#else
#include <cthreads.h>
#endif
#include <signal.h>
#include <stdio.h>
#include "sm.h"
#include "sm_decls.h"

#define CREATE              1
#define DISPLAY             2
#define APPEND              3
#define LOOPSOURCE          4
#define LOOPSINK            5

#define DEFAULT_HOSTNAME    ""
#define DEFAULT_OBJ_NAME    "client:memory_object"
#define DEFAULT_OBJ_KEY     ((sm_key_t) 631118)
#define DEFAULT_OBJ_PAGE    0
#define MAX_REGION_PAGES    20
#define DEFAULT_REGION_SIZE
        (vm_page_size*MAX_REGION_PAGES)
#define DEFAULT_OPERATION   DISPLAY

/*
 *    Important global variables.
 */
char            *Me;              /* this program's name */
port_name_t     sm_pager;        /* SM pager service port */
memory_object_t sm_object;       /* gotten from SM pager */
int             operation;       /* command for demo_sm */
sm_key_t        object_key;      /* encryption key for object */
char            *object_name;    /* object's ASCII name */
char            *hostname;       /* host running SM pager */
boolean_t       trace;           /* make pager print messages */
boolean_t       dealloc;         /* dealloc object when done */
int             page;            /* offset into object */
char            **text;          /* pointer into cmd-line args */

void            usage();         /* print message and die */
void            parse_args();    /* parse command line */
void            exit_program();  /* successful program exit */
int             sigdeath();      /* catch signals and exit */
extern void     kchk();          /* mach error checking */
extern void     mchk();          /* mach error checking */
```

```
extern void    fatal();              /* print message and exit(3) */
extern void    exception_handler();
extern void    sm_response_to_string();
extern char    *strcat();

main(argc, argv)
int    argc;
char   *argv[];
{
    port_name_t     task.exception_port;
    vm_offset_t     address;
    vm_size_t       region_size;
    boolean_t       create;
    kern_return_t   kr;
    sm_status_t     response;
    char            *err_msg;
    char            loopletter;
    int             length, length_seen;
#ifdef USE_PTHREADS
    pthread_t       pthread;
#endif

    /*
     *    Default values.
     */

    Me = argv[0];
    operation = DEFAULT_OPERATION;
    hostname = DEFAULT_HOSTNAME;
    object_name = DEFAULT_OBJ_NAME;
    object_key = DEFAULT_OBJ_KEY;
    page = DEFAULT_OBJ_PAGE;
    region_size = DEFAULT_REGION_SIZE;
    trace = dealloc = FALSE;

    /*
     *    Parse command line and set up global variables.
     */
    parse_args(argc, argv);

    /*
     *    Set up exception port to catch memory errors.
     *    We do not fix errors, only report them.
     *    Establish a thread on the exception port.
     */

    kr = port_allocate(mytask, &task_exception_port);
    kchk(kr, "port_allocate", "task exception port");

    kr=task_set_exception_port(mytask,task_exception_port);
    kchk(kr,"task_set_exception_port","set exception port");

#ifdef USE_PTHREADS
    if (pthread_create(&pthread, pthread_attr_default,
                    exception_handler,
                    task_exception_port) < 0) {
        perror("pthread_create");
        fatal("pthread_create");
    }

    if (pthread_detach(pthread) < 0) {
        perror("pthread_detach");
        fatal("pthread_detach");
    }
#else
    cthread_detach(cthread_fork(exception_handler,
                    task_exception_port));
#endif

    /*
     *    Ask the netmsgserver for the service port
     *    registered by the Secure Memory pager.
```

```
	/*
	 * When hostname is set to "", the search is
	 * confined to the local netmsgserver.
	 */
	kr = netname_look_up(name_server_port, hostname,
			SECURE_MEMORY_PAGER, &sm_pager);
	mchk(kr,"netname_look_up","locate secure memory pager");

	/*
	 * Contact the Secure Memory pager.  Request
	 * creation of or attachment to a memory region.
	 */
	create = (operation == CREATE);
	kr = sm_initiate(sm_pager, object_name, object_key,
			create, trace, &response, &sm_object);
	mchk(kr, "sm_initiate", "obtaining memory object");

	/*
	 * Check for service denial problem.
	 */
	if (response != SM_INIT_GRANTED) {
		sm_response_to_string(response, &err_msg);
		printf("%s: object %s (key %d) %s\n",
			Me, object_name, object_key, err_msg);
		fatal("sm_initiate");
	}

	/*
	 * Set up a simple signal handler to catch the
	 * most likely asynchronous death signals.
	 */
	(void) signal(SIGHUP, sigdeath);
	(void) signal(SIGINT, sigdeath);
	(void) signal(SIGQUIT, sigdeath);
	(void) signal(SIGTERM, sigdeath);

	/*
	 * We successfully obtained permission to use a
	 * secure memory region.  The port returned by
	 * sm_initiate may be used to enable secure paging
	 * service on a region of memory.  We permit the
	 * kernel to choose the first free region in the
	 * task's address space (searching from address 0)
	 * for the newly mapped memory.
	 */
	address = 0;
	kr = vm_map(mytask, &address, region_size, 0,
			TRUE, sm_object, 0, FALSE, VM_PROT_ALL,
			VM_PROT_ALL, VM_INHERIT_DEFAULT);
	mchk(kr, "vm_map", "vm_mapping object");

	/*
	 * Increase the initial address by the optional
	 * page offset value to permit operations on
	 * non-consecutive pages.
	 */
	address += page * vm_page_size;

	switch(operation) {
	case CREATE:
	case APPEND:
		/*
		 * Append command line arguments to the
		 * text in the sm region.  Even if no
		 * text has been written yet, the SM pager
		 * guarantees zero-fill memory so there
		 * will be a null at the beginning of the
		 * region so strcat will operate correctly.
		 *
		 * N.B. No check is made for overflowing
		 * the bounds of the allocated sm region.
		 */
```

```c
	*/
	while (text < &argv[argc])
		(void) strcat ((char *)address,*text++);

	break;

case DISPLAY:
	printf("%s: object contents, ", Me);
	printf(" page=%d:\n\t\"%s\"\n", page,
		(char *) address);

	break;

case LOOPSOURCE:
	/*
	 *	Loop forever writing characters into
	 *	the specified page.  This test shows
	 *	off shared memory.
	 */

	loopletter = 'A';
	for (;;) {
		*(char *)address++ = loopletter++;
		sleep(1);
	}

	/* NOTREACHED */
	break;

case LOOPSINK:
	/*
	 *	Loop forever reading characters from
	 *	the specified page.  Whenever the
	 *	string changes length, print out the
	 *	new string.  This test shows off
	 *	shared memory.
	 */

	printf("%s: watching memory contents:\n", Me);
	length_seen = 0;
	for (;;) {
		length = strlen((char *)address);
		if (length != length_seen)
			printf("found: %s\n",
				(char *) address);
		length_seen = length;
	}

	/* NOTREACHED */
	break;

default:
	break;
	fatal("internal command line processing error");
	}

}

exit_program();

}

/*
 *	Clean up resources and exit.
 */
static void
exit_program()
{
	sm_status_t	response;
	kern_return_t	kr;
	char		*err_msg;

	/*
	 *	Send the terminate message to the pager,
	 *	allowing the pager to clean up resources.  Check
	 *	the result of the terminate operation.
	 */

	kr = sm_terminate(sm_pager,sm_object,dealloc,&response);
	mchk(kr, "sm_terminate", "terminating memory object");

	if (response != SM_CLEAN_SHUTDOWN) {
		sm_response_to_string(response, &err_msg);
		printf("%s: object %s (key %d) %s\n",
```

463

464

```c
                Me, object_name, object_key, err_msg);
        fatal("sm_terminate");
    }

    /*
     *   Deallocate service and object ports.
     */
    kr = port_deallocate(mytask, sm_object);
    mchk(kr, "port_deallocate", "sm_object");

    kr = port_deallocate(mytask, sm_pager);
    mchk(kr, "port_deallocate", "sm_pager");

    exit(0);
}

/*
 *   Primitive command line processing.  Process options
 *   until encountering an unrecognized argument.  All
 *   arguments including and after the unrecognized one
 *   count as "text" to be written into the memory object.
 *   Almost no error checking.
 */
static void
parse_args(argc, argv)
int     argc;
char    *argv[];
{
    char    **arg, usage_buf[BUFSIZ];

    text = (char **) 0;
    for (arg = &argv[1]; arg < &argv[argc]; ++arg) {
        if (!strcmp(*arg, "create"))
            operation = CREATE;
        else if (!strcmp(*arg, "display"))
            operation = DISPLAY;
        else if (!strcmp(*arg, "append"))
            operation = APPEND;
        else if (!strcmp(*arg, "loopsource"))
            operation = LOOPSOURCE;
        else if (!strcmp(*arg, "loopsink"))
            operation = LOOPSINK;
        else if (!strncmp(*arg, "host=", 5))
            hostname = *arg + 5;
        else if (!strncmp(*arg, "name=", 5))
            object_name = *arg + 5;
        else if (!strncmp(*arg, "key=", 4))
            object_key = atoi(*arg + 4);
        else if (!strcmp(*arg, "dealloc"))
            dealloc = TRUE;
        else if (!strcmp(*arg, "trace"))
            trace = TRUE;
        else if (!strncmp(*arg, "page=", 5)) {
            page = atoi(*arg + 5);
            if (page < 0 || page>MAX_REGION_PAGES) {
                (void) sprintf(usage_buf,
                        "0 <= page < %d",
                        MAX_REGION_PAGES);
                usage(usage_buf);
            }
        } else {
            text = arg;
            break;
        }
    }

/*
 *   Both create and append must be followed
 *   by text on the command line.
```

```
	*/
	if ((operation == CREATE || operation == APPEND) &&
		text == (char **) 0)
		usage("create|append must have subsequent text");

	/*
	*	Display should have no other arguments.
	*/
	if (operation == DISPLAY && text != (char **) 0)
		usage("display takes no following text");
}

/*
*	Catch death-causing signals, clean up, and terminate.
*/
static int
sigdeath()
{
	exit_program();
}

static void
usage(message)
char	*message;
{
	printf("%s: %s\n", Me, message);
	printf("usage:  %s [options] * [operation]\n", Me);
	printf("\toperation=create|append [text]+\n");
	printf("\toperation=display\n");
	printf("\toperation=[loopsource|loopsink]\n");
	printf("\toptions: page=n|host=string|name=string");
	printf("|key=n|dealloc\n");
	exit(1);
}
```

Appendix C

System and Library Call Summary

This appendix contains the system call summary for the Mach interfaces presented throughout this book.

C.1   Mach Interfaces

This section describes the Mach system call and library interfaces. All functions outlined in this section are contained in the libmach library.

C.1.1   Interprocess Communication

This section describes the IPC and name server interfaces.

```
env_del_port(environment_port, name)                              242
port_name_t    environment_port;
env_name_t     name;

env_del_string(environment_port, name)                            244
port_name_t    environment_port;
env_name_t     name;

env_get_port(environment_port, name, port)                        242
port_name_t    environment_port;
env_name_t     name;
port_name_t    port;

env_get_string(environment_port, name, value)                     244
port_name_t    environment_port;
env_name_t     name;
env_value_t    value;

env_list_ports(environment_port, names, namecnt,                  245
               ports, pcnt)
port_name_t    environment_port;
env_name_list  *names;
port_array_t   *ports;
int            *namecnt, *pcnt;

env_list_strings(environment_port, names,                         245
                 namecnt, strings, strcnt)
port_name_t    environment_port;
env_name_list  *names;
env_str_list   *strings;
int            *namecnt, *strcnt;
```

APPENDIX C   SYSTEM AND LIBRARY CALL SUMMARY

```
env_set_port(environment_port, name, port)          242
port_name_t     environment_port;
env_name_t      name;
port_name_t     port;

env_set_ptlist(environment_port, names, namecnt,    246
               ports, pcnt)
port_name_t     environment_port;
env_name_list   names;
port_array_t    ports;
int             namecnt, pcnt;

env_set_stlist(environment_port, names, namecnt,    246
               strings, strcnt)
port_name_t     environment_port;
env_name_list   names;
env_str_list    strings;
int             namecnt, strcnt;

env_set_string(environment_port, name, value)       244
port_name_t     environment_port;
env_name_t      name;
env_value_t     value;

msg_receive(message_header, options, timeout)       75
msg_header_t    *message_header;
msg_option_t    options;
msg_timeout_t   timeout;

msg_rpc(message_header, options, rcvsize,           214
        sendtimeout, rcvtimeout)
msg_header_t    *message_header;
msg_option_t    options;
msg_size_t      rcvsize;
msg_timeout_t   sendtimeout, rcvtimeout;
```

```
msg_send(message_header, options, timeout)          84
msg_header_t    *message_header;
msg_option_t    options;
msg_timeout_t   timeout;

netname_check_in(name_server_port, name,            73
                 signature, checkin_port)
port_name_t     name_server_port;
netname_name_t  name;
port_t          signature, checkin_port;

netname_check_out(name_server_port, name,           240
                  signature, checkout_port)
port_name_t     name_server_port;
netname_name_t  name;
port_t          signature, checkout_port;

netname_look_up(name_server_port, host, name,       92
                lookup_port)
port_name_t     name_server_port;
char            *host;
netname_name_t  name;
port_name_t     *lookup_port;

netname_version(name_server_port, name)             240
port_name_t     name_server_port;
netname_name_t  name;

port_allocate(target_task, new_port)                70
task_t          target_task;
port_name_t     *new_port;

port_deallocate(task_task, old_port)                70
task_t          target_task;
port_name_t     old_port;
```

```
port_extract_receive(task_task, target, port)                    236
task_t          target_task;
port_name_t     target, port;
task_t          target_task;

port_extract_send(task_task, target, port)                       236
task_t          target, port;
port_name_t     target, port;

port_insert_send(task_task, port, target)                        235
port_name_t     port, target;

port_insert_receive(task_task, port, target)                     235
task_t          target_task;
port_name_t     port, target;
task_t          target_task;

port_names(target_task, names, name_count,                       232
        types, types_count)
task_t              target_task;
port_name_array_t   *names;
port_type_array_t   *types;
unsigned int        *name_count, *types_count;

port_rename(target_task, oldname, newname)                       231
task_t          target_task;
port_name_t     oldname, newname;

port_set_add(target_task, port_set, port)                        219
task_t              target_task;
port_set_name_t     *port_set;
port_name_t         *port;

port_set_allocate(target_task, port_set)                         218
task_t              target_task;
port_set_name_t     *port_set;


port_set_backlog(target_task, port, backlog)                     229
task_t          target_task;
port_name_t     port;
int             backlog;

port_set_remove(target_task, port)                               219
task_t          target_task;
port_name_t     *port;

port_set_status(target_task, pet, parray, count)                 220
task_t              target_task;
port_set_name_t     port_set;
port_name_array_t   *parray;
unsigned int        *count;

port_status(target_task, port, set, count,                       230
        backlog, owner, receiver)
task_t              target_task;
port_set_name_t     set;
int                 *count, *backlog;
boolean_t           *owner, *receiver;

port_type(target_task, name, type)                               233
task_t          target_task;
port_name_t     name;
port_type_t     *type;
```

C.1.2 Tasks and Threads

This section describes the Mach interfaces associated with tasks and threads.

```
task_by_unix_pid(target_task, child_pid,                          17
        child_task)
task_t          target_task;
pid_t           child_pid;
task_t          *child_task;
```

```
55   task_get_special_port(a_task, which_port,
                           returned_port)
     task_t       a_task;
     int          which_port;
     port_t       *returned_port;

50   task_info(a_task, which_info, info_array,
               info_array_size)
     task_t       a_task;
     int          which_info;
     task_info_t  info_array;
     unsigned int *info_array_size;

49   task_resume(a_task)
     task_t       a_task;

17   task_self()

54   task_set_special_port(a_task, which_port,
                           special_port)
     task_t       a_task;
     int          which_port;
     port_t       special_port;

49   task_suspend(a_task)
     task_t       a_task;

50   task_threads(a_task, thread_list, thread_count)
     task_t        a_task;
     thread_array_t *thread_list;
     int           *thread_count;

56   thread_abort(target_thread)
     thread_t     target_thread;

29   thread_create(parent_task, new_thread)
     task_t       parent_task;
     thread_t     *new_thread;
```

```
57   thread_get_special_port(th, which_port,
                             returned_port)
     thread_t     th;
     int          which_port;
     port_t       *returned_port;

31   thread_get_state(th, flavor, cur_state, count)
     thread_t     th;
     int          flavor;
     thread_state_t cur_state;
     unsigned int *count;

58   thread_info(th, which_info, info_array,
                 info_array_size)
     thread_t     th;
     int          which_info;
     thread_info_t info_array;
     unsigned int *info_array_size;

32   thread_resume(th)
     thread_t     th;

57   thread_set_special_port(th, which_port,
                             special_port)
     thread_t     th;
     int          which_port;
     port_t       special_port;

30   thread_set_state(th, flavor, new_state, count)
     thread_t     th;
     int          flavor;
     thread_state_t new_state;
     unsigned int count;

32   thread_suspend(th)
     thread_t     th;
```

```
thread_terminate(unneeded_thread)
    thread_t      unneeded_thread;                                289
```

C.1.3 Virtual Memory

```
vm_allocate(target_task, new_memory, size,
        find_space)
    task_t        target_task;
    vm_address_t  *new_memory;
    vm_size_t     size;
    boolean_t     find_space;                                      33

vm_deallocate(target_task, address, size)
    vm_task_t     target_task;
    vm_address_t  address;
    vm_size_t     size;                                           112

vm_copy(target_task, source_address, count,
        dest_address)
    vm_task_t     target_task;
    vm_address_t  source_address;
    vm_size_t     count;
    vm_address_t  dest_address;                                   114

vm_inherit(target_task, address, size,
        new_inheritance)
    vm_task_t     target_task;
    vm_address_t  address;
    vm_size_t     size;
    vm_inherit_t  new_inheritance;                                135
```

```
vm_map(target_task, address, size, mask,
        anywhere, memory_object, offset,
        copy, cur_protection, max_protection,
        inheritance)
    vm_task_t        target_task;
    vm_offset_t      address;
    vm_size_t        size;
    vm_offset_t      mask;
    boolean_t        anywhere;
    memory_object_t  memory_object;
    vm_offset_t      offset;
    boolean_t        copy;
    vm_prot_t        cur_protection;
    vm_prot_t        max_protection;
    vm_inherit_t     inheritance;                                 124

vm_protect(target_task, address, size,
        set_maximum, new_protection)
    vm_task_t     target_task;
    vm_address_t  address;
    vm_size_t     size;
    boolean_t     set_maximum;
    vm_prot_t     new_protection;                                 132

vm_read(target_task, address, size, data,
        data_count)
    vm_task_t     target_task;
    vm_address_t  address;
    vm_size_t     size;
    pointer_t     *data;
    unsigned int  *data_count;                                    119
```

```
vm_region(target_task, region_address, size,
          cur-protection, max_protection,
          inheritance, shared, object_name,
          offset);

vm_task_t        target_task;
vm_address_t     *region_address;
vm_size_t        *size;
vm_prot_t        *cur_protection;
vm_prot_t        *max_protection;
vm_inherit_t     *inheritance;
boolean_t        *shared;
port_t           *object_name;
vm_offset_t      *offset;
```
142

```
vm_write(target_task, address, data, data_count)
vm_task_t        target_task;
vm_address_t     address;
pointer_t        data;
unsigned int     data_count;
```
120

C.1.4   External Memory Management

```
memory_object_data_error(memory_control, offset,
                         size, reason)
memory_object_control_t   memory_control;
vm_offset_t      offset;
vm_size_t        size;
kern_return_t    reason;
```
313

```
memory_object_data_provided(memory_control,
                            offset, data,
                            data_count,
                            lock_value)
memory_object_control_t   memory_control;
vm_offset_t      offset;
pointer_t        data;
int              data_count;
vm_prot_t        data_count;
```
310

```
memory_object_data_request(memory_object,
                           memory_control,
                           offset, length,
                           desired_access)
memory_object_t           memory_object;
memory_object_control_t   memory_control;
vm_offset_t      offset;
vm_size_t        length;
vm_prot_t        desired_access;
```
308

```
memory_object_data_unavailable(memory_control,
                               offset, size)
memory_object_control_t   memory_control;
vm_offset_t      offset;
vm_size_t        size;
```
312

```
memory_object_data_unlock(memory_object,
                          memory_control,
                          offset, length,
                          desired_access)
memory_object_t           memory_object;
memory_object_control_t   memory_control;
vm_offset_t      offset;
vm_size_t        length;
vm_prot_t        desired_access;
```
319

```
memory_object_data_write(memory_object,
        memory_control, offset,
        data, data_count)
memory_object_t         memory_object;
memory_object_control_t memory_control;
vm_offset_t             offset;
pointer_t               data;
unsigned int            data_count;
                                                    316

memory_object_destroy(memory_control, reason)
memory_object_control_t memory_control;
kern_return_t           reason;
                                                    327

memory_object_get_attributes(memory_control,
                object_ready,
                may_cache_object, copy_strategy)
                                                    308
memory_object_control_t memory_control;
boolean_t               *object_ready;
boolean_t               *may_cache_object;
memory_object_copy_strategy_t *copy_strategy;

memory_object_init(memory_object,
                memory_control,
                memory_object_name,
                memory_object_page_size)
                                                    302
memory_object_t         memory_object;
memory_object_control_t memory_control;
memory_object_name_t    memory_object_name;
vm_size_t               memory_object_page_size;


memory_object_lock_completed(memory_object,
                memory_control,
                offset, length)
memory_object_t         memory_object;
memory_object_control_t memory_control;
vm_offset_t             offset;
vm_size_t               length;
                                                    323

memory_object_lock_request(memory_control, offset, size,
                should_clean, should_flush,
                lock_value, reply_to)
memory_object_control_t memory_control;
vm_offset_t             offset;
vm_size_t               size;
boolean_t               should_clean;
boolean_t               should_flush;
vm_prot_t               lock_value;
port_t                  reply_to;
                                                    320

memory_object_set_attributes(memory_control,
                object_ready,
                may_cache_object, copy_strategy)
memory_object_control_t memory_control;
boolean_t               object_ready;
boolean_t               may_cache_object;
memory_object_copy_strategy_t  copy_strategy;
                                                    305

memory_object_terminate(memory_object,
                memory_control, memory_object_name)
memory_object_t         memory_object;
memory_object_control_t memory_control;
memory_object_name_t    memory_object_name;
                                                    325
```

C.2   C Threads Library Calls

```
condition_alloc()                                              159

condition_broadcast(cond)
condition_t      cond;                                         168

condition_clear(cond)
condition_t      cond;                                         169

condition_free(cond)
condition_t      cond;                                         162

condition_init(condstruct)
struct condition      condstruct;                              168

condition_name(cond)
condition_t      cond;                                         170

condition_set_name(cond, name)
condition_t      cond;
char             *name;                                        170

condition_signal(cond)
condition_t      cond;                                         163

condition_wait(cond, mutex)
condition_t      cond;
mutex_t          mutex;                                        153

cthread_data(cth)
cthread_t        cth;                                          165

cthread_detach(cth)
cthread_t        cth;                                          161

cthread_exit(val)
int              val;                                          161
```

```
cthread_fork(func, arg)
void             *func();
any_t            arg;                                          160

cthread_init()                                                 159

cthread_join(cth)
cthread_t        cth;                                          160

cthread_name(cth)
cthread_t        cth;                                          170

cthread_self()                                                 165

cthread_set_data(cth, data)
cthread_t        cth;
any_t            data;                                         165

cthread_set_name(cth, name)
cthread_t        cth;
char             *name;                                        170

mutex_alloc()                                                  159

mutex_clear(mutex)
mutex_t          mutex;                                        169

mutex_free(mutex)
mutex_t          mutex;                                        162

mutex_init(mutexstruct)
struct mutex          mutexstruct;                             168

mutex_lock(mutex)
mutex_t          mutex;                                        161

mutex_name(mutex)
mutex_t          mutex;                                        170
```

```
mutex_set_name(mutex, name)                                     170
mutex_t        mutex;
char           *name;
mutex_try_lock(mutex)                                           166
mutex_t        mutex;
mutex_unlock(mutex)                                             161
mutex_t        mutex;
```

C.3 P Threads Library Calls

```
flockfile(a_file)                                               375
FILE           *a_file;
funlockfile(a_file)                                             375
FILE           *a_file;
pthread_attr_create(attr)                                       338
pthread_attr_t  *attr;
pthread_attr_setstacksize(attr, stacksize)                      338
pthread_attr_t  *attr;
long            stacksize;
pthread_cancel(a_thread)                                        358
pthread_t       a_thread;
pthread_cleanup_pop(execute_flag)                               359
int             execute_flag;
pthread_cleanup_push(my_cleanup_routine, arg)                   359
void            *my_cleanup_routine();
void            *arg;
pthread_condattr_create(nascent_cattr)                          345
pthread_condattr_t  nascent_cattr;
```

```
pthread_condattr_delete(unneeded_cattr)                         345
pthread_condattr_t  *unneeded_cattr;
pthread_cond_broadcast(cond)                                    346
pthread_cond_t  *a_cond;
pthread_cond_destroy(unneeded_cond)                             346
pthread_cond_t  *unneeded_cond;
pthread_cond_init(new_cond, cattr)                              344
pthread_cond_t  *new_cond;
pthread_condattr_t  cattr;
pthread_cond_signal(a_cond)                                     346
pthread_cond_t  *a_cond;
pthread_cond_timedwait(cond, mutex, abstime)                    348
struct          timespec *abstime;
pthread_cond_t  *a_cond;
pthread_mutex_t *a_mutex;
pthread_cond_wait(cond, mutex)                                  347
pthread_cond_t  *cond;
pthread_mutex_t *mutex;
pthread_create(thread, attr, start_routine, arg)                337
pthread_t       *thread;
pthread_attr_t  attr;
void            *arg;
void            *start_routine();
pthread_detach(thread)                                          340
pthread_t       thread;
pthread_equal(an_id, another_id)                                348
pthread_t       an_id;
pthread_t       another_id;
```

APPENDIX C   SYSTEM AND LIBRARY CALL SUMMARY

```
337   pthread_exit(exit_status)
      void        *exit_status;

339   pthread_join(thread, exit_status)
      pthread_t   thread;
      void        **exit_status;

354   pthread_getspecific(a_key, retrieved_value)
      pthread_t   a_key;
      void        **retrieved_value;

351   pthread_keycreate(a_key, destructor_routine)
      pthread_key_t  *a_key;
      void           *destructor_routine();

342   pthread_mutexattr_create(mattr)
      pthread_mutexattr_t mattr;

342   pthread_mutexattr_delete(mattr)
      pthread_mutexattr_t mattr;

341   pthread_mutex_destroy(unneeded_mutex)
      pthread_mutex_t  *unneeded_mutex;

341   pthread_mutex_init(nascent_mutex, mattr)
      pthread_mutex_t     *nascent_mutex;
      pthread_mutexattr_t attr;

341   pthread_mutex_lock(unlocked_mutex)
      pthread_mutex_t  *unlocked_mutex;

341   pthread_mutex_trylock(mutex)
      pthread_mutex_t  *mutex;

341   pthread_mutex_unlock(locked_mutex)
      pthread_mutex_t  *locked_mutex;

348   pthread_self()
```

```
358   pthread_setasynccancel(new_state)
      int         new_state;

357   pthread_setcancel(new_state)
      int         new_state;
      int         old_state;

354   pthread_setspecific(a_key, value)
      pthread_key_t  a_key;
      void           *value;

358   pthread_testcancel()

349   pthread_yield()

360   sigwait(setp)
      sigset_t    *setp;
```

Appendix D

References

Accetta, Michael; Robert Baron; et al., *A New Kernel Foundation for UNIX Development*, Proc. Summer 1986 USENIX Conference, pp. 93–112, June 1986.

Appel, Andrew W.; K. Li, *Virtual Memory Primitives for User Programs*, Proc. ACM Fourth Symposium on Architectural Support for Programming Languages and Operating Systems (ASPLOS IV), pp. 96–107, April 1991.

Barrera, Joseph S., *A Fast Mach Network IPC Implementation*, Proc. USENIX Second Mach Symposium, pp. 1–12, November 1991.

Bershad, Brian N., *The Increasing Irrelevance of IPC Performance for Micro-kernel-Based Operating Systems*, Proc. USENIX Microkernel and Other Kernel Architectures Workshop, pp. 205–211, April 1992.

Black, David L., *Scheduling and Resource Management Techniques for Multiprocessors*, Carnegie Mellon University Thesis, CMU-CS-90-152, Pittsburgh, PA, July 1990.

Black, David L., *Scheduling Support for Concurrency and Parallelism in the Mach Operating System*, IEEE Computer, Vol. 23, No. 5, pp. 35–43, May 1990.

Black, David L.; Jeff Carter; et al., *OSF/1 Virtual Memory Improvements*, Proc. USENIX Second Mach Symposium, pp. 87–104, November 1991.

477

Boyer, Fabienne, *A Causal Distributed Shared Memory Based on External Pagers*, Proc. USENIX Second Mach Symposium, pp. 41–58, November 1991.

Boykin, Joseph; Alan B. Langerman, *Mach/4.3BSD: A Conservative Approach to Parallelization*, Proc. USENIX Symposium on Experiences with Distributed and Multiprocessing Systems, pp. 105–126, October 1989.

Caswell, Deborah; David L. Black, *Implementing a Mach Debugger for Multithreaded Applications*, Proc. Winter 1990 USENIX Conference, pp. 25–39, January 1990.

Draves, Richard P., *A Revised IPC Interface*, Proc. USENIX First Mach Workshop, pp. 101–122, October 1990.

Draves, Richard P.; Brian N. Bershad; et al., *Using Continuations to Implement Thread Management and Communication in Operating Systems*, Proc. ACM 13th Symposium on Operating Systems (SOSP), pp. 122–136, October 1991.

Draves, Richard P.; Michael B. Jones; et al., *MIG—The Mach Interface Generator*, Unpublished Manuscript, Carnegie Mellon University, Pittsburgh, PA, July 1989.

Forin, Alessandro; Joseph Barrera; et al., *The Shared Memory Server*, Proc. Winter 1989 USENIX Conference, pp. 229–243, January 1989.

Goldberg, Arthur; Ajei Gopal; et al., *Transparent Recovery of Mach Applications*, Proc. USENIX First Mach Workshop, pp. 169–184, October 1990.

Golub, David; Randall Dean; et al., *UNIX as an Application Program*, Proc. Summer 1990 USENIX Conference, pp. 87–97, June 1990.

Golub, David; Richard P. Draves, *Moving the Default Memory Manager Out of the Mach Kernel*, Proc. USENIX Second Mach Symposium, pp. 177–188, November 1991.

Hoven, Rand, *Mach Interfaces to Support Guest OS Debugging*, Proc. USENIX Second Mach Symposium, pp. 131–148, November 1991.

Jones, Michael B., *Bringing the C Libraries with Us into a Multi-Threaded Future*, Proc. Winter 1991 USENIX Conference, pp. 81–92, January 1991.

Jones, Michael B., *Transparently Interposing User Code at the System Interface*, Proc. Third IEEE Computer Society Workshop on Workstation Operating Systems (WWOS-III), pp. 98–103, April 1992.

Jones, Michael B.; Richard F. Rashid, *Mach and Matchmaker: Kernel and Language Support for Object-Oriented Distributed Systems*, Carnegie Mellon University Technical Report, CMU-CS-88-129, Pittsburgh, PA, September 1986.

Langerman, Alan B.; Joseph Boykin; et al., *A Highly-Parallelized Mach-based Vnode Filesystem*, Proc. Winter 1990 USENIX Conference, pp. 297–312, January 1990.

Leffler, Samuel J.; Marshall Kirk McKusick; et al., *The Design and Implementation of the 4.3BSD UNIX Operating System*, Addison-Wesley, Reading, Mass., 1989.

LoVerso, Susan J.; Noemi Paciorek; et al., *The OSF/1 UNIX Filesystem*, Proc. Winter 1991 USENIX Conference, pp. 207–218, January 1991.

McNamee, Dylan; Katherine Armstrong, *Extend the Mach External Pager Interface to Accommodate User-Level Page Replacement Policies*, Proc. USENIX First Mach Workshop, pp. 17–30, October 1990.

Mitchell, David W., *Mach Resource Control in OSF/1*, Proc. USENIX Second Mach Symposium, pp. 123–130, November 1991.

Rashid, Richard F., *From RIG to Accent to Mach: The Evolution of a Network Operating System*, Proc. ACM/IEEE Computer Society Fall Joint Computer Conference, pp. 1128–1137, November 1986.

Rashid, Richard F., *Threads of a New System*, UNIX Review, Vol. 4, No. 8, pp. 37–49, August 1986.

Rashid, Richard F.; Avadis Tevanian Jr.; et al., *Machine-Independent Virtual Memory Management for Paged Uniprocessor and Multiprocessor Architectures*, Proc. ACM Second Symposium on Architectural Support for

Programming Languages and Operating Systems (ASPLOS II), pp. 31–39, October 1987.

Rashid, Richard F.; Daniel Julin; et al., *Mach: A System Software Kernel*, Proc. 34th IEEE Computer Society Internation Conference (COMPCON 89), pp. 176–178, February 1989.

Rashid, Richard F.; Robert Baron; et al., *Mach: A Foundation for Open Systems*, Proc. Second IEEE Computer Society Workshop on Workstation Operating Systems (WWOS-II), pp. 109–113, September 1989.

Subramanian, Indira, *Managing Discardable Pages with an External Pager*, Proc. USENIX Second Mach Symposium, pp. 77–86, November 1991.

Tevanian, Avadis Jr., *Architecture-Independent Virtual Memory Management for Parallel and Distributed Environments*, Carnegie Mellon University Thesis, CMU-CS-88-106, Pittsburgh, PA, December 1987.

Tevanian, Avadis Jr.; Richard F. Rashid, *Mach: A Basis for Future UNIX Development*, Carnegie Mellon University Technical Report, CMU-CS-87-139, Pittsburgh, PA, June 1987.

Tevanian, Avadis Jr.; Richard F. Rashid; et al., *Mach Threads and the UNIX Kernel: The Battle for Control*, Proc. Summer 1987 USENIX Conference, pp. 185–197, June 1987.

Van Sciver, James; Richard F. Rashid, *Zone Garbage Collection*, Proc. USENIX First Mach Workshop, pp. 1–16, October 1990.

Vaughan, Francis; Tracy Schunke, et al., *A Persistent Distributed Architecture Supported by the Mach Operating System*, Proc. USENIX First Mach Workshop, pp. 123–140, October 1990.

Young, Michael W.; Avadis Tevanian Jr.; et al., *The Duality of Memory and Communication in the Implementation of a Multiprocessor Operating System*, Proc. 11th Symposium on Operating System Principles, pp. 63–76, November 1987.

Young, Michael W., *Exporting a User Interface to Memory Management from a Communication-Oriented Operating System*, Carnegie Mellon University Thesis, CMU-CS-89-202, Pittsburgh, PA, November 1989.

Index